WORLD WAR TRUMP

WORLD WAR TRUMP

THE RISKS OF AMERICA'S NEW NATIONALISM

HALL GARDNER

Prometheus Books
59 John Glenn Drive
Amherst, New York 14228

Published 2018 by Prometheus Books

Cover design by Jacqueline Nasso Cooke
Cover design © Prometheus Books

Inquiries should be addressed to
Prometheus Books
59 John Glenn Drive
Amherst, New York 14228
VOICE: 716–691–0133 • FAX: 716–691–0137
WWW.PROMETHEUSBOOKS.COM

22 21 20 19 18 5 4 3 2 1

Library of Congress Cataloging-in-Publication Data Pending

Printed in the United States of America

CONTENTS

ACKNOWLEDGMENTS

Writing this book, has, like many of my previous works, been like shooting at a moving target. But in this case, the Trump administration has been zigzagging through ever-changing policies like a vampire in flight. I would like to thank the American University of Paris library staff for their assistance with my book projects over the years, and Nina Bechmann and Mohammad Abdalhaleem for their valuable assistance in volunteering to check over my endnotes, as well as Soyoung Park and Anita Maksymchuk for helping build my website. And once again I would like to thank Isabel, who had to put up with me working on this project from early morning to late at night for several weeks. And my daughters, Celine and Francesca, whom I have generally neglected in the process. I would also like to thank my editor, Steven L. Mitchell, Jade Zora Scibilia, Hanna Etu, Cheryl Quimba, and Jackie Nasso Cooke for their support and help in working with me on this project, and for those at Prometheus Books who originally proposed the title, *World War Trump*.

Let us hope that this project is not in vain—and that the Trump administration policies will not generate a global war. But, even then, it is crucial to begin to turn around the new arms race and concentrate on the real need for negotiated peace, development, and human fulfillment in the United States and abroad—and on a truly healthy and inhabitable planet.

INTRODUCTION
A SELF-FULFILLING PROPHECY

"Disarmament, with mutual honor and confidence, is a continuing imperative."

—President Dwight D. Eisenhower, 1961

"At this moment, for example, in 1984 (if it was 1984), Oceania was at war with Eurasia and in alliance with Eastasia. In no public or private utterance was it ever admitted that the three powers had at any time been grouped along different lines. . . . The enemy of the moment always represented absolute evil, and it followed that any past or future agreement with him was impossible."

—George Orwell, *1984* (1948)

"For the first time in all history, a great nation must go on arming itself more and more, not for conquest—not for jealousy—not for war—but for peace!"

—Sinclair Lewis, *It Can't Happen Here*, 1935

Toward the end of the Cold War, it became a cliché to cite the adage that the North Atlantic Treaty Organization (NATO) was created "to keep the Americans in, the Russians out, and the Germans down." Someone else later added as a joke: "to keep the French happy."[1] But this original rationale for expanding NATO (as a collective defense organization in such a way as to keep the new Russia out of Eastern

Europe and former Soviet states, the Germans/Europeans restrained, and the French happy, with the Americans fully in control) should have been thrown out the window once the Warsaw Pact dissolved in 1989. The Clinton administration should have put the whole NATO enlargement process on hold in the late 1990s and begun a full reassessment—just like one of the founders of the anti-Communist containment policy, Paul Nitze, among other officials and experts, had urged at the time.[2]

The Clinton administration was not entirely oblivious to the possibility that NATO enlargement could eventually provoke Moscow. And it did at least superficially consider a range of options for European security that could have provided an alternative to NATO as the primary supplier of European security. But in the process of expanding a large and complex political-military bureaucracy, President Clinton decided to hedge his bets and opt for what could be called the NATO "self-limitation approach."[3]

In the NATO self-limitation approach, NATO would not deploy foreign troops and nuclear weapons on the territory of new NATO member states. This approach was then confirmed by both NATO and Russia with the signing of the 1997 NATO-Russia Founding Act. The latter was intended to represent the basis for a closer NATO-Russia relationship, but Moscow saw it as almost immediately breaking down—given the fact that NATO's so-called exceptional war 'over' Kosovo, which was fought by NATO in 1999 against the interests of one of Russia's historical allies, Serbia, was not granted approval by the UN Security Council. Not only was that war in technical violation of the North Atlantic Treaty that had founded NATO, and against the spirit of the 1997 NATO-Russia Founding Act that Moscow had just signed, but the Clinton administration had opted to reject Russian proposals to deal jointly with the ongoing sociopolitical conflict in Kosovo—without even permitting Moscow to discuss those proposals thoroughly with either the United States or the other NATO members. And combined with the open NATO enlargement, this war represented one of the major factors that helped bring to power Vladimir Putin.[4]

For more than twenty years, I have been warning that the uncoordinated NATO and European Union enlargements into former Soviet space would result in a Russian revanchist backlash—and that the major focal point of dispute would be Crimea.[5] My argument was the following: If the Russian Federation was not fully included and engaged with both the United States and the Europeans in the formulation of the new post–Cold War security architecture, then the world could eventually expect a Russian backlash and the militarization of Russian behavior.

The militarization of Russian behavior would, in large part, result from the ambiguous nature of the 1997 NATO-Russia Founding Act. On the one hand, the expansion of NATO's integrated military capabilities and infrastructure to new members in eastern Europe, particularly once NATO proposed expansion to the three Baltic states, Georgia, and Ukraine in particular, risked a counter-military reaction by Moscow. On the other hand, the open NATO enlargement also made it more difficult to defend NATO's new members—that is, without the deployment of conventional forces coupled with direct threat to use of nuclear weapons the closer that NATO moved to the Russian border without a geostrategic "buffer" of neutral states.

That easily predictable Russian backlash against both NATO and European Union enlargement has now taken place. Much as NATO was seen by Moscow as containing Russia in geostrategic and military terms, Moscow also saw the European Union as seeking to isolate Russia in political-economic terms. And it is now the 1997 NATO-Russia Founding Act, among other international accords, that have been put in question in the aftermath of the early 2014 Russian annexation of Crimea, Moscow's political military interference in eastern Ukraine, and the buildup of Russian forces in the Baltic region. These Russian counteractions have led to the subsequent deployment of NATO forces in Poland and the Baltic states on a rotating, yet possibly permanently rotating, basis. In effect, rather than working together with Moscow to forge a new conjoint system of post–Cold War European security since the Gorbachev and Yeltsin administrations, the United States, NATO, and the European Union have achieved what can truly be considered a self-fulfilling prophecy by provoking a Russian backlash.

But that is not all. I also argued that along with a Russian backlash, a general militarization of interstate behavior would concurrently take place. Such a general militarization—which would include states such as the People's Republic of China in closer alliance with the Russian Federation, Iran, and other countries—would develop over time as the new powers that would emerge after Soviet collapse would soon resist US efforts to expand its global hegemony in eastern Europe, in the Indo-Pacific, and throughout the "wider Middle East" and much of the world.

Not only that, but these major and regional power rivalries are beginning to merge with the ever-expanding Global War on Terrorism that was initiated by George W. Bush against both anti-state organizations such as al-Qaeda and so-called rogue states including Afghanistan under the Taliban, Iraq under Saddam Hussein, and Libya under Muammar Gaddafi. The concern raised here is that the human and political costs of the US retaliation for the September 11, 2001, attacks—a retaliation which should have focused on al-Qaeda alone—have far exceeded the actual damage caused by those attacks, and that these wars on both "terrorism" and "rogue states" cannot be judged to be "successful" by any standard. Since 2001, approximately 370,000 people have been killed by violence in Iraq, Afghanistan, and Pakistan. At least 200,000 civilians have died in this fighting. Moreover, at least 10.1 million Afghans, Pakistanis, and Iraqis have been surviving as war refugees in other countries, or have been forcibly displaced from their homes.[6]

In terms of costs, the United States alone has spent or committed at least $4.8 trillion on the wars in Afghanistan, Pakistan, and Iraq—a sum paid for almost entirely by heavy borrowing. Depending on the costs of the ongoing wars against the Islamic State, future interest payments could total over $7.9 trillion by 2053.[7] Despite these huge costs, and despite the highly unlikely possibility that Washington can bring many of these conflicts to "successful" conclusions, the Global War on Terrorism is now being extended by President Donald Trump in Syria, Iraq, and Afghanistan, and countries such as Niger, among others. Trump has proclaimed that he would "eradicate" radical Islamist terrorism "from the face of the Earth"—but without necessarily pointing to feasible diplomatic solutions to establish peace in the long term in the aftermath of those military interventions.[8]

On the domestic side, the intensification of major power rivalries and sociopolitical struggles within states, coupled with the 2008 global financial crisis, has indirectly resulted in the rise of a number of authoritarian or "illiberal" democracies. Recall, President Bill Clinton had originally justified NATO enlargement as least in part on the basis that NATO would help to stabilize fledgling eastern European democracies—even if NATO was not exclusively democratic at the time of its conception. And yet, in contemporary circumstances, NATO members Hungary and Poland—and particularly Turkey—can now be considered authoritarian states, or in the new formula, "illiberal democracies." And NATO members Bulgaria, Hungary, the Czech Republic, and Turkey have all begun to flirt with Russia, for better or for worse.

On the international side, the ongoing conflict between major and regional powers and differing anti-state "terrorist" groups has increasingly taken place both outside and within domestic societies through new forms of hybrid warfare, cyber-sabotage, and acts of partisan "terrorism." The modernization of nuclear and conventional weaponry, combined with the deployment of advanced US missile defense systems, not to overlook the deceptive tactics of hybrid and cyber-warfare, have largely rendered the Cold War concept of mutual assured destruction (MAD) obsolete. As indicated by the tremendous risks involved in President Trump's nuclear brinksmanship with North Korean leader Kim Jung Un, it has become increasingly evident that any number of direct, or even indirect, conflicts in differing regions of the world could draw major and regional powers into a direct confrontation. The possibility of major power war—most likely with the use of nuclear weaponry—is real.

The danger that is now confronting the world is that these twenty-first-century hybrid wars against both "terrorists" and "rogue states," combined with major power rivalries, are now leading to the formation of two contending systems of alliances. The United States, NATO, Ukraine, Japan, Israel, and Saudi Arabia have all begun to take steps to align more closely with each other against Russia, China, or Iran. States such as Belarus, Bulgaria, Hungary, Turkey, the Czech Republic, Serbia, Qatar, the Philippines, Pakistan, and India, among others, have all been caught up in the cross fire and may either strengthen their present ties with either the United States/NATO or with Russia and China—or else switch to the other side, if they do not opt for neutrality. In any case, the very threat to switch sides further exacerbates regional and global tensions.

World War Trump argues that the new "America First" nationalism—coupled with Trump's largely unexpected and erratic foreign-policy flip-flops and willingness to use force—will provoke even greater regional sociopolitical-economic instability and interstate disputes than those that already exist. In essence, Trump's threatening actions and the general militarization of American policy could soon polarize much of the world into two rival alliances.

Trump's impatience; his Nixonian "madman" behavior; and his wild, unstatesmanlike foreign-policy flip-flops make both rival states and present allies automatically assume worst-case scenarios—as leaderships fear that the United States will not keep its promises or that Washington will radically alter its policies. Trump claims that he wants to bargain from a "position of strength," yet the United States is already seen as the predominant global power by far. America is already great and does not need to be "made great again"—at least not in Trump's militaristic manner of thinking. The risk is that Trump's "Peace through Strength" approach could soon spark a number of potential military confrontations—if his foreign policies are not accompanied by a sincere effort to seek out compromises and even make concessions through intense bilateral and multilateral negotiations. In this respect, Trump missed a major opportunity in his address to the UN

General Assembly on September 19, 2017, to formulate a concerted path toward global peace that would involve the United States, the Europeans, Russia, and China, among other concerned states.

In order to defuse a truly critical state of affairs, *World War Trump* proposes that Washington find ways to work with both Moscow and Beijing, in addition to other major and regional powers, through bilateral meetings and through multilateral Contact Groups, backed by the United Nations or the Organization for Security and Co-operation in Europe (OSCE), in the diplomatic effort to ameliorate political-economic tensions and disputes in key regional "hot spots" throughout the world. These multilateral Contact Groups need to prevent the global geopolitical system from polarizing into essentially two hostile systems of alliances, by seeking to better manage, if not resolve, key regional disputes that could potentially draw major and regional powers into direct conflict.

CHAPTER OUTLINE

Before we move forward, I want to present to you the general structure of *World War Trump*. As you have seen, this introduction, "A Self-Fulfilling Prophecy," argues that the Russian backlash to the uncoordinated NATO and the European Union "double enlargement" represents a self-fulfilling prophecy.

Chapter 1, "The Perils of the New 'American First' Nationalism," outlines the general arguments of the book and argues that Trump's "America First" nationalism and his often-contradictory foreign policies and policy flip-flops will prove destabilizing and provocative. The chapter discusses multiple tactics of the "hybrid warfare," including cyber-sabotage, "democracy engineering," and Russian "nationalist engineering." It argues that Trump-Pence policies, geopolitical rivalries between major and regional powers, and the new US-Russian arms race could lead the global system to polarize into two contending alliance systems. And that new techniques of hybrid warfare and acts of "terrorism"—which impact both the domestic and the international relations of differing states—could help spark a major power war.

Chapter 2, "Inauguration Tremors: Rifles, Tanks, and Nuclear Weapons," critically examines Trump's "Make America Great Again" budget and discusses the real social and political-economic costs of his proposed military buildup and the perverse impact of what President Eisenhower called the "military-industrial" (and congressional) complex on the American political economy and society.

Chapter 3, "The New Bogeymen: Russians, Immigrants, Muslims—and the Question of Impeachment," examines the domestic political impact on the United States of both the alleged Russian cyber-tampering and the accusations of Trump complicity with Moscow on the US presidential elections. The chapter critically discusses Trump-Pence policies and the apparently growing popular sense of alienation from the American system of democratic governance. Issues include the US electoral college system; the growing gap in wealth; Trump's opposition to the Affordable Care Act ("ObamaCare"); domestic violence, terrorism, drugs, and gun control; and Trump's controversial policies toward Mexican immigration and toward immigrants from Muslim-majority countries. The chapter concludes with a discussion of the prospects for Trump's impeachment.

Chapter 4, "Risks of the New American Nationalism for the European Union," discusses the impact of Trump's strong support for the British exit from the European Union ("Brexit") and for nationalist movements in general. The chapter examines Trump's approach to Germany; the impact of sanctions placed on Russia in the aftermath of its annexation of Crimea in 2014; the rise of anti-EU and anti-NATO movements in France and throughout Europe after Brexit and plans for strengthening the European Union; Russian and US attempts to influence elections in Europe; and Moscow's negative reaction to EU efforts to bring former Soviet bloc states into a closer political-economic partnership with Europe.

Chapter 5, "The Risk of War over Crimea, the Black Sea, and Eastern

Europe," examines why Trump suddenly flipped from opposing Ukraine's efforts to regain Crimea after the Russian annexation in early 2014 to supporting Kiev's efforts to regain Crimea, and why Trump no longer calls NATO "obsolete." The chapter discusses the sociopolitical ramifications of Trump-Pence efforts to press all NATO members to boost their defense expenditures in the effort to counter Russian military pressures in the Black Sea region and in eastern Europe in general. Given the rise of the authoritarian Erdoğan regime in NATO member Turkey, plus an authoritarian leadership in Hungary, NATO has begun to lose its "democratic" credentials. While Washington has begun to fear the potential breakup of NATO due to a potential Turkish defection, Moscow has begun to fear the potential defection of Belarus from the Russian-led Collective Security Treaty Organization (CSTO). These fears are leading both Washington and Moscow to attempt to tighten their alliance relationships against one another.

Chapter 6, "The Global Impact of the China-Russia Eurasian Alliance," explains how US defense and alliance policies have been pushing Russia and China into a closer alignment, not only in Eurasia but also throughout much of the world, including Mexico, Venezuela, and much of Latin America, where they intersect with the ongoing War on Drugs, thus impacting regional US and domestic interests. In analyzing the growing influence of China's Belt and Road Initiative (BRI) and its Regional Comprehensive Economic Partnership (RCEP) on Pakistan and on other states throughout the Indo-Pacific region, the chapter argues that India represents the key "pivot" state that could either move closer to a Russian-Chinese-Iranian Eurasian alliance or else toward a US-European-Japanese alliance—if New Delhi cannot remain neutral and become a potential mediator.

Chapter 7, "China, North Korea, and the Risk of War in the Into-Pacific," analyzes the regional implications of Chinese-Taiwanese-Japanese disputes and conflicts over the South China and East China Seas for the United States and Russia. The chapter then focuses on the real threat of nuclear war with North Korea, which could engulf the entire region—if the Trump administration does not soon engage in real negotiations involving the six powers most concerned, the United States, China, Russia, Japan, South Korea, as well as North Korea.

Chapter 8, "Syria and Widening Wars in the 'Wider Middle East,'" critically examines Trump's decision to bomb a Syrian airfield with 59 Tomahawk cruise missiles in April 2017 after the Syrian regime of Bashar al-Assad allegedly used poison gas against its own population. The chapter argues that Trump's strong backing for Saudi Arabia and his opposition to the Iran nuclear accord signed by the Obama administration will not only antagonize Iran but also divide the Europeans, and press Tehran closer to Russia and China—given the ongoing proxy war between Iran and Saudi Arabia that has enveloped most of the wider Middle East and that is spreading into new regions throughout the world.

Chapter 9, "Peace through Strength? Or World War Trump?" critically examines Trump's "America First" policies and argues that they could lead to polarization of the world into two rival alliances. To prevent the latter, the United States, along with the Europeans and Japan, must engage with both Russia and China in the effort to resolve disputes and conflicts over a number of regional hot spots. In effect, it is argued that geopolitical tensions will not be abated until the issues of Crimea, Kaliningrad, Kashmir, Taiwan, and North Korea are fully addressed by the major powers themselves through UN- or OSCE-backed Contact Group diplomacy—in a geostrategic context in which countries such as India and Turkey could play major diplomatic roles. Concurrently, the major powers need to bring Saudi Arabia and Iran into a rapprochement over the Israeli-Palestinian conflict and the ongoing wars in Syria, Iraq, and Yemen.

Chapter 10, "Defusing the Global Crisis," outlines ways to reduce, if not eliminate, nuclear weaponry. It argues for engaging in multilateral Contact Group diplomacy, backed by the United Nations and the OSCE, to help resolve a number of key regional disputes and conflicts. It emphasizes the need for NATO and the European Union to build effective peacekeeping forces that can work with Russia, China, and other major and regional powers under UN or OSCE mandates. In addition to arguing for implementing international legal norms to establish joint-sovereignty arrangements for territorial disputes, chapter 10 also critiques Trump's decision to drop out of the 2015 United Nations Climate Change Conference (COP 21) and argues that Trump's antediluvian emphasis on fossil fuels will amplify the global environmental crisis and exacerbate the very sociopolitical-ecological problems that could lead to wider wars—while also isolating the United States in the world community.

And, finally, America cannot truly help to resolve many of the world's problems unless it also engages in major social and political reforms at home—by reforming the electoral college system, by better controlling and reducing spending on the federally subsidized military-industrial-congressional complex, and by engaging in new approaches to the War on Drugs, gun control, and immigration reforms. If federal, state, and local debts (roughly $23.2 trillion in 2017) continue to skyrocket, more radical constitutional reforms of the US bicameral system of democratic governance and restructuration of the fifty-state system could be considered in order to reduce costs and provide fairer and more effective national, regional, and local governance that brings American leadership much closer to the needs and interests of the population. Most crucially, and in priority, the tremendous gaps in income need to be reduced through the implementation of practical and non-ideological systems of shared capitalism and workplace democracy in different kinds of enterprises.

World War Trump is primarily focused on reorienting American foreign and defense policy away from the pursuit of global America First hegemony and toward an omnidirectional peace-oriented diplomacy of interstate conflict resolution and inter-societal reconciliation intended to prevent a new arms race and the subsequent polarization of the world into two rival alliances. Nonetheless, the final chapter sketches a number of possible domestic US reforms that represent a practical alternative to those proposed by the Trump administration and that can hopefully be developed in greater detail in a sequel to this book. Given the depths of the global geopolitical and financial crisis now confronting the United States and the world, the point is that the prevention of major power war will also require radical reforms of the military-industrial-congressional complex, as urged by President Dwight D. Eisenhower in his January 1961 farewell address. The United States will not only need to reformulate its foreign and defense policy but also radically reform its system of governance and its domestic political-economy—if it is to both achieve peace abroad and work to mitigate tendencies toward even deeper social, economic, and political polarization within the United States itself.

CHAPTER 1
THE PERILS OF THE NEW "AMERICA FIRST" NATIONALISM

Even before Donald Trump's first one hundred days in office had finished, his administration was already confronted with a number of domestic and international crises. Trump's policy proposals—and efforts to implement those policies without full consultation with the parties involved—have been met with significant domestic and international political opposition.

Trump's hastily conceived and executed foreign- and domestic-policy decrees; his often-incoherent statements, tweets, and actions with respect to Russia, Ukraine, Crimea, China, and Taiwan, and the ongoing wars in Syria and Iraq; his strong criticism of President Barack Obama's nuclear accord with Iran; his attempts to impose a ban on immigration to the United States from six or seven Muslim-majority "countries of concern"; his policies toward "illegal" immigration and Mexico and Venezuela; his efforts to extend the Global War on Terrorism to Afghanistan (again); his rejection of the COP 21 United Nations Climate Change treaty on global climate change; his failure to strongly condemn the white supremacist and neo-Nazi "Unite the Right" demonstration in Charlottesville, Virginia; his threats to "totally destroy" the country of North Korea in response to its nuclear weapons and missile programs; coupled with many other issues, have all generated considerable domestic and international controversy, protest, and dissent.

TRUMP'S MAJOR POLICY FLIP-FLOPS ON RUSSIA AND CHINA

It was not a very long time after he had become president that Trump had begun to alter many of his presidential campaign pledges, at least in respect to US foreign and security policy. Trump, who had depicted himself in simplified terms as essentially "pro-Russian" and "anti-Chinese" during the US presidential campaign, soon began to flip-flop on both positions, thus creating confusion as to what US global strategy should be toward its two major rivals.

In August 2016, with respect to Russia, presidential candidate Donald Trump had warned that US efforts to regain Crimea on behalf of Ukraine against Russia could result in World War III.[1] Yet just two weeks after he became president, the Trump-Pence administration dramatically reversed course and took a much tougher approach toward the Russian annexation of Crimea and its political-military interference in eastern Ukraine. A year later, in August 2017, Trump reluctantly signed into law H.R. 3364, "Countering America's Adversaries through Sanctions Act," which strengthens sanctions placed on Iran, North Korea, and Russia.

Ironically, Trump's own contradictory foreign-policy proposals, plus congressional investigation into his alleged collusion and business deals with Moscow, and those of his associates, could potentially undermine his promised campaign efforts to achieve a deal with Russian President Vladimir Putin. In addition to Trump's newfound support for Ukrainian claims to Crimea, which Moscow had rapidly annexed in 2014, other policies that could alienate Moscow include Trump's massive nuclear and conventional arms buildup, his opposition to the Iran nuclear accord, and his strong support for Saudi Arabia against Iran. And, in the long term, his push for US shale energy development, coupled with his support for the 2016 Polish-Croatian "Three Seas Initiative," could potentially put the United States into direct rivalry with Russian energy exports to Ukraine and both eastern and western Europe.

Each of Trump's foreign-policy flip-flops are very problematic. Contrary to Trump's frequent declarations that NATO was "obsolete," the Trump-Pence administration soon claimed that it will strongly support NATO, although it still expected allies to spend up to 2 percent of their GDP on defense. And, contrary to Trump's statements that he was "indifferent" to the European Union (although this was dubiously the case), Trump spokespersons began to claim that they strongly supported the European Union. (See chapter 4.)

Prior to becoming president, Trump had stated that he did not care whether or not Ukraine joined NATO. Although Trump no longer appears to propose, as he did in November 2015, that Germany and the Europeans should play the major role in defending Ukraine, he has not yet stated whether he would seek to formalize Ukrainian neutrality or else bring Kiev into NATO. Instead of seeking a formal recognition of Ukrainian neutrality, the Trump administration, in part under congressional pressure, could decide to provide even greater US military assistance to Kiev in its struggle against Russian-supported "autonomists" in eastern Ukraine, thus further antagonizing Moscow—if no diplomatic solution can soon be found. (See chapters 5 and 9.)

Both NATO and the European Union are in dire need of major reforms. Trump's policy flip-flops and unstatesmanlike emotional outbursts are not very helpful when concrete proposals are needed to solve complex problems. Most important, as discussed in this book, Trump needs to address the key issues of the proposed enlargement of NATO to Ukraine and Georgia, as they impact vital Russian security concerns. The United States and Europeans need to explore with Moscow the question as to whether alternative security systems for the Black Sea/Caucasus region and Ukraine can be implemented. And the world still needs to find ways to reduce, if not eliminate, step-by-step, nuclear weaponry where possible—in the process of de-escalating nuclear tensions with North Korea. (See chapters 3, 4, 9, and 10.)

With respect to China, Trump had initially planned to take a very confrontational approach toward Beijing. But he suddenly backed off. Prior to becoming president, Trump had threatened to play the Taiwan independence "card" in an attempt to obtain political, military, and economic concessions from Beijing. Then, just a few weeks after becoming president, Trump suddenly engaged in an about-face in a phone call with the president of China, Xi Jinping, in early February 2017. This reversal of policy was taken after the Chinese president stated he would not agree to speak with President Trump until after Trump had publicly acknowledged the "One-China" policy.[2] Trump may have also suddenly switched positions due to his realization that Beijing was needed to help quell North Korea's nuclear weapons and missile programs. (See chapters 6 and 7.)

OTHER POLICY FLIP-FLOPS

Trump likewise flipped on his Syrian policy. In April 2017, in the midst of his dinner with Chinese President Xi, Trump opted for "cruise missile diplomacy" by firing 59 Tomahawk cruise missiles at a Syrian airbase. This action was ostensibly taken to punish the regime of Syrian leader Bashar al-Assad for the purported use of chemical weaponry against the Syrian people in the ongoing civil war. The irony is that Trump had previously opposed similar missile strikes against Syria when Obama declared that Syria had crossed the "red line" in August 2013 after Damascus had previously been accused of using chemical weaponry. While Obama had opted not to strike, Trump decided to act: For Trump, Syria had now crossed too many "red lines." Under domestic pressure to act, Trump felt he needed to show what he believed to be strength and decisiveness. But his cruise missile diplomacy did not result in any major changes in Syrian or Russian policies in that brutal war.

Trump has also threatened Iran if the latter does not live up to its promises not to develop a nuclear weapons capability in accord with the Joint Comprehensive Plan of Action (JCPOA). That accord has been strongly backed by Russia and China, as well as by US allies France, Germany, and the United Kingdom. Trump's strong criticism of the JCPOA, and US and Israeli threats to engage in missile strikes against presumed Iranian nuclear sites, not only threaten to undermine Trump's promises to achieve a positive relationship with Moscow but also could alienate Iran, particularly if Trump or the US Congress eventually decides to decertify the JCPOA without clear evidence of Iranian cheating. This could then encourage Teheran and other countries in the region to develop nuclear weaponry; Saudi Arabia, for example, could look toward nuclear-capable Pakistan for assistance. And Trump's major $110 billion arms sale to Saudi Arabia in May 2017, which was designed in part to counter Iran's missile testing and conventional weapons buildup, will only exacerbate Iranian-Saudi proxy wars throughout the wider Middle East, from Syria and Iraq to Yemen and up into Afghanistan. (See chapter 8.)

Not only that, but Trump's strong criticism of the Iranian nuclear accord could undermine the possibility that North Korea would accept a somewhat-similar future accord. The failure to press North Korea toward a nuclear freeze, and then hopefully toward denuclearization, could then lead to the further proliferation of nuclear weaponry in the Indo-Pacific—if not to a nuclear war that devastates the Korean Peninsula and much of the region. Here, Pyongyang heard the opposite message than that which Trump had intended in Syria: Pyongyang has continued to test a range of weapons systems in the aftermath of Trump's Tomahawk cruise missile attacks on the Syrian airbase—in preparation for a possible war with the United States. Likewise, in the aftermath of Trump's September 2017 speech to the United Nations, in which Trump called Kim a "Rocket Man . . . on a suicide mission," Pyongyang boosted the rhetoric by threatening to detonate a hydrogen bomb over the Pacific Ocean, and by calling Trump "a mentally deranged US dotard."[3] Put crassly, Trump and Kim have entered into a radioactive pissing match with potentially lethal consequences. (See chapters 7 and 9.)

Trump's anti-immigrant and America First protectionist stance also impacts countries closer to the US homeland and could further destabilize Mexico. In effect, given the ongoing social conflict in Venezuela, Trump-Pence policies toward Latino immigrants could impact US regional security by opening up Central America and the Caribbean to even greater Chinese and Russian political-economic influences—while exacerbating the drug wars and terrorist activities. The need for stability in the region—and for counterbalancing Chinese and Russian influence—is obtaining global attention. NATO has been considering making Venezuela's neighbor, Colombia, NATO's first Latin American partner.[4] In his September 2017 UN speech, rather than urging regional diplomacy, Trump threatened the possibility of US military intervention in Venezuela ostensibly in the effort to help "them . . . regain their democracy." An alternative is concerted mediation with Cuba, but Trump has downgraded US ties to Havana. (See chapters 6 and 10.)

Trump has, however, maintained at least one presidential campaign promise. He has sustained his hardline stance against the Islamic State (IS). The proof is the Pentagon's decision (most likely approved by Trump, although denied by the White House) to pulverize a network of Afghan caves that were occupied by IS fighters, with the use of the massive "Mother of all Bombs." Trump has thus demonstrated his potential to deploy massive force in the Global War on Terrorism by dropping the most powerful non-nuclear bomb in American arsenal. Not only will the use of such a weapon make it more likely that innocent people will be killed as so-called collateral damage, but it also lowers the threshold for the possible use of nuclear weaponry.

"AMERICA FIRST" NATIONALISM AND PROTECTIONISM

Trump has called his right-wing revolution "America First." But it is not certain what this means in a highly interdependent world—even if that interdependence is highly uneven. The United States may still remain the predominant or hegemonic power for a decade or more, but its global interests are being challenged in different regions of the world. It is a situation in which Washington cannot manage all complex political, economic, security, and ecological issues singlehandedly. Truly global problems cannot be managed or resolved without the full cooperation of other states.

By claiming that the whole world has been "ripping off"[5] the United States over the years, Trump has begun to criticize not only US rivals but US allies as well. He has threatened to place high tariffs not only on China but also on the US allies Germany, Japan, South Korea, Mexico, and other countries that have large trade deficits with Washington. These protectionist policies, if implemented, could result in new global and inter-allied trade and currency wars—and could potentially lead to an even deeper long-term recession/depression.

Trump's major economic concern has been the competition from China, with which Washington has a $310 billion trade deficit. Prior to becoming president, Trump attacked what he saw as unfair trade competition due to China's low wages, lack of environmental restrictions, and purported currency manipulation. These, he believed, were the major cause of the loss of an estimated 5 million US manufacturing jobs since 2001.[6] The Trump-Pence administration consequently threatened to counter China's (formerly) cheap labor advantage by raising tariffs.

The key issue, however, is how much of the US job loss is actually due to manufacturing import competition from China or from NAFTA or other trade pacts—and how much of the job loss is actually due to technological innovation and automation that reduce the need for manpower. It is not at all certain that an America First protectionist policy will help regain the considerable amount of manufacturing jobs lost since 2001; this is due to the fact that job loss has also been caused by technological modernization and automation. Another issue is that while import substitution does impact manufacturing and other jobs, those jobs cannot easily be shifted into other sectors. Assuming that US firms cannot fully enter the China market, they could then seek out low-cost trade with other countries. Putting up protectionist barriers on China or other countries could then cause dangerous trade and monetary wars as a result of globally interconnected industries and technologies.[7]

On the one hand, the US turn toward protectionism will press other states to also search for ways to reduce the types of interdependence that leaves them most vulnerable to economic coercion and financial sanctions. In this way, the search for new markets could be positive, in that it will provide states with greater freedom to pursue new markets other than the huge American market. On the other hand, it could also be negative, in that states might be less willing to abide by international laws, technical standards, and coordinated regulations—assuming that they can break somewhat free from corporate or technological interconnections. And by not forging multilateral trade agreements, states and their major corporations may have great difficulties in finding new markets and guaranteed access to increasingly scarce or expensive resources—hence opening the doors to both domestic and international conflict.

Trump's complaints about excessive Chinese imports, lack of US access to Chinese markets, and Chinese currency manipulation, not to overlook China's significant holdings of the US debt, represent a sign of major tensions between the two countries. With respect to Chinese imports, many goods are produced in China by US firms, to the greater profit of the latter. Both Washington and Beijing can be seen as manipulating their currency ratios, but these rates tend to fluctuate in differing cycles anyway, so that one side tends to criticize the other only when the terms of the exchange rate are not in that side's favor.[8] So in April 2017, when the dollar was at a relatively high value versus other currencies, Trump no longer accused China of currency manipulation. Yet the issue has not suddenly disappeared; either country could still opt take strong measures by devaluing their currencies against the other if there is no formal monetary cooperation between the two sides.

The possibility of a trade and monetary war with China is further augmented by the significant growth of the American national debt (over 100 percent of GDP since 2012) that has made the United States dependent, at least in part, on Chinese finance, along with that of Japan. Beijing has been the major foreign purchaser of US government bills, notes, and bonds, and it holds even more debt than the amount owned by American households. As such, Beijing owned $1.24 trillion of the US debt as of September 2016, but has begun to slowly sell its holdings.[9] The rest of the $19.5 trillion US gross federal debt (not including the fifty states and localities) is owned by either the American people or by the US government itself, in part in the form of trust funds for Social Security and for other programs such as retirement accounts. Combined with high levels of personal debt, the massive US debt could eventually impact the future well-being of the American population if the US economy goes into yet another tailspin after that of 2008. And a very large percentage of the US gross national debt is due to US investments in nuclear weaponry and infrastructure since the beginning of the Cold War, plus borrowing for the US-led military interventions in Afghanistan and Iraq since the September 11, 2001, attacks. (See discussion, chapter 2.)

The general danger is that the significant dependence of the United States upon foreign capital (primarily Chinese and Japanese), coupled with a substantial US current account and trade deficit, has historically resulted in an increase in domestic protectionist pressures. And this dependence on foreign capital could mean that the United States will be impacted by the vagaries of Chinese governmental policies—since China is not an US ally.[10] Beijing's control over a significant portion of the US debt accordingly makes it difficult for Washington to challenge Chinese policies and provides Beijing with considerable political-economic leverage over the United States, given its occasional threats to sell its dollar holdings.

It is true that, at the present time, Beijing's threat to sell its US dollar Treasury holdings would lead the value of the US dollar to drop and the price of Chinese exports to the United States to rise. So it is dubious that Beijing would act on those threats any time soon. But in the not-so-long term, Beijing could opt to sell its US Treasury holdings—likely only once it had sufficiently expanded China's domestic consumption for its own products by augmenting incomes, while also expanding its exports to the markets of countries other than the United States.

In this regard, China is, in fact, expanding its regional and global markets though its Belt and Road Initiative (BRI) and through the funds invested by the Chinese Investment Corporation and the Asian Infrastructure Investment Bank (which Beijing sees as a means to counter to the US-dominated World Bank and International Monetary Fund, or IMF). And, given Trump's own hastily conceived decision to dump the Trans-Pacific Partnership (TPP), China will be able to more easily pursue its major new trade accord, the Regional Comprehensive Economic Partnership (RCEP), which includes Russia and possibly India—and which could soon become the largest trading bloc in the world.

The danger is that this US political-economic battle with China could soon play itself out in real battle zones in the Indo-Pacific region. Such a scenario could prove plausible once China develops sufficient military capabilities, with Russian backing, to protect its political-economic interests throughout the Indo-Pacific and overseas, including in Latin America and the Caribbean. It also depends on how Japan will react to the Chinese quest for regional, if not global, hegemony. Already there are signs of increasing Japanese militarization in response to both China's burgeoning military capabilities and North Korea's missile and nuclear weapons provocations. And Tokyo could, somewhat like Beijing, try to use its own holdings of US debt as leverage to draw the United States to defend Japanese interests. (See chapter 6.)

FOCAL POINTS OF CONFLICT AND ALLIANCES

Trump believes that he will be able to preserve American hegemony by engaging in one of the greatest military buildups in US, if not in world, history. Such a major US military buildup, combined with a NATO and Japanese military buildup, Trump believes, will preserve peace with Russia, China, Iran, North Korea, and other states and anti-state movements that might attempt to challenge US hegemony in their specific regions. As he put it, "nobody will dare question our military might again. We believe in peace through strength, and that's what we'll have."[11]

Yet the situation is not quite so simple. Trump's foreign-policy flip flops over Crimea and Taiwan are extremely significant in that the primary geo-strategic, military, and political-economic tensions between the United States/NATO and Russia and between the United States, Japan, and China, revolve to a large extent around these two focal points respectively. In terms of geo-strategic and political-economic interests, both Crimea and Taiwan appear as crucial as the island of Gibraltar or the Falkland Islands for the United Kingdom, or the Panama Canal for the United States. In this perspective, Russian claims to Crimea appear to parallel Chinese claims to both Taiwan and islands in the South and East China Seas—as stated by US Secretary of State Rex Tillerson in his testimony before Congress.[12]

Focal points of conflict represent areas where differing powers struggle for access to raw materials and markets, seek to secure spheres of influence and security, and attempt to establish geostrategic positions for defense or attack. In addition to Taiwan and Crimea, other focal points include Russian-controlled Kaliningrad, which most immediately impacts Poland, the Baltic states, Sweden, the European Union, and NATO. Disputes in the Black Sea region and Caucasus (Russia vs. Georgia; Azerbaijan vs. Armenia; pan-Islamist movements in Dagestan and elsewhere in the Russian-controlled Caucasus) similarly impact directly or indirectly the global geo-economic interests of the United States, the European Union,

NATO, Turkey, and Russia. Disputes over differing islands in the South China and East China Seas impact the United States, Japan, and China, as well as the neighboring countries.

This is not to overlook how the burgeoning tensions over North Korea's nuclear program impact South Korea, Japan, and the United States, as well as China and Russia. The ongoing proxy wars in Syria, Iraq, and Yemen, and elsewhere throughout the wider Middle East between Saudi Arabia and Iran, represent focal points that have already drawn Russia, Iran, Turkey, Israel, Egypt, France, and the United States into the conflict in Syria, with many of the anti-Assad militias financed by Saudi Arabia and other Arab Gulf states or Turkey. US and NATO intervention in Afghanistan, and Indian-Pakistani rivalry over Kashmir, is beginning to draw in China and Russia. There is furthermore a real possibility that sociopolitical conflicts in Mexico and Venezuela, and other countries in Central America and the Caribbean, in part related to drug wars, could begin to draw the United States—if not NATO for the first time as well—into different forms of police or military intervention, as occurred during (and before) the Cold War.

The above areas all represent focal points of conflict that could either spark a major power war or else become theaters of conflict once a major power war breaks out. New regional or major power wars could soon be sparked if the geo-strategic, military, and political-economic disputes that surround these territories are not managed carefully and prudently. And in the background behind each of these conflicts there are deeper geo-strategic and political-economic concerns that are often combined with politico-economic instability and domestic crisis. One of these major issues that could generate major power war is the potential breakup of the Russian-led Collective Security Pact (CSTO), as feared by Moscow, and the potential breakup of NATO, as feared by Washington.

RECIPROCAL FEARS OF THE POTENTIAL BREAKUP OF NATO, THE EUROPEAN UNION, AND THE RUSSIAN-LED CSTO

After seeking to check the NATO and EU double enlargement into Ukraine by annexing Crimea and by supporting "autonomist" forces in the ongoing conflict in eastern Ukraine, Moscow now fears the "loss" of Belarus and the potential breakup of its Collective Security Treaty Organization (CSTO). Moscow likewise opposes the further encroachment of NATO influence into Russian-proclaimed spheres of influence and security in the Black Sea region. At the same time, Moscow fears the possibility that Russian Federation itself will begin to disaggregate in the face of the NATO and EU double enlargement, combined with the rise of pan-Islamist secessionist movements within Russia itself. This is not to overlook the pressure of so-called democracy movements inside the Russian Federation or else regional secessionist movements in Kaliningrad and in Siberia. (If the latter, for example, were to secede from the Russian Federation, Moscow would not be able to benefit from Siberia's significant oil and gas wealth.[13])

The possible disaggregation of the Russian Federation itself is exacerbated by the fact that certain regions are nearly bankrupt, a factor that caused protest in 2017 throughout the country, and not just in Moscow.[14] And unlike the disaggregation of the Soviet Union, the feared disaggregation of the Russian Federation could lead Moscow to engage in a full-scale Russian political-military buildup, which could involve more vengeful Russian actions that are intended to undermine US interests. Given the rise of a new Russian nationalism, it appears dubious that a new Russian reformer, somewhat similar to former Soviet president Mikhail Gorbachev, will be able come to power once Vladimir Putin eventually steps down.

While Moscow fears the eventual breakup of the CSTO, Washington somewhat similarly fears the potential breakup of NATO but for differing reasons. As Turkey becomes an illiberal democracy, it could potentially break away from NATO, for example. Some NATO members, such as Hungary, the Czech Republic, and Bulgaria, are beginning to seek closer relations with Moscow, while NATO member Poland appears to be sliding toward authoritarianism—even if it is a strong supporter of NATO. Most problematic, both the French far right and far left strongly oppose NATO membership, as do most far-right and far-left groups in Europe.

On the one hand, Trump-Pence administration pressures on NATO members to raise defense spending to 2 percent of their GDP could lead some states—specifically those that are in a dire financial situation—to drop out of the alliance. On the other, even an economically powerful state, such as Germany, could drop out of NATO if Berlin enters into a trade war with the United States over sanctions on Russia, among other disputes, and in the effort to forge an all-European system of security and defense. A relatively more independent Europe could then seek a separate accord with Russia or, more likely, with China. In fact, Trump's June 2017 decision to drop out of the 2015 United Nations Climate Change Conference (COP 21), coupled with major disputes with Russia, could help press the Europeans into closer political-economic and technological relations with China. Ironically, Trump's decision against the COP 21 appears to contradict his own concept of America First—that is, if that concept can be defined to mean that the United States should take leadership in innovation. (See chapters 4 and 10.)

Added to the US fear of a breakup of NATO is the potential breakup of the European Union after the United Kingdom's exit from the European Union (Brexit). Trump's proclaimed indifference to the European Union after Brexit—coupled with his ideological support for anti-EU, anti-NATO nationalist movements, combined with very strong criticism of Germany as the political-economic leader of the European Union—have risked undermining the European Union, even if Trump has attempted to backtrack from his previous positions.

One of the major reasons for the Trump-Pence administration to so suddenly reverse course and no longer call NATO "obsolete"—and to speak so highly of both NATO and the "wonderful" EU—is precisely to whip US allies into line. In effect, US efforts to boost NATO defense spending is intended to tighten the defense relations of NATO allies against their common foes. But high levels of defense spending will not resolve the financial crisis impacting European economies. Instead, high defense spending could exacerbate that crisis through increased government borrowing to pay for military capabilities. As the Trump-Pence administration seeks to press US allies (in Europe, in Asia, and in the wider Middle East) to spend more on defense (generally expecting those allies to "buy American"), Trump's America appears to be acting somewhat like ancient Athens as the latter tried to force its allies to pay their dues in the struggle against Sparta during the Peloponnesian War.

In effect, both Washington and Moscow have been attempting to whip their respective NATO and CSTO allies in line—while concurrently probing the weaknesses of the rival alliance. For its part, Moscow has sought to strengthen its ties to China and Iran while also boosting its own defense capabilities in an effort to strengthen the defense relations of its CSTO allies against their common foes. Moscow has also hoped to counter US nuclear and conventional force superiority by asymmetrical military means—leading to a new arms race.

THE NEW ARMS RACE

Initially, during his presidential campaign, and in the early days of his presidency, Trump had proposed to reduce US and Russian nuclear weaponry—in the optimistic assumption that he would be able to make an arms deal with President Putin that would then eliminate economic sanctions placed on Moscow after its annexation of Crimea in 2014, for example. Yet once becoming president, Trump has planned to surpass

Obama's own nuclear and conventional force military buildup—in order to pressure Moscow and other recalcitrant states to make deals on US terms in accord with the maxim: Peace through Strength.[15] Trump wants the Pentagon to engage in a much larger and costlier conventional and nuclear weapons buildup than that which Obama had reluctantly initiated in the midst of his second term.[16]

Obama had initiated a new nuclear and conventional arms race after his failure to "reset" US-Russian relations in 2009 in the aftermath of the five-day August 2008 Georgia-Russia war. This war was, in fact, initiated by Georgia after South Ossetian provocations, with Moscow waiting to pounce on the sidelines. And once Russian troops entered into Georgia itself, the Russian military then threatened Tbilisi, the Georgian capital. After Georgia fought very effectively for its size against Russia in the 2008 Georgia-Russia war, Putin opted for a major military modernization of its armed forces. This, in turn, combined with Beijing's push to militarize islands in the South China Sea and North Korea's nuclear weapons testing, led Obama to engage in a new nuclear modernization program. All of these factors led Obama to engage in a further buildup of US naval forces in what was called "rebalancing" to Asia.

Ironically, however, before announcing the new US nuclear modernization program, Obama had promised to abolish genetically genocidal nuclear weaponry altogether in his speech in Prague in April 2009. At that time, Obama had promised that the United States "would take concrete steps towards a world without nuclear weapons . . . and urge others to do the same."[17] (See chapter 10.)

Obama's efforts to "reset" US-European-Russian relations in 2009 had failed to pursue two proposals that might have opened the door to peace. The first was then Russian President Dmitri Medvedev's June 2008 call for a new European Security Treaty. The second was Turkish President Recep Tayyip Erdoğan's August 2008 call for a new Caucasus Stability and Cooperation Platform. If both of these proposals had been taken more seriously, and more thoroughly discussed and negotiated by the United States, NATO, and the European Union, with Turkey and Russia, then the present crisis might not have reached such a dangerous impasse. (See chapter 9.)

In sum, Trump has advocated building up US military power beyond Obama's military buildup—by means of advocating a Nixon-Reaganite policy of Peace through Strength. The goal of this military buildup is intended to put North Korea and Iran, as well as Russia and China, among other states as well, on their guard. By threat to use force, if not nuclear weapons, Trump has hoped to press these countries into making concessions on US terms, where possible. At the same time, in pushing for an American military buildup, the Trump-Pence administration has also planned to press the Europeans, Japan, and South Korea, Saudi Arabia, and other states to boost their defense spending as well—while concurrently waging the War on Terrorism against the Islamic State (IS) and affiliates of al-Qaeda, among others. The risk, however, is that this tremendous US and allied military buildup appears to be bringing Russia, China, and Iran, among other states, into an even closer alignment. (See chapters 4, 6, and 7.)

HYBRID WARFARE AND THE NEW GLOBAL RIVALRIES

The global rivalries between the United States, the Europeans, Japan, India, Russia, and China, among other regional powers and anti-state organizations, are becoming even more dangerous—precisely because a number of countries are trying to intervene in the domestic affairs of their rivals through techniques of "hybrid warfare." This new form of warfare includes both cyber- sabotage and the cyber-manipulation of popular opinion. Moscow, among other states and anti-state groups, has been accused of engaging in cyber-tampering in different countries. Russian military intelligence, the GRU, has, for example, been accused of intruding into both the US and French presidential elections, through its cyber-espionage group, APT 28 (also known as Fancy Bear). In addition to propagandizing against US policies through RT and Sputnik broadcasts, Moscow has likewise been accused of paying trolls to manipulate US and European public opinion through Facebook and Twitter accounts.

Evidently, this is not the first time that foreign governments have tried to manipulate the views of domestic populations or steal secrets or destroy assets. Throughout history, states and anti-state sociopolitical political movements have used techniques of propaganda, industrial warfare, sabotage, theft, and assassination. Both Washington and Moscow have interfered in the domestic politics of differing countries throughout the world—as well as each other's. Yet it is the United States that has sought to intervene in the elections of other countries roughly twice as much as Russia or the Soviet Union have, at least since 1945.[18]

From the Russian perspective, Moscow has opposed what it sees as US- and EU-inspired democracy engineering in countries with close ties to Russia or within the Russian Federation itself. Moscow considers this a form of "hybrid" or what it calls "nonlinear" warfare.[19] From the Russian perspective, democracy engineering can be traced to US-supported democratic revolutions in Warsaw Pact countries (1980s), Serbia's Bulldozer Revolution (2000), Georgia's Rose Revolution (2003), Ukraine's Orange Revolution (2004), and Ukraine's Euromaidan Movements (2013–2014). This is not to ignore the Cedar Revolution in Lebanon (against Syrian occupation in 2005) and the Arab Spring movements in 2011–2013. The latter prodemocracy movements appeared, at least in part, to be aimed at overthrowing Russian allies, such as Libyan leader Muammar Gaddafi and Syrian leader Bashar al-Assad.

At the same time, however, these sociopolitical movements were not controlled or perfectly manipulated by Washington. The Russian critique of the Arab Spring movement, for example, ignores the fact that US and Europeans allies, such as Ben Ali and Hosni Mubarak, were also overthrown by democracy movements in Tunisia and Egypt, respectively. This indicates that the United States is not entirely a puppet master that can manipulate the entire theater of events through democracy engineering.

Nevertheless, after what Moscow considers US and EU interference in the Ukrainian election process in 2013–2014, President Putin stills fears the possibility that US- and EU-supported democracy movements could eventually attempt to overthrow his own rule—and, perhaps more likely, that of his unstable ally in Belarus, Alyaksandr Lukashenka. In November 2014, Putin observed: "In the modern world extremism is being used as a geopolitical instrument and for remaking spheres of influence. We see what tragic consequences the wave of so-called color revolutions led to. . . . For us this is a lesson and a warning. We should do everything necessary so that nothing similar ever happens in Russia."[20] In effect, this statement implies that Moscow will try to repress such movements inside Russia, while also playing its own game of "nationalist engineering"—by supporting differing pro-Russian sociopolitical movements throughout the world and by interfering in the elections of other countries, if necessary. (See chapters 3, 4, and 5.)

Yet Russia is not the only country that has been accused of cyber-intrusions in American affairs. Chinese hacking into US military and corporate websites has been a major concern. Beijing has purportedly obtained access to US government, aerospace, military-technological, and corporate secrets, from Westinghouse and US Steel, for example. The latter included downloading 4.2 million government personnel files in 2015. The Chinese military purportedly possesses a 100,000-man cyber-espionage division.[21] Beijing has also been an effective political lobbyist in the US Congress, more so than Moscow. More recently, North Korea has been accused of devastating hacking into Sony Pictures, banks, and corporate accounts, ostensibly in order to raise funds for its military programs. North Korean hacking against Sony represented a protest against the film *The Interview*, a satire about a plot to assassinate Kim Jong Un.[22]

And while the United States has pointed the finger at Russia, China, and North Korea for allegedly engaging in differing forms of cyber-tampering and cyber-sabotage in the United States and other countries, Russia and Iran have pointed the finger at the United States and Israel for allegedly engaging in Stuxnet malware attacks against Iran's Natanz nuclear facility—where Iran had been suspected of enriching uranium for military purposes. Both Russian and Iranian officials denounced the Stuxnet cyber-attack as an "act of war." The key issue raised by the Stuxnet attacks is not so much that the computer virus could spread out of control but that state and anti-state actors that possess the appropriate know-how could soon develop similar malware that can be used for cyber-sabotage. These prototypes could then proliferate much easier than does nuclear weaponry—with potentially devastating results.[23]

The point here is that social-political manipulation of domestic societies by external powers is expanding beyond mere media propaganda and classical techniques like assassination and industrial sabotage. This manipulation is becoming part of a larger geopolitical struggle involving techniques of "hybrid" warfare and high-tech processes of manipulation and PSYOPS (psychological operations) that are intended, successfully or not, to transform domestic and elite opinion and mass social behavior. These manipulations are intended to influence the totality of a rival domestic society and its foreign policies and can thus impact a rival state's technological and industrial infrastructure, economies and banking systems, stock markets, corporations, state bureaucracy, governance processes, and international policies. Due to the deep interpenetration of each other's societies and political, economic, and financial processes, these new tactics make the prospects of new kinds of war even more likely. This means that the quest for American military superiority—short of being able to totally annihilate the enemy's military and its population through nuclear weaponry, as threatened by President Trump against North Korea—is impossible to obtain, given the new tactics of hybrid warfare that can engage in malevolent actions inside or outside the territorial perimeters of rival countries.

The danger is that these new forms of hybrid warfare coupled with the general rise of nationalism throughout the world—both of which are being exacerbated by the Trump-Pence administration's military buildup and America First doctrine—tend to press state leadership to demand presumed unilateral "solutions." Yet no conflict can be fully resolved unilaterally—all disputes and conflicts need concerted attention of the major and regional powers and representatives of the populations most concerned.

TOWARD A WORLD OF POLARIZED ALLIANCES?

If Washington—as the still globally hegemonic power—cannot, in the next few years, work to achieve a concerted and cooperative relationship with both Russia and China, then the post–Cold War constellation of major and regional powers could soon polarize into the formation of two rival alliance systems. On the one hand, Washington has already attempted to tighten its alliances with NATO, EU members, Japan, ASEAN states, Israel, Saudi Arabia, and the other Gulf states. On the other, Moscow and Beijing have begun to forge a new Eurasian alliance by means of linking the Russian-led Collective Security Treaty Organization (CSTO) with the Shanghai Cooperation Organization (SCO)—in addition to backing both Iran and Syria, while seeking out other potential allies, such as Brazil, South Africa, Qatar, and Turkey, if not both India and Pakistan, if possible.

As a burgeoning major power, India represents the key global pivot state that could join either alliance—as the United States, Europe, and Japan compete with Russia and China for New Delhi's political-economic and military allegiance. Should India join either alliance, that could represent a decisive shift in the global balance of power, norm, and strategic intent—which, in turn, could destabilize the global system, possibly leading to wider regional, if not major power, wars.

Without sustained steps toward a US diplomatic engagement with both Russia and China, a potential clash between two rival encircling and counter-encircling alliances appears to be in the making. These two essentially insular free trade versus continental protectionist alliances appear to be acting somewhat like the two opposing alliance systems, the British and French–led Triple Entente versus the German-led Triple Alliance, which unexpectedly exploded into major power war in August 1914.[24]

In this perspective, the possession of nuclear weaponry by major and regional powers will not necessarily deter major power war. Despite the lingering Cold War myth of mutual assured destruction (MAD)—that a rough equality of nuclear weaponry will prevent two states from engaging in major power warfare—war between major powers in the new polycentric post–Cold War global system, in which differing states and anti-state actors possess highly uneven power capabilities and influence, becomes even more plausible given the rise of new high-tech forms of combat, advanced stealth systems, renovated tactical nuclear weaponry, non-nuclear Prompt Global Strike missiles, and hypersonic and thermobaric weaponry, combined with cyber-sabotage that can destroy military and civilian infrastructure. It is theoretically possible for major powers to involve themselves in a direct but intermittent conflict, keeping nuclear weapons on reserve or using tactical nuclear weaponry with "low" explosive yields. By contrast, lesser powers might be tempted to use nuclear weapons first—in order to offset their relative military weakness vis-à-vis major and regional powers. The real possibility of major power war is furthermore being augmented by the fact the Global War on Terrorism since September 11, 2001, is beginning to merge with rivalries between major and regional powers that could lead to the polarization of the global system into two rival alliances.

In such circumstances that appear to be forging a proto-Sino-Russian alliance, Washington will not be able to play the "China Card" against Moscow as it did during the Cold War. Nor will the United States be able to play Russia against China, given their close financial, political-economic, energy, and burgeoning military relationship. In order to prevent a Sino-Russian alliance from more strongly backing a number of countries, which could possibly include North Korea, it is absolutely essential to better coordinate US and European policy toward North Korea and Iran, among other states, with both Beijing and Moscow. This means that the United States will need to engage in intensive diplomacy with both Moscow and Beijing so as to prevent an even tighter Sino-Russian military alliance, while preventing the outbreak of war on the Korean Peninsula, and in the wider Middle East.

Given the above, Washington needs to engage in a strategy intended to prevent two possible scenarios. The first is the polarization of the world into two rival alliance systems. The second is the feared breakup of the US systems of alliances that could take place—if the United States cannot work with the Europeans, Japan, India, Russia, and China, as well as key regional actors, to establish new systems of regional and global security. Either scenario could result in widening regional wars—if not major power war.

To prevent either of these scenarios, the Trump-Pence administration (or a future US leadership) needs to pursue a full-fledged and concerted diplomatic engagement with both friends and foes alike. In other words, the United States, the Europeans, and Japan must begin to engage in *a truly peace-oriented diplomacy* with *both* Moscow *and* Beijing. The concern raised in this book is that it is not at all clear that Washington can reach international agreements and forge solid alliances—a hope that President Trump himself has expressed—if all countries continue to assert their presumed national interests *above* the interests of other states.

As Trump put it in his inauguration speech: "It is the right of all nations to put their own interests first." But here, Trump makes no real distinction between vital and secondary interests. And he does not indicate whether so-called vital interests can be modified through diplomatic compromises and concessions.[25] Trump's threats and actions have additionally raised questions as to whether his policies are truly of the general American interest or those of his personal interests (or those of his associates). (See chapters 2 and 3.)

Trump's repeated statement that NATO is "obsolete" does not address the major issue and, in fact, makes the security situation even more precarious. The main issue should be how to reform NATO and permit it to retract gracefully from its promises of an open enlargement, while concurrently pressing for a rapprochement between NATO, the European Union, and Russia. The key problem is to put an end to Russian fears of encirclement and regime change, while also mitigating NATO fears of Russian efforts to probe NATO political and military weaknesses. More specifically, the fundamental question is whether NATO should continue to expand its "open" membership policy to Ukraine and Georgia or other countries (as promised in the 2008 Bucharest, 2010 Lisbon, 2012 Chicago, 2014 Wales, and 2016 Warsaw NATO summits) and how to bring NATO and the European Union into more positive relations with Moscow.

As to be argued, if bargained cautiously, a resource- and industrial-rich "neutral" and "decentralized" Ukraine with adequate self-defense capabilities, and with Crimea as an "free-trade zone" under Russian sovereignty, could begin to defuse tensions between the United States, the European Union, NATO, and Russia. It is essential that Russia and Ukraine learn to live side by side—as these two large and contiguous countries will remain in uneven political-economic, energy, and financial interdependence upon each other. Concurrently, it is crucial to find ways to bring China into a closer rapprochement with Japan—while all concerned states need to work to de-escalate the North Korea nuclear weapons and missile threat as soon as possible. (See chapters 9 and 10.)

Trump has rightfully hoped that NATO, the Europeans, and Russia can look for ways to cooperate in the Global War on Terrorism, yet such actions do not appear sufficient to prevent a new global arms race. Nor will such cooperation prevent the real potential for widening conflict—unless diplomatic cooperation between the major powers is soon expanded.

Here, the United States, Europeans, Russia, China, and Japan will need to find ways to reach a rapprochement between Saudi Arabia and Iran, India and Pakistan, and Israel and the Palestinians—if the Global War on Terrorism is ever to come to an end.

The concern raised here is that nationalist America First Trump-Pence administration ideology tends to undermine the crucial need for concerted multilateral diplomatic efforts to achieve global peace through international organizations such as the United Nations, the OSCE, and even more practically through multilateral Contact Groups, among other intergovernmental and nongovernmental inter-social and inter-religious forums that can help find solutions to disputes and conflicts between differing states and societies. The option of joint sovereignty arrangements, for example, backed by the United Nations, the OSCE, or a proposed Asian OSCE-like forum, may represent options that can help resolve interstate disputes over islands in the Indo-Pacific, if not over Crimea or elsewhere.

If the Trump-Pence administration continues to spout America First nationalism—*in such a way that Washington might not envision where and when it is absolutely necessary to compromise or concede on presumed vital interests*—World War Trump could well be the result.

Chapter 2

INAUGURATION TREMORS: RIFLES, TANKS, AND NUCLEAR WEAPONS

Most Americans—if not most of the world—were not expecting Donald Trump to be elected as the forty-fifth president of the United States.[1] Trump nevertheless obtained a solid victory in the electoral college by gaining the majority of Midwestern and Southern states. His rival, former Secretary of State Hillary Clinton, actually won the popular vote by a colossal 2.8 million votes. Yet Clinton's electoral college votes, primarily from coastal states, were not sufficient to win the presidency. Had she obtained roughly 80,000 votes to win a few key states, Michigan, Pennsylvania, and Wisconsin, she might have won the election.[2]

Much as was the case for the victory of George W. Bush, who had won his second presidential term in 2000 against his Democratic opponent, Al Gore, after winning the electoral college votes by a slim majority, Trump's victory once again raised significant questions as to whether the American system of democracy needs major reforms. Even though it was only the fifth time in US history that a president had won the election without winning the popular vote,[3] some form of electoral reforms appear necessary in the short run. In the longer term, a restructuration of the fifty-state system may prove necessary—given significant federal, state, and local debts and huge imbalances in the population sizes and industrial/rural areas across the fifty American states. (See chapter 10.)

PROTEST AT THE PRESIDENTIAL INAUGURATION

Trump's inauguration festivities were confronted by a predominantly peaceful protest of an estimated 500,000 demonstrators (with some estimates as high as 2 million) in Washington, DC—out of an estimated 4.5 million people also protesting throughout the country and much of the world. There were some acts of violence: in Washington, DC, some 209 of the 230 individuals arrested, including journalists, medics, and legal advisers, were charged with felony rioting. This raised fears that Trump could engage in a future crackdown on journalistic freedom.[4]

These inauguration protests attracted many more people than initially expected—and many more than those who came to hail Trump on the day of his inauguration—although this latter fact was denied by the Trump administration as "fake news." The demonstrators had marched on Washington to protest Trump's proposed policies with respect to women, ethnic minority groups, the LGBTQ communities, and in opposition to his campaign pledges to eliminate key environmental programs, develop highly polluting shale energy, and to make deep budget cuts in governmental programs that deal with social issues. (This is not to overlook opposition to his plans for funding a major military buildup.) The protests put Trump on warning that he does need to address the concerns of all Americans—even those who proclaim, "Trump is not my president!"

TRUMP'S DECREES

Once in power, Trump almost immediately launched an attack on the "progressive" or "egalitarian" domestic American policies that are generally demanded by both radical and liberal Democrats. In opposition to President Obama's essentially liberal policies, Trump's nationalist America First policy has generally opposed multilateralism, international trade pacts, arms control, high taxes on corporations and wealthy individuals, and strong federal-government regulation with respect to environmental protection, healthcare, gun control, and US-government backing for the political and legal rights and entitlements of women, minority groups, and immigrants.

Assuming Trump can eventually push his agenda through a Republican-dominated Congress—which will not be so easy, given the fact that not all Republicans necessarily support his policies—some of his proposed reforms appear to promise a boon for a number of corporations (depending on the sector), the banks, and the military-industrial complex in particular. In essence, Trump seeks to dismantle many federal government programs—in seeking budget cuts of up to $3.6 trillion over the next decade—while seeking to boost military spending considerably.

Trump's decrees are generally—but not necessarily—seen as welcome by a number of private enterprises and corporations, particularly given his promises to reduce corporate taxes significantly.[5] Trump initially promised major corporate tax cuts (down to 15-20 percent from 35 percent); cuts in federal regulations (including the banking/finance sector) by 75 percent, if not by more; and a controversial protectionist import or border tax of 20 percent to 35 percent. Yet Trump's tax cut proposals could increase the national debt by $3 to 7 trillion over the next decade.[6]

In order to reduce competition in the name of "economic nationalism," Trump furthermore promised to place a high tax on products from countries such as Germany, Japan, Mexico, China, and others. Trump likewise criticized American automobile firms that build cars in lower-cost foreign factories. Trump's proposals appeared to ignore the fact that many of these countries are highly dependent on the US market, and that many of these products are manufactured abroad by US-based multinational corporations. Moreover, his initial plans to tighten immigration controls were not necessarily seen as positive for agro-industrial firms, food services, restaurants, and retail concerns, as well as short-term construction projects or agricultural needs that often seek out both authorized and unauthorized immigrant labor. Here it has been argued that US firms need the influx of migrant labor, given the fact that the US harvest requires between 1.5 million and 2.2 million workers annually and at least 50–70 percent of farm laborers in the United States are unauthorized. If the United States did not actually face a shortage of labor in agricultural production, the US GDP would have grown by almost $12.4 billion in 2012 and would have produced almost $4.9 billion more in annual farm revenues.[7]

In his first hundred days of office, Trump issued more executive orders than any president since Harry Truman—despite previously criticizing Barack Obama for engaging in "major power grabs of authority."[8]

THE GROWING GAP IN WEALTH

One of the issues that is beginning to delegitimize the American system of governance both at home and abroad is the growing gap between the very wealthy in the United States and the rest of population. In a word, as it takes either tremendous wealth—or else access to finance—just to run for office, the United States is beginning to look like it is being run as a plutocracy. In the United States, the median top 5 percent of households possess more than ninety times the wealth of the median US family.[9] In his presidential campaign, despite his own considerable wealth, Trump himself had denounced outrageously high CEO pay. The chief executive officers (CEOs) of America's biggest companies can earn at least three times more than they did twenty years ago and at least ten times more than thirty years ago.[10] Some estimates put CEO pay at 373 times the average worker's pay.[11] Once he became president, however, Trump's proclaimed concerns with income inequities were quickly forgotten.

Ironically, the independent political machine of Donald Trump, the billionaire, actually spent less money to win the election than did the well-oiled Democratic machine of Hillary Clinton. The total amount spent for the election process is outrageous. Clinton spent almost $1.2

billion, and lost—because of the electoral college. Trump won the electoral college but spent only a little over half of what Clinton spent, roughly $650 million. Trump also needed less money because he was able to use some $66 million of his own money, his own private jet, and other Trump facilities.[12]

Trump has furthermore surrounded himself with wealthy advisers—showing a nepotistic penchant for members of his own family.[13] Trump has packed his Cabinet and administration with a number of individuals who are highly successful in financial terms but who do not necessarily possess significant (or any) governmental and political experience. Trump prefers to support those whom he believes represent real world "success"—as opposed to the input from academic and policy experts. And if Trump's appointees are not wealthy individuals, then they often possess considerable military experience—as has been the case with his National Security Council.[14] The careers of many of the latter individuals (including John Kelly as chief of staff, Jim Mattis as head of the Pentagon, and H. R. McMaster as National Security Advisor) appear heavy on military experience yet lighter on expertise in the areas of diplomacy and diplomatic engagement. Trump's dual emphasis on leadership from the corporate world and from military is taking place at the same time as he seeks to cut funding for the State Department and foreign service—all in a global situation in which effective diplomacy is most needed. At the time of Trump's first one hundred days of office, there were still about two hundred positions at the State Department that required Senate confirmation. The United States lacked ambassadors to NATO, the European Union, France, Germany, and Russia. For some very important diplomatic positions, Trump has been very slow to name nominees, while some of his appointments have questionable or politically biased qualifications.[15]

Yet the very fact that Trump has put the new captains of industry, high tech, and finance, and high-ranking military, in charge of governmental affairs, symbolically puts the capitalist system and the military-industrial complex on trial for the American population and the world.[16] In other words, Trump's success or failure could prove symbolic for the success or failure of capitalism and the American democracy as well. (See chapter 10.)

From this perspective, the very nature of the Trump administration serves as evidence that the United States is ruled by a wealthy plutocracy—and not by the neo-liberal myth of meritocracy.[17] Moreover, Trump's policies of high defense spending—what is called military Keynesianism[18]—appear to advocate a new form of supply-side trickle-down economics for the greater benefit of the defense-sector industries that are spread across most of the fifty US states. Trump has promised that the tremendous benefits accrued by the wealthy through tax reductions and for the military-industrial complex will eventually be passed down to the middle class and poor—but without any political guarantees whatsoever that that will prove to be the case.

POST-OBAMACARE AND THE PROSPECTS FOR DOMESTIC SOCIAL PROTEST AND VIOLENCE

In many ways, the growing gap in wealth in the United States is clearly illustrated by the lack of healthcare for many Americans. Trump's policies include the abolition of "ObamaCare" (the Affordable Health Care Act, or ACA), which is generally seen as very costly for business.[19] And while Trump has promised to remake the Affordable Care Act, given its costs, he also, at least initially, promised not to cut Social Security, Medicare, and other entitlements. Because Medicare and Medicaid provide coverage for around 70 million poor, disabled, and elderly people, it is politically risky to touch; but this has not stopped some Republicans from so doing. Yet the potential failure of Trump to deliver on his promises to achieve a more effective healthcare system could substantially augment social discontent in the United States—at the same time that federal, state, and local debts continue to skyrocket to over $23 trillion—which is now over 100 percent of the US GDP.[20]

By the end of September 2017, the predominantly Republican Congress was not able to find a way to replace the ACA. Influential Republicans such as Susan Collins, John McCain, and Lisa Murkowski, and libertarian Rand Paul, all opposed the Graham-Cassidy repeal measure to replace it.[21] Saner individuals realized that Republicans had not put together a viable option. Following the publication of the first version of Republican (GOP) healthcare plan in March 2017, it had been projected by the Congressional Budget Office that 14 million more people would be uninsured under the GOP legislation than under current law by 2018. Then, following the additional proposed changes to subsidies for insurance, the increase in the number of uninsured people relative to the number under current law was expected to rise to 21 million in 2020 and then to 24 million in 2026 under the March 2017 GOP proposal. If it had passed, the GOP plan could have meant that millions of people with preexisting conditions could find themselves priced out of the market.[22]

Those who supported the proposals argued that the first GOP plan would reduce the federal deficit by $337 billion in first decade—but most likely at the price of considerable domestic American discontentment and protest.[23] The failure to replace Obama's ACA divided the Republican Party and represented a major defeat for Trump. But this defeat will not prevent future efforts to reform ObamaCare, hopefully more prudently, with the advice of experts from both nongovernmental advocacy groups and healthcare providers, and with greater consideration for all political perspectives. Job insecurity and lack of health insurance are both factors that can undermine ideological support for the American system of democratic governance, resulting in social protest, if not increasing drug abuse, criminality, and violence. Washington must eventually work out a more fair and equitable deal on these issues.

US GOVERNMENTAL RESPONSE TO VIOLENCE

The Obama administration had to manage a number of mass urban protests and violence, somewhat reminiscent of urban protests of the 1960s and early 1970s. These protests were often in response to police killings of unarmed individuals—one factor that helped to generate the sociopolitical movement Black Lives Matter, among others. In the current situation, race relations appear to be deteriorating even further. And depending in part on the general level of employment, unemployment, and underemployment,[24] the situation could deteriorate even further.

It is consequently not surprising that a significant April 2017 opinion poll indicated that 36 percent of those interviewed believed that racism and bigotry are an imminent threat to the country (up from 29 percent from two years ago), while 23 percent thought it was serious (up from 22 percent). In other words, almost 60 percent of those interviewed believed racism was on the rise.[25] The poll also expressed concern that Americans believed that they were losing their rights to freedom of speech. If accurate, this poll forewarns of greater domestic American violence ahead. Such violence could be mixed with acts of differing forms of race-related "terrorism" for and against minority groups—combined with both pro- and anti-Islamist "terrorist" actions. And the poll had been taken prior to the violent clashes in which white supremacists, neo-Nazis, and the Ku Klux Klan took the offensive against peaceful counterprotesters in Charlottesville, Virginia, in a counterprotest that took place in August 2017 during a "Unite the Right" demonstration.[26]

The issue of dealing with protest and social discontent is complicated by the some of the completely understandable difficulties that the American police force will confront in dealing with new spates of urban protest. The problem is that even initially peaceful urban protests will tend to be tainted by fears of acts of terrorism. These fears could in turn generate excessive reactions by law enforcement officers, thereby resulting in unnecessary police violence and acts of repression. Trump's often crude, blatantly chauvinistic, and vociferous style of public speech has not done much to calm the situation, and a number of far-right groups and white supremacist leaders, such as former imperial wizard of the KKK David Duke and Richard B. Spencer, the president of the National Policy Institute (a white supremacist think tank), believe that they possess Trump's tacit support, given his refusal to strongly condemn their movements.[27] This belief is also due to Trump's ongoing relationship with his right-wing former National Security Advisor, Steve Bannon.[28]

In the effort to prevent police violence from reoccurring, Trump has promised to provide local police with sufficient resources to be able to build better relationships in their immediate community. At the same time, Trump has also threatened to engage in tougher measures than did the Obama administration in order to control urban violence, drug use, and crime. One of his proposals is to adopt the controversial and dubiously effective "stop-and-frisk" practice nationwide. This, however, implies an expansion of police powers that could be deemed unconstitutional, depending on the way the stop-and-frisk procedure is carried out.[29]

Backed by the National Rifle Association (NRA), one of the most powerful lobbies in the country, Trump has been a strong opponent of gun control, although he has publicly opposed the sale of assault weapons.[30] Yet if accepted into law, his proposed policies could make it easier for both "good" and "bad" guys to obtain weaponry and then carry that weaponry across the country.[31] Permission to take weapons across state lines is thus being proposed in an era in which mass shootings for different personal and ideological motives—and not only Islamist—appear to be becoming more frequent and more lethal in terms of the number of people killed, as illustrated, for example, by the October 1, 2017, mass shooting in Las Vegas.[32] (See chapter 3.)

At the same time, however, handguns and rifles are not the only problem. In the new age of hybrid warfare, everyday technologies and chemicals/substances can become weapons. Airplanes (as on September 11, 2001), trucks (as in Nice, France, on July 14, 2016 and in New York

City on October 31, 2017), and fertilizer bombs soaked in diesel fuel and other chemicals (as in the left-wing bombing of the University of Wisconsin-Madison Army Mathematics Research Center in protest of the Vietnam War in 1970 and the right-wing Oklahoma City bombing of the Alfred P. Murrah Federal Building in 1995), can also be used for purposes of mass killing—whatever the social or political cause might be.

Stricter gun control laws might not prevent all kinds of violence and criminality, but blocking access to assault weapons, among other forms of weaponry, including controlling cop-killer bullet sales, can help limit some mass killings. The 1994 assault weapons ban had expired on September 13, 2004—and subsequent efforts to renew the ban or propose alternative legislation have thus far failed.

Given the significant social problems related to unemployment and underemployment, job discrimination, high levels of drug-related crime, and other forms of criminality, which generally involve the spread of guns, will Trump be able to obtain the trust of urban communities? Or will Trump be confronted by the outbreak of mass urban protests against police violence of the kind that confronted the Obama administration in a number of major US cities? Or will there be more protests like those that took place in Charlottesville, North Carolina, in August 2017—in which a man drove a truck into a group that was counterprotesting the "Unite the Right" demonstration, killing one woman and injuring many others?

Trump's so-called solution to the problems of criminality and "terrorism" inside American society has largely been to justify the right of people to bear arms—rather than to seek ways to control weapons that do not necessarily infringe on personal freedoms. Trump's rhetoric does not appear to recognize the dangers that an even wider spread of heavy weaponry and their bullets will cause—if these weapons are not properly managed and controlled. Trump's so-called solution to both domestic and external threats has been to produce more rifles, tanks, and nuclear missiles, and the like.

TRUMP AND THE MILITARY BUILDUP

One can only speculate how the populations of the world might have reacted to the Trump team's decision to deploy tanks and missile launchers for his inauguration parade—if that had happened. This is actually what Trump's transition team initially proposed in a symbolic effort to show off American military power—as is the case for democratic countries such as France, which is a major arms producer, but which is also endemic for authoritarian and militaristic countries such as Russia, China, and North Korea.

Trump's team evidently did not think about the destructive impact that such heavy military equipment would have had on already heavily traveled Washington, DC, roads and infrastructure. Military flyovers, involving the latest US fighter jets, were approved instead, but they were ruled out at the last minute, ostensibly because of poor weather conditions.[33] Yet what message did Trump's team hope to convey by such a show of force? And how would those protestors, the American people, and the rest of the world, both US allies and rivals, have interpreted that message—if such a display of massive US military power—symbolic of the new America First nationalism—had taken place for the first time on the streets of the US capital, Washington, DC? And will Trump initiate a costly military parade for the future July 4th celebration of the Declaration of Independence, as he has indicated after his visit to France's July 14, 2017, Bastille Day celebrations?

It is clear that Trump's team believes that the United States must reassert itself on the global stage—if US interests and the "civilized world"[34] (in Trump's words) are to be defended and if America's global hegemony is to be sustained. Trump's choice of Mike Pence as his vice presidential running mate had already revealed his alignment with Christian conservatives who generally oppose domestic "political correctness" and "international cosmopolitanism." In terms of foreign policy, Christian conservatism advocates Peace through Strength—and the ostensible need for the United States to show leadership and intervene militarily, even unilaterally, when deemed necessary, but not necessarily, "legitimate."

Pence's formula for confronting Moscow, for example, can be summed up in his own words: "The provocations by Russia need to be met with American strength. . . . We are going to rebuild our military. This whole Putin thing, look, America is stronger than Russia. Our economy is 16 times larger than the Russian economy. Our political system is superior to the crony corrupt capitalist system in Russia it every way."[35] Yet given the fact that the Russian GDP is roughly the size of New York State's, building up the US defense budget—ostensibly in order to negotiate with Moscow (among other states) from a position of strength—is not the way to deal with Moscow, which will continue to react with countermeasures.

As furthermore indicated by its "America First: A Budget Blueprint to Make America Great Again,"[36] the Trump-Pence administration believes that the United States must reassert itself on the global stage through greater defense spending. In mid-February 2017, Trump proposed a major arms buildup that, he believed, would be able to more effectively assert US interests versus its adversaries—while engaging more deeply in the Global War on Terrorism. Trump accordingly proposed to augment defense spending above the already major increase sought by President Obama, to more than $639 billion. (See discussion, this chapter.)

The Obama administration had already planned to spend around $1 trillion on modernizing the US nuclear triad (land, sea, and air forces) over the next three decades against Moscow, China, North Korea, Iran, and other potential threats.[37] This military buildup involves the deployment of five new nuclear weapons systems and the deployment of new naval forces so as to better deter the possibilities of war with North Korea and China in the Indo-Pacific. Obama had initially intended to improve US force capabilities in the Indo-Pacific primarily. Yet Moscow's not-entirely-unexpected military intervention in Crimea and buildup of forces in eastern Europe in early 2014 forced the United States and

NATO to look toward ways to build up military capabilities in eastern Europe as well as in the Indo-Pacific. (See chapters 5 and 6.)

In his telephone call to Russian President Putin in February 2017, President Trump denounced the 2010 New START (Strategic Arms Reduction Treaty), a treaty that had been negotiated by the Obama administration—as a "bad deal," just after Putin had raised the possibility of extending that same treaty. New START permits both countries to possess no more than 700 deployed and 100 non-deployed land-based intercontinental and submarine-launched ballistic missile launchers and heavy bombers equipped to carry nuclear weapons. The treaty also limits each side to no more than 1,550 deployed warheads.[38]

Putin has asserted that Moscow has no intention of reneging on New START and on other arms control obligations. And yet Washington has accused Moscow of deploying a new intermediate-range ground-based cruise missile in violation of the 1987 INF treaty that bans the deployment of US and Russian land-based intermediate-range missiles. This, from a strategic perspective, would provide Moscow with an advantage in a military confrontation, as Russian intermediate-range missiles could be fired against targets in Europe and Japan, while Moscow would hope to protect itself from US retaliation with the threat to strike the US continent with its new intercontinental Topol'-MR (or RS-24 Yars) missile, which Moscow claims possesses multiple hypersonic warheads that can avoid missile defense systems.[39] In 2016, Washington had previously accused Moscow of adding more warheads and missiles, thereby surpassing the 1,550 warhead limit set by New START. But Moscow has until February 2018 to comply. (See chapter 10.)

This new buildup of American military capabilities has accordingly been aimed to cover a number of possible contingencies. Such capabilities would, it is believed, be sufficient to handle two major wars or "major regional contingencies" (MRCs) nearly simultaneously.[40] Trump also claims that he intends to develop a state-of-the-art missile defense system that includes the modernization of US naval cruisers with such antimissile capabilities. As part of this new military buildup, the Pentagon has been urging the Trump administration to consider a review of the US nuclear arsenal and force posture. The Pentagon also hopes to make the United States more capable of prosecuting a "limited" nuclear war—whether against North Korea, the Islamic State, Iran, Russia, China, or others—even if it is dubious such a war would remain "limited."[41]

For these scenarios, the US Army would need to increase in size to about 540,000 active-duty soldiers. This would represent an actual increase above the 460,000 active soldiers that the Pentagon itself called for in its $583 billion budget proposal for FY2017.[42]

In May 2017, Trump sent Congress a finalized proposed budget request for FY2018 of $639.1 billion. It would spend $574.5 billion for the base budget and allocate $64.6 billion for the Overseas Contingency Operations (OCO) budget, which is not included in the official defense base budget. The latter account pays for operations in Syria, Iraq, Northern Pakistan, and other regions. This overall budget request was $52 billion above the defense budget cap demanded by the Budget and Control Act (BCA) of 2011, and it does not fully include other defense-related costs to be discussed in this chapter.[43]

REAL DEFENSE COSTS

In 2016, official US defense spending for the base budget was already an astronomical $597 billion—almost as much as the next fourteen countries put together. China's budget of $145.8 billion, for example, was less than a third of the US budget.[44] Official US defense spending was thus roughly $385 billion more than China, $500 billion more than Saudi Arabia, and $530 billion more than Russia.[45]

But these official figures do not tell the whole story. To obtain total defense spending, one needs to add onto the Department of Defense budget those items related to defense spending in other government agencies. These include: veteran affairs (in the Veteran's Administration); military retiree payments and interest payments on money borrowed to fund previous military programs (in the Treasury budget); military aspects of the space program (in the NASA budget); energy programs that go for secret defense and nuclear weapons research, testing, and storage purposes (in the Energy budget); and foreign military aid in the form of weapons grants for allies (included in the State Department budget). Other defense costs include sales and property taxes at military bases (in local government budgets), plus the hidden expenses of tax-free food, housing, and combat pay allowances. One also needs to add on the costs of maintaining seventeen intelligence agencies, including Homeland Security, that are involved in international intelligence gathering and operations. If one adds all of these, the figure grows much higher, way above 20 percent of the total federal budget. And it averages per fiscal year about double what the Pentagon officially reports.[46]

But even then, the yearly DOD base budget does not account for the fact that the wars in Afghanistan, Pakistan, Iraq, and Syria represent supplemental spending, which is placed in the separate Overseas Contingency Operations (OCO) account, as mentioned above. The overall costs of these wars (plus other expenses that are not included the official DOD budget) from 2001 to 2016 added up to some $4.8 trillion in 2016 and are still rising.[47] And the costs of these wars would have been even greater if US interest rates had been higher since 2001.

QUESTION OF INTEREST RATES

The US Federal Reserve's controversial decision to keep federal interest rates artificially low in the period from 2002 to 2004 during the George W. Bush administration made the costs of borrowing for the Global War on Terrorism relatively much less expensive than what might have been the case otherwise. The Federal Reserve Bank is supposed to be independent of the US executive branch of government, yet the low interest rates at that time (whether or not they were made low "accidentally on purpose") just happened to make borrowing for the Global War on Terrorism in 2001 and the subsequent US-led intervention in Iraq in 2003 much cheaper. This is an issue that should be investigated. In the view of many economists who argued that interest rates should have been raised at the time of the dot-com crisis of 2000–2002, these low interest rates eventually had a severe impact on the economy. They represent one of the major causes of the 2008 global recession, as low interest rates provided cheap money to both China and US consumers, which in turn fueled the housing market bubble and its collapse, as illustrated in the subprime and "liars' loan" crisis, while assisting China's financial boom in the longer term.[48]

SOCIAL COSTS OF HIGH DEFENSE SPENDING

In order to help cover for the increase in defense spending, Trump has promised to cut governmental nondefense spending—instead of cutting the fat off military spending. Trump's proposed budget cuts include cuts in the State Department and foreign aid by some 30–37 percent, in addition to cuts in environmental protection programs, among other areas.[49] At present, roughly 60 percent of foreign aid goes to economic and development assistance, and 40 percent goes to security concerns. These cuts could impact US relations with a number of strategically important countries. The highest aid recipients in 2016 include Afghanistan, Israel, Egypt, Iraq, Jordan, and Pakistan, then Kenya, Nigeria, Tanzania, and Ethiopia.

Through such cuts, to a certain extent resisted by Congress, Trump has hoped to achieve a total reduction in federal spending by $10.5 trillion over ten years. In the past, increases in the Pentagon's budget have generally been financed by cuts in nonmilitary public spending, by borrowing from the Social Security Trust Fund, and by debt and deficit spending—

and at a tremendous cost for the overall economy. At the same time, this excessive government expenditure is justified by sustaining US superiority in arms and in arms sales to US allies so as to partially amortize the costs of public expenditure for the US military-industrial complex.

In 2015, the United States led in arms transfer agreements worldwide, making agreements valued at $40.2 billion (50.29 percent of all such agreements), up from $36.1 billion in 2014. The United States also led in the actual transfer or delivery of arms: In 2015, the United States ranked first in the value of all arms deliveries worldwide, making nearly $16.9 billion in such deliveries, or 36.62 percent of arms transfers. US arms sales have outpaced Russia's for the past eight years, with France in third place.[50] Yet even these sales do not amount to the total overall public costs of maintaining the military-industrial complex.

Coupled with the fact that defense spending is roughly double what is officially reported, assuming all defense budget categories are added up in their entirety, it is clear that the high costs of the defense program cut significantly into social needs. Trump's proposed cuts in nonmilitary affairs appear all the more absurd given the fact that defense spending dwarfs the mere 2 percent spent on the State Department (which also includes foreign military aid in the form of weapons grants for allies) and on international affairs—at a time when the United States and the world needs more diplomacy, with quality leadership at the head of the desks in key State Department positions. And defense spending furthermore dwarfs the amount the United States provides each year to the United Nations for peacekeeping, environmental protection, refugees, public health, and so on. The State Department should have been taking the lead in foreign affairs, but over the years, the military and intelligence agencies have gained predominance within the US governmental bureaucracy—much as President Eisenhower warned.[51] (See chapter 10.)

THE FAILURE TO MAKE SAVINGS

The Pentagon purportedly squashed a major study to restructure its approach to business operations. That 2016 study proposed that the United States could save $125 billion over five years and even more in the future. This could be done by streamlining bureaucracy, cutting back on the amount of high-priced contractors, and by making better use of information technology without necessarily reducing military forces or firing administrators.[52]

The Congressional Budget Office (CBO) also reported that the Pentagon could save tens of billions of dollars over the next ten years alone by delaying, reducing, or canceling deployments of a number of weapons systems.[53] These weapons systems include *Columbia*-class nuclear-armed submarines; a new intercontinental missile, the Ground-Based Strategic Deterrent; the new nuclear cruise missile, the Long-Range Standoff Cruise Missile (LRSO); and the Long-Range Strike Bomber. It is also possible to reduce or eliminate the numbers of B-61-12 "tactical" nuclear warheads (with 480 now scheduled for production by 2020). These weapons can be carried by the F-35 and the Long-Range Strike Bomber—in addition to already-existing fighter jets and bombers.[54] All of these systems can be questioned on both strategic (unnecessary or provocative) and financial grounds (excessively costly).[55] A number of these powerful weapons systems could be unilaterally reduced or eliminated, or else bargained down, as part of a general arms accord with Moscow and possibly with China. But to do that, the United States will need to engage in truly peace-oriented diplomacy.

During his presidential campaign, Trump had stated that he opposed the congressionally mandated sequestration process of the 2011 Budget Control Act that was aimed at cutting defense spending. From Trump's perspective, sequestration cut both wasteful and necessary military spending by equal percentages. This meant that absolutely necessary budget cuts due to excessive military spending might not necessarily make strategic or even practical sense.[56] At that time, before he became president, Trump claimed that he would not seek an across-the-board military buildup, but instead would build only those weapons systems that are truly "needed" by the military—and that are not pushed on the military by demagogic congressional demands of what should be called the "military-industrial-congressional complex."[57]

Once he became president, however, in seeking to abolish the sequestration process, Trump consequently tried to claim personal credit for reducing excessive expenditures on the F-35, for example. The F-35 advanced fighter is one of the most expensive defense boondoggles in US history, and is expected to cost upward of $1.45 trillion over its fifty-year life span.[58] But contrary to Trump's boasts, the Government Accountability Office (GAO) stated that the fifth-generation fighter still faces over $1 billion in cost overruns in FY2017 and is officially estimated to cost $10.3 billion in FY2018.[59] And there is some dispute about F-35 capabilities versus the Russian SU-35 and integrated air defenses. In fact, the United States, Russia, India, and China are all having both technological and cost problems with stealth fighter jets. And F-35s could also prove vulnerable to Russian-made anti-aircraft missiles, such as the S-400.[60]

TRUMP'S PLAN TO BOOST INFRASTRUCTURE INVESTMENTS

It is true that Trump's plans to boost defense expenditure will most likely generate high-skill high-tech work in the military-industrial complex throughout many of the fifty states, with some trickle-down effect. But increased defense spending risks reducing government funding available for other much-needed non-defense alternatives and alternative-energy projects, while augmenting the national debt. The irony raised here is that the roots of the US infrastructure crisis stems from mistakes that Ronald Reagan had already made with high military spending hikes and supply-side tax cuts. Reagan's policies did help expand the economy in the 1980s, but they also resulted in "insufficient investment in physical public capital such as highways, bridges, mass transit, waste water facilities, hazardous waste sites, and the like."[61]

To improve American infrastructure, Trump has proposed using $200 billion in public money as a means to leverage $1 trillion in private funding. This amount, for example, is expected to include some $40 billion in Saudi funding that was promised after the $110 billion arms deal with Saudi Arabia that was announced in May 2017.[62] Trump thus hopes to raise money by leveraging public funding, while replacing publicly supplied services and infrastructure with private-supplied goods and services. This approach will nevertheless continue to diminish and weaken the public sector—with uncertain consequences.

Perhaps more ironically, the Chinese Investment Corporation (CIC) has been looking to invest in Trump's infrastructure projects ostensibly in an effort to build trust between the two countries. Beijing's CIC claims that the United States will need as much as $8 trillion in infrastructure development, not just $1 trillion.[63] Contrary to Trump's anti-Saudi and anti-Chinese presidential campaign stances, it looks like both Saudi and Chinese finance are needed to save Trump's infrastructure program—and will help indirectly pay for his major military buildup while also exposing American politics to greater Chinese and Saudi political-economic influence.

It is furthermore not yet clear what kind of infrastructure projects would be funded—as Democrats oppose the use of healthcare as an infrastructure project, for example. Trump's ideology of "economic nationalism" emphasizes some areas of US "infrastructure development." These areas include the military-industrial complex and fossil fuels, for example, and roads, bridges, navigable waterways, and dams. But the Trump administration might not consider the infrastructure needed for mass transit, healthy drinking water, waste recycling, housing, alternative energy, and ecologically safe technologies. The dilemma is that much of the money spent on the defense buildup could be better spent on college scholarships for increasingly expensive education, for example, among other crucial nondefense needs.[64] Trump's emphasis on physical infrastructure development also overlooks the fact that a solid education in both practical studies and liberal arts provides the basis for all infrastructure development and for future innovations.

CONGRESS AND THE MILITARY-INDUSTRIAL COMPLEX

Not only does Trump's leadership and the US democratic process appear more closely linked with capitalist elites, but also it appears even more perilously linked with the military-industrial complex that President Eisenhower warned about in his 1961 farewell address: "we have been compelled to create a permanent armaments industry of vast proportions."

The problem is that the American system of spoils leads congresspeople to push for news arms projects. Arms lobbyists often try to press the US Congress to accept their policy, development, and even military-technology proposals upon promises of investment and additional jobs for the state—or else upon their particular definition of "national security."[65] On at least two occasions since the sequestering laws that seek to automatically cut defense costs went into effect in 2011, it was Congress (and not the Pentagon) that had decided to lift the spending caps so as to increase defense spending. The concern raised here is that the military-industrial complex operates and provides jobs in a vast majority of US states, so that the more weapons systems or parts of weapons systems that a state receives to construct, the more jobs (combined with the trickle-down effects of military Keynesianism) the state will support and more votes Congress can expect. The system is difficult to break, particularly because the House of Representatives is elected on two-year terms and congresspeople need show positive results as soon as possible. (This represents a significant reason to restructure the bicameral legislative system. See chapter 10.)

The fact that Vice President Mike Pence has supported the building of the extremely costly F-22 Raptor, among other excessively expensive and strategically unnecessary weapons systems, indicates the influence of the military-industrial-congressional complex.[66] Here, contrary to his pretended opposition to wasteful and excessive military spending, Trump himself has stated: "Accomplishing this military rebuild will be a fifty-state effort—every state in the union will be able to take part in rebuilding our military and developing the technologies of tomorrow."[67] Yet this linkage between the federally financed military-industrial complex and the fifty states is the root of the overspending!

POLITICIANS AND THE MILITARY-INDUSTRIAL COMPLEX

Perhaps more ironically, of the top five presidential candidates, it was the Democrat Hillary Clinton who obtained more money during the 2015–2016 election cycle from defense contractor employees than the next four presidential candidates combined. And the proclaimed democratic socialist Bernie Sanders actually obtained $100,000 more from defense contractors than did Donald Trump. And among Senators, Bernie Sanders also obtained more funding from defense contractor employees than Republican Senators Ted Cruz and John McCain—who are strong supporters of Peace through Strength.

To his credit, Senator McCain has criticized excessive defense spending on some projects, such as the extremely costly F-35 stealth fighter. Yet McCain also proposed a $640 billion base defense budget for 2017, much larger than that of Trump.[68] For his part, Sanders has nevertheless continued to argue for much deeper defense cuts than McCain—despite his continued support for the controversial F-35 fighter jet, which has three production plants based in Sanders's home state of Vermont.[69]

THE DOMESTIC AND INTERNATIONAL IMPACT OF A NEW ARMS RACE

How will Trump's America First military buildup impact American society? Will it really lead to a form of growth that more equitably distributes wealth, as Trump promised during his election campaign? Will excessive US governmental spending in the highly capital-intensive military-industrial complex really trickle down to benefit the general population, even if military industries are spread throughout most of the fifty states? Or will Trump's military buildup simply exacerbate the growing gap in the United States between rich and poor and indirectly press young people into state-financed military careers? And will Trump's display of a big stick necessarily result in peace—if the tools of diplomacy are undermined by excessive emphasis on military power?

The point is that government funding for the military-industrial complex—ostensibly in order to sustain US military superiority against all potential rivals alone—is not necessarily sufficient to keep the peace. On the international side, the dilemma is that the United States as a global hegemonic power cannot cover all regional contingencies where rival major and lesser powers and anti-state movements may possess a tactical advantage—or believe that they can seize one. On the domestic side, should Trump's new military Keynesian version of trickle-down economics fail to lift the economy, the result will be a major political-economic crisis and the augmentation of social and political conflict at home.

The danger is that Trump's massive military program will create more pork-barrel projects, significantly boost the national debt, and antagonize firms and workers who do not partake directly or indirectly in the military-industrial complex—while fomenting a global arms race among those state and anti-state partisan movements most opposed to America First policies. And because the United States still represents the predominant global power, a failure to lead the country at home will lead to even greater social and geopolitical strife abroad.

What is needed is a *greater*, not lesser, emphasis on omnidirectional peace-oriented diplomacy in an effort to prevent a new arms race—so as to thoroughly reduce excessive government spending on armaments and to foster positive conditions for national and international socioeconomic development and environmental protection. (See chapters 9 and 10.)

CHAPTER 3

THE NEW BOGEYMAN: RUSSIANS, IMMIGRANTS, MUSLIMS—AND THE QUESTION OF IMPEACHMENT

The fact that Donald Trump did not obtain a clear mandate from the American people—in an election in which only roughly 58 percent of eligible voters participated—has appeared to delegitimize the very nature of the American democratic system. Yet what has additionally worked to discredit the American elections have been accusations by both Trump and his opponents that foreign influence—both "illegal" immigrants and the "Kremlin"—had tampered with this important dimension of American society. This is not to overlook Trump's earlier allegations that the elections were supposedly rigged in advance—but he nevertheless won unexpectedly and without a majority of the popular vote![1] (See also chapter 10.)

THE ALLEGED ROLE OF MOSCOW

Just after the presidential vote count was in, President Obama rapidly accused Moscow of tampering with the US election process through cyber-intrusions. Obama ordered the FBI and five other law enforcement and intelligence agencies to start an investigation as to whether the Kremlin had attempted to influence the presidential election.[2] Republican Senator John McCain declared that alleged Russian hacking into American domestic affairs represented an "act of war."[3] Senator McCain, with Senator Lindsey Graham, then pressed for a full-fledged Senate Select Committee investigation. In response, Trump replied in a tweet that urged McCain and Graham to halt their investigation into Russia and to "focus their energies on ISIS, illegal immigration and border security instead of always looking to start World War III."[4] Nevertheless, both the House Committee and a Senate Select Committee continued to investigate Russian activities in the US elections and Trump's relations with Moscow, as have two other committees. For his part, Senator McCain also pushed for an independent inquiry.[5]

McCain not only sought to inflame the American public opinion against Russia, but also sought to condemn Trump for his ostensibly pro-Putin political stance. McCain did state that he would not, however, actually go to "war" with Russia over the issue. From a legal standpoint, such actions involving interference in the election process, assuming they could be proven, could not be considered a rationale for an initiation of armed conflict. At the same time, such intrusions would represent an "illegal" external intrusion in American internal affairs and could therefore invite some form of retorsion.[6]

By mid-May 2017, as events unfolded, and just after Trump fired FBI Director James Comey, who had begun to investigate Trump's alleged connections to Russia, former FBI Director Robert Mueller was appointed as a special counsel with the power to investigate whether Moscow had in any way covertly aided President-elect Donald Trump, and whether or not Trump himself, or any of his associates, were hoping to profit, for example, from its contacts with Russian officials. One accusation was that the Trump administration could put an end to the sanctions placed on Moscow in 2014 in the aftermath of the Russian annexation of Crimea and its political-military interference in eastern Ukraine, in exchange for business favors. Specific areas of investigation have included the alleged Trump compliance with the hacking and leaks of emails written by key figures in the Democratic Party; Donald Trump Jr.'s meeting with a lawyer with purported Russian government connections, in an effort to obtain "dirt" on Hillary Clinton; whether or not the Trump campaign was involved in Russian efforts to spread fake news targeted at voters in key states; and whether or not Moscow did attempt to hack into US election-related computer systems. Unlike the investigations of the congressional committees, Mueller has the power to file federal charges.[7] By late October, Mueller indicted three people, Trump's former campaign chief, a former Trump business associate, and Trump's ex-foreign policy adviser, with alleged crimes that included money laundering, lying to the FBI, and conspiracy against the United States.[8]

DOMESTIC ATTACKS AGAINST TRUMP

The key domestic dilemma for the Trump administration is that President Trump's campaign promises to engage in a rapprochement with President Putin immediately evoked strong congressional opposition. Both Republicans and Democrats have strongly opposed the lifting of economic sanctions on Russia without also seeking a guarantee that Moscow will withdraw its clandestine forces from eastern Ukraine and then return Crimea, which Moscow annexed in early 2014, back to Ukraine. This was seen in the passing of the August 2016 H.R. 3364 Act, "Countering America's Adversaries through Sanctions Act." Given its strong bipartisan congressional backing, Trump was pressed to sign the bill into law despite the fact that he considered it to be "flawed"; Trump argued that the bill "encroaches on the executive branch's authority to negotiate" and "makes it harder for the United States to strike good deals for the American people and will drive China, Russia and North Korea much closer together." The bill could also "hinder our important work with European allies to resolve the conflict in Ukraine," he argued.[9]

In American domestic debates, the crisis in Ukraine has generally been blamed on Moscow *alone* due to the Russian annexation of Crimea and its political-military interference in eastern Ukraine. American observers tend to downplay issues concerning the highly centralized nature of the Ukrainian domestic power structure and Kiev's discrimination against the Russophone Ukrainian minority. There is thus a tendency for Moscow *alone* to be blamed for the continuation of the conflict in eastern Ukraine by arming the autonomist movements—as opposed to Kiev's failure to follow up on the Minsk II accords and its refusal to negotiate directly with the "autonomist" factions in the Donbas region due to Kiev's strong opposition to federalism and decentralization of power. (See chapters 5 and 9.)

That Trump has realized that his efforts to seek a rapprochement with Russia are not "good" for him in political terms is seen in his following statement: "If we could get along with Russia, that's a positive thing. We have a very talented man, Rex Tillerson, who's going to be meeting with them shortly, and I told him, I said, 'I know politically it's probably not good for me. . . . I would love to be able to get along with Russia. Now, you've had a lot of presidents that haven't taken that tack. Look where we are now."[10]

Trump has largely based his hopes on greater cooperation with President Putin through concerted cooperation in the Global War on Terrorism—in the hope that such cooperation will lead to cooperation in other areas. Trump accordingly said: "I respect a lot of people, but that doesn't mean I'm going to get along with him. He's a leader of his country. I say it's better to get along with Russia than not. And if Russia helps us in the fight against ISIS, which is a major fight, and Islamic terrorism all over the world—that's a good thing. Will I get along with him? I have no idea."[11] In his own eccentric way, Trump has argued that his efforts to deal with Putin are not personal—but a national security issue, an affair of the state. Nevertheless, Trump has been suspected of seeking personal profit from his dealings with Moscow.

Trump's off-the-wall and off-key statements regularly bring him political trouble. When a journalist insisted that Putin was a killer, Trump replied: "There are a lot of killers. We have a lot of killers. . . . Well, you think our country is so innocent?"[12] It has been alleged without absolute proof that that Putin had ordered the death of Russian journalists (including Anna Politkovskaya, who reported on human rights abuses during the brutal Russian military intervention in Chechnya) and other opponents of the regime (such as Boris Nemtsov, an opposition politician who strongly denounced Putin's corruption and Russian intervention in Crimea and in eastern Ukraine).[13] Putin has also been accused of killing Alexander Litvinenko, former FSB and KGB agent, who denounced Putin as coming to power with the help of the Russian secret police, the FSB.[14] Litvinenko was murdered by the use of the radioactive substance polonium in a London restaurant in 2006—an affair that soured Anglo-Russian diplomatic relations for years. Litvinenko had openly accused Putin of killing the Russian investigative journalist Anna Politkovskaya and engaging in other criminal actions.

Although it does not justify murder, of course, the fact of the matter is that Putin is far less repressive, in comparative historical terms, than Lenin or Stalin, or even previous tsars. And Washington has had to negotiate with the leadership of far more repulsive regimes (including Joseph Stalin and Mao Zedong, among others, who have engaged in mass murder) as part of geopolitical realities. And although Trump could have replied more tactfully, the Central Intelligence Agency (CIA) has, in fact, been accused of assassination, both before and after the Cold War, and has engaged in so-called targeted killing, with the use of drones in Pakistan and Afghanistan. The US government has also been accused of torturing or attacking journalists critical of US policy. NATO, for example, as the US-led defense organization, bombed Radio Television Serbia in downtown Belgrade, Serbia (a Russian ally) in 1999 during the war over Kosovo, for example, killing sixteen people.[15] Washington has likewise been accused of killing and torturing Al Jazeera journalists, among others. In addition to the use of so-called enhanced interrogation techniques (which included waterboard torture) at Guantanamo Bay, the Abu Ghraib prison scandal—which involved torture, rape, and murder—has represented a national disgrace.[16] Since the scandals at both prisons have worked to undermine fundamental American values, the United States cannot claim the higher moral ground versus Putin's Russia. Moreover, Putin's preclusive interventions in Crimea and eastern Ukraine in 2014 without a UN mandate have not caused even close to the same degree of death and destruction as has George W. Bush's so-called preemptive decision to engage in a major military intervention in Iraq in 2003, for example, also without a UN mandate. In this sense, one cannot point the finger at Putin alone.

ALLEGATIONS OF RUSSIAN TAMPERING IN US ELECTIONS AND IN US DOMESTIC AFFAIRS

Trump has consequently faced severe criticism at home and abroad for his hope to achieve a more positive relationship with Russia—and with Russian leader Putin, in particular. The dilemma is this: Even if Trump is finally able to reach out to Putin and Russia—even in such a way that appears consistent with American national security interests—there will nevertheless be a cloud of suspicion that he did so with his own personal interests, or those of his business associates, in mind.

As the so-called Russia-gate has evolved, the Kremlin has been accused of cyber-tampering in an effort to embarrass Hillary Clinton and the Democrat National Committee, allegedly to help Trump be elected president. These alleged actions resulted in the releasing of private emails of key Democratic leaders that exposed the Democrat's campaign tactics and political manipulations.[17] Moscow (or someone) had also allegedly tapped into Republican Party communications, but these materials were not released.

Alleged Russian meddling in US elections is a major issue that Trump himself made much worse when he urged Russian hackers to target Hillary Clinton's nonsecure personal email server, saying: "Russia, if you're listening, I hope you're able to find the 30,000 emails that are missing."[18] It has been alleged that Moscow used WikiLeaks and other critical media to divulge information that was intended to embarrass Clinton and the Democrats. This accusation has, however, been denied by WikiLeaks founder Julian Assange—even though he himself was not absolutely certain who was ultimately responsible for distribution of the information.[19] But it does appear plausible that disgruntled Democrats who opposed Hillary Clinton may have leaked some materials. In short, Moscow's Fancy Bear espionage group may possibly have engaged in cyber-intrusions, but so did others. In May 2017, Russian President Putin claimed that the Kremlin was not responsible, but that "patriotic-minded" Russians could have been responsible for the alleged cyber-attacks.[20]

At the same time, on the US side, some leaks of highly classified materials at the highest level of government appear to be ignored by Washington, while other leaks have been investigated and prosecuted with the fullest intensity of the law, such as the significant information leaked by Chelsea Manning.[21] In general, the dilemma is that some of these leaks may represent a legitimate reaction to perceived negative government policies that seek to perpetrate conflict or that augment governmental powers. But other leaks may be a result of the opposition by special interest groups to positive state efforts to mitigate conflicts or solve disputes or deal with controversial issues, but which do not serve the interests of those particular groups or individuals. Some leaks may thus be self-serving and done to settle scores. Other leaks may be mis- or dis-information intended to divert attention and shift the focus of journalistic investigations—what Trump himself has called "fake news"—but which is an area in which he himself excels by exaggeration, distortion, or invention of so-called information.

It has been argued that Moscow's alleged cyber hacking was one of the causes in the decline of popular support for Hillary Clinton's bid for the presidency. For her part, Clinton herself did blame Russian President Putin, at least in part, for undermining her presidential campaign, but she also blamed FBI Director James Comey for the way he handled the federal investigation into her use of a non-secure email account for US government purposes. Comey's accusations against Clinton were accordingly seen as impacting voters just days before the election—more so than Russian influence.[22]

But it has not yet been proved whether the alleged Russian hacking or the FBI investigation into Clinton's use of a non-secure email account—if either—was truly responsible for impacting the votes in three key states in Michigan, Pennsylvania, and Wisconsin. Had Clinton obtained roughly 80,000 votes in the aforementioned states, then she might have obtained a large enough number of electoral college votes to win the presidency. Clinton did not even campaign in Wisconsin, because she believed it was solidly blue-collar pro-Democrat state—even though many blue-collar voters were shifting toward Trump.[23] It will be very difficult to prove whether Russian influence and/or the FBI investigation were really the primary reasons for some 80,000 people not to vote for Clinton. Some people did not vote at all or backed third-party candidates simply because they disliked both Trump and Clinton.

MOSCOW LOSES FAITH IN TRUMP

Whether or not Moscow had any real influence in helping Trump get elected appears dubious. It is certain that Moscow did attempt to influence popular opinion in the United States and elsewhere, but to what extent is not clear. Moscow did propagandize against US policies through Russian Television (RT) and Sputnik broadcasts. Moscow most likely paid trolls (as can any group or state) in an effort to secretly manipulate US and European public opinion through Facebook and Twitter accounts. Yet whether and to what extent Russian military intelligence, the GRU, intruded into the US presidential elections, through its cyber-espionage group, APT 28 (also known as Fancy Bear), is not certain.

If, and to what extent, Trump himself might have colluded with Moscow is a major dimension of the FBI investigation. The fact that Trump fired FBI Director Comey in May 2017—ostensibly for the poor way he had handled the Clinton email investigation—even if Comey's actions may have helped Trump and cost Clinton some votes—raised real questions as to the possibility that Trump obstructed justice.[24] Comey was fired just a few days after he had purportedly demanded more resources for the FBI investigation into the alleged ties of Trump and his associates to Moscow. (Comey's alleged demands were denied by the Justice Department but affirmed by a number of congresspeople.) Moreover, Trump had previously urged Comey to kill the investigation of the alleged ties of former National Security Advisor Michael Flynn to Russia (an allegation first denied by the White House). Another possible reason for Comey's firing was that the FBI had begun to investigate Jared Kushner, Trump's son-in-law. Kushner has been accused of opening a secret back channel to Putin, ostensibly to discuss global strategy—an action on the surface that appears appropriate, given the dangerous state of the US-Russian relationship. Yet Kushner; Trump's son Donald Trump Jr.; and Trump's campaign chairman at the time, Paul J. Manafort, all attended a meeting with a lawyer who claimed to possess close connections to the Russian government, in the hope they could obtain damaging information on Hilary Clinton.[25]

Interestingly, while Trump's team was attempting to find dirt on Clinton, Clinton was obtaining dirt on Trump. It is now known that the controversial Fusion GPS report on Russian influence on Trump, which was completed by former British MI6 intelligence agent Christopher Steele, was paid for in part by Hillary Clinton's campaign and the Democratic National Committee.[26] While the Fusion GPS report does not absolutely prove collusion between Trump and the Russian government, and argues that Moscow possessed information that could blackmail Trump, and while fact can be mixed with fiction, the report did point the way to engage in even deeper investigations, given Trump's extensive and long-term connections to Russia.[27]

What gives at least some credence to the Fusion GPS report, and what is not generally stated by the media, is its analysis of the differing factions inside the Russian government. It sounds credible that Prime Minister Dmitri Medvedev, for example, was purportedly furious over the Russian hacking of the Democratic National Council and the subsequent anti-Russian backlash in the United States. The Russian Ambassador to the United States Sergei Kislyak; the Ministry of Foreign Affairs; and independent foreign-policy adviser Yuri Ushakov, had purportedly urged caution. As evidence of tampering came out, Putin's chief of staff, Sergei Ivanov, purportedly argued that the only thing to do was sit back and deny everything—and the blowback would amount to nothing. But then Ivanov was sacked as chief of staff in August 2016, with no public explanation, and was replaced by Anton Vainov, who had no role in the operation. This indicates that Putin may have realized his mistake, although Russian foreign minister Sergei Lavrov, who may also have played a role, remains in office. In effect, some Russian elites, in opposition to Ivanov and Putin, had feared Trump's erratic character and preferred Clinton as the "devil you know" rather than the "devil you don't know."[28] Now, after Trump's election, US-Russian relations are at their lowest level since the end of the Cold War.

Despite alleged clandestine efforts of the Kremlin to support Trump and despite Trump's initially strong support in the Russian government-controlled media, Trump's popular and official backing in Russia began to diminish almost immediately once he became president—in part due to some of his Cabinet choices.[29] By early February, the Trump-Putin dating game was at an end. The tone of the new Trump administration changed dramatically after the new US ambassador to the United Nations, Nikki Haley, issued her first salvo against Russia. Haley condemned Moscow for the upsurge in violence in eastern Ukraine at that time and demanded that Russia return Crimea to Ukraine.[30] (See chapters 1 and 5.) Concurrently, accusations of Russian cyber-tampering in the US presidential elections hit the news headlines and Moscow continued to deny governmental involvement in the US election process.

THE RUSSIAN PERSPECTIVE

In Russian eyes, it was the Obama administration who had acted first by trying to influence the outcome of both the Russian and Ukrainian national elections. In December 2011, Hillary Clinton had publicly supported mass protests against the results of the Russian elections after Putin's party, United Russia, had suffered significant losses. At that time, Putin claimed that hundreds of millions of US dollars were being distributed to influence those elections. Putin accused Clinton of publicly declaring that the elections "were not honest and not fair" before she had even "received the material from the observers"; according to Putin, Clinton "set the tone for some actors in our country and gave them a signal" and "with the support of the US State Department, [they] began active work."[31] Putin further resented Clinton's public remarks and US and news media accusations that Putin, his family, and his associates, had become billionaires. Clinton's criticisms, and those of others, made Putin believe that Washington was seeking "regime change" in Russia.[32]

Putin likewise criticized the influence of NGOs (nongovernmental organizations) backed by the US State Department. Moscow passed legislation to make the paperwork much more difficult for all NGOs to register in Russia. In 2012, Putin signed the so-called foreign agent law. This law required NGOs that received funding from outside Russia to register as foreign agents. NGOs would then be subject to mandatory audits. Moreover, Putin raised the penalties for those caught protesting at unauthorized rallies.

Then, during the Euromaidan protest movement of late 2013–2014 in Ukraine, Moscow intercepted and broadcast comments made by then

Assistant Secretary of State Victoria Nuland. In what has been called "democracy engineering," which backs ostensibly democratic sociopolitical movements that hope to change authoritarian governments into democracies, Nuland's comments indicated US support for specific Ukrainian leaders and expressed her disdain for the less assertive policies of the European Union, for example, in a four-letter word.[33] The Euromaidan movement, backed by the United States, then succeeded in ousting the kleptocratic regime of Ukrainian President Viktor Yanukovych, who was seen as backed by Moscow—even if Yanukovych did always not support Putin on all issues. Yanukovych, for example, refused to join the Russian-led Collective Security Treaty Organization (CSTO), Russia's much weaker version of NATO.

Nevertheless, angered by perceived American efforts to undermine Yanukovich through democracy engineering, Moscow retaliated by using Washington's interference in Ukrainian politics to rationalize its own clandestine military intervention into Crimea and into eastern Ukraine in early 2014—in the effort to check NATO and EU enlargement into its self-defined "near abroad." At that time, Clinton, who was no longer secretary of state, compared Putin's annexation of Crimea with Hitler's annexation of the Sudetenland—but qualified that analogy by stating that she did not think Putin himself was like Hitler.[34] It was nevertheless a remark that must have infuriated Putin—and represented one of the factors that could possibly have led him to engage in alleged Russian cyber-tampering and social-media propaganda in the US elections against Clinton.

THE TRUMP ADMINISTRATION, RUSSIA, AND ENERGY INTERESTS

As the congressional investigations into the Russia-Trump relationship continued, a number of members of Trump's team have been shown to have had some form of close ties to Russian officials or businessmen. And if allegations can be proved to possess some veracity, such a major scandal could easily be used by both Democrats and Republicans in Congress to block any potential Trump efforts to "appease" Moscow. In fact, the publication of the "Paradise Papers" in November 2017 shows the extent to which a number of Trump administration officials are linked financially to offshore financial paradises and to Russian business interests.[35] These disclosures warrant open congressional hearings.[36]

Initially, it was believed that former ExxonMobil CEO Rex Tillerson, whom Trump nominated as Secretary of State, would attempt put an end to the sanctions on Moscow once he took the post. This belief was due to the fact that ExxonMobil had lost more than $1 billion in 2015 on account of US sanctions placed on Russia in 2014, and that ExxonMobil could lose hundreds of billions in the future if it cannot sustain many of its large-scale energy projects in Russia.[37] Yet Tillerson, who had received the Russian Order of Friendship Award from Putin for his role in setting up ExxonMobil's extensive investments in Russian energy reserves, took a very tough stance against Moscow's actions in Crimea and eastern Ukraine during his Senate confirmation hearings for US Secretary of State. Tillerson strongly criticized Obama's policy as being too weak from the outset. Obama, Tillerson asserted, should have advised Ukraine to move all available military assets to its eastern border and provide those assets with defensive weapons, US or NATO air surveillance, and intelligence.[38] Yet had such an approach been taken by Obama, it could have drawn the United States, NATO, and Russia directly into the conflict in eastern Ukraine, as Moscow would seek to fend off Ukrainian forces and foreign surveillance too close to its borders.

Tillerson's tough stance on both Moscow and Beijing at his Senate confirmation hearing helped him to obtain the post as secretary of state. Tillerson was also able to survive congressional scrutiny, in large part by arguing in favor of maintaining sanctions on Moscow—a position that he has generally sustained since becoming secretary of state.[39] Nevertheless, this did not prevent ExxonMobil from applying to the Treasury Department in April 2017 for a waiver from US sanctions on Russia in a bid to resume its joint venture with state oil giant Rosneft. And Tillerson's stance on sanctions has not prevented ExxonMobil from eventually suing the Treasury Department in July 2017 over a $2 million fine for purportedly violating US sanctions against Russia in 2014 at the time when Tillerson was CEO. In general, Trump and Tillerson appear less supportive of sanctions on Moscow than does Vice President Pence.[40]

Yet the first person to fall as a part of this so-called Russia-gate scandal was not Tillerson but Trump's pro-Russian former National Security Advisor Michael Flynn.[41] The key issue here is that Flynn appeared to be setting up a political network inside Ukraine that would attempt to undermine Ukrainian President Petro Poroshenko's rule and his policies toward eastern Ukraine and Crimea and toward Russia—and then forge a new Ukrainian-Russian accord and put an end to sanctions.[42] This is significant, since Washington will eventually need to find a path for both Ukraine and Russia to compromise over eastern Ukraine and Crimea in the near future—even if Flynn's plans have been thrown to the garbage heap.

In addition to his paid role to represent Turkish interests for a company with close ties to the Turkish government, and his work for RT, Flynn may have been in trouble for another reason. It was Flynn, as director of the Defense Intelligence Agency at the time, who claimed that Washington had made a willful "decision" set up a "Salafist principality" in eastern Syria to counter the Assad regime.[43] This frank statement implied that Washington, along with its Arab Gulf allies, supported radical Islamist groups, including al-Qaeda, and may have helped to create the Islamic State. Such an affirmation by a former high-ranking intelligence officer may have enraged a number of invisible faces in US governmental agencies in Washington against him. (See chapters 5 and 9.)

SANCTIONS ON MOSCOW

A number of US senators, both Republican and Democrat, have accordingly wanted to make it extremely difficult for Trump to reduce or eliminate sanctions on Russia—even if those sanctions have ostensibly hurt the profits of major US and European businesses and oil or agricultural interests. Senator John McCain has warned that if President Trump did not soon put an end to speculation that he is still willing to ease sanctions on Russia, "for the sake of America's national security and that of our allies," McCain would work with his colleagues "to codify sanctions against Russia into law."[44]

Senator McCain, and Democratic Senate Minority Leader Chuck Schumer, accordingly initiated the bipartisan effort to require congressional approval before Trump lifts any sanctions against Moscow. "Sectoral sanctions" on Russia that impact major energy companies and banks were due to expire in December 2017—unless extended by Congress.[45] (See chapter 4.)

COUNTER-ALLEGATIONS OF ILLEGAL IMMIGRANTS AND TERRORIST INFILTRATION

Trump and his spokespersons denied the general consensus among US intelligence agencies that Moscow had, with high probability, tampered in the US presidential elections. Instead, Trump repeatedly countered with claims that "3–5 million" unauthorized immigrants had voted "illegally" for Clinton.[46] Trump then stated he would begin an investigation of purported voter fraud once he became president. Such an investigation raised the prospects that the fifty US states would try to implement more restrictive voting regulations (such as voter ID laws) that could further limit the ability of the poor and minorities to vote.

Trump's claim that unauthorized immigrants were permitted to vote for Clinton in the millions is evidently false. But what is true is that when states count all residents for purposes of redistricting, whether or not those residents are eligible to vote, that can change the social and political balance of the election districts at the time of the census. This fact can lead the party who is in the majority in each state's district to try to fix the size and shape of those districts in that party's favor, using the process of gerrymandering.[47]

Yet Trump's negative approach to illegal and unauthorized immigration overlooks the fact that many immigrants fill seasonal and other low-paying jobs that most Americans generally do not want. Trump has nevertheless threatened to expel illegal and unauthorized Mexican and other immigrants. He has furthermore demanded that Mexico pay for the border wall/fence that he plans to extend between the two countries. And he has also threatened to block the remittances that are sent back to the families of undocumented workers living in the United States—an action that would be probably be ruled illegal.

Nevertheless, if Trump is able to force large numbers of aliens to leave the United States, this act could destabilize Mexico and other Central American countries whose populations depend on those remittances. As some 50 percent of Mexicans live in poverty, the remittances of undocumented workers accounted for as much as 2.1 percent of the Mexican GDP in 2010, and they considerably exceeded earnings of Mexico's oil exports in 2016. In fact, immediately after Trump threatened to block bank transfers and helped to erode confidence in the peso during his campaign, Mexicans abroad sent nearly $2.4 billion in transfers in November, 24.7 percent higher than in 2015—the fastest expansion since March 2006.[48]

Trump's threats have generally hurt the Mexican economy. A weak Mexican economy will augment the power of the mafia and the fees of coyotes who take immigrants across the US border, and who will not necessarily be stopped by a wall or fence. A weakened Mexican economy would concurrently strengthen the hands of drug lords in Mexican society, and create greater socioeconomic instability that could impact US urban areas as well. This is true given the degree of violence, political corruption, money laundering, and arms trafficking that takes place as drug traffickers attack each other's gangs for control over territories and populations, and engage in extortion from industries, such as avocado production. This appears plausible given the link between higher remittances and lesser crime rates in Mexico.[49]

A politically unstable failed state on or near US borders could potentially require US police, if not military, interventions. Trump purportedly warned the Mexican president that Mexico was not doing enough to stop those "bad hombres down there"; he said, "You aren't doing enough to stop them. I think your military is scared. Our military isn't, so I just might send them down to take care of it."[50] Jest or not, in December 2010, Mexican drug smugglers were involved in a controversial gun battle with US Border Patrol agents that killed a US officer in a remote canyon in southern Arizona. Incidents like the latter, which involved US government efforts to trace US manufactured guns sent to Mexican drug gangs, could drag the United States into more overt intervention along the border. Such a jest could become a self-fulfilling prophecy—if relations between the United States and Mexico continue to deteriorate—along with the relations between the United States and Venezuela, among other Latin American countries—in part due the perverse political-economic regional impact of the illegal drug trade and the War on Drugs, which results in drug addiction and the spread of guns and criminality in many US cities. (On Venezuela, see chapter 6.)

By contrast, a major change in US policy that would legalize some drugs, and treat the drug epidemic as a social and health issue, could help wind down the War on Drugs, improve US relations with Mexico and Latin America, reduce the number of prisoners in US jails, permit law enforcement authorities to focus on other forms of criminality (including white-collar financial crime and terrorist groups), while concurrently helping to reduce the spread of guns throughout the United States.[51] (See chapter 10.)

FEARS OF DOMESTIC ISLAMIST TERROR

To add to this heightened sense of paranoia, Trump's accusations against millions of "illegal" immigrant voters, who purportedly voted in favor of Hillary Clinton, have been combined with Trump's claims that Islamist terrorists have been trying to infiltrate into American society—by means of both legal and illegal immigration.

In January 2017, Trump activated a ninety-day immigration ban on individuals from seven "countries of concern" and which happened to be Muslim-majority countries. Five of these were predominantly Sunni: Sudan, Libya, Somalia, Yemen, and Syria. And two were predominantly Shi'a: Iran and Iraq. Yet after his first immigration ban was blocked in the courts, Trump issued a new order in March 2017 that dropped Iraq from the list—after reassurances from the Iraqi government that it would provide increased information sharing with the United States. But this shift also appears to have resulted from the fact that US businesses and the US military have major interests in Iraq.[52] The new order would not include American green card holders or previous visas, for example, and it would no longer permanently ban Syrian refugees. At the same time, Trump authorized new decrees that would make it easier to deport any illegal or unauthorized aliens.[53]

Ironically, however, Trump's efforts to ban immigrants from six or seven Muslim-majority countries do not impact the nationalities of the individuals who were directly involved in the September 11, 2001, terrorist attacks: Saudi Arabia had nineteen citizens involved; the United Arab Emirates, two; Egypt, one; and Lebanon, one. In addition, the September 11 attacks were not even orchestrated from Saudi Arabia, or even from Afghanistan—which the United States, under a UN mandate, then attacked in December 2001; the attacks were coordinated by an al-Qaeda cell operating out of Hamburg, Germany—a NATO ally.

Trump has denied that the immigration ban is aimed at Muslims alone. He has claimed that his administration has only been pinpointing those individuals from "countries of concern" who could engage in extreme violence. Nevertheless, the fact that Trump had demanded a "total and complete shutdown of Muslims entering the United States" in December 2015 during his election campaign after the San Bernardino killings by Islamic State sympathizers—and that he plans to "eradicate" radical Islam from the face of the earth, as stated in his January 2017 inauguration address—project the public image that Trump intends to engage in a crusade against the whole Muslim world.

THE QUESTION OF DOMESTIC TERRORISM

Even if some form of immigration ban is eventually upheld by the courts, it is not at all clear that such a ban would necessarily address the real security problem involving acts of terrorism inside the United States. This is because acts of extreme violence are not always influenced by radical Islamist theology, and many of these acts have been carried out by US citizens, not by immigrants or Muslims.

Such acts of terrorism, among many others, include the 2012 mass shooting in Aurora, Colorado, in which the killer was not an Islamist. They also include the 2013 attack in Orlando, Florida, in which the killer purportedly pledged allegiance to the Islamic State. What the two cases had in common was that both killers were mentally disturbed "lone wolves"—with very different personal and social grievances. And both had legally purchased semiautomatic weaponry as American citizens.[54] While al-Qaeda and Islamic State represent organized groups that can provide some technical know-how and information to individuals, lone wolves often act in the hope that their violent actions will be disseminated by the media and then inspire others.[55]

The issue raised here is that given Trump's near-obsessive focus on Islamist militants, the real dangers of "right-wing," anti-Semitic, Islamophobic, and other forms of violent fanaticism and xenophobia must not be ignored. The Norwegian Anders Behring Breivik, for example, murdered seventy-seven young Norwegians on July 22, 2011, at a Labour Party Youth summer camp in the hope that the media attention he would obtain would help his fascist cause gain support in Europe and in Russia. Breivik had hoped to spark a war against both politically correct "cultural Marxism" and against Islamist movements.[56] Breivik's attack and his right-wing ideology then influenced the American Adam Lanza, who shot and killed twenty-six people (including twenty children) at Sandy Hook Elementary School in Newtown, Connecticut. Lanza then shot himself.[57]

In August 2017, white supremacists, neo-Nazis, and the Ku Klux Klan organized a "Unite the Right" demonstration in Charlottesville, Virginia, to protest a decision to remove a statue of Confederate General Robert E. Lee; the violence at that demonstration, which resulted in the death of one counterprotester and the injuring of nineteen others, shows that these right-wing movements are coming out of the closet in the belief that Trump has appeared to sympathize with their cause. Trump did not strongly condemn the white supremacist movement and its racist and neo-Nazi slogans, and instead affirmed that the violence was caused by "hatred, bigotry and violence on many sides."[58] Former imperial wizard of the Ku Klux Klan David Duke stated that protesters were "going to fulfill the promises of Donald Trump" to "take our country back."[59] (Further, other acts of terrorism have been influenced by ideologies other than political Islamism. The killings of police officers in Dallas and Baton Rouge in 2016 by two disturbed US veterans, Micah Johnson and Gavin Long, respectively, were facilitated by the access to assault weapons. These acts appeared to be more inspired by the Black Lives Matter movement and black nationalism than by Islamist ideology.[60])

And finally, Trump was absolutely silent on the issue of gun control when a deranged individual, Stephen C. Paddock, engaged in a mass shooting in Las Vegas, using a device that turned semiautomatic weapons into automatic. Paddock killed himself, and no one seems to know the motivation for the shooting, except perhaps that he had lost a significant amount of wealth and feared losing his casino "high-roller status." Armed with at least twenty guns, Paddock was able to bring four thousand rounds of ammunition into his hotel room before killing at least fifty-eight people and wounding 546.

TRUMP'S CONTINUING FOCUS ON MUSLIMS

In his February 2017 address to Congress, Trump became the first president to use the term "radical Islamic terrorism." He purportedly overruled his newly appointed National Security Advisor, Lt. Gen. H. R. McMaster, who had argued that these groups are better described as "un-Islamic"—even if they claim to represent Islamist beliefs. Neither George W. Bush nor Barack Obama officially referred to "Islamic terrorism." This is because the term conflates Islam as a religion with terrorist organizations that manipulate Islamic beliefs for their own political purposes. In addition, anti-state partisan groups that engage in acts of terrorism and violent extremism might or might not possess "Islamist" ideologies. Trump reiterated the same offensive term in his September 2017 speech to the UN General Assembly, when he proclaimed that he would "stop radical Islamic terrorism."

The issue raised here is that because Trump is focusing on what he has called "radical Islamic terrorism" primarily, US policy might avoid focusing its attention on far-right-wing or far-left-wing or other individuals/groups that are also plotting the use of extreme violence—but that do not possess Islamist ideologies (e.g., the Charlottesville attack and the Las Vegas mass shooting). Yet the October 31, 2017, attack in a Lower Manhattan bike path by Sayfullo Saipov, an Uzbek citizen whom Trump claims had won the green card—but who had ostensibly converted to Islamist extremism only since living in the United States, and who was then praised by the Islamic State for his actions—has permitted Trump to once again go on the attack against violent Islamist movements and immigrants in general, while trying to avoid crucial issues raised by right-wing violence in Charlottesville and by the mass shooting in Las Vegas.

The problem is that the official US government use of the term "radical Islamic terrorism" can be manipulated by militant groups with Islamist ideologies to augment recruitment. This is very problematic because one the major sources of pan-Islamist recruitment is the very high un- and underemployment rate of youth throughout much of the Arab/Islamic world, plus police repression. In addition, these youths are often attracted to militant Islamist movements because Islamists argue that the tremendous Arab oil wealth, which is controlled by the royal families of these countries, which are in turn backed by the United States, European (or Russian) military-industrial complexes, could be better invested in job creation and development of the poorer Arab states. Groups like al-Qaeda and IS oppose not only the United States, Europeans, Russia, China, and Israel but also the Arab Gulf monarchies. (See chapter 8.)

In sum, Trump is doing much too little to unite the country against "hate and evil" in all forms. On the contrary, his anti-Muslim propaganda and perceived sympathy for extreme right-wing movements appear to be helping to spread "hate and evil" and to polarize American society.

THE QUESTION OF IMPEACHMENT

Many of the allegations against Trump discussed in this chapter could be used to impeach him, but the process could prove to be very long and make it even more difficult to pursue US diplomatic initiatives that are truly intended to foster regional and global peace.[61] All accusations against him have, of course, been denied by Trump as "fake news - a total political witch hunt."[62]

Nevertheless, there appear to be viable grounds for the alleged complicity of a number of Trump's political advisers with Russian officials, but it really depends on what was the precise purpose of those contacts between the Trump team and Moscow. The Trump team has been accused of complicity with Moscow in the effort to find damaging information on Hilary Clinton, with information allegedly provided by Russian intelligence services. There have been further allegations that Trump and/or his associates might have obtained significant stock shares in the Russian government's Rosneft Gas Company (close to Putin) in exchange for the lifting of sanctions against Moscow and downplaying the Ukrainian question.[63] As previously mentioned, the disclosure of the "Paradise Papers" could open the door to further congressional investigations of alleged Trump administration corruption.

While a number of the previously mentioned charges have not yet been proved, Trump and his associates have engaged in major business deals with Chinese firms—which has also raised ethical and constitutional questions. In March 2017, for example, Chinese officials rapidly approved thirty-eight new Trump trademarks, including branded businesses from hotels to insurance to bodyguard and escort services.[64]

In May 2017, Trump was additionally accused of allegedly sharing US secrets with Russian Foreign Minister Sergey Lavrov. In this meeting, Trump was said to have revealed the city in the Islamic State's territory where the US intelligence partner, Israel, had detected the purported IS threat to laptops. This sharing of information, which is the president's prerogative, apparently did not go through the appropriate intelligence channels and was not approved by Israel, which feared that it could expose the source of the information. This action, by itself, did not present a case for Trump's impeachment, but it could be considered a violation of his oath of office, in addition to representing an example of presidential incompetence.[65] If it is proven that Trump's firing of FBI Director James Comey did represent obstruction of justice, then this could provide at least one basis for impeachment.

If Trump were impeached, or forced to step down by his own cabinet under Article 25 of the US Constitution, Christian conservative Vice President Mike Pence—who is at least partly responsible for Trump's turn toward a more hardline anti-Russian position—could take his place. But these scenarios will take time to carry out and it is not clear that the Republican-controlled Congress wants Trump out yet—at least not until its radical tax-reduction proposals are implemented into law, after the Republicans failed to defeat ObamaCare and implement a new plan.

More likely, Trump will continue to use both external and internal "threats" such as illegal immigrants, Islamist terrorists, and North Korean nuclear weapons testing to deflect criticism away from the investigation into his affairs with Russia for as long as possible. At the same time, critics of Trump will point to Russia as the predominant "threat." Not all of these "threats" are imagined, and Russia, along with China, could soon represent a real danger—but only because of the failure of US diplomacy to deal with Russia, China, and other perceived threats more effectively.

THE IMPACT OF DOMESTIC THREATS ON FOREIGN POLICY

In sum, allegations of the Kremlin's influence in the US election process, combined with accusations of "illegal" immigrant votes taking part in the US elections, plus fears of Islamist "terrorist" infiltration into American society, not to overlook Beijing's and Pyongyang's alleged cyber-intrusions, all appear designed to illustrate purported foreign threats to the sacrosanct American democratic process and to the safety and security of American society as a whole. On the one hand, Senator John McCain was not alone in decrying alleged Russian cyber-tampering as an "act of war." On the other, President Trump himself has made both "illegal" immigration and fears of "Islamic terrorist" infiltration into American society major issues of his presidency—while Trump's public pronouncements have worked to escalate nuclear tensions with Pyongyang.

If steps are taken to impeach Trump, the danger in such a situation is that Trump's presidential decisions that impact both domestic and foreign policy could be made for domestic tactical reasons, to protect Trump himself—and not for any greater national or international purpose that could serve the greater cause of global peace. As events continue to play out under the looming possibility of Trump's impeachment process, any of these foreign "threats" could be manipulated by the president, his cabinet, or Congress in such a way as to start a war, either accidentally or accidentally on purpose, in the effort to divert American popular attention away from domestic controversies that involve the ongoing struggle for power within Washington and with rival states abroad. A major war could break out—particularly if a rival or anti-state organization engages in something, correctly or incorrectly, interpreted by Washington to represent an action hostile to US interests.

Much as Aristotle pointed out more than two thousand years ago, it is when the "distant threat" can be brought home, and into one's daily life, that the possibility of war with a distant power or powers becomes much more viable.[66] And once the distant threat is brought home, then the burdens of militarization, if not the sacrifices of war, can be met with greater toleration by the society once the general population can actually see how that otherwise "distant threat" actually challenges their safety and way of life. And the possibility of war abroad is then further exacerbated by the perceived threat of "enemies" at home—who are seen as opposing, whether peacefully or violently, the politics and goals of those in power—thus undermining the legitimacy and effective ability of the powerful to rule.

CHAPTER 4

RISKS OF THE NEW AMERICAN NATIONALISM FOR THE EUROPEAN UNION

There is a real risk that a number of Trump administration policies that tend to encourage US protectionism and "economic nationalism" will likewise help to legitimize both far-right-wing and far-left-wing anti-EU and anti-NATO political parties throughout Europe. And if Trump continues to push for increased military expenditure for an ongoing NATO enlargement, coupled with a policy of strong US and EU sanctions on Moscow that are seen as harming European political-economic interests, such a policy could backfire. This could cause some states to abandon EU and/or NATO membership—without necessarily implementing constructive and viable alternatives. Wolfgang Ischinger, head of the Munich Security Conference, and a former German senior diplomat, warned: "Is President Trump going to continue a tradition of half a century of being supportive of the project of European integration, or is he going to continue to advocate EU member countries to follow the Brexit example? . . . If he did that, it would amount to a kind of non-military declaration of war. It would mean conflict between Europe and the United States. Is that what the US wants? Is that how he wishes to make America great again?"[1]

Likewise, the president of the European Commission, Jean-Claude Juncker, warned that the collapse of the European Union could, for example, lead to war in the western Balkans. Juncker further stated that Trump's America First doctrine was scaring Europeans into thinking that the United

States no longer cared for Europe.[2] Soon after, Trump suddenly changed tune and claimed that the European Union was a "wonderful" organization.[3]

Prior to becoming president, Trump initially claimed to be "indifferent" to the European Union—in addition to asserting that NATO was "obsolete." But he nevertheless appeared to be actively seeking to undermine the European Union by encouraging states to leave that international regime, given his strong support for the United Kingdom's exit from the European Union (Brexit). Trump also engaged in strong attacks on Germany, which he sees as the major global economic competitor to the United States, given Germany's roughly $65 billion trade surplus with the United States. The risk is that Trump's America First policies could eventually open the door for Beijing and Moscow to play their own games of offering finance and trade (China) and energy and resources (Russia) to needy countries—in their effort to obtain greater political-economic influence inside Europe. And in destabilizing Europe—coupled with Russia's overt and covert backing for anti-EU and anti-NATO movements—Trump's policies could destabilize much of the world. (See chapter 1.)

With respect to NATO, Trump had initially argued that NATO was obsolete due to the fact that it had been created during the Cold War, and because of its ostensible lack of relevance for the Global War on Terrorism, combined with the fact that not all of its membership spends the expected 2 percent of its GDP on defense. From Trump's perspective, this has forced Washington to remain the predominant provider of European and global security; the United States contributes some 70–75 percent of NATO's military capabilities—a fact that implies that the Europeans were free riders, paying for only 25–30 percent of total defense costs. Trump therefore made the provocative argument that the United States might not defend allies who did not pay their fair share of the NATO defense burden. Trump's statements accordingly appeared to downplay NATO's Article V defense commitment.

Trump's negative positions toward NATO and the European Union appeared, at least on the surface, to reverse themselves by February 2017, once Vice President Pence spoke up for both NATO and the European Union. Countering European fears that Trump would abandon NATO and the European Union, Vice President Mike Pence rushed to Brussels in late February 2017 to declare "unwavering" US support for NATO and "unequivocal" support for the European Union—in a speech before an audience of skeptical European elites. The Belgium capital, Brussels, ironically, houses the offices of both the European Union and NATO. But the two rarely speak together, and when they do, they generally cannot find a common understanding!

Vice President Pence accordingly gave a resounding "yes" to three crucial questions from EU Council-Consilium President Donald Tusk. The first question was whether the Trump administration was committed to maintaining an international order based on rules and laws. Tusk's second question was whether Trump was committed to NATO and to "the closest possible trans-Atlantic cooperation." The third question was whether Europe could count, "as always in the past, on the United States' wholehearted and unequivocal, let me repeat, unequivocal support for the idea of a united Europe."[4] By mid-February 2017, Trump himself suddenly changed tune, stating his strong support for the European Union and claiming that it was a "wonderful" organization.[5]

Nevertheless, the Trump-Pence administration continued to warn that the alliance might cease to function altogether if allies did not contribute their share of the defense burden. This possibility was due to the fact that underspending on NATO eroded "the very foundation of our alliance," in Mike Pence's words.[6] Secretary of Defense Gen. James Mattis, put it this way: "America will meet its responsibilities, but if your nations do not want to see America moderate its commitment to the alliance, each of your capitals needs to show its support for our common defense."[7] At the May 2017 NATO summit in Brussels, Trump argued that even 2 percent of GDP (roughly $119 billion) would be "insufficient to close the gaps in modernizing, readiness, and the size of forces. Two percent is the bare minimum for confronting today's very real and very vicious threats."[8]

Vice President Pence likewise stated that some of the largest US allies still lacked "a clear and credible path" in order to build up their military capabilities to 2 percent of GDP.[9] Here Germany, the main political-economic power in Europe, and major arms exporter to Qatar and Saudi Arabia (along with the United States[10]) is still below the mark and is considered "short of everything" from manpower to military equipment.[11] And even though France spends more for defense than other NATO members, it has nevertheless reduced its actual capacities by roughly 50 percent under Presidents Nicolas Sarkozy and François Hollande.[12]

Yet the problem is that even an increase in European defense spending will only prove helpful if is better coordinated by a European defense organization. Of the five countries that spend more than 2 percent of GDP on defense—the United Kingdom, Estonia, Poland, Greece, and the United States—Greece is more concerned with NATO member Turkey than it is with Russia. For its part, the United Kingdom still retains a global empire, as does the United States—so that European NATO is not its only defense and security concern. Romania has declared that it will reach 2 percent of GDP in 2017, while Latvia and Lithuania will also reach 2 percent. All three of the latter are primarily concerned with a potential Russian "threat," as are Estonia and Poland. At the same time, it is not clear whether all NATO allies, including Germany, can or will fall in line with US demands to increase defense spending.[13]

The real problem is that the two sides, the United States and Europeans, continue to divide on a number of key political and strategic questions. These questions involve the nature and costs of a NATO/European defense buildup, the Global War on Terrorism, as well as policies toward Russia, Ukraine, Iran, and China, and others. Here there are many issues where the United States and Europeans disagree and where the Europeans themselves disagree, as eastern European states generally want NATO and the European Union to focus on Russia, while states such as France want NATO and the European Union to focus on the issues confronting the Mediterranean and the Global War on Terrorism. The question as to whether or not Ukraine and Georgia should become NATO members, for example, remained the unspoken "elephant in the room" in the NATO summit of May 2017. And, as to be argued, another option to forcing individual NATO countries to augment their defense spending would be to implement a post-Brexit European defense entity that would better coordinate defense spending. (See chapter 9.)

TRUMP AND THE EUROPEAN UNION

The new American nationalism risks playing with fire if Trump continues to engage in policies that would even indirectly support "economic nationalism" in Europe. The demise of the European Union risks the return of rabid nationalist rivalries inside Europe. This is because the rise of the European Union has played a historical role in helping to bring rivals France and Germany into cooperation with other the European powers—following the formation of the European Coal and Steel Community in 1957 and the Franco-German decision to forge a common currency, the Euro.

Trump had fully supported the British exit from the European Union (Brexit), and he stated his belief that other countries could soon leave the European Union as well.[14] The so-called PIIGS states of Portugal, Ireland, Italy, Greece, and Spain—whose political economies need significant reforms in order remain in the Euro monetary system—could possibly drop out of the European Union. Greece is still suffering after reaching a crisis point at which it almost left the European Union.[15] European austerity measures have resulted in cutting public expenditures, high unemployment, loss of pensions, the sale of public assets, plus efforts to raise taxes—in a situation in which the Greek economy has lost 25 percent of its former value. International efforts to bail Greece out have been promised only after Athens engages deep structural reforms and further austerity measures.[16] Having already accumulated over €300 billion in bad loans, the possible collapse of Italian banks could impact much of Europe, including Austria, Greece, Spain, and Portugal.[17] And if Italy fails, France may be next.

Despite the election of the liberal-centrist and pro-EU Emmanuel Macron as president of France in April 2017, there is still a real possibility of a French exit from the European Union in the next five to ten years. If so, this would risk tearing apart the remaining Franco-German-EU political-economic and defense relationship. In dividing Europe, such an option is even more dangerous than the British exit—as the United Kingdom never shared a common currency with the European Union. Brexit and Frexit are not the same thing!

While the United Kingdom will most likely continue to work with the Europeans through bilateral national security accords and through NATO, even if it is no longer a member of the European Union, it is highly unlikely that other states that leave the European Union will necessarily remain in NATO. Unlike the British conservatives, like Theresa May who backed Brexit, but who underscored the importance of NATO in her meeting with President Trump in January 2017, many continental Europeans, on the left, right, and even center, are anti-NATO.

BREXIT AND THE EUROPEAN UNION

Brexit nevertheless opens up a number of complex questions with respect to the United Kingdom's security and defense relationship with Ireland and Scotland and with the European Union as a whole; questions that indirectly impact NATO. As of September 2017, London plans to leave the European Union by March 2021—at a cost of about £40 billion and a slight loss of Britain's credit status thus far.

First, the United Kingdom, which accounted for roughly 20 percent of European defense, will no longer be able to block all-European defense plans. This theoretically permits EU to press ahead with an all-European defense system, if France and Germany, the next two major EU actors, can gradually coordinate policies.[18] At the same time, however, bilateral UK-French strategic nuclear accords reached at the 1998 Saint Malo agreement indicate the continuing need for bilateral UK-French nuclear-strategic and defense cooperation.[19] In 2016, London and Paris agreed to deepen their joint efforts to develop missile technology. How Brexit will politically impact these bilateral UK-French accords, which are outside the NATO and EU context, remains to be seen.[20]

Brexit also opens up a number of questions for Ireland and Scotland as members of the United Kingdom. Brexit raises border questions with Ireland, and once again raises the question of Northern Ireland's independence, given the fact that hundreds of thousands of Irish live in the United Kingdom and hundreds of thousands of UK-born and eastern European citizens reside in Ireland. Brexit also raises the issue as to how to regulate trade and traffic along the border of UK-controlled Northern Ireland and EU member Ireland. This concern led to UK Prime Minister Theresa May and Irish Prime Minister (the taoiseach) Enda Kenny reconfirming the 1998 Good Friday accords in Northern Ireland, which has led to peace through power-sharing between the Unionists (who want to remain in the United Kingdom) and the Irish nationalists.

The issue of border controls has brought back memories of the Troubles—as British military outposts and customs posts were often attacked by the Irish Republican Army. If new border controls are implemented, and if the borders are not perceived to be free and "fluid," they could once again become targets of new violent anti-UK movements by Irish militants who still hope to leave the United Kingdom—particularly if the aforementioned power-sharing arrangement reached in the 1998 Good Friday agreement continues to break down periodically, as it did in January 2017, for example.[21]

Brexit could also lead to Scottish independence from the United Kingdom. This was proposed by Scottish Prime Minister Nicola Sturgeon, who has planned a second independence referendum for the fall

2018 to the spring 2019. Scottish nationalists have generally wanted to remain in the European Union, but not necessarily in the NATO "nuclear alliance"—given the Scottish National Party's (SNP's) opposition to nuclear weaponry. The Scottish independence issue impacts the future of the United Kingdom's Trident nuclear submarine system, which is based on the Clyde. Many Scots oppose Trident, as well as NATO/UK airbases in Scotland.

An independent Scotland may also need to reapply to join the European Union, which could open monetary questions concerning the Scottish use of the British pound after Brexit. And if Scotland wants to remain in NATO, it might need the approval of the all NATO members. This could possibly be opposed by some states that do not want to encourage independence movements. NATO members Spain, Greece, Romania, and Slovakia, for example, did not want to recognize Kosovo independence, which was backed by the United States. Some sort of intermediary arrangement could possibly be worked out with both NATO and the European Union—but not without time-consuming negotiations.

Brexit has also opened questions as to whether the United Kingdom or EU member Spain will control Gibraltar, which guards the gates of the Mediterranean. Like the people in Northern Ireland, the population in Gibraltar fears the possibilities of economic instability once they leave the European Union's external border. In addition, UK disputes with Argentina over the Falkland Islands appear to be returning. This is because Argentina believes that the European Union may no longer back British control over the islands after the 1982 UK-Argentine war. Argentina may seek to bargain post-Brexit bilateral accords with Britain in exchange for a return of the islands to Argentina. The region around the Falklands is rich in fishing, resource deposits, and oil. These concerns were responsible, at least in part, for the 1982 sea battle over the Falklands between Argentina and the United Kingdom. Just prior to that conflict, the option of joint sovereignty had been proposed as a way to forge a compromise and prevent war—but it failed to be implemented. (See chapter 10.)

GERMANY

Trump has argued that the European Union represents an "instrument of German domination designed with the purpose of beating the United States in international trade."[22] And largely because he sees the European Union as a mere instrument of German political-economic power, Trump claims that he is basically "indifferent" as to whether or not the European Union will break up. Germany does represent a major economic competitor of the United States (in automobiles, for example, and given Germany's huge $65 billion trade surplus with the United States). But while it is true that Germany may dominate the economy of the European Union, that by itself is more reason to engage in political and economic reforms of the European Union, rather than lending support to those who want to break up it entirely. (For EU reform options, see chapter 9.) After discussions with Chancellor Angela Merkel, Trump stated: "Nevertheless, Germany owes vast sums of money to NATO & the United States must be paid more for the powerful, and very expensive, defense it provides to Germany!"[23]

The issue raised here is that Trump's harsh criticism of Germany's immigration policy, plus his demands that Germany spend at least 2 percent on defense (Germany spent roughly 1.19 percent of GDP on defense in 2016), combined with threats to impose up to 35 percent border taxes on German products,[24] could unleash a wave of thus far hidden anti-American nationalist forces in Germany and elsewhere, particularly after the right party, Alternative for Germany party (AfD), entered the Bundestag with roughly 13 percent of the vote in September 2017. (See discussion on right-wing parties, this chapter.)

Although Germany hopes to diversify its energy sources, it has opposed strong US sanctions on Moscow that might interfere with the construction of Nord Stream 2, an energy pipeline that would run through the Baltic Sea, circumventing Ukraine. US sanctions could also hurt the financing of European firms doing business in Russia. Berlin has called the sanctions imposed by the "Countering America's Adversaries through Sanctions Act" in August 2017 as illegal and has urged the European Union to take countermeasures—a step that could enter into a trade war if the United States and the European Union do not coordinate sanctions policy and negotiate the eventual lifting of sanctions together.[25]

American threats not to support NATO and Brexit, alongside Russian threats to Ukraine and eastern Europe, could then press Germany and the new European Union (without the United Kingdom) to forge tighter political-economic, if not military, ties with China, with which Germany has already established a "special relationship,"[26] in which China believes that Berlin will strengthen its influence in the European Union to China's political and economic advantage. Germany has, for example, been lobbying the European Union to put an end to the EU arms embargo placed on China since the June 1989 repression of the Chinese democracy movement. In exchange for the European Union ending its arms ban, Beijing has promised greater finance to European countries, and greater trade and investment opportunities. Beijing has been investing heavily, for example, in nuclear energy plants in the Czech Republic, Hungary, and Poland, in rivalry with both the United States and Russia, and Beijing is looking to the Bulgarian nuclear energy market as well. Because the United Kingdom had been one of the strongest supporters of the arms embargo on China, the lack of a British presence in the European Union could then open the door to closer European-Chinese defense relations.[27] Such an approach would ostensibly be intended to attempt to draw China away from closer defense ties to Russia, but to the chagrin of the Japanese, while it could be interpreted as an act of "encirclement" by Moscow. Such an EU-China defense linkage could occur if NATO does start to fall apart, and assuming that Germany and the new European Union (without the United Kingdom) cannot reach a separate accord with Russia over Ukraine, among other EU-Russia disputes.

Prior to Trump, the Obama administration had been encouraging Germany, France, and the Europeans to look toward Japan and India for closer political-economic ties, including arms sales—despite Germany's already close ties to China. Closer German-Japanese political-economic relations in Europe and the Indo-Pacific would then represent a counterpoint to China's Belt and Road Initiative (BRI), which seeks to expand Chinese trade and investment between Asia and Europe.[28] Both Moscow and Beijing, however, see this approach as seeking to forge a new "encircling" alliance in Europe and in the Indo-Pacific. (See chapters 6 and 9.)

IMMIGRATION INTO EUROPE

The general financial crisis in the European Union since 2008, coupled with the immigrant crisis, and US and EU sanctions on Russia, has been making it even more difficult for the European Union to function—as a number of states have decided to strengthen their borders. In mid-2016, among EU countries, Hungary possessed the most asylum applicants per capita, followed by Sweden and Germany. In terms of numbers, Germany has accepted the most migrants, then Sweden, Italy, France, the Netherlands, and the United Kingdom. Ironically, Germany's decision to take in at least 1.1 million immigrants, due, in large part, to Germany's growing need for labor, has been criticized by Trump, even though this is a German, and not an American, affair, and should be of no concern to Trump.

One of the main issues that has caused an anti-EU backlash has accordingly been the failure of the European Union to deal effectively with the post-2015 immigration crisis from Syria, Afghanistan, Iraq, and other North African countries. Waves of immigrants followed in the wake of the Arab Spring movements in 2011, the French- and UK- led military intervention in Libya (backed by NATO) in March 2011, and then the Syrian civil war, which began in 2011. More than a million refugees arrived in Europe in 2015 alone.[29] The failure of the European Union to check the wave of refugees at the edges of the European Union in Greece and Italy, as well as into Hungary through the Balkans, then led many

European states to close their national borders. This led to the building of a whole series of national walls/fences/barriers in Europe, as generally demanded by rising right-wing nationalist groups.

Ironically, refugees were blocked in Calais, France, unable to travel to the more liberal United Kingdom, where they believe they will find jobs—as the United Kingdom was not part of Schengen group that oversaw immigration policy inside the European Union. The large immigrant camps in France were then broken up by force by the government of François Hollande, and most immigrants were forced to move to different locations or flee the country. France was in the ironic situation of trying to keep in the country refugees who did not want to stay! Here, although fears of immigration were a factor in Brexit, it was largely opposition to immigration from eastern Europe that was believed to have impacted the jobs of English citizens—and not the fear of non-European refugees who had entered the Schengen zone of continental Europe.

SANCTIONS ON MOSCOW

By contrast with east European states (with the exception of Serbia, Hungary, Slovakia, and perhaps Bulgaria and the Czech Republic), many western European states (Germany, Italy, and France, among others) have generally wanted to maintain positive relations with Russia. These states were initially reluctant to place strong sanctions on Moscow's banking, oil, and defense sectors in 2014.

For its part, the United Kingdom has generally taken the toughest stance on Russia in part due to the poisoning of former Russian agent Alexander Litvinenko. But British legal investigations into that affair, plus sanctions placed on Russia in the energy sector, have not, for example, prevented British Petroleum (BP) from making profitable deals with the Russian energy firm Rosneft by 2016.[30] Likewise, German Chancellor Merkel has nevertheless insisted that the United States and the European Union sustain sanctions on Russia in response to its annexation of Crimea and political-military interference in eastern Ukraine, while likewise denouncing Putin for his support of Syrian leader Bashar al-Assad.[31]

Europeans who argue against sanctions generally argue that sanctions have no impact on Russian policy in Ukraine. Contrary to the Americans, who trade less with Moscow, many businesses did not want to lose access to Russian markets. And when Moscow unexpectedly placed counter-sanctions on European agricultural exports to Russia, those counter-sanctions generally hurt Europeans more than Americans. European farmers have subsequently been hurt significantly by counter-sanctions placed by Moscow on European farm products. Trade between Russia and the European Union consequently dropped by over €180 billion between 2013 and 2015 while EU farmers and agricultural cooperatives claim that they have lost their main export market worth €5.5 billion. EU agriculture was additionally hurt by a general drop in Chinese demand due to a downswing in the Chinese economy.[32]

While some US auto companies and banks have been hurt by sanctions on Moscow, a number of American food companies, including MacDonald's, Yum! and Burger King, and the agro-industrial firm, Cargill, have actually been benefiting from them—as Moscow began to engage in import substitution (which it claimed to be beneficial) while also seeking to import food products from Brazil, Argentina, and Asia.[33] Israeli agriculture has also hoped to benefit—a factor drawing Israel and Russia closer together.[34] The enterprises of states that do not agree to placing sanctions on Russia, most importantly China, but also Japan, Turkey, Brazil, Argentina, Qatar, and South Africa, have begun to benefit.

In June 2016, the German and Austrian foreign ministers began to have second thoughts. They stated that EU sanctions on Russia should be gradually phased out as the peace process progresses. This represented an effort to reverse previous positions that sanctions could be lifted only once the Minsk peace plan is fully implemented. Both France and Greece have likewise sought a change in policy toward sanctions as well. EU sanctions have reduced Russian GDP by 1 to 1.5 percent, and the EU's own GDP by 0.1 percent. The EU has lost an additional 0.3 percent of its GDP as a consequence of the Russian counter-embargo on EU agricultural products. The Baltic states, Finland, and Poland are paradoxically the most supportive of sanctions but also the ones to suffer most from them. This is while Italy, for example, has been less harmed.

For its part, the United States, which most strongly supports sanctions, has lost a mere 0.005 percent of its GDP because of its own sanctions on Russia and the counter-sanctions imposed by Russia on the United States. Yet despite the harm done to European agriculture, EU ambassadors nevertheless agreed to first extend their economic sanctions against Russia to January 2017, and then later to July 2017, and again to January 2018.[35] These renewed sanctions were due to Moscow's perceived lack progress on Minsk II accords that has been intended to establish peace in eastern Ukraine—and even if not all the problems can be blamed on Moscow for not following through on the Minsk accords.

THE RISE OF ANTI-NATO ANTI-EU MOVEMENTS

The US and European financial crisis since 2008 has led a number of left-wing and right-wing political parties to demand that their countries drop the Euro as a currency, dump their creditors, and then exit the European Union—rather than attempting to further reform the European Union itself. The Austrian, Dutch, and French elections have, however, appeared to have stemmed the tide of nationalist-populist movements for the moment, but they might not be able to hold out for long—if political-economic conditions do not eventually improve in the European Union as a whole. In this regard, the rise of the German far right, which seeks to break monetary ties with France and other countries, in the September 2017 elections is very worrying. In general, both far-right and far-left movements have gained in strength as a result of the decline of traditional parties, due in large part to the rise in social inequity and the decline of the middle classes.

In 2016, in the Austrian presidential elections, the Green Party and European Federalist candidate Alexander Van der Bellen just barely defeated far-right party Freedom Party candidate Norbert Hofer. In the Netherlands, in the March 2017 elections, three centrist parties (People's Party for Freedom and Democracy, VVD; Labour Party, PvdA; and Democrats 66, D66)—which are all pro-European and pro-NATO, but with some differences on immigration—ran against the nationalist anti-EU Party for Freedom (PVV) of Geert Wilders. The PVV only won 13.1 percent of the votes, but due to the pluralist party system, the PVV still became the second largest party.

In April 2017, Emmanuel Macron of the new, liberal Federalist party En Marche! (Onwards!) won the French presidential elections by 67 percent. But Macron will nevertheless face an uphill battle to obtain popular support for his proposed liberal market-oriented reforms. The far-left presidential candidate, Jean-Luc Mélenchon, refused, for example, to publicly endorse Macron against Marine Le Pen in the second round of the French elections and called for an international conference to adjudicate border conflicts in eastern Europe. Along with the far right, Mélenchon has continued to oppose Macron's liberal labor policies, calling for strikes in September 2017.[36] (See discussion on France, this chapter.)

Chancellor Angela Merkel, whose pro-immigration policies were also denounced by Donald Trump, won her fourth term in September 2017. The Social Democrats (SPD) had surged briefly in popularity since choosing left-wing Martin Schulz to run against Angela Merkel, but he nevertheless lost the elections. The SPD then announced that it would no longer sustain an alliance with Merkel's CDU (Christian Democratic Union of Germany). This will make it difficult for Merkel to forge a coalition in the Bundestag particularly as the extreme right-wing party, Alternative for Germany party (AfD), gained roughly 13 percent of the Bundestag. The CDU will hold 246 MPs in the Bundestag, and the SPD, which scored poorly, has 153. The right-wing AfD took 94 seats; the FDP, 80; the Left, 69; and the Greens, 67.[37]

The rise of the far right in Germany negates what were otherwise more or less positive signs. In addition, there is a real concern that Trump's policies of economic nationalism, his support for Brexit, his strong criticisms of Germany, and his pretended support for the European Union, plus the general financial crisis, combined with sanctions on Moscow—and US pressure on NATO members to spend more on defense—are all encouraging a number of anti-EU, anti-NATO left-wing, populist, and nationalist parties to rise to power in Europe. These movements have been given ideological support by Steve Bannon, one of Trump's advisers, who has remained behind the scenes even after he was pressed out of the US National Security Council in April 2017.[38] And behind a number of these populist movements, there are a number of even more overtly fascist/ racist movements that could follow in their footsteps.

After winning the presidency, Trump had met with Nigel Farage of the right-wing UK Independence Party, even before meeting with Theresa May, the British Prime Minister.[39] Trump himself gave far-right-wing candidate Marine Le Pen a tacit endorsement just before the April 2017 French presidential elections, by saying that she was "strongest on borders, and she's the strongest on what's been going on in France. . . . Whoever is the toughest on radical Islamic terrorism, and whoever is the toughest at the borders, will do well in the election."[40] Trump's statement proved completely wrong, since the liberal-centrist Emmanuel Macron won the election.

Some of these right-wing and left-wing movements are backed by Moscow; others oppose Moscow. But both left-wing and right-wing movements have stated their opposition to NATO and the European Union. On the right, these include the Front National (France); FPÖ (Austria); Golden Dawn (Greece); KSCM (Czech Republic); and Jobbik (Hungary). On the left: Front de Gauche (France); AKEL (Cyprus); and Die Linke (Germany).[41]

In 2014, in Hungary, for example, the pro-Russian Prime Minister Viktor Orbán's nationalist Fidesz-KNDP party had won 44.5 percent of the votes, but the far-right Movement for a Better Hungary, Jobbik, won 20.54 of the vote, meaning far-right-wing parties possess some 65 percent of the vote in that country. In 2015, in Poland, the right-wing Law and Justice Party has begun to challenge the separation of powers between the state and legal system. While anti-Russian and pro-NATO, Poland's Prime Minister Beata Szydło may also oppose the European Union's new project—a European Pillar of Social Rights.[42]

Many left-wing movements tend to take a pro-Russian stance on many issues, even if Putin's politics are far from being "left-wing." European left-wing movements have gained strength following the 2008 financial crisis, but they tend to lose support on account of the fear of a massive influx of foreign immigrants entering Europe. Among left-wing movements, European United Left/Nordic Green Left (GUE/NGL) in the European Parliament generally supports the Russian position in the Council of Europe, and in OSCE general assemblies—especially on issues related to Ukraine and Syria. Greece's Syriza party, in coalition with the right-wing populist ANEL, often backs Russia on energy, foreign affairs, and defense. The left-wing Podemos rapidly became the third largest party in Spain since 2014, while Die Linke is strong in eastern Germany. The Cyprus Communist AKEL party has obtained as much as 30 percent of the vote in parliamentary elections. Sinn Fein, the political wing of the IRA, is one of the top three political parties in Ireland.[43] In September 2017, as previously mentioned, the populist Alternative for Germany (AfG) party entered the Bundestag for the first time, with ninety-four seats.

Moreover, given the fact that the far-right nationalist-populist parties possess very different goals, such movements will not be able to forge a unified policy—except for their general opposition to the European Union and NATO. There are, however, a few nationalist parties (primarily from eastern Europe, but also the Scottish, who want to remain in the European Union once the United Kingdom leaves) who want to not abolish the European Union but reform it. Most of the Euro-nationalist parties thus oppose EU bureaucracy but disagree on other issues. The Alternative for

Germany (AfG) party, for example, regards Le Pen's National Front (NF) as a national socialist movement in that the NF does not believe in the free-market, pro-business, and national-libertarian policies that the German AfG party supports. The AfG tends to be anti-immigrant, anti-Muslim, anti-EU federalism, anti-NATO, anti-Ukraine, and pro-Russian.

In general, far-right parties in countries in close proximity to Russia tend to oppose Russian influence, while far-right parties farther away from Russia are generally more supportive of Russian interests. Far-right parties in Finland, Latvia, and Romania tend to be hostile to Russia, while those in Germany, Croatia, Denmark, Hungary, Poland, and Sweden tend to be more open or neutral. Pro-Russian parties in Estonia are influential due to strong ethnic Russian influence, but these groups are not necessarily pro-Putin. Hungary's Prime Minister Viktor Orbán and Slovakia's Robert Fico have taken pro-Russian stances, and so has the Czech Republic's new prime minister, Andrej Babis, the billionaire "Czech Trump."

Other right-wing parties tend to be strongly pro-Russian in the rest of Europe—most crucially, the National Front in France and the UK Independence Party (UKIP) and the British National Party (BNP) in the United Kingdom; in Germany, the Alternative for Germany (AfG) and the Nationalist Democratic Party (NPD); and in Italy, the Northern League. Even the populist Italian Five Star Movement (M5S), which claims to go beyond left-wing and right-wing schisms, has shifted in a pro-Russian direction. A M5S foreign-policy spokesperson stated that M5S was neither pro-Russian nor pro-American, but it has opposed NATO "aggression" and called for the end of EU sanctions against Russia. It has also called for the strengthening of intelligence ties between the European Union and Russia.[44]

Like left-wing movements, right-wing nationalist movements have been gaining political capital from high unemployment. But these nationalist movements have also been gaining support due to the failure of the European Union and the Schengen system of border controls inside Europe to deal with the post-2015 immigration crisis.[45]

FRANCE AS THE KEYSTONE OF THE EUROPEAN UNION

The fate of the European Union could well depend on the nature of French politics in the coming five to ten years, after liberal-centrist pro-EU Emmanuelle Macron was elected president in May 2017. The United Kingdom's decision to leave the European Union has put the focus on French politics. It is now France that could eventually determine the future of Europe, as the outcome of the September 2017 German elections means that Merkel will probably have to concentrate on domestic issues, with the rise of the far-right AfG party and the alienation of the SPD. Macron and Merkel appeared to have established a good working relationship in support of a more effective European Union, but may profoundly disagree on the details. Berlin has thus far opposed French proposals to integrate European budgets, to create a European Monetary Fund and a minister of finance and the economy to surpass the economic crisis, coupled with a common European defense. Instead Germany, contrary to French counsel, has sought to impose austerity on Greece, for example, to the benefit of German banks, for example, with Greek airports and ports under German administration.[46]

Both the far right and the far left in France have highly criticized, if not opposed, French membership in the European Union and NATO. Out of nineteen French presidential candidates, only Emmanuel Macron was supportive of NATO and the European Union; the rest were critical of both international regimes. But even if Emmanuel Macron won the French presidential elections by 66.1 percent, an estimated 43 percent voted for him only in an effort to block Le Pen—with 8.6 percent of the voters voting blank or nul, and with high abstention at one-quarter (25.4 percent) of the voting population.[47]

After the May 2017 French presidential elections, all the political parties were shaken up by Macron's victory and are in the process of reconstituting themselves. Macron possesses a strong federalist vision of the European Union. He is calling for a banking union and an integrated EU budget that all EU states must follow, overseen by an EU finance minister. And yet, given the social and political divergence of the EU membership, only a limited degree of political and social integration has thus far taken place that would fit into this mold. It seems a more decentralized and interstate model of cooperation would be more appropriate, one that addresses the EU "democracy deficit" at both the local and national level. Whether Macron will try to push through a more centralized model or one that is more decentralized remains to be seen. He says he is open to discussion. And much depends on Merkel and Germany. (See chapters 9 and 10.)

RUSSIAN (AND AMERICAN) EFFORTS TO INFLUENCE EUROPEAN ELECTIONS

Just like it had been claimed that Moscow was supporting Trump against Clinton, it is believed that Moscow had been supporting the French Republican candidate François Fillon, whose political career as prime minister had brought him in close contact with Vladimir Putin, and who has been critical of NATO and US policy toward Russia. Moscow was also said to support the anti-EU, anti-NATO National Front candidate Marine Le Pen over any other candidates. Le Pen met with Putin in March 2017. In addition to being accused of interfering in the American elections, Moscow has also been accused of both overtly and covertly (through cyber-attacks) interfering in the elections and the domestic politics in Holland, Montenegro, Germany, and France in 2016–2017, in addition to in Estonia and in Georgia in the past.[48]

Marine Le Pen was able to borrow funds from a Czech-Russian bank after being unable to borrow from banks in the European Union, but she has had problems paying her debts after failing to win the presidential election.[49] In addition to demanding a national referendum of France's membership in the European Union and NATO, the National Front has recognized Russia's annexation of Crimea and sent observers to the Crimean referendum, which was intended to legitimize the Russian annexation. But what was perhaps even more disturbing than Russian support for Le Pen was the fact that Marine Le Pen was seen at Trump Towers prior to the presidential inauguration in January 2017 in effort to gain political support and financing from some of Trump's associates.[50] As Trump tacitly endorsed Le Pen just prior to the April–May 2017 French presidential elections, it was consequently feared that Trump associates (along with Putin) were still supporting a French exit (Frexit) from the European Union for nationalist-ideological reasons. In France, Le Pen was seen as an all-American "Trumpette." But Le Pen then claimed that it is Trump who has been following French National Front policies of "economic patriotism." Yet Trump's steps away from a positive relationship with Russia since February 2017 have greatly deceived Le Pen.

In France, Richard Ferrand, the secretary-general of Macron's En Marche! (Onwards!) stated that the Macron campaign had been hit by "hundreds, if not thousands" of attacks that were attempting to probe the campaign's computer systems from locations inside Russia.[51] If true, this sounds much like what has been called a "cyber riot" involving angry individual hackers, as opposed to a direct Kremlin-sponsored "cyber-attack." Moscow was said to strongly oppose the Liberal-Centrist Emmanuel Macron, who is pro-EU, even though he had opposed further NATO enlargement, but so might be "patriotically minded" Russian hackers, as Putin himself has claimed, in reference to attacks on the United States.[52] (See chapter 2.)

Then, just two days before the French presidential elections, Macron's offices were hacked once again, purportedly by APT 28 (also known as Fancy Bear)—a cyber-espionage group tied to Russian military intelligence, the GRU, which may have also been involved with hacking during the US elections. The involvement of Russian military intelligence, of course, was vehemently denied by the Kremlin.[53] After the French elections, Putin met with Macron at Versailles in late May 2017—but without making any major changes in French-Russian policy—in part as the G-7 opted to sustain sanctions on Moscow. There was, however, despite Macron's not-very-warm encounter with Putin at Versailles, a general recognition by Macron that many problems, including that of Syria and the battle against the Islamic State, could not be resolved unless Moscow was involved.

MOSCOW AND THE EU PARTNERSHIP WITH EASTERN EUROPEAN STATES

In 2008–2009, Moscow had begun to oppose stronger EU efforts to expand its political-economic interests into former Soviet bloc states by means of the EU Eastern Partnership and neighborhood program. Before that time, even though the European Union began to implement a visa regime that blocked the entry of Russian citizens, Moscow generally did not consider the European Union a potential "threat." Yet the European Union concurrently developed a common security and defense policy and mutual defense clause based on Article 42 (7) of the Treaty of the European Union, introduced in 2009. This treaty, in effect, links the defense of NATO members with the defense of EU members—and could potentially mean that both NATO and EU members could be drawn into support of both non-NATO members and partners of the European Union.

Moscow soon began to interpret the 2008–2009 EU Eastern Partnership as being aimed at bringing its six Eastern European, yet former Soviet bloc, neighbors away from Russian spheres of influence and security. The EU partnership thus limits Russian political-economic influence over its six post-Soviet Eastern European neighbours—Armenia, Azerbaijan, Belarus, Georgia, Republic of Moldova, and Ukraine. In such a way, the European Union was seen as redirecting the political-economic orientation of Ukraine and other former Soviet republics toward Europe and away from Moscow—as the latter's political-economic and energy interests were not taken into account.

This leads to questions as to how, and if, the European Union will balance its relations with Russia and with the new EU "Eastern Partners." Although EU supporters do not like to admit it, it had been EU efforts since 2008 to 2014 to bring Ukraine—along with other post-Soviet states into EU Associate Agreements—that represented one of the major factors that provoked the Russian annexation of Crimea in early 2014. It is possible that the Russian response would have been very different if there had been greater political-economic coordination between the European Union, Ukraine, and Russia.

Kiev did, however, sign the EU Association Agreement after the Russian annexation of Crimea in 2014 despite the ongoing conflict in the Donbas region—only to see that association accord rejected by a referendum in a European state, Holland, in April 2016.[54] Georgia and Moldova already possess association agreements with the European Union. Moldovans, Georgians, and Ukrainians obtained visa-free access to the European Union in the spring of 2017, while Armenia and Azerbaijan should complete negotiations on somewhat-similar partnership deals.

Even Belarus could soon participate in Eastern Partnership summits—as the European Union hopes to distance the country from Moscow, despite its authoritarian leadership under President Alyaksandr Lukashenka. In February 2016, the European Union had lifted sanctions against Lukashenka and other Belarus defense-sector officials for human rights abuses. This was true even though UN observers have seen no substantial improvement in the treatment of journalists and others who have criticized the government.[55] The fact that Belarus has been attempting to facilitate the Minsk accords between Moscow, Kiev, Paris, and Berlin has represented a sign that Belarus wants to move closer to Europe, in part due to fear of Russian irredentist claims to Belarus. At the same time, Minsk needs to closely balance its relations with Moscow and Brussels, as Moscow opposes the defection of Belarus from the CSTO and the Eurasian Economic Union.

A BREAKUP OF THE CSTO?

One of Moscow's key concerns is the fear that Belarus could break away from the Russian-led Collective Security Treaty Organization (CSTO) and Eurasian Union and shift toward the European Union. Part of Russia's militarization has been intended to prevent the breakup of its system of alliances as the bitter conflict in Ukraine also indirectly impacts Russian ally and trading partner, Belarus, given Russian irredentist claims to Belarus and Ukrainian territory. Belarus could well be the next former Soviet state to enter into a political succession crisis similar to that which took place in Ukraine.

A political succession crisis in Belarus appears highly likely given strong social opposition to President Alyaksandr Lukashenka, his difficulties in finding ways to balance political-economic relations between the German-backed EU association promises and Polish influence, and the Russian difficulties in subsidizing the Belarusian economy. The drop in world energy prices, and the imposition of US and European sanctions since 2014, has led Moscow to fear the breakup of its CSTO—which represents a mini-version of the Warsaw Pact.[56]

Moscow is also in competition with the European Union in Serbia, which is both a candidate for the EU Stabilization and Association Agreement (SAA) and a candidate for membership in the Russian Eurasian Union. Interestingly, this presents the same dilemma for Serbia as that which faced Ukraine in the choice between the EU Associate Partnership and the Russian-led Eurasian Union. In theory, Belgrade could join both. In practice, however, it might not work because once it joins the EU Associated Partnership, Serbia would have to implement the exact same tariffs on trade with the Russian-led EEU, which the European Union, as a single trade bloc, does.[57] Perhaps much like EU efforts to bring Ukraine into a closer partnership in 2013–2014, steps to bring Serbia into a closer partnership with the EU also forewarns of potential political-economic instability in Serbia as the latter splits between those who want closer ties to Russia and those who want closer ties with Europe, which dominates Serbian imports and exports—that is, if the European Union and Russia cannot begin to forge some form of compromise deal. (See chapter 9.)

The general problem is that it is not certain the European Union can offer by means of these Association Accords anything that is truly better than what Russia or China or other countries can offer.[58] In addition, Russia could react by force once again with respect to Belarus, for example, if it sees its interests threatened by an expanding European Union, like it did in Ukraine in 2014. Will the European Union renew economic sanctions against Russia, which are set to run out by the end of January 2018, thus risking the further alienation of Moscow? Will all EU countries continue to abide by the sanctions regime? Will the United States and the European Union be able to continue to align their policies toward Moscow? Or will US and EU policies diverge? Could the European Union then look to closer security and defense relations with China? Or will it seek an accommodation with Moscow without US input?

RISKS OF EU COLLAPSE

In sum, the Trump administration's encouragement of economic nationalism could facilitate the breakup of the European Union (after Brexit)—if not the disintegration of NATO as well—particularly if Italy enters into a financial crisis and/or if France veers to the left-wing or right-wing and opts to break out of the European Union in the next in five to ten years.[59] A collapsed European Union would then be preyed upon by US, German, Russian, and Chinese political, economic, and military pressures. Both Russia and China have been attempting to draw a number of states closer to the Eurasian orbit—hoping to further splinter Europe and weaken its global influence.

European Council President Donald Tusk, the former premier of Poland, has warned that acts of Russian imperialism, an assertive China, anarchy in the Middle East and Africa, plus the threat posed by radical Islamist groups—combined with the economic nationalism of Donald Trump—all represent threats to European unity. For his part, despite very strong policy differences toward global warming, for example, and how to handle the Iranian and North Korean disputes, President Macron has thus far sought a close working relationship with Trump, while seeking to convince Trump that alternative multilateral strategies, as outlined in Macron's address to the UN General Assembly, are plausible if France, the European Union, and the United States can work together. For Macron, it is urgent to "rebuild multilateralism" with regard to the conflicts in Syria, Ukraine, Iran, and North Korea, and to sustain the COP 21 process to reduce global warming.[60]

Both Macron and Tusk mentioned above realize that a breakup of the European Union and NATO could lead individual states, including Germany, potentially under the pressure of the far right, to "re-nationalize" their defenses while renewing old territorial and nationalist/ethnic rivalries within Europe. Already, after Brexit, the United Kingdom appears willing to rebuild its special relationship with the United States, if the United States is willing to do so as well. Yet the complex process of the United Kingdom's withdrawal from the European Union could potentially leave Brussels relatively impotent and unable to work toward greater unity. The United States, Germany (after breaking out of the European Union), Russia, and China would then begin to compete to obtain political, economic, and financial, if not military, influence over a divided Europe in turmoil.

If this latter scenario is to be avoided, the United States, NATO, and a more effective European Union (with close French-German cooperation) need to begin to find ways to work with, and not against, Russia. The United States/NATO, Europeans, and Russians also need to begin to defuse political-military tensions and reinitiate efforts to reduce the ongoing buildup of nuclear and conventional arms in Europe, while trying to find as many political-economic and ecological areas as possible where they can work in common both in Europe and abroad. (See chapters 9 and 10.)

CHAPTER 5

THE RISK OF WAR OVER CRIMEA, THE BLACK SEA, AND EASTERN EUROPE

In August 2016, presidential candidate Donald Trump had warned that US efforts to regain Crimea on behalf of Ukraine against Russia in the aftermath of Moscow's annexation of the Ukrainian-controlled Crimea in early 2014 could result in World War III.[1]

But in February 2017, the Trump administration appeared to have completely reversed position. The new US ambassador to the United Nations, Nikki Haley, condemned Moscow's military support for the autonomists in eastern Ukraine: "We do want to better our relations with Russia, however the dire situation in eastern Ukraine is one that demands clear and strong condemnation of Russian actions. The United States . . . calls for an immediate end to the Russian occupation of Crimea. Crimea is a part of Ukraine. Our Crimea-related sanctions will remain in place until Russia returns control over the peninsula to Ukraine."[2]

Ambassador Haley's statement caused resentment in Moscow since the fighting had only begun to escalate once again after Kiev's forces engaged in a "creeping offensive" since mid-December 2016 into the buffer zone closer to the positions of the eastern Ukrainian autonomists in the Donbas region. (See further discussion on eastern Ukraine, this chapter.) These forward actions, in which Russia was then blamed for the outbreak of the fighting, took place at a time when Kiev feared that Trump would make a separate deal with Moscow over US sanctions on Russia, Crimea, and eastern Ukraine, but without Kiev's participation.

Haley's statement thus appeared to have reversed Trump's previous position, that, in order to improve US-Russian relations, and prevent a possible major power war, the United States would seek out a new "deal" with Moscow. In the aftermath of the US ambassador's address to the United Nations, Trump did, however, promise to "work with Ukraine, Russia, and all other parties involved to help them restore peace along the [Russian-Ukrainian] border."[3] But it was not clear how this would be achieved. Nor was it clear what how the Trump administration would approach the issue of Moscow's annexation of Crimea.

At this point, Trump had been proposing the possibility that the United States would lift the fairly tough economic and political sanctions that had been placed on Russia in the aftermath of Russia's annexation of Crimea—if Moscow would, in turn, begin the process of reducing the size of its strategic nuclear forces. The issue was that some of the major sanctions against Russia were due to expire in December 2017—if Congress did not renew them.[4] The problem with this approach, from the perspective of Trump's critics, was that it appeared to delink the sanctions issue away from Russia's illegal annexation of Crimea and its political-military interference in eastern Ukraine. Moreover, Trump's proposal to remove sanctions on Russia appeared to be tied to the "Russia-gate" controversy in which Trump and his associates have been accused of collusion with Moscow. (See chapter 3.)

SANCTIONS AND ENERGY QUESTIONS

Yet a deeper factor that underlies the debate as to whether or not to sustain or lift sanctions on Russia is another debate raised by Trump's America First nationalist ideology. Is it better to sustain US-based multinational corporate energy investments in Russia for the long term? Or would it be better to invest in the development of US shale energy industry? (The real debate, however, should be on how to fully develop alternative sources of energy that produce jobs and that are more ecologically sustainable, but this does not appear to be on the Trump-Pence administration agenda. See chapter 10.)

On the one hand, ExxonMobil, for example, has claimed that it has been taking considerable losses due to US sanctions placed on Moscow. Some elements in the Trump administration want to eliminate, or at least minimize, sanctions and safeguard ExxonMobil's considerable joint investment deals in the Arctic Kara Sea, western Siberia, Sakhalin island, and the Black Sea, which had been reached with Russian-government energy company, Rosneft, in 2012–2013, given the massive size of Russian reserves.[5] In April 2017, ExxonMobil applied to the Treasury Department in April 2017 for a waiver from US sanctions on Russia in a bid to resume its joint venture with state oil company Rosneft. In July 2017, ExxonMobil sued the Treasury Department over a $2 million fine for purportedly violating US sanctions against Russia in 2014. In fact, a number of energy deals sought by ExxonMobil, Chevron, Royal Dutch Shell, Repsol, and Petrochina, with Kiev and with its state-owned Chornomornaftogaz, have been placed in jeopardy and in legal limbo due to the Russian annexation of Crimea.[6] This makes it nearly impossible for Moscow to legally make deals with these same companies, among others, over formerly Ukrainian owned assets—until there is a political and legal settlement between Kiev and Moscow.

Specifically, both the American-based multinational Chevron and Royal Dutch Shell pulled out of their promised investments in Ukraine. Shell pulled out in part due to the annexation of Crimea and the outbreak of war in eastern Ukraine and in part due to the fact shale oil and gas reserves in both Poland and Ukraine were not as large as previously believed. ExxonMobil, among other oil companies, will need to renegotiate its Black Sea energy exploration deals with Moscow, after it annexed Crimea, if possible—as the area is still disputed with Kiev. But Chevron had actually pulled out in December 2014 due to, in large part, Ukraine's complex tax laws, and not the conflict in eastern Ukraine.[7]

For its part, Moscow has nevertheless hoped that it can ride out US and EU sanctions. Moscow still believes that it can eventually develop Black Sea energy and other resources seized from Ukrainian jurisdiction that are potentially worth trillions of dollars. Moscow hopes to obtain finance and investment from Swiss, Qatari, and Chinese, if not Japanese and South Korean, banks and corporations that are not subject to US and EU sanctions. Moscow also hopes to engage in trade with countries in Latin America, in the Middle East (including Israel and Turkey), and in the Indo-Pacific (including China and Japan) that have not imposed sanctions. Moscow wants to believe that the United States and/or the European Union will eventually abandon sanctions altogether.

The sanctions have initially tended to cut off Russia's access to Western capital markets and know-how and scare off foreign investors, even though the Russian economy began to strengthen in 2016.[8] Coupled with generally low global oil prices, the general economic crisis has cut real incomes, fueled inflation, and caused significant capital flight. Since 2012, consumer prices in Russia have risen by 50 percent. There had been a drop in the value of the ruble against the dollar, and average salaries fell by 36 percent from 2012 to 2016 in dollar terms. Inflation has been officially described at 5.4 percent but is probably much higher.[9]

Even though it does open some opportunities for non-US and non-EU firms, the Russian annexation of Crimea comes at a major political-economic cost to Moscow. It also undermines US and EU trust in the Russian leadership—which it makes it even more difficult to build a positive relationship.

IDEOLOGICAL DIVISIONS IN THE TRUMP ADMINISTRATION

The Trump administration appears divided into two ideological camps. Against the globalists, there is a general move among other America First economic nationalists to reduce, or at least minimize, multinational energy investments in Russia in favor of the development of US shale oil and gas. Trump's nationalist America First ideology stands against multinational corporate investments, such as those of ExxonMobil in Russia, and wants ExxonMobil to invest back in the United States.

This group generally wants to further develop the US domestic energy market through strong support for the Keystone XL pipeline, through cutbacks on strict Environmental Protection Agency regulations, and by opening public lands for energy development purposes. Shale energy supporters see US and European sanctions on Russia as an opportunity to export shale gas to Europe, including Poland and Ukraine, and thus reduce eastern European dependency on Russian energy. In addition, shale energy supporters want to support the Baltic states to reduce their dependence on Russian energy, by helping to supply the technology to build regasification plants. Despite the ongoing Ukrainian-Russian conflict, Kiev is still dependent on Moscow for about 50 percent of its natural gas. Expanded exports of highly polluting US shale gas and oil to Europe are furthermore seen as a means to potentially undercut one of Moscow's major sources of revenue, which represents some 68 percent of Russia's total exports.[10] American energy companies also hope that they can eventually break the Organization of the Petroleum Exporting Countries (OPEC), which seeks to control energy pricing. The US effort to export shale energy to Europe (despite the heavy debts involved in shale oil and gas production) could soon put the United States and Russia into direct competition for former Russian energy markets.

In effect, Trump's "energy dominance" plan was written into the August 2017 H.R. 3364 act, "Countering America's Adversaries through Sanctions Act." As mentioned in an earlier chapter, Trump appeared to be forced to sign this bill into law, given its strong bipartisan congressional backing, despite the fact that he publicly stated it to be "flawed."[11] H.R. 3364, Trump argued, "encroaches on the executive branch's authority to negotiate" and "makes it harder for the United States to strike good deals for the American people and will drive China, Russia and North Korea much closer together" and could additionally "hinder our important work with European allies to resolve the conflict in Ukraine."[12]

Trump claimed to have opposed the "Countering America's Adversaries through Sanctions Act," but he nevertheless more strongly backed America First energy interests against those of Moscow by supporting the 2016 Polish-Croatian Three Seas Initiative. The latter initiative is intended to foster trade, infrastructure, energy, and political cooperation among the ex-Communist countries bordering the Adriatic, the Baltic, and the Black Seas. Nearly all the countries involved—Poland, Hungary, the Czech Republic, Slovakia, Romania, Bulgaria, Lithuania, Estonia, Latvia, Croatia, Slovenia, and Austria—are heavily reliant on Russian gas and oil imports. The Three Seas Initiative seeks to minimize these states' dependence on Russian energy imports, and thus could clash with Russian interests.

It is predicted that by 2040, given significant and risky investment, US shale oil production will increase 45 percent from 2015 levels to 7.1 million barrels a day—and it most like grow rapidly with the assistance of Trump's pro–fossil fuels policies.[13] Over the past decade, shale gas has risen from 2 percent to 37 percent of US natural gas production. After surpassing Russia, the United States is now the world's largest producer of natural gas and is beginning to develop its export capabilities. On January 24, 2017, President Trump signed presidential memoranda to revive both Keystone XL and Dakota Access pipelines in order to speed the process after President Barack Obama had rejected the fourth phase of the Keystone XL pipeline in November 6, 2015, in an effort to reduce greenhouse gases.

The Keystone XL pipeline has been opposed by both ecology groups and Native Americans. In November 2014, the Rosebud Sioux Tribe had called the US decision to build the pipeline "an act of war" and had vowed to block the project from crossing its lands.[14] The debate has, in part, revolved around the social, health, and economic impacts of potential pipeline leakage and whether or not the pipeline will generate a significant number of long-term jobs, while also raising the question of whether these risky investments are creating new debt bubbles. Perhaps most important, the Trump administration support for the project raises real questions as to whether the government will be able to move energy producers away from carbon emissions that exacerbate the dangerous trends toward global warming, and toward nonpolluting and healthier energy options. (See chapter 10.)

TRUMP TAKES AN ANTI-MOSCOW STANCE

It was only once Trump became president that he began to stress the importance of NATO as a collective defense organization. Throughout his presidential campaign, and in the early days of his presidency, Trump repeatedly called NATO "obsolete." On the one hand, this raised Moscow's hopes that Trump would begin to reform NATO, a collective defense organization that dates from the Cold War. On the other hand, Trump's critical statement raised the fears of eastern European countries that the United States and NATO might no longer back them against ongoing and future Russian military pressures and threats in accord with NATO's Article V security guarantees.

Prior to becoming president, Trump had appeared to ignore NATO's role as a collective defense organization against potential threats from Russia or other states. And even though NATO has thus far played only a limited role in the fight against the Islamic State, Trump also appeared to ignore NATO's role in Afghanistan and Libya as part of the Global War on Terrorism. At that time, Trump appeared unaware of the debate inside NATO as to how many resources to concentrate on defenses to the north and east against Russia and how much to concentrate on defending Europe to the south in relationship to immigration, refugees, and terrorist movements.

At the same time, however, Trump did agree to accept the Balkan state of Montenegro into NATO membership. This action was taken in order to check Russian influence inside the country and for NATO to secure the coast of the Adriatic—angering Moscow, which purportedly tried to stage a coup, assuming the government did not pretend to stage a coup itself, as has been alleged in this age of disinformation.[15] But it nevertheless remains unclear how NATO should or could deal with the high level of corruption in Montenegro, including counterfeit Euros in the country, plus the strong pro-Russian sentiment among the population.

THE QUESTION OF RUSSIAN "AGGRESSION" AND THE THREAT OF WAR

For understandable historical reasons, most eastern European states are afraid of Russia and believe that Moscow is inherently "aggressive." Yet the term "aggression" does not fully explain *why* Russia has acted in the way it has—and at that particular moment. As Moscow had made what it believed to be reasonable deals with the previous Ukrainian Yanukovych leadership, a better explanation is that Russian military intervention in Crimea and political-military interference in eastern Ukraine was intended as a *preclusive action* that has sought to check further enlargement by both NATO and the European Union into the Russian-defined "near abroad." Here, Moscow believes the EU expansion since 2008 has sought to undermine Russian political-economic influence in the former Soviet states of Belarus, Ukraine, Moldova, Georgia, Armenia, and Azerbaijan.

Since at least March 2014, if not earlier, Moscow has been engaging in provocative overflights and submarine incursions into the territories of NATO and EU members, including EU member states Sweden and Finland. As a consequence, the latter countries have been considering closer ties to NATO. Likewise, in mid-March 2014, Moscow engaged the Russian Baltic Fleet in exercises along the Baltic coast, while also placing infantry, air force, and Spetsnaz troops on alert throughout the Russian Federation and along the borders of NATO member states from the

Arctic region to the Baltic and Black Seas. A Russian military buildup has accordingly been taking place in Kaliningrad, where Moscow's warships are not as vulnerable as they are when they sail from Saint Petersburg and pass between Estonia and Finland. In addition to threatening to deploy nuclear weapons in Kaliningrad, Moscow has also threatened a nuclear and conventional weapons buildup in the newly annexed Crimea.

These are just a few of many incidents that have taken place since the Russian annexation of Crimea in 2014 that could spark conflict. Somewhat-similar incidents involving both Russian and Chinese overflights have taken place in the Asia-Pacific region as well, while both Russia and China point to the buildup of NATO and US (and Japanese) military capabilities in Europe and Asia. From the Russian perspective, such repeated overflights into European, Japanese, and US airspace have been justified by the fact that the number of nuclear-capable fighters in the NATO Baltic air-policing mission had been significantly increased in early March 2014. In Moscow's view, advanced NATO fighter jets with potential nuclear weapons capabilities now patrol regularly along the sensitive Baltic state border only a few minutes by supersonic flight to Saint Petersburg and Moscow.

Moscow has also opposed NATO membership for EU members Sweden and Finland, who are no longer technically neutral, having joined the European Union. Should Finland join NATO, Moscow would fear the rebirth of Finnish irredentist claims, backed by NATO, to territories taken by the Soviet Union after the Winter War and the Continuation War.[16] Finland has claimed that it has no irredentist claims, yet Moscow nevertheless fears that if Finland joins NATO, then NATO might back Finnish claims to Karelia, Salla, and Petsamo. Claims to Petsamo, if pursued, could give Finland access to the Barents Sea—which will become a major sea line of communication in the coming years as the polar ice caps, unfortunately, melt. (This issue might be better addressed by bilateral Finnish-Russian negotiations than by drawing NATO into the picture.)

Russia already feels "encircled" by NATO in the Arctic region. Out of the eight Arctic Circle states, in addition to Russia itself, five are NATO members: Norway, the United States, Canada, Denmark (Greenland), and Iceland (where it passes through the small offshore island of Grímsey). As previously mentioned, two are EU members considering NATO membership, Sweden and Finland.

There are a number of major legal and defense issues here. The close overlapping links between NATO and EU members raises a delicate political-legal-security question. If an EU member is attacked, the United States and NATO could automatically become involved. This is because NATO and the European Union possess close overlapping memberships, which themselves possess mutual defense clauses. The EU defense clause, however, is much tighter than the NATO Article V clause.

BUDAPEST ACCORDS AND NATO-RUSSIA FOUNDING ACT

Russian actions raised the question as to whether the United States, France, and the United Kingdom were necessarily obliged to provide military assistance to Ukraine in accord with the Budapest Memorandum of 1994, but which was not a formal treaty. The United States and the European Union did agree to apply economic sanctions on Russia in 2014, but they are not legally mandatory for all states.[17] Nevertheless, Moscow's ostensible violation of the Budapest Memorandum, among the other international agreements, including the 1997 NATO-Russia Founding Act, which had established the NATO-Russian relationship, led the United States and the European Union to argue that Russian actions in Crimea and eastern Ukraine could not be permitted without some form of punishment. (See the introduction.)

The 1994 Budapest Memorandum had provided security assurances (not security guarantees) to Ukraine that obliged its signers, the

United States, Russia, and the United Kingdom (plus France and China later and separately), "to respect the independence and sovereignty and the existing borders of Ukraine" once Kiev gave up its nuclear weaponry left over from the ex–Soviet Union.[18] But "respect for borders" was not intended as an absolute guarantee of military assistance to Ukraine.

The NATO-Russia Founding Act of 1997 stated, "Any actions undertaken by NATO or Russia, together or separately, must be consistent with the United Nations Charter and the OSCE's governing principles."[19] From the Russian perspective, this principle was already broken by NATO itself after it declared war on Serbia over Kosovo in 1999 without a UN Security Council mandate.

The 1997 NATO-Russia Founding Act had also promised that NATO had no plans to deploy troops or nuclear weapons on the territories of the new members—at least at that time.[20] In terms of conventional forces, the Founding Act stated that "the Alliance will carry out its collective defense and other missions by ensuring the necessary interoperability, integration, and capability for reinforcement rather than by additional permanent stationing of substantial combat forces."[21] Both sides were to "prevent any potentially threatening build-up of conventional forces in agreed regions of Europe, to include Central and Eastern Europe."[22]

The Russian military intervention into Crimea and eastern Ukraine has accordingly threatened to tear apart the 1997 NATO-Russia Founding Act. For this reason, the option to support Kiev through direct military assistance to counter eastern Ukrainian secessionists secretly backed by Moscow is a decision of individual states—not of NATO or the European Union as a whole. Under the Obama administration, Washington decided to provide only limited US training and support for Kiev's military units—instead of providing significant arms shipments.

Since 2014, Russian military pressures have led NATO to consider a rotating deployment of troops on the territory of the new NATO members, so as to not technically violate the NATO-Russian Founding Act, with the questionable rationalization that the "rotation" of forces did not represent a "permanent" deployment of forces. By January 2016, the US Congress mandated the European Reassurance Initiative, which promised $985 million for the Pentagon to augment a "rotational" US troop presence in Europe for NATO activities and to preposition US military infrastructure and assets in Europe. President Obama then requested $3.4 billion for 2017 for the deployment of an additional "rotational" Armored Brigade Combat Team (ABCT) to central and eastern Europe, plus the prepositioning of combat equipment, and additional training and exercises in Europe.[23]

US aid has also been allocated to help build the defense capacity of new NATO members in addition to assisting potential NATO members, which include Georgia, Macedonia, Moldova, and Ukraine. Yet proposed NATO membership for the latter states continues to fuel tensions with Moscow. The latter interprets US calls for greater NATO defense spending as an anti-Russian gesture that is intended to force Moscow to spend much more on defense against the combined forces of NATO in return.

Nevertheless, members of the US Congress, the Pentagon, and European hardliners have continued to argue for a permanent NATO deployment, while Russia already considers the decision to be a "permanently rotating" deployment—and thus a violation of the NATO-Russia Founding Act. Hardliners have also argued for NATO to display a nuclear capability in military maneuvers in order to symbolically counter Russian threats to deploy tactical nuclear weapons in Kaliningrad, for example. But these measures would most likely be met by Russian counter-threats. And the risk is that Ukraine's 1,300-mile-long and porous border with Russia can only be defended by NATO's use of nuclear weapons if relations between Ukraine and Russia remain acrimonious. A NATO defense of Georgia, Moldova, Ukraine, and the Baltic states could easily escalate into a nuclear conflict given the Russian tactical advantage in each area.

In effect, President Obama had argued that Ukraine was part of Russia's vital interests, but not those of the United States—and left the situation dangerously ambiguous.[24] Obama did not seek to formally renounce

NATO enlargement. Nor did he seek to formally establish Ukraine as a neutral country. Despite the fact that Ukraine is not a NATO member, NATO has become involved in defending Ukraine with what it considers defensive assistance. This is in part because NATO and Ukraine formed the NATO-Ukraine Commission just after NATO first formed the NATO-Russia Council in 1997.[25] In 1997 the idea was to approach both sides and suggest cooperative measures but give Russia priority. Now NATO appears to be granting Ukraine priority in its conflict with Russia. Members of the US Congress, the Pentagon, and some members of the Trump administration, have been considering greater military supports for Kiev, including lethal aid, which Russia could easily counter.[26] NATO Secretary General Jens Stoltenberg and other European leaders have proposed a policy of "defense and dialogue" vis-a-vis Russia. But the question remains: How much defense? And how much *real* dialogue?

WAR OVER CRIMEA AND EASTERN UKRAINE

From the Russian perspective, the events that resulted in the Russian annexation of Crimea and Russian political-military interference in eastern Ukraine in 2014 stem from US and European attempts to expand their spheres of influence into the Russian "near abroad." In effect, Moscow feared that its naval base at Sevastopol would fall into the hands of NATO, while its political-economic interests in eastern Ukraine would be undermined by the more competitive European economy.[27]

Moscow not only opposed US and European efforts to engage in "democracy engineering" against former Ukrainian Prime Minister Viktor Yanukovych in 2013–2014, but also opposed any political-economic deal between the European Union and Ukraine that did not also incorporate Russian gas, Ukrainian debts to Moscow, and other political-economic interests. Moscow then pressured Yanukovych to refuse to sign the EU Association Accord—which helped spark the Euromaidan protests in Kiev in 2013–2014. Moscow then took advantage of the chaos once the kleptocratic, but not always pro-Russian, Yanukovych leadership collapsed.

The general chaos then taking place in Ukraine permitted Moscow to engage in preclusive actions intended to rapidly annex Crimea by means of deploying "little green men" without insignias in strategic locations throughout the isthmus. Moscow also began to engage in clandestine political-military intervention in eastern Ukraine in support of Ukrainian "autonomists." This also meant that Moscow seized waters surrounding Crimea in which Ukraine had just offered US and European multinational energy companies, such as ExxonMobil, to explore.

By March 2014, Moscow had formally annexed Crimea after staging a public referendum that ostensibly legitimized Russian actions. This put an end to Kiev's controls over the peninsula and thus safeguarded the Russian Black Sea fleet from possible eviction by the new government in Kiev. Moscow, of course, denied any wrongdoing in that it saw Yanukovych as being overthrown by an "illegal" coup (even if Ukrainian lawmakers backed that "coup" by opposing Yanukovich's corruption and kleptocracy).

In effect, Moscow claimed that it was fighting Ukrainian "fascists" by supporting the right of self-determination for the ethnic Russian majority of the Crimean populations, according to its own national security interests defined during the Yeltsin administration. At the same time, whether Moscow has been able to improve the living conditions, quality of life, and sociopolitical freedoms of both Russian and non-Russian minorities, such as Tatars and Ukrainians, living in Crimea after the annexation is another question. The potential failure to do so could undermine Moscow's rationale for the annexation.

As fighting intensified between pro–Ukrainian government supporters and Russian-backed autonomists in the Donbas region, the Minsk I accords were signed in September 2014 talks between representatives from Russia and the opposing two Ukrainian factions under the auspices of the Organization for Security and Co-operation in Europe (OSCE). The Minsk I agreement, which had followed previous attempts to stop fighting, tried, but failed, to implement a cease-fire. These accords were then followed by the February 2015 Minsk II accords between Ukraine, Russia, France, and Germany, once again under the auspices of the OSCE.[28]

The February Minsk II accords urged greater "decentralization" by means of a reform of Ukraine's Constitution. By mid-July 2015, the new Ukrainian Prime Minister Petro Poroshenko introduced a bill to the parliament that would ostensibly devolve powers to localities. Poroshenko insisted that these constitutional changes would not turn Ukraine into a "federation" or "special status" as demanded by Moscow. Kiev has opposed greater "autonomy" or "federation"—a position opposed by many in the Ukrainian parliament and violently opposed by right-wing centralists—in the fear that greater autonomy for the Donbas could eventually lead to political secession and independence. On March 16, 2017, three of Ukraine's major far-right groups—Svoboda, Right Sector, and National Corps—signed a manifesto that called for "establishing and developing a great national state."[29]

Nevertheless, Poroshenko has claimed that he would grant local authorities more power throughout the country.[30] But this is to be done by the strengthening of presidential control over local self-governments by means of "centrally assigned 'prefects' with broad powers."[31] Kiev's efforts to find an in-between position that will somehow satisfy both centralists and "autonomists" who demand a special status (while actually asserting presidential powers over localities in the process), appears to have failed miserably with the resumption of fighting in mid-2016. At the same time, despite pressures from the World Bank and NGOs pressing for greater governmental transparency, corruption runs high. Ukraine is tied with Russia as two of the most corrupt states in the world, with a rating of 131 out of 176 countries.[32]

In May 2015, Moscow's own propaganda in favor of the Novorossiya movement for a potential union with the Donbas region and other southern Ukrainian regions suddenly ceased.[33] Not only was such an option opposed by France and Germany in the Minsk II accords, but the costs of such a venture, coupled with strong Ukrainian resistance, the probable need for a long-term Russian occupation force, the costs of long-term Russian political-economic isolation from the United States and Europe, and the general collapse of global energy prices, appeared to put a damper on such imperialist expansion. In an effort to show that it does not possess an imperial design, Moscow had permitted a series of Ukrainian overflights under the Open Skies Treaty in March 11, 2014, and it likewise granted Ukraine's request to conduct an inspection of a "non-declared military activity" in a border region.[34] (NATO, however, was not impressed by what it called Moscow's "selective" implementation of the Open Skies Treaty.[35])

Moreover, the very fact that Moscow has been unwilling to admit to its own population the role of Russian special forces in Ukraine appears to indicate that Moscow does not want to take over the burden and responsibility for the entire region, as has been the case for Crimea. Moscow does not want an unpopular war in which it must enlist the general population. Whether or not the killing was orchestrated by Putin, as alleged, one of the purported rationales for the assassination of Boris Nemtsov, an opposition politician, in February 2015 was that he was attempting to make public proof that Russian forces were involved in the intervention in eastern Ukraine.[36] (See discussion, chapter 3.)

Ukrainian autonomists have still not given up their struggle, despite the fact that they are not obtaining full backing from Moscow. In August 2016, Russian-backed forces engaged in a major military buildup around Ukraine (to north in Bryansk, to the east near Rostov, to the south in Crimea, and to the west in the Transnistria area of Moldova) after it claimed that Kiev had engaged in a military incursion and terrorist sabotage in Crimea. This incident followed a number of sabotage attempts—which may or may not be backed by Ukrainian authorities. These include efforts to disrupt the supply of electricity to Crimea and to blockade transportation routes and water supplies.

Kiev does not appear willing to accept the loss of Crimea and has sought US and NATO support to regain it. The Trump administration has now supported Kiev's position since February 2017—particularly after conflict flared up again after Kiev engaged in a "creeping offensive" in mid-December 2016, which has nonetheless stepped deeper into the grey zone between the two sides. This offensive was ostensibly intended to check supplies going to the Russian-backed autonomists, while trying to preempt militias from the Donetsk and Luhansk "people's republics" from seizing more territory.[37] The autonomists have, in turn, begun to expropriate Ukrainian businesses in the Donetsk and Lugansk regions.[38] For its part, Kiev has claimed that Moscow was building up its forces in Crimea to turn it into an "isolated military base" and was attempting to justify "aggressive actions of [Russian] military units . . . on the territory of the currently occupied peninsula."[39]

Kiev's strategy has been intended to further divide and then defeat the "autonomist" Russophone forces that have generally split between those seeking independence (the self-proclaimed yet unrecognized "republics" of Donetsk and Lugansk) and those seeking greater autonomy from Kiev's centralized controls, but who are not necessarily pro-Putin. The dilemma is that Ukrainian President Petro Poroshenko appears incapable of implementing the February 2015 Minsk decentralization proposals, which would involve changes to the constitution and would permit local elections.

Concurrently, Moscow appears reluctant to make good on its security commitments because of its commitment to eastern Ukrainian autonomists. The latter see the open border with Russia as key to their survival. At the same time, Kiev has, particularly in 2015–2016, insisted on being able to control the Ukrainian-Russian border first before implementing the Minsk accords. This is a major factor that has led to a breakdown in discussions—and which, in addition, led to Kiev's December–February 2016 "creeping offensive" into the grey zone between the two sides that is in or near the war-ravaged cities of Avdiivka, Debaltseve, Dokuchaievsk,

Horlivka, and Mariupol, closer to the positions of the eastern Ukrainian autonomists. Control of the Mariupol region for the autonomists appears key in geo-economic terms—as it opens up the possibility of trade and transportation links with Russian-held Crimea.

The United States and European states have appeared to have granted Kiev sufficient financial and military assistance in order to counter autonomist movements that are not-so-secretly backed by Russia. Yet the fighting in the Donbas has moreover proved very costly for all sides, and rebuilding the region will prove very difficult. A collapsed Donbas region that is potentially separated from a partitioned Ukraine could soon become a much larger and unstable version of Russian-backed Transnistria, South Ossetia, and Abkhazia combined. Such political-economic instability will continue to pollute the whole area with black marketeering, weapons smuggling, and other forms of criminality.

Moreover, a failed "state" in eastern Ukraine would prove very troublesome not only for an essentially bankrupt Kiev and the rest of the region, but for Moscow as well—as the latter, for example, will need to deal with refugees fleeing to Russia. Some 1,554,497 people have already fled the country, with the vast majority (1,226,104) moving to the Russian Federation—which has not necessarily accepted them with open arms. Roughly 148,867 have gone to Belarus.[40] The costs of reconstruction and development in the aftermath of the conflict will be considerable.

Putin's annexation of Crimea has been proving unexpectedly costly for Moscow to achieve rapidly in the short term—and even more so with US and European sanctions in place. Moscow has needed to augment salaries and pensions of the Crimean population to Russian standards, while tourism will remain much lower than normal until the situation stabilizes. The Kerch bridge that is needed to supply Crimea from Russia will probably cost much more than the officially estimated $4.5 billion and may not prove long-lasting due to the harsh nature of the surrounding climate.[41] In addition to the need for Moscow to supply Crimea with gas and electricity, Kiev's blockade of the North Crimean Canal has negatively impacted Crimean agriculture, as well as the overall Crimean economy, ecology, and population.

By blocking the North Crimean Canal, for example, Kiev has prevented as much as 85 percent of Crimea's water supply from entering Crimea. In this new form of hybrid and environmental warfare, these actions have already provoked a crisis in agricultural production and could force migration back to Russia—if Moscow cannot soon find ways to provide water for the isthmus.[42]

THE FAILURE OF US POLICY

The NATO-Russia Founding Act—which was intended to bring NATO and Russia into closer post–Cold War cooperation—is now being challenged. The breakdown of the NATO Founding Act could potentially result in the permanent deployment of troops and nuclear weaponry in eastern Europe. This could not only result in a new partition of Europe but also provoke an even more dangerous Russian backlash—if the crisis cannot soon be abated. It could also lead to a major arms race in which Moscow will seek to counter US military superiority by asymmetrical and "hybrid" methods. Not only do "rotating" deployments risk undermining that fundamental NATO-Russia Founding Act, but so does the deployment of the F-35 stealth fighter, which is capable of carrying the renovated B-61-12 tactical nuclear bomb, in NATO military exercises along the Estonian-NATO border, for example. Although this is not the official explanation, these exercises are designed to demonstrate capabilities that could counter a potential Russian advance into the region.[43]

The essential dilemma is this: As long as NATO, Ukraine, and other countries "will not" recognize Russian sovereignty over Crimea, and as long as Moscow claims it "will not" give up that sovereignty, there will be no lasting peace. Other diplomatic options to a military buildup and arms race must be forthcoming, and yet not only is the State Department divided, but the White House and Congress appear totally at odds on this issue—as the passage of the "Countering America's Adversaries through Sanctions Act" in August 2017 has indicated. There is a real risk that an eventual partition of Ukraine, coupled with the permanently rotating deployment of NATO forces in the Baltic region, could in turn lead to a new partition of Europe though Ukraine—followed by the polarization of the world into two rival alliances. (See chapters 9 and 10.)

CHAPTER 6

THE GLOBAL IMPACT OF THE CHINA-RUSSIA EURASIAN ALLIANCE

US and NATO policies have thus far been pushing Russia and China closer together. While Trump was initially right to seek a rapprochement with Russia, despite the controversial way he has gone about it, the dilemma is that the Trump administration's policy flip-flops could push Beijing and Moscow even closer together. This is true given the Trump-Pence administration's newfound support for Kiev's claims to Crimea combined with Trump's initial threat to support Taiwanese independence (even though he backed off to support the One-China policy). Washington has also been seeking to check China's access to islands in the South and East China Seas, while concurrently threatening trade sanctions against both North Korea and possibly China itself—if Beijing cannot convince North Korea to give up, or at least freeze, its nuclear weapons program.

On a geostrategic level, Washington has been raising China's suspicions of a US-inspired "encirclement" by calling on India to join the United States, Japan, and Australia to deal with common security challenges in the Indo-Pacific region, through the Quadrilateral Security Dialogue (or Quad). For its part, Japan, China's historical rival, has called for the formation of a "democratic security diamond" that would include Japan, the United States, Australia, and India to counterbalance China. Washington's threat to build up naval forces and alliances in the Indo-Pacific region, plus the deployment of US missile defense systems in

Europe, the Middle East, and Asia since the Obama administration, has accordingly begun to press Russia and China into an even closer defense relationship against US conventional and nuclear weapons superiority. China has furthermore opposed US-South Korean, THAAD missile defense deployments.[1] A close Sino-Russian defense relationship could then lead to tighter Sino-Russian defense relations with Iran—and possibly with India.

For its part, Beijing has hoped to overcome its century of humiliation since its Opium wars with Great Britain and its subsequent political-economic exploitation by the Europeans, by the United States, and particularly by Japan. Now China wants to establish itself as a major power in the twenty-first century. Beijing first seeks to make itself a major political-economic and financial actor by expanding its global political-economic hegemony through its Belt and Road Initiative (BRI) and by working to develop a massive trading bloc, the Regional Comprehensive Economic Partnership (RCEP). China's huge financial, economic, and technological capabilities will then permit it to develop significant military capabilities.

China's Belt and Road Initiative (BRI), which was initially said called "One Belt, One Road," comprises the Silk Road Economic Belt and the Twenty-First-Century Maritime Silk Road. Beijing's objective has been to develop a trade and infrastructure network that connects Asia with Europe and Northern Africa along the ancient Silk Road routes.[2] These routes cover more than 60 countries and regions from the Far East to Europe and the Middle East (with Egypt and the Suez a key geo-economic focal point). The BRI countries currently account for some 30 percent of global GDP and more than 35 percent of the world's merchandise trade.

By 2050, Beijing hopes that the BRI will contribute up to 80 percent of global GDP growth and bring as many as three billion more people into the middle class. In many ways, the legitimacy of the Chinese Communist Party ironically depends to a large extent on its ability to expand the share of its economic pie to as many Chinese citizens as possible.

By 2020, Beijing aims to double the yearly average personal disposable income of roughly $3,000 in 2010 (20,000 yuan) to roughly $6,000 (40,000 Yuan) for at least one billion people.[3] And in the process, China is straining regional, financial, and global resources (as well as the health of its population through excessive pollution)—in rivalry with US, Japanese, and European incomes and mass consumerism, while concurrently risking conflicts with its neighbors and with the United States itself.

Concurrently, Beijing has been finalizing the RCEP negotiations with the ASEAN states (Indonesia, Malaysia, Philippines, Singapore, Thailand, Brunei Darussalam, Cambodia, Laos, Myanmar [Burma], and Vietnam), plus India, Japan, South Korea, Australia, and New Zealand. If the RCEP is finalized by the end of 2017 as expected, and assuming India, Japan, South Korea, and Indonesia do not stall progress, the RCEP would create the largest trading bloc in the world, covering nearly one third of the global economy. But it would exclude the United States and Europeans.

TOWARD CLOSER RUSSIAN AND CHINESE POLITICAL-ECONOMIC AND MILITARY INTEGRATION

To achieve their long-term goals, China and Russia appear to be moving into a closer political-economic and strategic Eurasian alliance. At the roots of this Sino-Russian rapprochement was the final border delimitation of 2004. This had been the fruit of negotiations since 1986, when Gorbachev initiated the Soviet rapprochement with China. Since at least since 2005, Russia and China have been engaging in major military maneuvers in the framework of the Shanghai Cooperation Organization (SCO). By 2012, they announced their Strategic Partnership, followed by the comprehensive 2014 Strategic Partnership. The latter has been symbolized by closer Sino-Russian defense collaboration involving joint naval maneuvers in the eastern Mediterranean in May 2015—in which China appeared to backing Russian military actions in Syria.[4] Russia and

China likewise engaged in joint naval maneuvers in September 2016 in the contested waters of the South China Sea.

It was in Moscow on May 8, 2015, that Moscow and Beijing stated their combined intent to integrate the Chinese-led Silk Road Economic Belt and the Twenty-First-Century Maritime Silk Road with Russia's Eurasian Economic Union (EEU). This accord took place at the ceremony that commemorated the end of World War II—but which was boycotted by most US and European leaders, due to Moscow's annexation of Crimea in 2014. The boycotting of this event, at least in the Russian perspective, appeared to denigrate Moscow's crucial role in defeating Hitler.

For its part, Moscow has additionally tried to widen its markets and build a stronger economic infrastructure by forging its new Eurasian Economic Union. The EEU is to include Armenia, Belarus, Kazakhstan, Kyrgyzstan, and Russia. Moscow has also been attempting to press Moldova, Kyrgyzstan, Tajikistan, and Serbia into joining. Moscow, however, has failed to incorporate Ukraine, which joined the EU Association Agreement in late 2014 after the Euromaidan movement overturned the kleptocratic government of President Viktor Yanukovych, but after Russia had annexed Crimea and supported the autonomist movements in eastern Ukraine.

Moscow has also hoped to enlarge the Collective Security Treaty Organization (CSTO), which represents a Russian effort to mimic NATO. The CSTO thus far includes Russia, Belarus, Kazakhstan, Kyrgyzstan, and Tajikistan, but Moscow has invited China, India, Iran, Mongolia, and Pakistan to be CSTO observers. Afghanistan and Serbia are already observers. Pakistani observer status was, however, surprisingly rejected by Armenia due to Pakistan's support for Azerbaijan and its refusal to recognize Armenia.[5] (Even before 2014, Ukraine had remained out of both the CSTO and the Eurasian Union—giving preference to possibility of joining NATO and the EU Association Agreement.)

REASONS FOR A CLOSER SINO-RUSSIAN ALLIANCE

The first major rationale for closer Russian ties to China is a consequence of Russian fears of isolation in Europe in response to the double expansion of NATO and the European Union into former Soviet spheres of influence and security. In the Indo-Pacific, the US-Japanese alliance has been tightening relations with South Korea and Australia, while seeking to strengthen relations with India, if possible. In effect both Moscow and Beijing fear that Washington will reactivate its policy of containment or "encirclement."

Moreover, both Moscow and China tend to see US and European ideological appeals to "democracy" and "human rights" as a threat both to one-party Communist leadership in the case of China and to the dynamic authoritarian duo of Vladimir Putin and Dmitri Medvedev in the case of Russia—a situation in which Putin's political party, United Russia, predominates over all other Russian political parties, with more than 3/4 of the 450 seats in the Russian Duma. From Beijing's perspective, the student-led Chinese democracy movement in Tiananmen Square and throughout the country in April–June 1989, and the more recent Hong Kong democracy movements (the Umbrella Revolution, since 2014), have been seen as backed by US and European (and Taiwanese) democratic ideology, media, and secret financial supports.

Rather than engage in necessary reforms designed to check corruption and open the decision-making processes to greater civil-society inputs, both Moscow and Beijing see these democracy movements as an essentially US-directed tool of hybrid warfare primarily aimed at undermining the Russian and Chinese power structure and ultimately aimed at breaking up both countries. (On Russian views, see chapter 3.)

THE QUESTION OF RUSSIAN ARMS SALES TO CHINA

Moscow has, for the first time in years, begun to sell China advanced weaponry. In 2016, Moscow promised to sell four advanced Russian Su-35 fighter jets to Beijing—with a total of twenty-four jets to be completed in three years. And China will probably obtain more than just the initial twenty-four Su-35s. This significant arms sale has generated tensions with India, Taiwan, and Japan.[6] In addition, Moscow has also been considering the sale of *Amur*-class submarines to China, plus advanced aircraft engines and radars. Moreover, Russia is expected to deliver its S-400 surface-to-air missile to China by 2018. Overall, Beijing and Moscow had signed roughly $8 billion in defense contracts as of November 2016.[7]

In effect, Russian technology could boost China's air defense capability significantly—even though Moscow still fears Beijing could clone Russian military technology. In 2014, Beijing was seen as copying the Su-27/30 fighter—which then became the J-11. The Chinese have also been accused of cloning US military technology. The Chinese J-31, for example, looks like a US F-35—as the Chinese were believed to have hacked into the files of F-35 sub-contractors.[8] Yet Russian fears of Chinese high-tech copying appear less worrisome due to the fact that Moscow expects to deploy the even more advanced S-500 surface-to-air missile and T-50 fighter in the near future. Nevertheless, these major arms sales to China are significant in that they appear to put to an end Moscow's own informal ban on selling advanced weapons systems to Beijing, which had in place since roughly 2004.[9]

Moscow elites do fear that Russia could, in the not so-distant future, become a junior partner of China in military terms. Already, China possesses world's largest land army, and it is rapidly developing its blue-water navy, plus ICBM missile capabilities. For this reason, many Russian elites have called for restraining the sale of advanced military technologies to China. These elites worry that Russian arms sales to China could backfire, if Beijing eventually turns against Russia.[10] By contrast with this view, other Russian elites have hoped to co-opt China by means of working closely with the leadership. They consider it futile to confront Beijing.

The dilemma is that the long-term ability of Russia (and of the United States) to stay ahead of China in the game of military innovation is not guaranteed. There are still some items Russia will not sell China—such as technology that allows the Iskander cruise missile to maneuver at extremely high speed, making it difficult to intercept. Moscow will also not supply Beijing with satellite systems that could detect ballistic missile launches.[11] At the same time, Russian arms sales to China are helpful in permitting Moscow to obtain a better conception of real Chinese military capabilities. The nature of Russia and Chinese defense relations indicates that the two countries could deepen military-to-military trade through the joint development of new space technology, airplanes, and helicopters.[12] Advanced Russian arms sales appear designed to support China militarily as Beijing has begun to confront the US-Japanese alliance—while both Moscow and Beijing have hoped to splinter ASEAN where possible. Cambodia, Laos, and Myanmar, but more importantly Malaysia, even Vietnam, and now the Philippines, appear to be moving closer to both Russia and China.

ENERGY COOPERATION

Russian arms deals with China were bargained just when Russia and China were finalizing their "historic" gas deal worth $400 billion in May 2014, just after the Russian annexation of Crimea. Even though there have been ongoing price disputes over the gas deal, China and Russia also worked out a series of energy agreements involving the doubling of oil supplies and the construction of a natural gas pipeline to China from Russia. Additionally, the two agreed to develop Russian coal resources for China's benefit.

In this case, Russian-Chinese rivalry could be seen in the fact that

China had previously sought to block Russia's attempts to establish a Russia-based energy infrastructure in Central Asia, by establishing contracts with a number of Central Asian states to build gas and oil pipelines directly to China.[13] The fact that this deal came just after the United States and the European Union imposed sanctions on Moscow after its annexation of Crimea, however, indicated that Moscow could find financing for its major projects from other sources. From the Russian perspective, defense and security issues are now overriding political-economic concerns and previous disputes with China. Likewise, major Chinese banking deals with Russia to develop the Yamal liquefied natural (LNG) gas venture in the Arctic permit Russia to reduce its reliance on gas-export sales to Europe, while supplying China and opening up LNG shipping exports to Asia. And these deals once again show that Moscow can still find financing for a major project despite US and EU sanctions, but at the risk of too great a dependence on Beijing.

In late September 2017, CEFC China Energy purchased a 14.16 percent stake ($9.1 billion) in the Russian oil producer Rosneft, a firm closely linked to Putin, which will provide China access to eastern Russian oilfields near the Chinese border. It is the first time China has acquired a significant stake in a major Kremlin-controlled corporation.[14]

Moreover, these deals will boost not only China's economy but also its energy security. This is because the energy supply chains, particularly over land but also on the sea, tend to avoid the maritime choke points dominated by the United States and its allies.[15] This latter strategic economic fact provides a major rationale for China to sustain its close Eurasian relationship with Russia in the future.

COMMON VALUES

What appears very significant is that Russia and China have begun to enhance cooperation not only by means of cultural exchanges but also by cooperation in the actual making of domestic policies. In early 2016, Russian President Vladimir Putin and Chinese leader Xi Jinping urged the legislative bodies of their respective countries to enhance their exchanges and mutual experience so as to further strengthen China-Russia ties. This resulted in the agreement of the Russia's Federation Council and Russia's State Duma, and China's National People's Congress to strengthen their cooperation on legislative initiatives and supervision, so as "to enhance coordination on regional, municipal and industrial development policies and plans."[16]

While it is generally argued that Russia and China are not compatible in ideological terms, as China is still run by the Chinese Communist Party, the above factors have tended to bring China and Russia even closer together rather than to tear them apart. While potential disputes and a "quiet rivalry"[17] does exist between the two Eurasian powers, the two countries appear to be moving beyond a marriage of convenience and toward a proto-alliance in opposition to the United States and its allies—as indicated by their June 2016 joint statement on strengthening global strategic stability.[18]

RUSSIA AS A JUNIOR ECONOMIC PARTNER TO CHINA

By reaching out to China, Russia is not so gradually becoming to China a junior partner in political-economic and financial terms. And Moscow could become even more financially dependent on China if Russia remains isolated from US and European sources of capital for too long. It has been argued that a close Chinese-Russian relationship is probably more important to Russia than to China, but Beijing also hopes to avoid the possibility that the United States will also impose sanctions on China in the future.

In March 2013, China, along with the other BRICS countries of Brazil, Russia, India, and South Africa, set up the New Development Bank. In October 2014, China set up the Asian Infrastructure Investment

Bank (AIIB).[19] Founded in September 2007, the China Investment Corporation (CIC), which, with $813.5 billion in assets in June 2017, is the third largest soverign wealth fund, after that of Norway and the United Arab Emirates, and possesses a capital funding that dwarfs the Japanese-led Asian Development Bank (ADB) and the World Bank.[20] China's AIIB and the CIC also possess assets that Russia cannot match—particularly with world energy prices down from their previous heights before 2008. Since 2014, and particularly in 2015, Russia has become one of the five largest recipients of Chinese outbound direct investment, in relation to the Chinese government's BRI that connects Asia with Europe. Meanwhile, China was Russia's largest bilateral trade partner in 2015.

In September 2016, the China-Russia dialogue emphasized principles such as the "rule of law." The two countries hoped to promote new tax and legal concepts for enhancing investments, investment protection, privatization, and providing state guarantees on finance for projects. There was also dialogue on how to deal with differing interpretations of legislative concepts, such as public-private partnerships and concession agreements.[21] While Washington has often reiterated that Russia and China do not accept the "rule of law," Russia and China appear to be developing their own laws and rules!

RCEP VS. TPP

Russia has augmented its support for China to build the BRI. China is also implementing its major trade accord, RCEP, which would tighten its political-economic relationship with Russia and other Eurasian states. These trade pacts were initially forged to counter the US-led Transatlantic Trade and Investment Partnership (TTIP) and Trans-Pacific Partnership (TTP). But Trump unilaterally abandoned the TPP, while the TTIP has been in limbo—although the Trump administration talked about reviving it in May 2017 through a joint US-EU task force.[22]

In terms of the international political economy, the Trump decision not to implement the TPP could actually permit Beijing to play a more significant political-economic role in the Indo-Pacific relative to Japan and the United States, particularly if it can implement the RCEP. Moreover, Trump has been seeking Chinese investment in the United States, with China's CIC and Goldman Sachs promising to co-partner in a five-billion-dollar fund, which is also intended to expand US exports to China.[23] Contrary to his own campaign rhetoric, Trump has looked to both Saudi Arabia and China to finance his infrastructure projects, which will augment Saudi and Chinese political-economic influence in the United States.

At the same time, however, Beijing could nevertheless threaten to back away from its significant financial supports for the over-indebted US economy and its promised investments in the United States—if Trump administration continues to threaten sanctions against China due to Beijing's efforts to expand its regional sphere of influence and security through the BRI—coupled with Beijing's efforts to implement a Chinese version of the US Monroe Doctrine. (See discussion on China's holding of US debt and the possibility of a trade and monetary war, chapter 1.)

As China expands its political-economic influence in the Indo-Pacific, one dilemma is that ASEAN countries find themselves caught between the promises of Chinese trade and finance versus the uncertain American promises of security and defense assistance. ASEAN countries need strong US political-economic backing if they are to also engage in military commitments. Given Trump's decision to dump the TPP, ASEAN states do not feel confident that Trump will continue to back the Obama administration's policy of "rebalancing to Asia" that sought to strengthen the US political-economic and defense role in the Indo-Pacific.

Both Singapore and Japan had essentially argued that the TPP would provide economic "substance" through trade to the US military efforts to rebalance the region. TPP had thus been seen as a means to counterbalance China's massive political-economic influence in the region that impacts all states, from Cambodia to the Philippines to Australia. It had also been hoped that the formation of TPP would have pressed China to reform its generally poor labor standards and upgrade its environmental standards, among other concerns. Seen in this way, the TPP was intended to press China to reform its own economy so that Beijing could have eventually joined.[24]

Ironically, now that Trump threw the TPP out the window, it is the "liberal democratic" United States that appears to be advocating economic protectionism under Trump's new America First nationalism. And it is Communist China that appears to be arguing for liberal exchange and international trade. Chinese President Xi Jinping affirmed at the Davos Forum in 2017: "We must remain committed to developing global free trade and investment, promote trade and investment liberalization and facilitation through opening-up and say no to protectionism. Pursuing protectionism is like locking oneself in a dark room. While wind and rain may be kept outside, that dark room will also block light and air. No one will emerge as a winner in a trade war."[25] After this speech, the motto of the Chinese President Xi Jinping could be called "People First." For Trump it is "America First"—or even "Trump First." (For French President Macron it is "Planet First." See chapter 10.)

Yet China's approach is not altogether altruistic. While China claims that its investment deals do not come with political strings attached, countries that want to trade with China must drop their recognition of Taiwan. China can drive hard bargains on interest rates for loans. And Chinese investment projects, which Beijing insists on controlling, often bring in Chinese labor via "gated communities" of workers who live and eat on the premises—instead of hiring local workers.

When he had signed the TPP, Obama stated,

> Today, these countries signed the Trans-Pacific Partnership—a new type of trade deal that puts American workers first. Right now, the rules of global trade too often undermine our values and put our workers

> and businesses at a disadvantage. TPP will change that. It eliminates more than 18,000 taxes that various countries put on Made in America products. It promotes a free and open Internet and prevents unfair laws that restrict the free flow of data and information. It includes the strongest labor standards and environmental commitments in history—and, unlike in past agreements, these standards are fully enforceable. TPP allows America—and not countries like China—to write the rules of the road in the 21st century, which is especially important in a region as dynamic as the Asia-Pacific.[26]

In effect, despite Obama's warnings and Trump's anti-Chinese rhetoric, it looks like Trump's anti-TPP policy will actually permit China to write the rules of the future as it develops the BRI and RCEP step-by-step in an effort to dominate world trade by 2050. This appears true unless India, Japan, South Korea, and Indonesia stall the RCEP, and if Japan and New Zealand can put together a revised TPP to counterbalance China. But here, the proposed participation of Taiwan in a revised TPP could spark tensions with China, as Taiwan could escape from Beijing's efforts to force countries not to recognize Taipei and thus isolate Taiwan in the global economy. Taiwan has formal state-to-state relations with only twenty countries, after Panama shifted to recognize Beijing in June 2017.[27]

The question remains: if Trump does convince Beijing to invest heavily in the United States in the near future, and augment US exports to China, what political strings will be attached?

MEXICO, LATIN AMERICA, AND CHINA AND RUSSIA

From a global standpoint, America First protectionism also opens the door for Mexico to sell its products to China, and for China, India, and Russia to enter the Mexican market—in addition to obtaining greater political-economic influence in the rest of the Caribbean and Latin America—as is already the case in the highly unstable country of Venezuela.

Trump's threats to expel Mexican immigrants, for example, and make Mexico pay for a US border wall/fence, in addition to threatening to place a "border tax" on imports from Mexico, could further destabilize a highly inequitable Mexican society.[28] Such threats could exacerbate the drug and mafia wars inside Mexico and on the streets in urban America. They could furthermore force Mexico to look toward China, India, and Russia for trade, aid, and assistance.[29] A Chinese geo-strategic foothold in Mexico, Venezuela, or elsewhere in the region could eventually be regarded as a challenge to the US Monroe Doctrine—particularly if China, backed by Russia, is eventually seen by Washington as trying to go too far.

Beijing has rapidly extended its influence in Latin America. In 2000, the Chinese share of Latin American trade was merely 2 percent, while the US share was 53 percent. By 2010, the Chinese share had grown to 11 percent of the total; the United States share dropped to 39 percent. By 2016, the United States was still Latin America's overall top trade partner, but China became the top trade partner of Brazil, Chile, Peru, and Venezuela. China has also been expected to overtake the European Union as the second largest trade partner of Latin America and the Caribbean in 2016.[30] China has, for example, already initiated a new multilateral forum in 2014 with the CELAC (the Community of Latin American and Caribbean States)—a forum that excludes the United States. And in addition to looking to China for trade, investment, and finance, Latin American states such as Brazil, Venezuela, Peru, Bolivia, Nicaragua, and Argentina have begun to import Chinese arms.

CHINA'S EFFORTS TO CONTROL GLOBAL SHIPPING

In addition to its port investments in Asia (see discussion in this chapter), Beijing has sought to expand its interests in the geo-strategically sensitive region of the Panama Canal zone, acquiring Panama's largest seaport, Margarita Island Port, in May 2016. Margarita Port is part of the Colón Free

Trade Zone, the largest free-trade zone in the Western Hemisphere and one of the world's major cargo distribution centers with sea-land-air-rail multimodal transport.[31] Chinese elites are also looking to Nicaragua, given the proposed canal through the latter despite difficulties involving domestic opposition and environmental concerns.[32] Chinese shipping companies have likewise been investing in Darwin, Australia; Athens, Greece (the Port of Piraeus in Greece is a gateway to Asia, eastern Europe, and North Africa); Istanbul, Turkey; and Venice, Italy—all as part of its BRI.

The concern raised here is that Chinese shipping and port investment ventures raise questions in a global situation in which geostrategic/security issues and political-economic issues are becoming intertwined. The close ties between the Chinese government and Chinese shipping and investment firms raises questions as to whether these firms are operating in Beijing's military interests or strictly in China's economic interests.[33]

CHINA AND RUSSIA ARE STILL IN CUBA

With respect to China and Russian influence in Cuba, President Putin signed ten bilateral economic and commercial agreements in Cuba in July 2014 and then promised to forgive more than $35 billion in Cuban debt to the former Soviet Union, during a time when President Obama was seeking to formally recognize the country (the latter was achieved one year later, on July 1, 2015). Russia announced that it would invest in Cuban offshore oil exploration, while hoping to help other Caribbean countries develop energy sources as well. It has been reported that Moscow could also be seeking basing rights to refuel its long-range bombers in Venezuela, Cuba, and Nicaragua. Moscow and Havana have purportedly been seeking a deal to permit Russian intelligence-gathering vessels to operate off of the US East Coast and in the Gulf of Mexico through proposed logistical outposts for resupply, shore leave, and repairs.[34]

Russian and Chinese backing for the Cuban government represents one factor in leading Trump to reverse some of Obama's policies that were intended to open US relations with the country. As of November 2017, Trump intends to restrict the ability of American citizens to engage with those Cuban businesses, restaurants, and hotels that possess close ties to Cuban government officials and the security services, as determined by the State Department.[35] Yet such policies are likely to strengthen, not weaken, Cuban ties to China and Russia.

THE CRISIS IN VENEZUELA

Since 2007, China has loaned as much as $60 billion to Venezuela alone, out of more than $120 billion in Chinese loans and investments over Latin America as a whole. Access to Venezuelan oil has been the focal point of Chinese investment. Without Chinese finance, it is unlikely that the governments of Hugo Chavez and Nicolás Madder could have paid for their welfare and social programs that helped them to stay in power. Beijing has also been able to obtain many of the legal rights to Venezuelan oil and other natural resources throughout Latin America. In such a way, China has become the new social imperialist—once critiqued by Maoists.[36]

The burgeoning civil war in Venezuela, has begun to impact the entire region. President Donald Trump labeled Venezuela's ongoing political and economic turmoil "a very very horrible problem" and placed sanctions on a number of corrupt government officials.[37] Criminal human- and drug-trafficking organizations have begun to take advantage of black-market activities and the flight of refugees from the country. In a presumed effort to help provide stability in the region, NATO has been considering making Venezuela's neighbor, Colombia, NATO's first Latin American partner. NATO's rapprochement comes just after the historic peace deal between the Colombian government and the Revolutionary Armed Forces of Colombia FARC that ended the five-decade war that had killed more than 220,000 people and had left nearly eight million people as internal refugees. In addition to seeking to shield Colombia from sociopolitical instability from Venezuela, and securing the peace, NATO could seek to counterbalance Chinese and Russian influence in the near future.[38]

Now that Venezuela is embroiled in civil conflict, it is not certain how either China, Russia, or the United States will react to the possibility of growing instability there and throughout the region. As the state collapses, Venezuelan finance from its oil exploitation will no longer provide funding for mismanaged countries in the region—thus exacerbating social tensions throughout Central and Latin America and the Caribbean. For its part, Moscow sees Venezuela as a strategic partner in the area, while China seeks Venezuelan oil and holds significant amounts of Venezuelan debt, which are generally repayable in oil and other forms of investment. At the same time, one can expect more problems in the Caribbean, which represents a major entry point for terrorist and drug financing.[39]

In his September 2017 speech at the United Nations, President Trump threatened to intervene militarily, ostensibly in the effort to help Venezuelans "regain their democracy."[40] Yet a much better option would be for Washington to negotiate a domestic peace settlement in Venezuela by working with Havana, even if Trump may have spoiled relations with Cuba by placing sanctions on the country, as previously discussed. If the United States and Cuba can work together to resolve the domestic crisis in Venezuela, that approach may help the United States and Cuba to make amends as well.[41] But if Trump does not attempt, or cannot obtain, a negotiated domestic settlement in Venezuela, his threats to intervene militarily could further polarize the world into rival alliances, with Latin America destabilized and Venezuela looking to Russia and China for arms.

INDIA: THE KEY PIVOT STATE

In addition to Latin America, Moscow and China appear to be working somewhat in tandem particularly in Eurasia. Moscow had initially hoped to work with China in the Chinese-inspired Shanghai Cooperation Organization (SCO), founded in 2001, which seeks to expand security cooperation in Eurasia. The SCO is expected to include India and Pakistan as new members in 2017.[42] This prospect has been symbolized by the annual trilateral summit between India, China, and Russia.[43]

At the same time, however, Chinese-Russian strategic and energy ties today have become far more extensive than Russian-Indian ties as Russia and China increasingly coordinate their global policies. This has raised a question that will impact the global strategic balance: Will a presently neutral India reach out to a possible Eurasian alliance with China and Russia? Or will India move closer to the United States, Europeans, and Japan in opposition to China and Pakistan in particular? Or can India remain neutral and a potential mediator between the two blocs?

Both China and Russia have been attempting to counter the tightening US-French-Japanese-Australian alliance, but China has been checking Russian efforts to draw India into a closer three-way defense collaboration despite Russian, Chinese, and Indian summitry; for example, Russia itself has moved closer to China than to India. China has vetoed India's application to join the Nuclear Suppliers Group (NSG), despite Russia's request. As membership in the NSG would help legitimize New Delhi as a nuclear power, India sees China's attitude as representing an effort to keep India down as a major global actor. China also refused to permit India from participating in an April 2017 defense meeting with Russia.[44] And a highly protectionist India has been hesitant to join the Chinese-backed RCEP, making it the potentially largest trade bloc in the world.

In response to Russian efforts to forge a closer trilateral defense relationship with China and India, the United States and France have hoped to draw India away from Russian political-economic influence through arms sales. In addition, the United States, Japan, and Australia hope to work with India to deal with common security challenges in the Indo-Pacific region, through the Quadrilateral Security Dialogue (or Quad). For its part, India has only slowly begun to expand its defense ties with Japan and southeast Asian states. Indian Prime Minister Narendra Modi renamed India's policy toward the region from "Look East" to "Act East" in 2014. India is now the largest recipient of Japan's $35 billion overseas assistance for infrastructure development and for its "Make-in-India" manufacturing programs. Overall, India is seeking high technology to boost its defense-industrial base.[45]

In March 2016, India held one of its largest military exercises on its territory, involving all ten ASEAN member states. ASEAN possesses close economic relationships with both India and China, yet the ASEAN countries generally remain wary of what they see as a Chinese policy of counter-encirclement through its "string of pearls" strategy. And China is the largest arms supplier for most of India's neighbors.

The aforementioned "string of pearls" expression refers to port construction along the Indian Ocean, from Chittagong in Bangladesh, to Colombo Port City and Hambantota in Sri Lanka, to Gwadar in the Baluchistan province of Pakistan, and to the Maldives. Fears of China's military usage of these ports were raised in 2014 when a Chinese military submarine docked at the Chinese-owned facility at Colombo Port City, Sri Lanka—which represents a key trading hub between East Asia, the Middle East, and Africa, and thus one of the most prominent financial and commercial centers on China's Twenty-First-Century Maritime Silk Road (or BRI).[46] New Delhi has additionally been highly critical of Beijing's efforts to check freedom of the seas and has protested Chinese nuclear submarine patrols in the Bay of Bengal.

India is additionally reaching out to Mongolia, Vietnam, the Philippines, Australia, Indonesia, Singapore, Malaysia, Thailand, Cambodia, Laos, and Brunei—in part in an effort to establish maritime patrols to counter terrorism, piracy, and smuggling, and in part to counter Chinese influence.[47] The Thai and Indian leadership have, for example, stated their intent to "enhance the ASEAN-India Strategic Partnership."[48] Thailand had reached out to China in 2015, yet relations with India appear to be taking priority. The two governments intend to prioritize the completion of the India-Myanmar-Thailand trilateral highway. This would establish a land route to Southeast Asia through India's northeast and help to counter Chinese political-economic influence in Pakistan.

To counter China's influence in Southeast Asia and to affirm India's status as a rising global power, New Delhi needs to secure sea lines of communication, enhance security in the Malacca Strait trade route, and strengthen its trade relations with ASEAN. The problem, however, is that India, as compared to China, lacks the infrastructure that is required to support more trade with ASEAN. Until India enacts land and labor reforms to encourage manufacturing investments, China's trade with ASEAN will continue to surpass that of India. India likewise possesses difficulties in competing with China in Nepal, Bhutan, and other regional countries. China is the top source of imports for Pakistan, Sri Lanka, and Bangladesh, for example, as well as for India; between 2010 and 2015, China's exports to Pakistan doubled.[49]

In the summer of 2017, the Chinese and Indian militaries engaged in a face-off over the Siliguri "Chicken Neck" corridor in western Bhutan where the Chinese were constructing a mountain road seen as a potential strategic threat to India. New Delhi fears that if China would bring tanks and troops to the corridor, it could cut off India from its northeastern states in case of war. Tensions, however, calmed by the time of the Brazil, Russia, India, China, and South Africa (BRICS) summit in September, but the issue of burgeoning Chinese political, economic, and military influence in Bhutan, Pakistan, and other regions remains.

RUSSIAN AND CHINESE RELATIONS WITH INDIA

Throughout the Cold War and immediately after, Moscow has largely sought to counterbalance the interests of India with those of China. In the past, Moscow wanted to make certain that India had a favorable military-technological balance vis-a-vis China. Now, however, Russia appears to be switching toward support of China, if not Pakistan as well. In terms of joint exercises, for example, Russia's military exercises with India take place in the context of international UN peacekeeping operations. By contrast, Chinese-Russian military exercises have included maneuvers in which China and Russia have engaged in potentially offensive exercises.[50]

Moscow thus appears to be tilting somewhat away from India as its preferred partner in defense sales and military cooperation. As previously discussed, Russia has been selling relatively more advanced weaponry systems to China—a fact that aggravates Indian security concerns.[51] Yet as the United States and France and other arms suppliers have begun to enter the India defense market, Russia risks losing not only its arms market in India but also contracts for high technology. India has recently sought American economic and technological assistance to expand its own military and naval position in the Indian Ocean region. And it has purchased some $14 billion worth weapons and technology from the United States over the past decade, in seeking to augment its capabilities vis-à-vis China on the Himalayan border and in the Indian Ocean.[52]

Given India's importance in Russian arms sales and foreign policy, Moscow accordingly fears that the Americans, French, and Japanese are beginning to cut Russia out of arms markets and other deals in India.[53] This appears true even if the French Rafale may not hold up against China's (Russian-made) Su-35s, according to some experts.[54] In short, both Moscow and Beijing have begun to support Pakistan more strongly, with Russia beginning to step back from its previous strong support for India.

KASHMIR

Indian-Pakistani conflict over Kashmir and other regions is concurrently beginning to interlink with the ongoing war in Afghanistan. Given the poor nature of US-Pakistani relations, at least since the US assassination of Osama bin Laden in May 2011 on Pakistani territory, Russian President Putin has begun to open discussions with Pakistan and even with the Taliban—to the chagrin of India and other regional powers that fear the potential formation of an Islamist state in Afghanistan or in other places in southwest Asia. For its part, China has opposed a number of differing Uighur Islamist movements in Xinjiang province—which China hopes to make the hub of its BRI in Central and South Asia.

The key issue is that Pakistan has been supporting differing pan-Islamist movements in Afghanistan and in Indian-controlled Kashmir. In Afghanistan, Pakistan's goal has been to somehow achieve "strategic depth" versus India by aligning itself with pan-Islamist forces. In Kashmir, Pakistan hopes to press Indian troops out of the Indian occupied zones. Pakistan has likewise supported various major terrorist strikes on Indian territory. Indian-Pakistani conflict came close to going nuclear in the dispute over Kargil in 1998—a conflict that was largely mitigated by US diplomacy.

Moscow's rapprochement with Pakistan appears to be in accord with Moscow's close alliance with China and Beijing's plans to extend the BRI into Pakistan—but in areas that India finds strategically sensitive. Relations between Putin and Indian Prime Minister Modi thus far appear to be positive in the areas of general economic cooperation, defense and arms sales, and nuclear energy.[55] Moscow claims it wants to sustain its "special" relationship with India, and that its relations with Pakistan are strictly economic.[56] Yet the Indian concern is that Russian and Pakistani relations appear to be warming. This was illustrated by joint Russian-Pakistani military exercises in Pakistan in September 2016—at a time when relations between New Delhi and Islamabad were tense. Moscow has also begun to discuss with Islamabad a wide range of regional issues and key areas of mutual interest—but which may or may not coincide with Chinese interests as well.

Beijing has additionally been expanding its sphere of influence and security into Pakistan, raising Indian concerns. As part of China's BRI, China is implementing the China-Pakistan Economic Corridor (CPEC). This means the development of transport and energy infrastructure roads, from China's western Xinjiang province to the Chinese-built port of Gwadar, Pakistan, on the Indian Ocean. This consequently creates an alternative direct transport link between western China and the Indian Ocean. It permits China to bypass the South China Sea by land, if strategically necessary, while developing areas of western China along the historic Silk Road from China's Xinjiang province.

While China's plans in Pakistan have not been entirely finalized, there is a possibility that some elements of the CPEC project will cross into the highly insecure and militarized territories of Pakistan Occupied Kashmir (PoK) and Gilgit-Baltistan—areas that are still claimed by India. Given the uncertain nature of security in this entire region, Beijing has been urging the Pakistan Army to take the leading role in CPEC, as opposed to civilian authorities. This could make China "a major target of Pakistani extremists and separatists,"[57] in which some secessionist groups could possibly be backed by India. In addition to perceived manipulation of the Pakistani military, China's tendency to use its own engineers and a large Chinese labor force while only hiring a minimum number of Pakistani workers could cause a popular backlash among local impoverished populations.

On the one hand, if the CPEC project succeeds, and the Chinese economy does not face its own financial meltdown in its global efforts to finance such a large number of gargantuan overseas projects, while Beijing also attempts to boost domestic incomes, repress domestic protest, and put its severe problems of pollution under control, then the CPEC could benefit Pakistan's infrastructure development and economy in the long run. But the CPEC project could also entangle Pakistan in China's global network. This could link the Pakistani military and police to Chinese political-economic and military interests. In effect, Chinese BRI and CPEC ambition raises the Kashmir dispute to the forefront of Chinese and Indian relations.

KASHMIR: FOCAL POINT OF CONFLICT

Initially, when the Hindu nationalist Bharatiya Janata Party (BJP) government came to power in 2014, Prime Minister Narendra Modi appeared to offer an olive branch to Pakistan. But the quest for peace did not last very long. In August 2016, terrorist attacks by Pakistan-based militant groups such as Lashkar-e-Taiba and Jaish e-Mohammed, among many previous attacks, led India to engage in a crackdown on the Indian side of Kashmir.[58] At that time, India crossed the "line of control" that divides Kashmir and purportedly engaged in "surgical strikes" on the Pakistani side. Concurrently New Delhi threatened to block Pakistan's water supply by means of speeding up the building of new hydropower plants along the three rivers that flow into Pakistan.[59] If so, this would have been in violation of the 1960 Indus Waters Treaty. And it could cause a negative counteraction by Pakistan's ally, China, which controls much of the water that flows into India before it enters Pakistan.

On Pakistani Independence Day, August 14, 2016, Prime Minister Nawaz Sharif called directly for the freedom of Kashmir. In effect, this statement overtly admitted Pakistani support for Kashmiri insurgence against India. In response, on Indian Independence Day, August 15, Prime Minister Modi then sent his greetings to "people of Baluchistan, Gilgit [and] Pakistan-occupied Kashmir."[60] This statement in effect raised the prospects that India could more overtly support anti-Pakistan movements, such as the Baluchistan Republican Army and the Sindhudesh Liberation Army, in the Pakistani province of Baluchistan. If India does strongly support these movements, such actions would in turn raise tensions in the Pakistani-controlled regions of Azad Jammu and Kashmir and Gilgit-Baltistan, which are in turn claimed by India.

By contrast with his 2016 India Independence Day speech, in August 2017, Prime Minister Modi pledged that he would focus on domestic development and social issues that are confronting Indian society, so that India could be "free of terrorism, corruption, dynasty politics, communalism and casteism."[61] But on Kashmir, he stated: "Neither gaali (abuse), nor goli (bullet) will bring a change. The change will take place when we embrace every Kashmiri." For his part, on Pakistani Independence Day, Prime Minister Sharif criticized the "expansionist designs of India" and urged the "international community to play its role in the resolution of the regional conflicts, particularly the Kashmir dispute in conformity with the UN Resolutions on the subject with a view to ensuring durable peace in the region."[62] Here it appears essential for the Trump administration to address the Kashmir question despite Indian reluctance, and before it is too late to prevent the conflict from escalating. (See chapter 9.)

WAR? OR CONCERTED DIPLOMACY?

Russian and Chinese ties to Pakistan and to the Taliban consequently raise major concerns for India—despite the invitation of both India and Pakistan into the Chinese-led Shanghai Cooperation Organization (SCO) in 2017. But while the SCO will provide a forum for bilateral discussions, and could possibly help build relations between Indian and Pakistani military forces and intelligence, it appears dubious that the SCO will help India and Pakistan to find a solution to the question of terrorism and counterterrorism, and to the Kashmir problem. Nor will the SCO help find a solution of their nuclear disputes.

In addition, any Russian deal with Pakistan tightens Russian relations with China as well. Russia may hope to play intermediary between China, Pakistan, and India, but this will not prove easy, as the United States and its allies will seek to draw India closer to their geostrategic and political-economic interests through security cooperation and arms sales. These include the major sale of the thirty-six advanced French Rafale fighter jets to India in 2016—at the same time that the United States has cut assistance to Pakistan. France has also been limiting arms sales to Islamabad, while selling to New Delhi. The US Senate had blocked a deal with Pakistan for eight F-16 fighter aircraft in May 2016 and refused $300 million in defense aid to Islamabad in August 2016. These steps have led Pakistan to buy Chinese JF-17 fighter jets.[63]

In accord with US and Japanese policy, India has strongly opposed China's maritime and naval buildup. New Delhi has moreover rejected China's claims to islands in the South China Sea, in the demand for freedom of navigation for all states in the region—which corresponds with US concerns. Despite Russian efforts to bring India into closer relationship with China, the above factors could press India closer to the new global alliance that is forming between the United States, France, Australia, and Japan.

In sum, India is hesitant about joining the Chinese-backed RCEP, and while New Delhi has hoped to maintain strong ties to Russia, Moscow appears to moving closer to China. Moreover, India's skepticism of the goals of China's CPEC and BRI combined with Modi's provocative statements with respect to Baluchistan and Gilgit-Baltistan against Pakistani claims to support Jammu and Kashmiri independence raise the risk of Indian conflict with Pakistan.[64] And since India additionally claims Aksai Chin and Shaksgam Valley, which are presently controlled by China and because China claims Arunachal Pradesh (calling it South Tibet), which is controlled by New Delhi, Indian-Pakistani conflict could potentially set off a wider confrontation.

Chapter 7

CHINA, NORTH KOREA, AND THE RISK OF WAR IN THE INDO-PACIFIC

Trump's Indo-Pacific policies have flipped like a fish in a frying pan since he came to power in January 2017 up until his visit to South Korea, China, Vietnam, the Philippines, and Japan in November 2017. Whether he will obtain a better grasp of the region after his visit remains to be seen, but Trump has so far flipped from supporting Taiwan, to fawning upon China, to threatening to "totally destroy" North Korea. Kim Jung Un upped the ante by repeating threats that he would soon explode a hydrogen bomb over the Pacific Ocean in the process of developing nuclear missiles capable of striking the continental United States.[1]

But, perhaps even more incredibly, Trump actually told Secretary of State Rex Tillerson not to engage in even a half-hearted attempt at diplomacy. As he put it in one of his (in)famous tweets: "I told Rex Tillerson, our wonderful secretary of state, that he is wasting his time trying to negotiate with Little Rocket Man."[2] In effect, Trump's tweet signals to North Korea that the United States is interested not in a diplomatic solution but in regime change.

In addition, even if Trump does eventually opt for a diplomatic path, his tweet has already helped to undercut the credibility of his secretary of state, at the same time that Tillerson is attempting to restructure the State Department in accord with Trump's directives, by shutting down more than thirty special envoys offices and trying to eliminate at least 2,300 employees.[3] This situation creates a tense working atmosphere that will make it even more difficult for the State Department to effectively deal with a number of critical issues discussed in this book, including the truly existential threat posed by North Korea.

The argument of this chapter is that there is absolutely no alternative to diplomacy with North Korean leader Kim Jung Un except for a war that could kill more than a million people. It is crucial for the United States to engage in effective diplomatic leadership that would seek a settlement between South Korea and North Korea through multilateral negotiations, and that would involve Japan, Russia, and China; and that would soon lead to direct US-North Korean talks.

TRUMP AND HIS TAIWAN-CHINA FLIP-FLOPS

As presidential candidate, Trump had questioned the One-China policy that has governed US, Taiwanese, and Chinese relations since the Shanghai Communiqué of 1972 and that is fundamental to sustaining positive US-Chinese relationship. In an effort to obtain political, military, and economic concessions from Beijing, which Trump has seen as the primary threat to the US economy and US interests abroad, Trump threatened to play the Taiwan independence "card." By backing Taiwan, Trump had hoped to obtain the support of anti-Communist Asian American voters. Trump also hoped to alter China's expansionist political-economic and military policies in the Indo-Pacific region.

In opposition to the One-China accord, Trump had stated that he did not see why he must be "bound by a 'one China' policy" unless the United States could make a deal with China "having to do with other things," including trade, devaluation, border taxes, their military buildup in the South China Sea.[4] He continued, "and, frankly, they're not helping us at all with North Korea. . . . You have North Korea, you have nuclear weapons, and China could solve that problem. And they're not helping us at all." But Trump also added as part of his bargaining strategy: "I wouldn't want them to know what my real thinking is."

Trump then offended Beijing by accepting a phone call from the Taiwanese president, Tsai Ing-wen, whom Beijing has refused to recognize as a leader.[5] This is because Beijing sees Taiwan as a secessionist province that must eventually be reunified with the mainland—and by the use of force if necessary. Trump's efforts to play the Taiwanese card against Beijing consequently caused great popular resentment and protest in China—and continues to raise China's suspicions.

In mid-December 2016, much as it has done in the past at the beginning of the administrations of both George W. Bush and Barack Obama, Beijing flashed its dragon claws. Just after Trump's telephone conversation with Taiwanese president, Beijing sailed its (former Ukrainian) aircraft carrier, the Liaoning, accompanied by three guided missile destroyers and two frigates, into the South China Sea. This resulted in a symbolic crossing—for the first time—through the waterway between Okinawa and Miyakojima Island near Japan. The aircraft carrier thus sailed only twenty nautical miles outside Taiwan's air defense identification zone (ADIZ) in the Bashi Channel between Taiwan and the Philippines. This action forced Taiwan to deploy an unspecified number of F-16 fighter jets.[6]

China was also purported to have flown a nuclear-capable Xian H-6 bomber along the so-called Nine-Dash Line which outlines China's territorial claims to roughly 90 percent of the South China Sea. Chinese claims clash with the claims of Vietnam, Malaysia, Indonesia, Brunei, and the Philippines to their own exclusive economic zones as determined by the international law of the sea. China's Nine-Dash Map, which is ironically based on Chinese nationalist Kuomintang party claims, sets China's boundaries in permanent dispute with the claims of almost all of China's neighbors, whose claims in the same area are not as extensive. Even if the Chinese bomber did not possess nuclear weaponry, these actions nonetheless represented symbolic statements that were intended to demonstrate that Beijing would be willing to use nuclear weaponry in order to defend its territorial claims. The incident also involved Japan, which reportedly sent out two of its fighter jets in response to the flight of the Chinese bomber.[7]

Trump's Secretary of State, Rex Tillerson, had already warned China during his congressional confirmation hearings: "We're going to have to send China's leaders a clear signal: that, first, the island building stops and, second, your access to those islands is not going to be allowed."[8] And according the US reports, China has appeared to be upping the ante, at least since Trump came into office, by installing antiaircraft and antimissile systems, among other weaponry, on all seven of the artificial islands it has built in the South China Sea. With Beijing ramping up the pressure, Trump suddenly backed off and was forced to capitulate just a few weeks after becoming president. This reversal of policy was taken in large part as the Chinese President Xi Jinping would not agree to speak with Trump until after he had publicly acknowledged the One-China policy. Both Tillerson and Trump then radically softened their statements toward China.[9]

THE ONE-CHINA POLICY

Trump's policy reversal was largely due to the fact that the One-China policy has been at the heart of a more or less stable US relationship with the People's Republic of China since at least the 1972 Shanghai Communiqué, when President Richard Nixon and Secretary of State Henry Kissinger began to reach out to China. At that time, Washington brought the People's Republic of China into the UN Security Council (UNSC) by way of dismissing the Republic of China (Taiwan) from UNSC membership. The One-China policy is deliberately ambiguous in that it permits a Sino-US *modus vivendi*. In other words, the United States has publicly agreed to accept Chinese claims to unify with Taiwan, but Washington is nevertheless permitted to sell arms to Taiwan, without formal recognition of Taiwan as a sovereign state. Yet there is another essential issue: as Washington did not press Beijing to renounce the use of force against

Taiwan when agreeing to the One-China policy, US defense support for Taiwan gives China more reason to look to Russia for arms. And it gives Moscow more reason to play the China card against the United States—so as to obtain greater concessions. Pressing China and Taiwan to mutually renounce the use of force will be key to peace. (See chapter 10.)

Beijing fears that Taiwanese independence would undermine the Communist Party's legitimacy to control "all" of China, and that US support for Taiwanese independence would impact China's claims to sovereignty and territorial integrity. Beijing furthermore fears that Taiwanese demands for independence could spark other independence movements inside the mainland (e.g., Tibet, Xinjiang province, and Inner Mongolia). For Beijing, Taiwan is nonnegotiable: Taiwan cannot be part of a Trump bargaining strategy that swaps trade and financial questions.

Trump has nevertheless appeared to be offering China a positive trade deal if Beijing will help "contain" North Korean nuclear ambitions. On the one hand, Trump's threats to engage in economic sanctions and military actions against China give Beijing very little incentive to pressure North Korea, even if Beijing does fear that the North Korean nuclear program could lead both Japan and South Korea to develop nuclear weaponry that would in turn threaten both North Korea and China itself. On the other, Trump's efforts to forge a new trade deal with China, as a possible reward for its role in dealing with North Korea, could be opposed by the US Congress as well as by Trump's domestic Republican and Independent base of support, who oppose Chinese economic competition.

Another dilemma is that Beijing represents the second most powerful political-economic actor in the world, if not the very first in some categories. In 2015, for example, China possessed the world's four biggest banks. And among the world's one hundred largest banks, China possessed the most at the top, with thirteen banks in total, while the United States placed second, with eleven banks.[10] By some measures, China will surpass the United States in terms of gross domestic product by 2018, after already surpassing the country in terms of purchasing power parity in 2014–2015.[11] And given its burgeoning financial, economic, and technological prowess, Beijing could, in just another decade, challenge the United States and its remaining allies in military terms, particularly in its own region—if Washington does not play its cards right. (See chapter 6.)

THE REGIONAL CHALLENGE

For Beijing, the state that possesses hegemony over Taiwan in turn possesses control over what the US Navy calls the "sea lines of communication" from Japan to the Arab-Persian Gulf and to the Suez Canal. Japan, South Korea, and Australia all rely upon shipping routes that pass close to Taiwan, through which an estimated \$5–\$7 trillion worth of goods are transported each year. Some two-thirds of South Korea's energy supplies, nearly 60 percent of Japan's and Taiwan's, and 80 percent of China's crude oil imports, flow through the South China Sea.[12]

In addition to the geo-economic importance of who controls the sea routes through the South China Sea, there are significant amounts of resources in the region. Optimistic estimates claim that the South China Sea may contain 17.7 billion tons of crude oil. Pessimists claim that the proven reserves of oil may be only about 1.1 billion tons. For China's energy needs, cheaper alternatives are readily available, particularly given the currently low oil prices. But for the Philippines and Vietnam, losing access to the South China Sea's potential oil and gas wealth would be far more significant in economic terms than it would be for China. Another major concern is that fish stocks in the South China Sea area have fallen 70 to 95 percent from their levels in the 1950s, and in the next twenty years they could decline an additional 59 percent from their 2015 levels.[13] The decline of fish stocks has already led China to look in waters beyond the South China Sea and as far as West Africa.

According to the Pentagon, Beijing has built up more than 3,200 acres of islands by dumping rocks in at least seven areas it occupies in the waters, in strategic positions near the disputed Spratly Islands. This provides China with long-term "civil-military" outposts from which it can project power.[14] In addition to expanding its claims to fishing areas, resources, and energy deposits in the South China Sea and elsewhere, one of the main reasons for China to construct artificial islands in the South China Sea, which are far more extensive than those of Vietnam, for example, is to provide a barricade to protect its fleet of advanced nuclear submarines, which is based on the southern tip of Hainan Island.[15]

China has not yet formally declared an Air Defense Identification Zone (ADIZ) in the South China Sea, as it did in the East China Sea in 2013. (See further discussion, below.) An ADIZ would identify, monitor, and control all civilian and military aircraft in the region—in a form of anticipatory self-defense. Nevertheless, Beijing has repeatedly threatened to declare an ADIZ, particularly after the Hague Permanent Court of Arbitration (PCA) ruled unanimously in July 2016 in a suit filed by the Philippines against the legal basis for China's Nine-Dash Line territorial claims to the South China Sea.[16] China sees the PCA's decision against its irredentist claims as illegitimate: In effect, China is seeking to justify its demands to establish a Chinese version of the Monroe Doctrine for the East and South China Seas.

Beijing furthermore sees itself as potentially "encircled" by the United States, Japan, and India; this is because China considers all three to be strengthening their military presence in the Indo-Pacific. China's fears of encirclement have led Beijing to develop the concept of "forward edge defense." This is China's new strategic doctrine that calls for the projection of its strategic capabilities from land toward the ocean. This new defense concept appears designed to establish a Chinese "arc-shaped strategic zone that covers the Western Pacific Ocean and Northern Indian Ocean."[17] Beijing has accordingly sought to develop a defense umbrella to counter US military strategies involving anti-area denial and air-sea battle concepts that could bring a potential conflict to the Chinese mainland. (See chapter 6.)

The major focus of China's defense spending remains building its capabilities to seize Taiwan—particularly in the assumption that the latter country will be defended by Washington. The problem is that, in Beijing's view, Taiwanese independence continues to represent a real "threat" that has been given greater credence by Trump's conversation with the Taiwanese president. In addition, Moscow's rapid yet relatively peaceful annexation of Crimea may have given Chinese elites the idea that they might be able to capture Taiwan in a somewhat-similar way—but only if the United States is distracted by other events or if Washington appears willing to appease Beijing.

JAPAN AND CHINA

Tokyo has sought to bolster its alliance contributions through the revision of the US-Japan Defense Cooperation Guidelines in April 2015. Tokyo has also insisted that the United States extend its nuclear deterrent to cover Japanese claims, including the Senkaku/Diaoyu Islands, rather than simply relying on the US nuclear umbrella.[18] In addition to developing its own missile defense system involving the deployment of US Patriot and Aegis missile defense systems (but not yet THAAD, Terminal High Altitude Area Defense), Tokyo has increased its military spending for the past five years since 2012.[19] At the same time, the Abe government has urged the revision of its "pacifist" constitution. So far, Tokyo has extended the ability of its self-defense forces to engage in overseas operations under the United Nations—or alongside allied forces.

To this goal, Tokyo has acquired surveillance drones, fighter jets, naval destroyers, and amphibious vehicles to counteract China's military activity in the region. In 2016, the Abe government sought to purchase an additional submarine and new fighter aircraft. The government proposed deploying roughly 1,300 soldiers from Japan's Self-Defense Force on the southern islands of Kagoshima and Okinawa—which are close to the Senkaku/Diaoyu Islands also claimed by China.[20] Tokyo has deployed a new amphibious unit modeled on the US Marines. The latter could be called on to respond to Chinese naval and aerial activity near the disputed Senkaku/Diaoyu Islands.[21]

One of the main concerns that could provoke war between China and Japan has been the Japanese "nationalization" of the Senkaku/Diaoyu Islands in 2013. This nationalization (the purchase of three islands from their private owner by the Japanese government) then inadvertently led to a confrontation between contending Chinese and Japanese claims. Japan has claimed the islands since the 1895 Sino-Japanese War, at a time when they were said to be uninhabited. Chinese claims go back to the Ming period, when they were said to be linked to Taiwan. China has considered Taiwan to be an inalienable part of its territory—even if the Taiwanese do not see it that way.[22]

China then proclaimed an Air Defense Identification Zone (ADIZ) for the East China Sea in late 2013. Here it can be argued that international law has ironically begun to force a number of confrontations. Even though international law (the United Nations Convention on the Law of the Sea, UNCLOS) is intended to help states resolve disputes, international organizations have also begun to insist that states define their territorial boundaries instead of emphasizing joint sovereignty. Due to the complex situation and emphasis of national sovereignty over territorial control, both Japan and China would probably have preferred to let the Senkaku/Diaoyu issue rest in its ambiguous format.[23]

China's claims to an ADIZ not only clash with Japanese claims over the Senkaku/Diaoyu Islands but also, to a limited extent, South Korean and Taiwanese ADIZ claims.[24] Foreign aircraft must now identify themselves before entering the Chinese air-defense zone. The Pentagon responded with what it calls Freedom of Navigation Operations, which are intended to demonstrate that China cannot try to maintain these areas as an exclusive defense zone. As a provocative demonstration that the United States does not accept China's ADIZ, the Pentagon flew a nuclear-capable B-52 bomber over the East China Sea. With respect to Sino-Japanese conflict over the Senkaku/Diaoyu Islands, Rex Tillerson said the United States had "made a commitment to Japan in terms of a guarantee of their defense."[25] Tillerson stated that Beijing's unilateral declaration in 2013 of an air defense identification zone overlapping Japanese airspace over the Senkaku/Diaoyu Islands was "illegal"—even if it was Japan that had first declared its own ADIZ. Tillerson nevertheless affirmed that the United States needed to defend Japan in accord with Article 5 of the US-Japanese security treaty. This Article 5 is similar to the Article V of the North Atlantic Treaty.

Japan has consequently accused China of violating international law, while Tokyo has also tightened its defense relations with the United States. Washington has clearly backed the Japanese position and has not attempted to play honest broker. At the same time, a Japanese conventional military buildup is not sufficient to defend Japanese interests unless the United States is also pressed into playing the role of nuclear gendarme—a role that Trump appeared *not* to want to play as presidential candidate, but has threatened to play after becoming president.

RUSSIA, CHINA, AND ASIA-PACIFIC COUNTRIES

Joint Russian-Chinese military exercises have in part been intended to press regional states to work more closely with both China and Russia. Throughout the Cold War and up until recently, Moscow has largely sought to counterbalance the interests of Vietnam with those of China—but now it seems to be somewhat tilting toward China. For its part, China has used Russian military backing to support its own claims to expansion in the South China Sea and East China Sea (Senkaku/Diaoyu Islands), against Japan and against Taiwan, in addition to seeking to divide the ASEAN alliance. In many ways, due to Chinese "sweet and sour" policies (promises of trade and investment, coupled with military threats), Cambodia, Malaysia, Vietnam, and now the Philippines appear to be moving closer to both China and Russia—in part because of China's promises of financial assistance through the Asian Infrastructure Investment Bank (AIIB). (See chapter 6.)

Moscow has only recently begun to open political-economic relations with Southeast Asian countries. At the same time, while seeking trade with Japan, Russia continues to pressure Japan through a military buildup on the Kurile Islands/Northern Territories, largely in response to the Japanese military buildup. Concurrently, Moscow has also been keeping a rising China on guard. Moscow has, for example, doubled the number of S-400 air defense systems that it deploys in its Far East region, while it has also deployed the S-400 system in its southern coasts near Japan, while its S-500 system is in development. These systems could potentially be used against either Japan or China.

Russia has likewise been building up its Pacific Fleet. The main goal of its Pacific Fleet is to control the Northern Sea Route in the Arctic—which creates tensions with the other Arctic powers, which are primarily NATO members. This includes the stationing of new offensive missile complexes on the Kurile Islands/Northern Territories.[26] (Because the United States is to head the Arctic Council until 2017, US-Russian cooperation will be key to avoiding conflict.)

While Moscow has not overtly backed China's claims in the Indo-Pacific, Moscow has wanted to demonstrate to the United States that Moscow and Beijing are now working together militarily in both the Mediterranean and the Indo-Pacific. This cooperation is intended to provide a possible Sino-Russian joint defense of China's Belt and Road Initiative (BRI). For its part, Beijing may want to engage in joint Sino-Russian maneuvers in order to demonstrate, to countries such as Vietnam, that Russia, despite its promises, might not protect them—in case of potential conflict with China.

Nevertheless, despite Japanese-Russian disputes over the Kurile Islands or Northern Territories, Japan's primary security concern is with

North Korea and China—and not with Russia. This is due to North Korea's close political-economic ties to China, plus China's not-so-long-term threat to control sea lines of communication to the Arab-Persian Gulf. In August 2016, for example, after China had sent a warship close to the Senkaku/Diaoyu Islands in June, North Korea fired a submarine-launched ballistic missile toward Japan. Throughout 2017, North Korea launched a number of missiles over Japanese airspace, while concurrently testing its nuclear weaponry.

The dual North Korean and Chinese "threats" have consequently led Tokyo to try to prevent Russia from more strongly backing China. These factors accordingly led Japanese Prime Minister Shinzo Abe in May 2016 to advocate an eight-point plan for Vladivostok that was designed to ameliorate Russia-Japanese tensions. In effect, due to its assessment of a truly threatening situation, Japan began to both break the US and EU sanctions regime placed on Moscow after its annexation of Crimea in 2014 and engage in a rapprochement with President Vladimir Putin (See chapter 9.)

PHILIPPINES

By May 2016, the election of Rodrigo Duterte, as Philippine president, has led to a new Filipino-style of rebalancing to China and Russia in response to Obama's policy of "rebalance" or "rebalancing" to Asia.[27]

In the case of the US ally, the Philippines, Manila has looked to China's Asian Infrastructure Investment Bank (AIIB) to provide it with $24 billion in economic assistance—even if it is not certain whether China can fulfill its promises given its present economic downturn.[28] While Washington has hoped that it could help Manila to stand up to China in the South China Sea, backed by the ruling of the Hague Permanent Court of Arbitration, Washington has not concurrently been able to provide sufficient aid and assistance to help improve Philippine infrastructure. Nor has Manila perceived the United States (and the World

Bank and the International Monetary Fund, IMF) as helping to improve living conditions in that highly impoverished country—in part because US and World Bank loans generally require countries to engage in significant market-oriented domestic-economic reforms.

In addition, President Barack Obama's criticism of Philippine President Duterte's repressive actions against individuals accused as being involved in the underground drug trade has led the Philippines to try to better balance its relations (including arms purchases) between the United States and the authoritarian states of China and Russia. Duterte hopes Beijing can put pressure on China's drug mafias that deal in the Philippines so as to better control drug-related criminality. How long Manila's balancing act can continue remains to be seen.

Given Obama's strong criticism of Duterte's human rights abuses in his war on drugs (which include an estimated seven thousand extrajudicial killings by March 2017[29]), Trump purportedly told Duterte, "I just wanted to congratulate you because I am hearing of . . . what a great job you are doing and I just wanted to call and tell you that." When Duterte replied by calling drugs the "scourge of my nation," Trump responded: "I . . . fully understand that and I think we had a previous president who did not understand that."[30] Trump's approach appears to represent a vulgar realist effort to draw Duterte closer to the United States, but will dubiously succeed.

VIETNAM

In the case of the former US rival Vietnam, Moscow and Hanoi became strategic partners in 2001. That relationship was then upgraded to a comprehensive strategic partnership in 2012. A Russia-Vietnam military cooperation pact then formalized the two governments' defense cooperation. Moscow promised arms to help to protect Vietnam's offshore energy interests and defend its claims in the South China Sea.[31] Yet, in order to hedge its bets, Vietnam has also sought defense cooperation with India, the Philippines, and the United States—in the aftermath of then President Bill Clinton's diplomatic recognition of Vietnam in 1995—largely to counter Beijing's claims to portions of the Spratly Islands, which are also claimed by Hanoi.

RISK OF ANOTHER KOREAN WAR

In one 2016 interview, Trump had stated in reference to the 28,500 US troops deployed to South Korea: "We get practically nothing compared to the cost of this. Why are we doing this?"[32] Yet he would subsequently reverse this position by February 2017, after he became president. When North Korea threatened to test an ICBM (intercontinental ballistic missile), Trump tweeted what appeared to be a "red line"—suggesting that if North Korea does test an ICBM, the United States will somehow be able stop it: "it won't happen." But then Pyongyang tested a number of nuclear weapons systems anyway.

One of the rationales for Trump's decision to bomb Syria in April 2017, after the latter purportedly used chemical weaponry against its own population, was to send a message to North Korea, China, and Russia that Washington was prepared to use force to assert its interests and values. As a show of force, Trump made the decision to bomb Syria at the very time that he was dining with Chinese leader Xi Jinping in Florida. Issues discussed with Xi included the $310 billion US trade deficit with China; Taiwan; Tibet; and China's military expansion in the South China Sea. Before Xi arrived in Florida, Trump had warned that he was prepared to go it alone to remove the threat presented by North Korean nuclear and missile programs—if China fails to control its closest ally.

In April–May 2017, Trump's Peace through Strength policy was blatantly challenged by North Korea in a show of conventional forces. Yet Trump's display of force in Syria did not halt North Korean missile and nuclear testing. Although Pyongyang's missile launches failed go off on schedule in April, Pyongyang successfully tried again in May with a long-range missile that could potentially strike the US military base in Guam. It has been estimated that North Korea will be capable of deploying as many as one hundred warheads by 2020 (up from twelve in 2017)—if its nuclear weapons and long-range missile program cannot be frozen in the near future by diplomatic agreement. In addition to developing a long-range missile that could strike the US continent, North Korea has purportedly been able to miniaturize its nuclear warheads.[33]

In Trump's September 2017 UN speech, Trump threatened to "totally destroy" the state of North Korea and its population of 26 million, in rhetoric that went way beyond the George W. Bush's threats to Pyongyang in his "Axis of Evil" speech (in which Bush aimed to engage in regime change in the name of democracy). In addition to effectively blaming the North Korean people for not standing up to overthrow Kim Jung Un ("If the righteous many don't confront the wicked few, then evil will triumph"), Trump criticized the North Korean leader in an apparently improvised attack—against the advice of his advisers, who argued that Kim would take such comments personally. Trump dubbed Kim a "rocket man . . . on a suicide mission." Not surprisingly, Pyongyang then boosted rhetoric against the "mentally deranged US dotard" by threatening to detonate a hydrogen bomb over the Pacific Ocean.[34] However, it appears that Trump cannot handle personal insults very maturely either: In addition to signing an executive order to introduce new sanctions against those who trade with or finance Pyongyang, Trump upped the ante by flying B-1 Stealth bombers and F-15s to the farthest point north of the Korean demilitarized zone (DMZ) that any US fighter or bomber aircraft has flown since the George W. Bush administration, according to the Pentagon.[35] (See chapter 9.)

MISSILE DEFENSES

Both Beijing and Moscow have opposed the deployment of the US Terminal High Altitude Air Defense (THAAD) missile-defense system on Japanese and South Korean territory. THAAD is viewed as representing a means to counter China's strategic missile deterrent though a potential preemptive strike. And to the south and west, China also sees as a major threat India's deployment of sophisticated BrahMos cruise missiles in areas of Arunachal Pradesh that are close to disputed borders with China. At the time of this writing, Japan has purchased the Patriot and Aegis antimissile systems, among others, but has not yet decided to purchase the THAAD system.

In denouncing North Korean provocations, which are in large part intended to break US alliances with Japan and South Korea, Trump proposed accelerating the deployments of missile defense systems for Japan and South Korea.[36] The United States had already begun to deploy advanced Terminal High Altitude Area Defense (THAAD) missile defense systems in South Korea, with the backing of the interim South Korean government, prior to the election of President Moon Jae-in. When the decision to deploy THAAD was announced, Chinese relations with South Korea plummeted—despite the US caveat that the MD systems would be designed only to counter North Korean missiles. Nevertheless, Beijing began an unofficial boycott of South Korean products. Both Beijing and Pyongyang have purportedly augmented cyber-attacks against South Korea.[37]

From Beijing's perspective, the THAAD deployments symbolized a closer defense relationship among the United States, South Korea, and Japan. The United States additionally appears to be forging an encircling alliance against China in the Indo-Pacific by also reaching out for defense accords with Australia, New Zealand, Vietnam, the Philippines, and China's major rival, India. Both Beijing and Moscow fear that US advances in missile defenses and radar systems, coupled with the speed and accuracy of US nuclear missiles, could permit Washington to launch preemptive strikes. Both Moscow and Beijing have accordingly engaged in overflights designed to test US-Japanese defense capabilities, but such actions appear to be further militarizing Japan.

In addition to the political-corruption scandals that confronted the government of South Korean President Park Geun-hye, who was impeached and forced to step down, the THAAD deployment is generally not popular among the South Korean population—even though Beijing's meddling in the affair may possibly have led more people to accept it. Trump himself further exacerbated domestic tensions in South Korea by stating that South Korea must pay $1.1 billion for the THAAD—an issue that US officials tried to downplay. In effect, South Korea would have to pay for a system that protects Seoul, but the THAAD system that would protect US forces from attack would be "free," as the United States would pay for it![38] One can imagine that Trump might not have been happy with that prospect either.

The winner of the South Korean presidential elections in May 2017, Moon Jae-in, initially stated that he would reconsider Seoul's previous agreement to host the THAAD, if possible—given the fact that the corrupt Park government and the United States had rushed to sign the contract. But by September 2017, he reversed his previous stance and agreed to limited THAAD deployments, despite public opposition.[39] President Moon Jae-in has likewise hoped to bring back former president Kim Dae-jung's Sunshine Policy, which sought greater diplomatic and political-economic engagement with Pyongyang. He has also sought to revive the Kaesong industrial project that involved South Korean investment in North Korea. If possible, he would like to engage in direct talks.[40]

To help improve relations with North Korea, Moon hopes to encourage greater South Korean investment in Russia, in the hope that by reaching out to Moscow, the latter would help facilitate a new dialogue between Seoul and Pyongyang. Japan and now South Korea both appear to have adopted a more cooperative approach to dealing with Moscow.

This position opposes US and European sanctions on Russia. At the same time, Moon Jae-in wants to press for greater South Korean input into Trump's America First policy orientation as it relates to Seoul's interests.

Here it cannot be ruled out that Moscow might want to play the game of spoiler, in taking advantage of disputes between China and North Korea. Moscow could then seek to expand its economic and financial cooperation with North Korea, which has included support for transportation networks, fuel supplies, and employment. But it appears unlikely that Moscow would support North Korea to the extent that it would alienate Beijing. More likely, the two powers would pursue a more coordinated approach, much as they did with the Iranian nuclear question. (See chapter 9.)

Before the April 2017 Chinese-American summit, Trump appeared convinced that China could do much more than not just purchase North Korean coal exports—in order to change North Korea's nuclear policy. Yet Chinese President Xi was said to give Trump a ten-minute lecture on relations between China and North Korea. The lecture appeared to convince Trump how difficult it was for China to pressure North Korea: "I felt pretty strongly that they had a tremendous power over North Korea. . . . But it's not what you would think."[41]

Washington has accused Chinese companies of supplying North Korea with European- and Chinese-made dual-use and military technology and hardware. Washington has demanded that these sales be stopped, given estimations that show that trade between China and North Korea has increased and that secondary banks continue to provide North Koreans with loans. At the same time, Beijing and Washington have reportedly begun to share intelligence, which could permit the interdiction of arms and other illicit trade to North Korea.[42]

As previously discussed, soon after the US missile strikes on Syria, on April 15, 2017, North Korea displayed new weaponry—which included what appeared to be a new ICBM and a new submarine-launched ballistic missile—during the Day of the Sun military parade. The Day of the Sun parade celebrated the birthday of North Korea's founder, Kim

Il-Sung, who had launched the Korean War in 1950, with Soviet and Chinese backing.

Just after Pyongyang displayed its new weaponry, Washington tested an unarmed Minuteman III intercontinental ballistic missile (ICBM) from Vandenberg Air Force Base off the coast of California as part of a series of testing.[43] Then, in May 2017, the Pentagon deployed two supersonic B-1B Lancer bombers to conduct military operations with Japan and South Korea. The United States has furthermore engaged in major military exercises with South Korea that North Korea had ritually denounced as provocative.

In regard to US military actions, China has repeatedly asked that the Pentagon stop such exercises, in order to reach a peace accord. In April 2017, when the United States appeared to be threatening an attack on North Korea, Beijing warned Trump not to engage in a Syrian-like strike against North Korean nuclear facilities—as Pyongyang would most likely strike back against South Korea, Japan, and/or US bases in the region. At the same time, despite their 1961 mutual assistance clause, it was not clear whether Beijing would be obliged to assist North Korea in the case of a US attack. This is true given Beijing's view that Pyongyang's development of nuclear weapons appears to represent a breach in their bilateral pact.[44] Nevertheless, there is still a danger that Pyongyang will try to draw Beijing to support North Korea against Washington.

One way for North Korea to draw in China for support in case of war would be to expand the conflict to as many countries as possible. North Korea has accordingly hoped to build missiles as rapidly as possible to penetrate US, South Korean, and Japanese missile defenses. This can be accomplished by firing multiple missiles in rapid succession or simultaneously—in a tactic called "salvo fire." Enough simultaneous launches could then overwhelm the THAAD missile defense system, which requires that several antimissiles be fired in order to be assured that a missile will be destroyed, and hence increase the possibility that a nuclear missile could reach its target in South Korea.[45] Patterns in North Korea's missile testing behavior since 2014 indicate the regime's possible intention of deploying nuclear weapons to missile units throughout the country.[46]

At what point North Korea might use nuclear weapons is not certain, but Pyongyang appears to want to make a war as destructive as possible, in the hope that this will force its opponents to seek peace on North Korean terms. And attacking South Korea's twenty-four nuclear power plants with conventional weapons, for example, could prove an option. Even given the heavy damages that the United States inflicted upon North Korea during its invasion of the south in 1950, through the use of Napalm, for example, Pyongyang continued its struggle until 1953, until Stalin's death. Because there has never been a peace treaty between the North and South, Pyongyang has been preparing for the next round of conflict ever since. Yet a war could result in 1 million casualties, at the cost of $1 trillion. And it could go nuclear.[47]

Given the fact that North Korea wants formal recognition as a "nuclear state,"[48] the major question for the Trump administration is whether the era of "strategic patience" is truly "over" as Vice President Mike Pence declared.[49] Should the Trump administration attempt preemptive strikes now, at the risk of a very bloody war? Or should it engage in diplomacy that is intended to freeze Pyongyang's nuclear program where it is in 2017—as it appears unlikely that North Korea will totally denuclearize, at least in the near future?

The problem is that multilateral talks have yet not gone anywhere. The efforts of the six-party talks (between the United States, Japan, Russia, China, South Korea, and North Korea) to achieve peace ended in 2009. Tensions between North and South Korea since the end of the Cold War appear to be surging—and particularly once North Korea repeatedly tested nuclear weapons in 2006, 2009, 2013, and 2016. North Korean nuclear and missile threats, China's reluctance to drop North Korea as an ally, China's coercive tactics in the South China Sea, plus its military buildup aimed primarily at Taiwan, are all factors that are seen by Trump as threatening war in the Indo-Pacific.

WAR WITH NORTH KOREA? AND WITH CHINA?

Trump appears ready to extend Obama's "rebalancing to Asia" policy (originally called by Obama the "pivot to Asia") with his Peace through Strength buildup of US military power in the region, as illustrated by his November 2017 visit to the region. But here, Trump appears to be taking a more forward-deployed stance than did Obama. Trump appears to be directly threatening North Korea with unilateral preemptive strikes instead of engaging in Obama's neo-realist strategy of "offshore balancing."[50] This latter, more defensive, approach uses regional allies to counter China and North Korea, while relying on a large offshore US naval presence in the Asia-Pacific region to deter a threatened attack. By contrast, as part of a forked strategy, while pursuing a forward military approach that threatens Pyongyang, Trump has hoped to influence China to engage in quiet diplomacy with North Korea.

The dilemma is that Trump's efforts to engage a reluctant China in diplomacy with North Korea could lead Beijing to demand considerable concessions from Washington in exchange. Moreover, China sees US policies at fault and has urged Washington to engage in direct bilateral diplomacy with Pyongyang, which will in effect legitimize the regime. Washington has been afraid that direct diplomacy will not lead North Korea to give up its nuclear weapons program.

Furthermore, given Trump's ideology of "economic nationalism" and his threats of a trade war with China, there is a real danger that Washington will not respond to Chinese political-economic demands due to Beijing's ostensible lack of assistance on the North Korean question, and that a Sino-American economic war could break out. China then could decide not to buy American products, and instead choose European products, such as Airbus over Boeing, for example. China has already been slowly selling American treasuries and can continue to do so if it begins to establish new markets in the Asia-Pacific through the Chinese-led Regional Comprehensive Economic Partnership (RCEP), which could soon represent the largest market in the world without US participation, while Beijing concurrently tightens its political-economic and military alliance with Russia. (See chapter 1.)

If tensions grow even greater, Beijing could begin to threaten Taiwan by cutting off joint economic agreements. It could further increase the number of intermediate-range nuclear missiles aimed at Taiwan, while militarizing islands and strategic positions in the South China Sea by deploying air-defense systems and advanced fighter jets on a number of China's artificially constructed islands. And if China threatens to attack Taiwan, Taipei has threatened to attack the massive Three Gorges Dam in return so as to flood vast areas.

These actions and threats could be combined with a formal declaration of an Air Defense Identification Zone in the South China Sea, much like how Beijing had established an ADIZ in the East China Sea in late 2013.[51] Beijing, along with North Korea and Russia, could augment its cyber-attacks against private corporations, financial institutions, government agencies, and military and intelligence networks in the United States.

And, finally, if tensions really escalate, Beijing could decide not to sanction North Korea, while increasing Chinese economic aid (and possibly covert military aid) to Pyongyang.[52] In such a way, an economic war could lead to a military conflict with both North Korea and China—as China has not given up its goal to unify with Taiwan, by force, if necessary.

The above sketch of the possible outbreak of war in Asia is of course hypothetical and hopefully will not take place. Nevertheless, after Trump's visits Asia in November 2017, a number of key questions remain: How might US frictions with China over Taiwan and North Korea, among other political-economic issues, impact the Sino-Russian relationship? Will Trump's policy toward China bring Russia and China even closer together? Or will Trump be able to draw Beijing and Moscow away from closer defense ties, if not an alliance? Will all three powers cooperate with Japan and South Korea as well, to prevent North Korea from wreaking havoc?

In sum, it is crucial for the United States to find ways to work with South Korea to open the doors to discussions with the North. Concurrently, Washington must engage with both China and Russia in such a way that not only seeks a peaceful resolution to the disputes with North Korea, but also concurrently sets the stage for a more fundamental rapprochement between the United States, Japan, China, and Russia as well. And as multilateral diplomacy between the United States, South Korea, Japan, Russia, and China with North Korea progresses, Trump will eventually need to meet directly with Kim Jung Un in order to mend relations and provide security assurances that the US will not attempt to destabilize or overthrow the regime.

But is the flip-flop Trump administration and presently demoralized State Department capable of such a sophisticated diplomatic engagement in the quest for peace? (See chapter 9.)

Chapter 8

SYRIA AND WIDENING WARS IN THE "WIDER MIDDLE EAST"

It has been estimated by different sources that the ongoing war in Syria has killed between 321,358 and 470,000 people and has turned millions into internal or external refugees, as of July 2017.[1] Some 13.5 million people require humanitarian assistance, including 4.6 million who are trapped in besieged and hard-to-reach areas, as of September 2017.[2]

The possibility that the conflict could provoke a major power conflagration is illustrated by the shooting down of a Russian military aircraft by NATO member Turkey in November 2015 as a Russian jet passed out of Turkish airspace. US efforts to coordinate effective military actions among the partners in the Global Coalition against Daesh (Islamic State), which was formed in September 2014, and which possesses 73 partners,[3] have proved difficult, to say the least. This is true given the fact that many coalition partners oppose Jabhat al-Nusra (or al-Nusra Front), an al-Qaeda affiliate, and the Islamic State, as well as the Assad regime, while some countries, such as Saudi Arabia, Qatar, and Turkey, have been accused of secretly supporting either the al-Nusra Front or the Islamic State, or ignoring private funding that supports or trades with those terrorist organizations.[4] In addition, Israel, for example, is not a coalition member, yet it periodically intervenes militarily in Syria, primarily against Hezbollah, when Tel Aviv sees its interests being threatened, while Iran, which is not a member of the coalition, supports Hezbollah in Lebanon and other Shi'a militias in Syria and Iraq. Concurrently, Turkey, which is a member of the coalition, has opposed US military support for Kurdish militias that are fighting against IS in Syria and Iraq. While most NATO member countries have participated in the Global Coalition against Daesh, it was not until the May 2017 NATO summit that NATO countries agreed to engage in that Global Coalition as a collective NATO operation. This represented a political statement designed, in large part, to obtain greater political support for NATO from Donald Trump, who had been highly critical of what he saw as NATO's lack of participation in the Global War on Terrorism. (See chapters 4 and 5.)

For its part, Moscow, since its entry into the war in support of Bashar al-Assad's regime in September 2015, but which is not a member of the Global Coalition against Daesh, targeted not only the Islamic State but also most of the Syrian opposition forces. The latter have been backed by Saudi Arabia, Turkey, the United States, and other states, plus Syrian Kurds, as they fight the regime of Assad. Yet the Trump-Pence administration upped the ante by bombing a Syrian airbase in April 2017 after the Assad regime had allegedly used chemical weapons in a region largely controlled by Jabhat al-Nusra (or al-Nusra Front).

President Donald Trump's April 2017 decision to engage in so-called limited Tomahawk cruise missile attacks represents yet another flip-flop in Trump foreign policy. In September 2013, before Obama ruled out the use of airstrikes against Syria in the aftermath of the Assad regime's alleged use of chemical weaponry in favor of diplomacy with Russia, Trump had tweeted: "Again, to our very foolish leader, do not attack Syria - If you do many very bad things will happen & from that fight the US gets nothing!" Then, two days later, Trump tweeted: "President Obama, do not attack Syria. . . . There is no upside and tremendous downside. Save your 'powder' for another (and more important) day!"[5]

On April 7, after months of domestic American criticism for being "soft" on Putin and on Russian allies, including Syrian leader Bashar al-Assad, Trump opted to strike a Syrian airbase with fifty-nine Tomahawk cruise missiles—after ostensibly weighing all of the options in his new National Security Council cabinet.[6] Trump, as he later admitted, reversed his previous opinions about Assad and Syria—to the chagrin of some of his strongest supporters and to the praise of his political opponents. Trump's adviser, Steve Bannon, had purportedly opposed the strikes, but was apparently overruled by Jared Kushner.[7]

But in firing fifty-nine Tomahawk cruise missiles (at roughly one million dollars each[8]) at an airbase used by Russian military aircraft, Trump took the tremendous risk that he would not provoke some form of a Syrian or Russian retaliation at some point in the future. Putin's style is not to react immediately but to wait until conditions are in Russia's favor before he strikes back. And without UN Security Council backing, or even a legal justification on the grounds of self-defense, the Tomahawk strike nevertheless represents a unilateral decision that could open the door to additional unilateral and illegal actions—with potentially unexpected and dangerous consequences.

The Pentagon is now engaged in at least seven very different, yet increasingly interrelated, wars in the "wider Middle East" in Afghanistan/Northern Pakistan, Iraq, Syria, Yemen, Libya, and Somalia, while also imposing sanctions on Iran. Trump's actions (and particularly his backing for Israel and Saudi Arabia against Iran, as to be argued) risks a further widening of these conflicts. The problem is that even the use of more massive airstrikes will not address the root causes of these wars. A real strategy involving concerted diplomacy is needed. (See chapter 9.)

In many ways, Trump's cruise missile attacks were intended to send a message that the United States is back in the game of global geopolitics, and that Washington would now be able to negotiate with Syria and Russia and other states from a "position of strength." Washington hoped it would help press Moscow to reconsider its support for the Assad regime.[9] (See discussion of US policy, this chapter.)

Yet this ostensibly "limited" US military action has showed no sign of drawing Syria and Russia to the bargaining table: Moscow has not shown itself to be less willing to back the Assad regime. And the Tomahawk cruise missile strikes have definitely not changed North Korean, or even

Iranian, policies. The question remains: why did Trump not ask for congressional or UN authorization?[10] How will this action help to achieve peace—if it was intended to do so?

One of the major reasons that President Obama had pulled backed from military intervention in Syria in 2013, after the Syrian regime allegedly used chemical weaponry at that time, was the fear that the intervention could result in the collapse of the Assad regime and rise of radical pan-Islamist forces without an effective government to take Assad's place. This issue has been made more complex by the fact that a number of so-called moderate forces (generally backed by Saudi Arabia or other Arab Gulf states) nevertheless possess ties with the militant Jabhat al-Nusra (which is linked to al-Qaeda), among other militant partisan movements that may oppose the United States, Europeans, Russians, Israel, and Saudi Arabia. Because al-Nusra, among other militant Islamist groups, often possesses the best trained and effective fighting forces against the Assad regime, both Qatar and Saudi Arabia have often been seen as turning a blind eye to the private networks that support these groups financially. This was true at least in the past, before Riyadh and Doha joined the Global Coalition against Daesh in 2014. At the same time, suspicions between Qatar and Saudi Arabia still remain.[11] (See discussion on the rupture of Saudi-Qatar relations, this chapter.)

Not so ironically, Trump's Tomahawk cruise missile attacks in April 2017 were accordingly supported by the Islamic State and al-Nusra. One member of the Jaysh al-Islam faction argued that a single strike was "not enough"—as there were twenty-six airbases that strike civilians. In addition, IS appeared to take advantage of the strikes in a failed effort to retake the ancient city Palmyra in Syria's Homs Province. The Shayrat Airbase, located southeast of Homs city, which was attacked by the United States, was ironically the airbase that was being used by the Syrian Army to protect Palmyra against its destruction by the Islamic State, which had razed at least three temples and destroyed or tried to sell ancient artifacts from the World Heritage Site protected by UNESCO (the United Nations Educational, Scientific and Cultural Organization).

Other non–al-Qaeda, non-IS groups, such as the Southern Front, saw the attacks as "political" and aimed primarily at Russia. A member of a Turkish-backed Sultan Murad group stated that it would "welcome any action that will put an end to the regime that is committing the worst crimes in history."[12] The National Coalition of Syrian Revolution and Opposition Forces welcomed the strike and urged Washington to neutralize Syria's ability to carry out air raids. In general, the strikes were seen by opposition forces as much too limited to really engage in regime change—but regime change was evidently not the goal.

Yet now that Trump (and not Obama) is in command, will there be "no upside and tremendous downside," as Trump himself had previously warned when he had urged Obama not to engage in a military response to the alleged Syrian use of chemical weaponry? What would happen if the Syrian regime is accused of using chemical weapons again or else engages in a major massacre? Would this represent another "red line"? What would Trump do then?

The major issue raised here is that even the use of force by the Trump-Pence administration will not necessarily bring about diplomatic compromise with either Syria, Russia, or other countries. In fact, after the cruise missile strikes, the Syrian regime purportedly offered the United States access to the airfield that the Pentagon had bombed; this was done only on the condition that the rebels likewise offer access to the site where the poisonous sarin gas was deployed, but which lies in territory held by the rebels.[13] In addition, the Syrian regime was believed (although it was unclear which planes did the actual bombing) to have attacked the same opposition positions in Khan Shaykhun the very next day, from the same airbase that had just been hit by US cruise missiles. These attacks were aimed at the very same positions where the Syrian regime had allegedly used chemical weapons less than a day before.[14]

The first issue is that Trump's attack blocked the possibility that the United Nations could rapidly begin to investigate who was actually behind the use of deadly chemicals. Some experts argue the evidence at the site of the attack tends to show that the regime did do it.[15] The October 2017 Seventh Report of the Organization for the Prohibition of Chemical Weapons–United Nations Joint Investigative Mechanism was "confident that the Syrian Arab Republic is responsible for the release of sarin at Khan Shaykhun on 4 April 2017."[16] Yet the evidence provided by the latter UN report is not absolutely verified.[17]

Even though the Trump-Pence administration has claimed that it had intercepted Syrian messages that stated the plans to use chemical weaponry, Trump still could have waited and exposed the horror to the world. And Trump's action has not stopped the Syrian regime from continuing to kill by other means (including chemicals used in barrel bombs) in opposition to UN Resolution 2139, which had ordered all parties to the conflict in Syria to end the indiscriminate use of barrel bombs and other weapons in populated areas.[18] The point is that a more concerted international approach to the use of chemical weaponry could have put even more diplomatic pressure on the Syrian regime.

The second issue is the question, Why didn't Moscow use its advanced S-400 Triumph antimissile systems, which it had installed in 2015 on the Syrian coast in Latakia and that have raised Israeli security concerns? Could Putin have actually been complacent with Trump's decision to use force, after Trump gave Moscow notice of the cruise missile attacks? Or, more likely, did Moscow not want to demonstrate the S-400 system's capabilities—*or* its lack of capabilities? This issue raised a debate in Iran as to whether Russia's S-300 and S-400 air defense systems were even capable of thwarting the US Tomahawk missiles.[19] And it also raises questions whether the US attack could now pressure Moscow to deliver more advanced weapons systems to Iran and other countries if US-Russian relations sour even further. Since 2014–2017, Moscow has considered sales of its advanced S-400 Triumph antimissile system to Iran,[20] to China and India, as well as to close US allies Turkey and Saudi Arabia, as the latter hope to diversify their arms suppliers and not rely only on US weapons systems. With regard to both Iran and Saudi Arabia, the eventual deployment of more advanced Russian antimissile systems and other weaponry to these two countries could intensify Iranian proxy wars with Saudi Arabia in Syria, Iraq, and Yemen.

US unilateral actions certainly made Moscow look weak. Moscow then cut off the US-Russian "hotline"—but then restored it after Secretary of State Rex Tillerson's discussions with Putin in April 2017. Yet despite the reinitiation of US-Russian talks in April, Moscow has nevertheless promised to bolster defenses with deployment of its most advanced Black Sea "carrier-killer" frigate into the eastern Mediterranean, which is to be deployed at its Tartus naval base. Moscow has increased the size of its naval and air force in the eastern Mediterranean—but these deployments are still not sufficient to counter US and NATO deployments.[21]

The other issue is whether this attack represented an opening salvo for more attacks. Some congressional spokespersons have claimed that this was "one-time attack"[22]—a symbolic attack. But the US ambassador to the United Nations contradicted that statement. Ambassador Nikki Haley threatened Moscow with the following: "[The United States] is not going to have you cover for this regime anymore. And we're not going to allow things like this to happen to innocent people."[23] Haley further stated that the United States took a "moderate approach" but is still capable of doing much more. The question remains whether this action represents a first step toward "regime change," perhaps more like Libya in 2011 than like Iraq in 2003. Or will Moscow be able to hold Assad in power?

National Security Advisor H. R. McMaster has called for Moscow to rethink its support for the Syrian president, to reevaluate its actions, and to see that Russia could actually be part of the "solution" instead of part of the "problem."[24] But if the United States does not soon show how it can lead Moscow out of its Syrian debacle by means of a general settlement over all of the issues that divide the two sides—from Crimea to tactical nuclear weapons and missile defenses—then the confrontation between the United States, Europe, and Russia will only continue to augment, particularly if the two sides do not effectively coordinate strategy and end up "accidentally" striking each other's forces.

INTERNATIONAL REACTIONS

The US attack on Syria was met with strong public support from the United Kingdom, France, Germany, Canada, Poland, Saudi Arabia, Israel, Turkey, and much of the Sunni world, plus Japan, Australia, NATO, and the European Union. It was condemned by Russia, Belarus, Venezuela, Bolivia, Iran, and North Korea, while Brazil, Ireland, Switzerland, and China urged UN diplomacy.

German Chancellor Angela Merkel and French President François Hollande, for example, had issued a joint statement that declared that Bashar al-Assad "bears sole responsibility" for the US strike following the suspected chemical attack.[25] But by contrast to the French and German positions, Washington pointed to Russian responsibility for not enforcing a 2013 agreement it brokered with Syria to eliminate its chemical weapons—in an effort to shame Moscow. As Rex Tillerson put it bluntly: "Clearly, Russia has failed in its responsibility to deliver on that commitment from 2013. . . . So either Russia has been complicit or Russia has been simply incompetent in its ability to deliver on its end of that agreement."[26]

The issue raised here is that the American position appears to put Putin in a bad light. Blaming Russia could make it more difficult for Putin to save face. The Trump-Pence administration may hope that Putin would put the blame on Assad for the use of such weaponry, in which case the United States and Russia could put joint pressure on Assad to step down. Yet so far this does not appear to be the case.

For its part, Beijing warned against the "further deterioration of the situation"[27] while also opposing the use of chemical weaponry under any circumstances. Nevertheless, Beijing stated that it would have preferred that the Trump administration conduct a complete investigation under

UN auspices before engaging in the use of force. Beijing insisted that all parties continue to search for a "political solution."[28] Yet President Trump probably made too much over the fact that China abstained on the UN Security Council vote that dealt with the alleged use of chemical weaponry by the Syrian regime in April 2017. China has vetoed six UN resolutions related to Syria since the civil war began in 2013. But even if China did turn away from joining Russia in vetoing UN resolutions, it did not oppose Moscow's position either. At the same time, Beijing was worried that Trump might engage in cruise missile strikes against North Korea—given the fact that Bashar al-Assad's Syria is not the same as Kim Jong Un's North Korea. (See chapters 1 and 7.)

UN Secretary-General António Guterres called for a diplomatic settlement. Guterres warned that there was "no other way to solve the conflict than through a political solution." He continued, "Mindful of the risk of escalation, I appeal for restraint to avoid any acts that could deepen the suffering of the Syrian people."[29] The diplomatic dilemma has been how to get Moscow to withdraw support from Assad—but also to find a way to ensure a stable transition to an effective and more inclusive and legitimate new government.

THE ISRAELI RESPONSE TO THE CRUISE MISSILE ATTACKS

Israel's prime minister, Benjamin Netanyahu, stated that Trump had "sent a strong and clear message" that "the use and spread of chemical weapons will not be tolerated"; Israel has feared that such "game-changing" weapons, and more than 100,000 short-range missiles, armaments, could reach Hezbollah based in Lebanon.[30] Israel has also engaged in military strikes in Syria when it believed that Syria or Iran was backing Hezbollah. Yet Israel is also aware of the fact that the US focus on the conflict in Syria tends to deflect criticism away from Israel—which has not yet made any progress toward resolving its conflict with the Palestinians. Yet lack of progress in peace negotiations between Israel and the Palestinians, coupled with a Saudi-Israeli rapprochement, helps to fuel the propaganda machines of differing Islamist movements. (See chapter 9.)

THE SAUDI RESPONSE

A Saudi foreign ministry official praised Trump as "courageous" for taking action when "the international community has failed to put a halt to the regime's actions."[31] Riyadh not only has supported Syrian opposition forces but also has been involved in a proxy war with Iran throughout the wider Middle East, in Iraq and Yemen, while secretly seeking closer strategic cooperation with Israel.

In Yemen, Riyadh has been accused of severe human rights violations in its battle against Iranian-backed Houthis. As of 2016, more than ten thousand civilians have died in the conflict in Yemen, which has been confronted with a major cholera epidemic that has infected over 600,000 people and mass starvation as a result of the Saudi embargo.[32]

In effect, Riyadh fears Iranian efforts to infiltrate Yemen through its support for Houthis. Riyadh's brutal military intervention is intended both to cut off the Iranian arms supply and to make the Houthis think twice about aligning with Iran. The Saudis fear that Iran could ultimately gain a geostrategic foothold in the Gulf of Aden. The UN Special Envoy to Yemen, Ismail Ould Cheikh Ahmed, has hoped to convince Abd-Rabbu Mansour Hadi, president of Yemen, that a UN-sponsored peace agreement, "including a well-articulated security plan and the formation of an inclusive government, is the only way to end the war that has fuelled the development of terrorism in Yemen and the region."[33] The UN plan would strengthen the powers of the vice president, who would oversee elections that would lead to a coalition government that would provide Houthi representation on the basis of power-sharing. A domestic political settlement could then help to end Saudi-Iranian rivalry over which state controls Yemen and the narrow Bab el-Mandeb maritime chokepoint, which in turn oversees naval access and trade to and from the Red Sea. Riyadh fears an Iranian or an al-Qaeda foothold in the region that could potentially block the passage of commercial shipping through the Red Sea and the Suez Canal, in which approximately 3.3 million barrels a day of oil cargoes pass from the Gulf to Western ports.[34]

If all sides can cooperate, a concerted internationalized control over the Bab el-Mandeb chokepoint by means of US, French, Indian, Japanese, Saudi, and Chinese naval deployments in Djibouti appears in the making. Yet as Djibouti is China's first overseas "support facility," the United States believes that China is engaging in military expansionism to protect its overseas trade and investments.[35]

IRAN AND SAUDI RIVALRY

For its part, Iran, as the strongest ally of Syria, condemned the Tomahawk attack as "dangerous, destructive and a violation of international law."[36] Iran condemned the US attack even if it should likewise be concerned with Syria's alleged use of chemical weaponry after Saddam Hussein used such weaponry against Iranian, Iraqi Kurdish, and Iraqi Shi'ite forces during the Iran-Iraq War.

And, angering Iran, Trump has additionally begun to escalate the war in Yemen in support of the Saudi position against the Houthis. While the United States has ostensibly focused its airstrikes and Special Forces operations on al-Qaeda affiliates in Yemen, it has also provided considerable military support to Saudi Arabia. Obama transferred more than $100 billion in over forty different arms sales to Saudi Arabia. And President Obama made a major military sale to Saudi Arabia just as the US Congress overrode his veto and adopted the Justice Against Sponsors of Terrorism Act (JASTA). The latter permits US citizens to sue Saudi Arabia for the damages and death caused by the September 11, 2001, attacks. This bill was passed on the still-unproven presumption that Saudi officials may have supported al-Qaeda or that Riyadh may have known something about the attacks. Saudi Arabia is now facing a $6 billion lawsuit. US attorneys are also investigating whether Iran may have assisted al-Qaeda members by letting them pass through Iranian territory, for example.[37]

Obama had tried to veto the JASTA bill in the belief that it could further alienate Saudi Arabia from US policy and thus intensify the conflict in the wider Middle East. In addition, Riyadh had threatened to pull hundreds of millions of dollars in assets and investments out of the United States in response to the lawsuits. Perhaps most crucially, the law opens the United States itself to lawsuits from people in other countries who have been impacted by US military interventions.

For his part, Trump had strongly opposed Obama's veto of JASTA. Yet Trump then opted for a major arms sale to both Saudi Arabia and Bahrein, which had initially been delayed by the Obama administration on account of human rights concerns resulting from the unconventional way Riyadh is fighting in Yemen. In 2015, Trump had tweeted, "Saudi Arabia should be paying the United States many billions of dollars for our defense of them. Without us, gone!"[38] On his trip to Riyadh in May 2017, however, Trump opted to sell Saudi Arabia seven THAAD missile defense batteries, over 100,000 air-to-ground munitions, and billions of dollars' worth of new aircraft, among other weapons and satellite systems, in addition to assistance in border security and counterterrorism, maritime and coastal security, air force modernization, and cyber-security and communications upgrades. This deal, initiated by Obama, is potentially worth a total of $110 billion, assuming the US Congress does accept all proposed sales to the kingdom.[39] Yet Riyadh, seen as hedging its bets on long-term US support with the particularly fickle Trump presidency, also raised eyebrows in Washington when it sought to purchase the Russian-made S-400 antimissile system.

THE RUSSIAN RESPONSE

Putin's immediate response was to call the April 2017 Tomahawk strikes on Syria a violation of international law and a "significant blow" to the Russian-American relationship.[40] The strikes were not necessarily interpreted by Moscow as a legitimate means to punish the Assad regime for its alleged use of chemical weaponry against its own population. Russian diplomats furthermore condemned the United States for being a "partner of Daesh [that is, IS] and al-Nusra Front terrorist groups operating in Syria." Former US Defense Intelligence Agency director Michael Flynn, who lost his post as one of Trump's National Security Advisors, had affirmed that Washington, along with its Arab Gulf allies, had made a willful "decision" set up a "Salafist principality" in eastern Syria to counter the Assad regime.[41]

One Russian diplomat described the US Tomahawk strike as a ploy to distract attention from the "tragedy" that the so-called US-led Coalition Against Daesh has created by targeting Iraqi civilians in the Iraqi city of Mosul. Russian Prime Minister Dmitry Medvedev stated the strikes had been only "one step away from military clashes with Russia"; Russian Foreign Minister Sergei Lavrov stated: "It reminds me of the situation in 2003 when the United States and Britain, along with some of their allies, attacked Iraq."[42] Yet Lavrov hoped that "this provocation will not lead to irreparable damage" to the ties between Washington and Moscow.

One of the reasons for Moscow's direct military intervention in Syria in 2015 was to compel the United States and Europeans to recognize Moscow as a strong equal partner and to better respect Russia's perceived "vital" national security interests. Moscow hoped to signal that it does not want to lose its spheres of influence and security either in the Black Sea region or in the eastern Mediterranean and Levant region. In essence, Moscow has feared that the collapse of the Assad regime could permit pan-Islamist movements to undermine Russian controls not only in the Northern Caucasus but also in Muslim areas of the Russian Federation and in Central Asia.

The Russia intervention in Syria also represented an effort to help deflect US and European attention away from its *fait accompli* in Crimea—while also hoping to use Syria as a form of bargaining chip to press the United States and Europeans to put an end to the political and economic sanctions that were placed on Moscow after the annexation of Crimea.

NATO MEMBER TURKEY AND RUSSIA

With respect to the states closest to the conflict, Turkey's Foreign Minister Mevlut Cavusoglu affirmed that Ankara saw the US intervention in Syria as appropriate but that if the intervention was limited only to a missile attack on a Syrian air base, then it represented only a "cosmetic intervention" unless it eventually removed President Bashar al-Assad from power. NATO ally Turkey welcomed the missile strikes as "positive."[43] Syrian relations with Turkey and the Arab Gulf states had begun to deteriorate in 2011 when the Assad government engaged in a brutal repression of Arab Spring protesters, who were seen by Damascus as supported by the Muslim Brotherhood, among other pan-Islamist groups. At that time, Ankara abandoned its ties to Assad when it began to implement its idealist policy of "zero problems with its neighbors." In November 2015, after Moscow entered the Syrian conflict, Ankara shot down a Russian military aircraft that was flying out of Turkish airspace, after it had ended its mission over Syrian territory near the Turkish border. The Russian jet had struck Turkmen villages that Moscow believed were engaged in the war against Assad. It was the kind of incident that could spark World War III—if NATO had backed Turkey.

Nevertheless, NATO member Turkey, despite previous Turkish opposition to Moscow's support for Assad, began to look toward Moscow for several reasons. First, Turkey began to turn against the United States in the belief that Washington was behind the failed Gülen coup attempt in the summer of 2016. Fethullah Gülen, who lives in the United States, is a self-exiled Islamist who used to be Turkish President Recep Tayyip Erdoğan's ally when the two were engaged in curbing the political power of the military in Turkey's secular "deep state." But Erdoğan broke with Gülen in 2013—who was accused by Ankara of masterminding the coup. Erdoğan has subsequently initiated a major purge of an estimated 150,000 civil servants, teachers, prosecutors, judges, journalists, army officers, and police who have been suspended or dismissed. At least 52,000 have been put in prison. In April 2017, Erdoğan was able to pass a close and disputed referendum that augmented the powers of the presidency by revising the Turkish constitution.[44]

TURKEY, RUSSIA, AND THE KURDS

Despite his unexpected rapprochement with Moscow since 2016, Erdoğan stated that he did not see Trump's strikes as going far enough. Turkey's Foreign Minister Mevlut Cavusoglu said Assad's government "must be removed from leading Syria as soon as possible, and the best way to do that is by starting the transitional process."[45] In addition, Ankara called for the United States and its allies in the Global Coalition against Daesh to set up a no-fly zone in Syria in the wake of the April 2017 US Tomahawk cruise missile strikes. Yet this proposal has not been realized.

Second, US support for Kurdish factions in Syria to fight against IS also has also enraged Turkey. Ankara believed correctly or incorrectly that Kurdish political parties and militias in Syria, such as the Democratic Union Party (PYD), are linked to the radical Kurdish PKK in Turkey. These Kurdish groups have been seen by Turkey as demanding independence and not "autonomy" as they claim.[46] When US airstrikes helped the Syrian Kurdish People's Protection Units (YPG)—whom Ankara saw as aligned with the Kurdish PKK inside Turkey itself—to defend the town of Kobani from the Islamic State, Erdoğan suddenly flipped sides. Turkey then began to align more closely with Russia in the fear that US support for Kurdish opponents of the Syrian Assad regime could ultimately result in the formation of independent Kurdish state that could break away from Syria and then support the PKK inside Turkey.

US support for Syrian Kurds then led Turkey to bomb US-backed Kurdish fighters in northern Syria and in Iraq, in April 25, 2017, for example, as Ankara also did in October 2016.[47] These actions were denounced by Washington, which stated that these strikes were not approved by the Global Coalition against Daesh. And despite strong Turkish objections, the Trump administration decided in early May 2017 to provide weaponry for the Syrian Kurds of the YPG to take on fortified Islamic State fighters in Raqqa, Syria.[48]

Third, Turkey was also impacted by Russian blackmail: Moscow could also threaten support the PKK and Assad against Turkey much as Moscow did in the past—if the two sides are not able to reach a compromise. Accordingly, Moscow has wanted Ankara to begin to work with Assad again, as Ankara had done prior to the 2011 Arab Spring movement. Moscow would then reopen mutually beneficial trade, tourism, and energy deals that had been cut off when the two sides broke off relations in November 2015 after Turkey shot down a Russian military aircraft. Russia had also threatened to cut off the South Stream energy pipeline that would provide rents for Turkey.

This situation has been made even further complex by the fact that the Turkish government considers as "terrorists" the Syrian and other Kurdish factions that are supported by the United States to fight IS. At present, the main focus of the United States is not Assad but the Islamic State (IS). In the past two and a half years, as of mid-2017, Washington has spent some $12 billion in fighting IS alone. The United States has hoped to defeat IS but by putting the fewest boots on the ground as possible. This means that not only has the Pentagon bombed IS positions since 2014, but it has also worked with both Shi'a groups in Iraq and Kurdish groups in Syria and Iraq.

The dilemma is that US support for Syrian and Iraqi Kurds has raised

Ankara's fears that the United States could purposely or inadvertently be supporting Kurdish independence movements inside Turkey—even if the Pentagon has promised to closely monitor its supplies of weapons and ammunition to the Kurds. The Turks have accordingly moved across the border into Syria to control Syrian Kurdish forces and prevent them from linking to the PKK. They have periodically bombed PKK forces in northern Iraq. Turkish attacks against the Kurds come at a time when the Turkish PKK ostensibly no longer claims "independence" from Turkey. Instead, it is the Kurdistan Regional Government (KRG) leadership that has begun to demand independence. In mid-September 2017, Massoud Barzani, the president of the KRG, held a nonbinding referendum on independence of Iraqi Kurdistan; this was done against the advice of the US government, and it is strongly opposed by Iran, Syria, Turkey, and Iraq itself—but it has been backed by Israel.[49] Also in September, the US Senate blocked the sale of $1.2 million in small arms to Erdoğan's personal security guards after accusing them of using excessive force against primarily Kurdish protesters in May. This was seen as another pro-Kurdish step by Washington against Ankara's interests.

The "threat" of an Iraqi Kurdish independence movement accordingly opens a new can of worms that could further splinter Iraq, Syria, Iran, if not Turkey itself, and can exacerbate ongoing regional conflicts, since Turkey has threatened an energy blockade and Iran has purportedly mobilized troops along the Iraqi-Kurdish border. The more the United States is seen as supporting the Kurds, the more Turkey will threaten to turn to Moscow. In addition, given growing sociopolitical tensions between Germany and Turkey in part due to immigration and human rights issues, plus the fact that the European parliament threatened to suspend EU accession talks with Ankara in mid-2017 after President Erdoğan cracked down severely on the alleged Gülen coup attempt, likewise presses Turkey closer to Russia.

Close ties to Moscow are moreover indicated by Turkish interest in purchasing Russian-made S-400 antiaircraft missiles. These weapons, which would require much closer Turkish-Russian military training and cooperation, could permit Ankara to diversify its military capabilities so that Turkey is not entirely under NATO oversight.[50] Such a sale could also open Russian arms sales to the Arab Gulf countries or to other US allies. The sale would have proved much more acceptable to Washington and NATO, that is, if the United States, NATO, and Russia were on better terms, but it now threatens the relationship between NATO and Turkey.

Because the United States and Europeans, with their close ties to Saudi Arabia, were unable to reach an accord with Russia and Iran over Syria, Turkey joined with Russia and Iran for peace talks in Astana, Kazakhstan. The three countries then brokered a cease-fire for Syria in the effort to create "de-escalation" zones, which took effect (more or less) on December 30, 2016.[51] But these talks took place without US, European, or Saudi participation, raising questions as to whether they can be successfully implemented. By not working with both Russia and Turkey, Washington risks letting Moscow control the show. Washington also risks the rupture of relations with Turkey—in exchange for the not entirely certain benefits of working with Syrian Kurds to try to defeat the Islamic State. Washington will eventually need to work with both Russia and Turkey, and the Kurdish factions, if not Iran as well, in the effort to find mutual accords—if a Syrian settlement is to be found.

Despite the above concerns, Trump nevertheless claimed that the Turkish president "is becoming a friend of mine" and that "he is running a very difficult part of the world."[52]

INDIA: A MORE NEUTRAL RESPONSE

India made no strong comments about the US cruise missile attacks, so as not to offend the United States. India also did not want to offend Russia, its traditional ally. But New Delhi additionally does not want to make statements that could possibly enrage Muslim populations inside India itself.

New Delhi has generally seen Assad as an ally; for example, when in 2016 there was a UN vote on a Syrian cease-fire, New Delhi abstained from voting. Despite the ongoing conflict, Syria has sought contracts with Indian companies in the effort to build electrical plants, iron and steel mills, and oil and gas refineries. Syria has also sought Indian financial support to help reconstruct the country—which will prove a daunting task.[53] India appears to be trying to balance itself between the US and Russian positions. But for how long it can do so remains to be seen. (See chapter 6.)

THE IRAN NUCLEAR ACCORD AND THE THREAT OF US INTERVENTION

In addition to intervening militarily in Syria and striking an IS target in Afghanistan with the Mother of all Bombs, Trump has likewise threatened to strike Iran, which is directly involved in defending the Syrian regime and in supporting Hezbollah—if the latter does not fully comply with the Iran nuclear accord, or the Joint Comprehensive Plan of Action (JCPOA), which seeks to prevent Tehran from acquiring a nuclear weapons capability.

In effect, the JCPOA took at least a decade for the UN Security Council plus Germany to negotiate through concerted Contact Group diplomacy. The Obama administration argued that the JCPOA was absolutely crucial in that it would limit the chances of a regional nuclear arms race. And it would also limit the possibility that Iran would develop a covert weapons-grade enrichment program.[54] Trump, however, has claimed that the Iran JCPOA nuclear deal puts "limits on [Iran's] military nuclear program for only a certain number of years, but when those restrictions expire, Iran will have an industrial-sized, military nuclear capability ready to go and with zero provision for delay, no matter how bad Iran's behavior is."[55] The truth, however, is that the Iran nuclear deal promised fifteen years of Iranian compliance, plus international inspections. Trump's concerns appear to be less about the Iran nuclear accord itself and more about his opposition to Iran's actual foreign policy toward Israel and Saudi Arabia, and its support for Syria.

Iran further angered Trump with the testing of a new intermediate-range missile in January 2017.[56] For its part, however, Iran claimed that its missile test did not violate UN Resolution 2231. The missile was ostensibly not designed to carry nuclear weaponry and was only to be used for purposes of conventional "deterrence." The JCPOA nuclear deal is strongly backed by the Russians, Chinese, and Europeans. The problem is that Iran's missile test violated the spirit, but not the actual letter, of the JCPOA accord. Neither Russia, China, nor the Europeans would permit Washington to apply language that would prohibit all kinds of missile tests. Only tests for those missiles capable of carrying nuclear warheads would be prohibited.[57]

A possible Trump-Pence administration or a US congressional decision[58] to reject the JCPOA accord could (1) undermine US credibility; (2) start a new nuclear arms race in wider Middle East with Saudi Arabia, Turkey, and possibly with Egypt; and (3) make it more difficult, if not impossible, to achieve a nuclear arms accord with North Korea. Alienating Iran so that it does decide to engage in a nuclear weapons program could furthermore make it more difficult to find ways for Teheran and Riyadh to establish a *modus vivendi* that would seek to dampen the "terrorist" proxy wars between the two rivals and thus attempt to achieve regional political settlements. A rejection of the JCPOA not only would threaten to undermine Trump's promises to achieve a positive relationship with Moscow but also could further alienate Beijing, if not the Europeans—who are just as close as Israel to a possible Iranian missile attack. And a possible US or Israeli attack on the suspected Iranian nuclear program could work to mobilize the Iranian population against the United States, as it did during the 1980–1988 Iran-Iraq War.

By criticizing the nuclear accord, the Trump-Pence administration is ironically putting pressure on Iran just when Iran rejected a fundamentalist

Shi'a leader and elected an ostensibly reformist leader, Hassan Rouhani, and just when Boeing has signed two aircraft deals worth $22 billion that could supply an estimated eighteen thousand American jobs.[59] Given the fact that part of the Boeing deal was signed when Trump was president, it appears highly unlikely that Trump would strike Iran. Nevertheless, the proxy war between Saudi Arabia and Iran could continue to escalate. And in response to Saudi military purchases from the United States and to the threat of potential new US economic sanctions on Iran, or if Washington should brand the Iran's Revolutionary Guards as a terrorist organization, then their commander, General Mohammad Ali Jafari, warned that US military bases in Bahrain, Iraq, Oman, and Afghanistan would be at risk of an Iranian missile attack.[60]

Prior to Trump's arrival to power, the Obama administration had hoped that the JCPOA nuclear accord would eventually open the door to better US-Iranian relations, trade, and a settlement of regional conflicts. Yet the JCPOA nuclear accord was also signed at a time in which there was no apparent progress toward a resolution of the Israeli-Palestinian conflict, nor a resolution of regional disputes that involve a surrogate war between Iran and Saudi Arabia. The risk is that Trump's major $110 billion arms sale to Saudi Arabia in May 2017, as previously discussed, may have jeopardized any possibility of a Saudi-Iranian rapprochement in the near future and could turn Iran even closer to Moscow and Beijing for arms.

Here a new dimension of the global rivalry manifests itself. The fact that Iran has been moving closer to both Russia and China in the post–Cold War era raises questions as to whether the three countries could forge a new Eurasian Alliance. This appears plausible, given the fact that Iran has been considered for membership in both the Russian-led CSTO military alliance and also the more security and cooperation–oriented Chinese-led Shanghai Cooperation Organization (SCO)—even though it has not yet joined either. Teheran has thus far closely aligned with Moscow and Damascus in the conflict raging in Syria and Iraq.

THE RUPTURE BETWEEN SAUDI ARABIA AND QATAR

One of the most recent signs of the polarization of the world was the decision in June 2017 by Saudi Arabia, the United Arab Emirates, Bahrain, Yemen, and Egypt to isolate Qatar for its ostensible support for Iran, al-Qaeda, the Islamic State, and the Muslim Brotherhood. This effort to isolate the super-wealthy country, which is not much bigger than the size of the state Delaware, could represent a prelude to a much larger conflict for control over finance, oil, and gas resources throughout the wider Middle East—if diplomacy cannot eventually settle the dispute. Here, Turkish troops have been deployed in Qatar to protect it from a potential Saudi invasion. But more likely, the country could be threatened by an internal pro-Saudi coup d'état intended to replace the present emir of Qatar, Tamim bin Hamad al Thani.

The dispute with Qatar is threatening to splinter the Gulf Cooperation Council (GCC) of Saudi Arabia, Kuwait, the United Arab Emirates, Bahrein, and Oman, in which the latter finds itself trying to resist Saudi pressures. The dispute is also beginning to polarize countries in Africa and the wider Middle East. Already, Djibouti, Somaliland, Chad, Senegal, Maldives, and Mauritania have tended to side with Saudi Arabia and the United Arab Emirates. States such as Sudan, Ethiopia, Somalia, Eritrea, Guinea, and the Seychelles have tried to remain neutral, while Turkey is Qatar's strongest supporter. The United Arab Emirates is building a naval base in Eritrea (a country that also has close ties to Qatar), which worries Ethiopia. The United Arab Emirates has also obtained the backing of three semiautonomous regions inside Somalia, which is strategically crucial for providing airspace for Qatar. The United Arab Emirates removed its ambassador from Somalia when it declared neutrality. Riyadh is building a naval base in Djibouti, along with the United States and China. Israel likewise opposes Qatari foreign policy in the region, given Qatar's close relations with Hamas, Hezbollah, and Iran. In spreading its portfolio, Qatar has also invested in Russia's Rosneft energy company, as well as other strategic investments in Russia, so that Qatar is hedging its bets by maintaining closer ties not only to Iran, but to Russia as well—despite the fact that the US maintains its major Al Udeid military base in Qatar. Yet according to Trump, the United States "would have 10 countries willing to build us another one, believe me, and they will pay for it."[61]

THE WAR IN IRAQ: THE MOSUL OFFENSIVE

In October 2016, the United States and forces of the Global Coalition against Daesh—involving Iraqi forces, Kurdish Peshmerga fighters, Sunni tribesmen, and Shi'a militiamen backed by Iraq and Iran—began a major offensive against IS in Mosul, Iraq. This is the location of Great Mosque of al-Nuri, where IS leader Abu Bakr al-Baghdadi had initially proclaimed the creation of a "caliphate" in July 2014.[62] This major battle resulted in 420,000 refugees. Mosul was ostensibly "liberated" in January 2017; yet fierce fighting continued until July, raising questions as to how to reconstruct the devastated city.[63]

Although IS is being defeated step-by-step in battles with the Global Coalition against Daesh, its fighters have begun to spread out in small numbers throughout the wider Middle East—from Libya to Egypt and Afghanistan. In mid-January 2017, US B-2 bombers struck IS positions in Libya, which is divided into at least two major warring factions, plus splinter groups. Concurrently, Egyptian forces have tried to eradicate IS in the Sinai. Trump bombed proclaimed IS fighters with the Mother of All Bombs in Afghanistan. The military dilemma is that air strikes do not control the ground, thus airpower does not necessarily prevent the Islamic State or pro-al-Qaeda forces from dispersing to new regions and regrouping to engage in a nomadic style of hybrid warfare.

THE ONGOING WAR IN AFGHANISTAN

The US effort to reconstruct a corrupt and essentially insolvent Afghanistan has represented the largest expenditure to rebuild a single country in US history. Despite a $70 billion US investment in the Afghan security forces, only 63 percent of the country's districts are under Afghan government control or influence. And since 2001, 2,247 US military personnel have died and more than 20,000 have been wounded in Afghanistan alone. And Afghanistan still leads the world in opium production—despite $8.5 billion in US counter-narcotics investment.[64]

The September 11 attacks had actually been masterminded in Hamburg, Germany, and in not Tora Bora. Osama bin Laden—who was the leader of these terrorist attacks—was killed a decade later in 2011 by US Navy SEALs in his hiding place in Pakistan, which is ostensibly a major non-NATO ally but which has not given up its secret supports for differing radical Islamist factions in Afghanistan or in Kashmir. (See chapter 6.) Although al-Qaeda has lost some influence since bin Laden's assassination, affiliated groups are still influential in Yemen and in Syria, for example.

Further, if the actual goal of the US intervention in Afghanistan since 2001 was to set up energy pipelines and gain access to an estimated $1 trillion worth of strategic raw materials, as some analysts have argued, US firms are not necessarily in the forefront for gaining those contracts. Chinese and Indian firms appear willing to take the risks. One could argue that the 2001 intervention in Afghanistan, followed by the 2003 intervention in Iraq, which reduced US resources for Afghanistan, has done nothing but spread pan-Islamist movements—while also doing very little to resolve the domestic sociopolitical problems for either Iraq or Afghanistan, despite the billions invested.

Moreover, the US struggle against the Taliban, al-Qaeda, and now the Islamic State in Afghanistan, ironically, has served Russian interests more than American interests—while US intervention did not achieve its initial goal to destroy al-Qaeda. On the one hand, Moscow has sought to force NATO out of the Black Sea region; on the other, Putin has urged NATO to stay on in Afghanistan since 2014. This is because NATO has helped stabilize some key regions of the country while preventing the Taliban from returning to power. Yet the Russian position toward the Taliban has been shifting.

FACTORS LEADING TO POTENTIAL CONFLICT

The situation in Central and Southwest Asia, in Afghanistan and Kashmir, has accordingly begun to heat up again due to a number of factors. First, Obama promised that the United States and NATO would to leave Afghanistan during his administration. Yet Trump has been considering a significant increase in NATO and US troops in the country. The main purpose of a renewed surge would be to shore up Afghan troop morale—but it would also provide the Afghan government with greater firepower. Trump would, in the process, put an end to Obama's restrictions that had limited the ability of the US military to act on the battlefield. And he would give the Pentagon greater authority to use air strikes, such as the April 2017 MOAB (Massive Ordnance Air Blast, or Mother of All Bombs) attack against an IS tunnel complex. Trump would purportedly authorize the Pentagon, not the White House, to set troop numbers in Afghanistan.

Trump's National Security Advisor, H. R. McMaster, who had led anticorruption efforts in Afghanistan, is said to be one of the main backers of the new Afghan strategy. McMaster was also one of the architects of President George W. Bush's generally failed troop surge in Iraq.[65] Donald Trump had initially claimed that he opposed—and would continue to oppose—unnecessary, if not disastrous, US military interventions, such as those in Iraq and Libya, but these initial assertions appear completely false. And it was only after the fact, that Trump argued that the George W. Bush administration's decision to invade Iraq may have been the worst foreign-policy decision in US history.[66] Trump has also stated that he would attempt to limit the exposure of US servicemen and servicewomen to combat situations, but will he?

Despite his campaign statements, Trump appears to be engaging in yet another futile military intervention after the Bush administration had severely maltreated American service members during the wars in both Afghanistan and Iraq. Ironically, in 2013 Trump had tweeted that the United States should leave Afghanistan immediately, or, "if we have to go back in, we go in hard & quick."[67] But it does not look like the United States will be going in hard and quick. And, at the same time, by unleashing the Pentagon rather than pressing for renewed diplomacy, Trump may actually end up extending this seemingly endless war.

Trump's call to deploy more US and NATO forces (as many as five thousand above the already eight thousand present) is a due to the fact that the Taliban appear to be making advances concurrent with the arrival of the Islamic State in the region. In effect, this will complicate US calculations as it attempts to fight both movements, which in turn will fight each other—unless they join forces. (It is possible that the new IS groups could be disgruntled Taliban elements who have formed their own groups and have declared themselves to be IS.[68])

Moreover, Moscow appears to be seeking a rapprochement with the Taliban—given the Obama administration's promises to withdraw from Afghanistan, which Moscow believes might then lead to a Taliban takeover. In 2014, the Taliban almost took over Kunduz, after NATO began to phase out of Afghanistan. At that time, Pakistan had concurrently sought to clear Islamist militants out of the North Waziristan tribal area; this forced those groups into Afghanistan, even though there are still Taliban sanctuaries on Pakistani territory, which make it almost impossible to achieve peace.[69]

The dilemma for Russia is that if the United States and NATO do eventually pull out of Afghanistan, as Obama had promised, it appears unlikely that the Afghan government will survive for long. On the other hand, if the United States and NATO do engage in a new troop surge, as Trump has indicated, Moscow could play the role of a spoiler that attempts to sabotage US foreign policy wherever possible, given thus far unproven US accusations that Russia has begun to provide the Taliban with weaponry—a charge vehemently denied by Moscow.

Moscow may have decided to make a deal with the Taliban "devil."[70] It is accordingly possible that both Beijing and Moscow might try to make some deal with the Taliban so that the latter (which has begun to struggle with the Islamic State in Afghanistan) will not support the Muslim Uighurs in Xinjiang province in China (former East Turkestan). As they build BRI together, neither Beijing nor Moscow want the Taliban to support those Islamists who want to destabilize Muslim regions in southwest Asia or in the Russian Federation itself. The problem then for Moscow and Beijing is to buy off the Taliban and to play the Taliban against the Islamic State—while also countering the United States and NATO in Afghanistan.

Yet the new Russian policy could also lead the United States to negotiate with the Taliban, which the State Department does not formally designate as a "terror organization." Proposed negotiations with the Taliban, which Secretary of State Rex Tillerson appeared to support at a NATO conference in March 2017,[71] could have two different results. Either the United States could return to the Obama policy of supporting an "Afghan-owned, Afghan-led" negotiation, or the United States could take the lead in negotiations with the Taliban, which the Taliban have claimed they would prefer. Such negotiations could take place in US-led multilateral framework, with countries such as Russia, China, India, Pakistan, Afghanistan, and Qatar involved.[72] But unfortunately it will take much more time, death, and destruction before such negotiations begin, because there is no trust between the opposing sides after years of warfare. And these talks could be further delayed if Trump does unleash the Pentagon so that it is no longer under State Department controls.

THE WIDENING OF THE GLOBAL WAR ON TERRORISM

In his first public speech in Saudi Arabia in May 2017, Trump argued that the Global War on Terrorism was "not a battle between different faiths, different sects, or different civilizations. . . . This is a battle between barbaric criminals who seek to obliterate human life, and decent people of all religions who seek to protect it."[73]

While Trump did not then use the term "radical Islamic terrorism" in this speech (which he did use in his address to the United Nations in September 2017), he also did not define what he meant by "terrorists and extremists." (See chapter 3.) Nevertheless, Trump urged that "they" (whoever "they" are) be driven "out of this earth" by all the Sunni Arab states and societies that are involved in the Global War on Terrorism. It is not clear how the terms "terrorists and extremists" will be interpreted in the Sunni Arab/Islamic cultural context—as these terms could be interpreted to mean those who believe in Shi'a Islam or other "unbelievers" and atheists.

In his May 2017 speech in Saudi Arabia, Trump had focused on Shi'a Iran, as if Tehran were the source of all the problems: "From Lebanon to Iraq to Yemen, Iran funds, arms, and trains terrorists, militias, and other extremist groups that spread destruction and chaos across the region. For decades, Iran has fueled the fires of sectarian conflict and terror." So instead of seeking a way to end the regional arms race and urge Saudi Arabia and Iran to settle their differences—which is absolutely fundamental if it will ever prove possible to put an end to the Global War on Terrorism—Trump appears to have sided fully with Riyadh. In effect, rather than attempting to play honest broker, Trump has greased the fire.

On the one hand, Trump's speech (accompanied by promises of $110 billion in arm sales, plus $300 to $400 billion in mutual investments[74]) could lead some pro-Saudi holy warriors, among others, to shift their focus from the United States, Europeans, Russia, and Israel to fight against Shi'a Iran and the Syrian regime. Saudi Crown Prince Mohammed bin Salman, who has been designated by the eighty-two-year-old King Salman to run the country, has initiated major political, social, and economic reforms so that Saudi Arabia can attempt to sustain its regional hegemony in the long term by diversifying the economy away from oil production by 2030. At the same time, Salman has begun to purge potential domestic rivals (some two hundred individuals arrested on corruption charges, including members of his own ruling al-Saud family).[75] In addition to seeking to isolate Qatar, due in part to its ties to Iran, Salman has militantly opposed Iranian efforts to increase its political-economic influence in Lebanon, Iraq, Syria, Bahrain, and Yemen, and along the Red Sea in the Gulf of Aden. Trump appears to be falling into Salman's game plan.

On the other hand, Trump's speech will not stop IS or similar groups from recruiting young Muslims and converts—particularly those individuals who oppose what they see as the corrupt Saudi Kingdom, which controls Mecca and Medina and whose regime they believe is backed by US and European weaponry. This creates a tacit alignment between these groups and Tehran, which opposes Saudi Arabia, which is seen as the major supporter of pan-Sunni movements that could destabilize the northern Caucasus, Central Asia, and other areas in the wider Middle East against Iranian and Russian interests. At the same time, Tehran also opposes a nuclear-capable Israel, which is threatening to preempt Iran's "peaceful" nuclear program in large part due to Iran's support for the Shi'a militias of Hezbollah in Lebanon.

And despite US/NATO efforts to fight the Taliban, al-Qaeda-affiliated movements, and IS, both Moscow and Beijing see the United States as indirectly backing a number of pan-Sunni Islamist movements throughout the wider Middle East via bilateral US alliances with Saudi Arabia and the other Sunni Arab Gulf countries. US policy has led Russia, and increasingly China, to support Shi'a Iran and Syria. At the same time, Pakistan may be shifting sides, looking to both China and Russia.

Trump's propaganda risks once again falling into the trap first set by bin Laden's attack on the World Trade Center and Pentagon and that sought to draw the United States and other countries into wider wars within the Islamic world. But in this case, Trump's speech represents a call to arms for a war with Iran and those pan-Islamist groups that oppose Saudi Arabia as well. As long as Trump's pro-Saudi, anti-Iranian policies and America First, anti-"radical Islamic" ideology prevails, the Global War on Terrorism appears doomed to last a very long time.

Chapter 9

PEACE THROUGH STRENGTH? OR WORLD WAR TRUMP?

In his book *Trump: The Art of the Deal,* Trump stated: "My style of deal-making is quite simple and straightforward. I aim very high, and then I just keep pushing and pushing and pushing to get what I'm after." But he also said, "I never get too attached to one deal or one approach. . . . I keep a lot of balls in the air, because most deals fall out, no matter how promising they seem at first."[1]

For all of his pro-Russian and anti-China rhetoric expressed during his presidential campaign, the Trump-Pence administration has totally reassessed his negotiation strategies with both Russia and China, among other states—much like his book *The Art of the Deal* suggested he might. In the case of Russia, is Trump now taking a much tougher line in which he fully expects Moscow to hand over Crimea to Kiev? Or is he taking a hardline stance on Crimea in order to make a compromise deal? And if so, what kind of compromise? In the case of China, can Trump be tough after initially backing down on the One-China policy? Or will Trump need to make concessions—and if so, which ones? And how will North Korea impact Trump's calculus? Will China agree to play a key role in mediation with North Korea? Should he renew the six-party talks? Or should Trump meet directly with Kim Jung Un? Or both? What will be the impact of China's Belt and Road Initiative (BRI) and Regional Comprehensive Economic Partnership (RCEP), which could become the major trading bloc in the world, without US involvement? And will Moscow and Beijing be able to forge a full-fledged Eurasian military alliance?

Will his potential deals succeed or "fall out," in Trump's language? And if it is true that "most deals fall out, no matter how promising they seem at first," as he himself had affirmed—then the world is in real trouble. Gambling with war and nuclear weapons is not quite the same thing as gambling in Trump's casinos; although one can lose a fortune in a casino, *everyone* loses in a nuclear war.

INITIAL DISCUSSIONS WITH MOSCOW

Despite his policy flip-flops and feigned efforts to engage in Nixonian madness in order to keep all sides guessing as to his actual policies and tactics, Trump has been more or less correct that the United States needs to begin to engage in a rapprochement with Russia, otherwise the situation could spiral out of control. But he initially moved much too fast to reach out to Moscow and raised suspicions that he sought to profit personally from his Russian contacts, while Putin's alleged efforts, whether effective or not, to interfere in the US elections caused a significant, and hopefully not irreconcilable, American backlash. (See chapter 3.) Given these circumstances, how is a more concerted US-European-Russian relationship to be established?

Based on Russian reports of the January 2017 Putin-Trump conversation, the issues the two presidents began to consider included: The creation of an anti-IS coalition; the establishment of a US-Russia partnership on an equal basis; and the possible "restoration" of trade and economic relations. This implied that sanctions imposed on Moscow after its annexation of Crimea could be reconsidered—but coupled with a *quid pro quo* with respect to a reduction of nuclear weapons.[2] Putin and Trump accordingly reviewed possible cooperation on a wide range of issues, including Syria, Ukraine, Iran, the Korean Peninsula, and nuclear nonproliferation.[3]

At the same time, it was clear even then that the conditions were still not ripe enough to reach out for a full-fledged US-Russian accord. On the one hand, Trump's approach was opposed by US and European critics who argued that it was too soon to consider lifting sanctions, given the perceived Russian failure to implement the Minsk II agreements, and without pressing Russia to give Crimea back to Ukraine. On the other hand, Moscow did not completely accept Trump's proposals, either. Moscow was not prepared to give up elements of its nuclear weapons capability without a *quid pro quo* on the part of the Americans. Nor was Putin willing to give up Crimea.

Despite the backlash caused by Moscow's efforts to influence the American elections, the dilemma now is how to put US-Russia relations back on course so that they do not spin totally out of control. A first step to ameliorate tensions would be a US-Russia summit that would address all the disputes between the United States and Russia (ranging from Ukraine, to the wider Middle East, to China and North Korea), while seeking measures to reduce, if not eliminate, nuclear weaponry, and finding ways move away from putting nuclear missiles on high levels of alert and launch-on-warning. Such a summit would lead both sides to pledge to engage in concerted cooperation to resolve these disputes and other issues of concerns where possible. (See discussion, chapter 10.) Perhaps most crucially, from an American domestic standpoint, a Trump-Putin summit could also issue a sincere pledge of noninterference in each other's domestic politics, given allegations that both sides have interfered in each other's elections. (See discussion, chapter 3.)

A US-Russia summit should then be followed by a revival of talks between the NATO-Russia Council. The concern raised here is that the buildup US and NATO power capabilities through the deployment of "permanently rotating" forces in the Baltic region, as has been pushed by the Trump-Pence administration since February 2017, risks undermining the 1997 NATO-Russia Founding Act and will only result in a counter Russia military buildup. This buildup will in turn further escalate US-European-Russian (and Chinese) tensions—if such an approach is not simultaneously accompanied by a detailed plan for an alternative system of European security and a full US, NATO, and EU willingness to compromise with Moscow over what some NATO members might consider to be "vital" interests.

The point is that the United States/NATO and Europeans need to define clear objectives so that they can convince Moscow that they are sincerely seeking to forge a grand compromise on Euro-Atlantic security. The United States and Europeans thus need to provide positive incentives and enticements and not just threats and sanctions in order to convince Moscow that a general militarization is not in Russian interests and that a closer Russian military alliance with China is not in Russian interests either. The promise to lift economic sanctions, for example, must be only one of the levers of a much larger and coordinated bargaining strategy that is intended to reduce overall NATO-EU-Russian tensions. The dilemma is how to implement a systemic approach to these issues of contention and show how they relate to each other, while seeking to find compromises or concessions where possible. (Nuclear-weapons issues are discussed in chapters 2 and 10.)

EASTERN UKRAINE

In many ways, it does not seem that Germany and France possess enough political leverage to press both Ukraine and Russia into a compromise in the Minsk discussions that have been facilitated by Belarus. For this reason, the United States, and possibly Turkey, should soon join the Contact Group discussions between Germany, France, Ukraine, and Russia—since this conflict cannot be completely resolved unless the issues of both the NATO and EU enlargements are also on the table.

One major goal (backed by Moscow but thus far opposed by Kiev) is to work toward the "decentralization" of the country. Kiev has opposed what it calls federalism, or what is really "asymmetrical federalism," in the not-entirely-unjustified fear that federalism could eventually lead regions to demand independence. The dilemma, however, is that no one can really force *from the outside* the two sides to cooperate—so the situation in the Ukraine needs to move toward one of a "mutually hurting stalemate,"[4] in which each side realizes on its own volition that it needs to agree to a mutual accord. Once again, Washington should join the process to help press both sides into an agreement.

From the Russian perspective, Ukraine has not yet fulfilled its part of the February 2015 Minsk II agreements.[5] The latter involves the parliamentary vote on decentralization—a vote which was postponed in 2016, but which is a crucial part of the Minsk process. But more constitutional reforms may be needed in order to ensure that Ukraine develops a true separation of powers and a true "decentralization."[6] German proposals for a special status law, a broad amnesty law, and a special election law for the Donbas appear possible to implement—but only if the Ukrainian coalition government under President Poroshenko can press for a resolution to the conflict in eastern Ukraine. But these already-difficult-to-implement measures are taking place in the midst of a Ukrainian financial crisis and need for deep structural and anticorruption reforms.[7] Once again, a more engaged US diplomatic presence is needed.

To achieve peace, Kiev (backed by the United States and Europeans) needs to take official steps to meet with autonomist leaderships in order to negotiate peace settlement. Efforts to meet with the leadership of Russia-backed eastern-Ukrainian autonomists, as proposed by Ukrainian lawmaker Nadia Savchenko (and former prisoner of war in Russia), and to engage in prisoner exchange or other issues, need to be officially backed by Kiev, rather than denounced as "negotiating with terrorists."[8]

If a political settlement can be found, one possibility is the deployment of a "multinational brigade of neutral but armed peacekeepers with unrestricted access throughout the Donbas"[9] in order to enforce Minsk II—otherwise Minsk II will fail. This proposal has merit, and Russia and Ukraine have considered the possibility of deploying peacekeepers. Thus far, Moscow has agreed only to a temporary and limited presence, but which does not control the territory linking Russia with the autonomist movements. For its part, Kiev wants to set up a more permanent and expanded peacekeeping force.

But if these steps, as proposed by the Minsk II accords, fail, another more pessimistic scenario might result in a highly instable partition of the country, which will not benefit either side and which will create permanent tensions beyond Ukraine. This possibility becomes more probable if the United States does provide lethal assistance to Kiev. (See chapter 5.) A partition of the country could, ironically, force Moscow to financially subsidize the secessionist region—which would prove to be a more daunting task than holding up the Russian-supported breakaway republics of Transnistria (claimed by Moldova), South Ossetia, and Abkhazia (claimed by Georgia), and it could further militarize Russian actions. This represents yet another reason for a concerted international solution.

There is a real risk is that an eventual partition of Ukraine, coupled with the permanently rotating deployment of NATO forces in the Baltic region, could in turn lead to a new partition of Europe—followed by the polarization of the world into two rival alliances. (See chapter 5.)

TOWARD UKRAINIAN NEUTRALITY

Once, and if, the Minsk II accords can be implemented (assuming Kiev can eventually implement the necessary constitutional changes and negotiate directly with the Donbas "autonomists"), the United States, Europe, and Russia then need to establish Ukraine as an internationally recognized neutral and "decentralized" country—with Crimea as a free-trade zone, yet under Russian sovereignty, while providing aid and assistance for Ukraine's development.

Both former US Secretaries of State Henry Kissinger and Zbigniew Brzezinski have called for a "neutral" Ukraine. Yet the Kissinger proposal for the formal "neutralization" of Ukraine, coupled with the non-recognition of Crimea, will not put an end to US-Russian-European geostrategic and political-economic tensions. And the crisis will continue unabated if Kiev does not finally grant some form of decentralization or autonomy arrangement for eastern Ukraine, as demanded by the Minsk II accord. There will also be no settlement if Kiev, backed by the United States and NATO, continues to demand that Crimea be returned to Ukraine as well, while Kiev concurrently develops a strong independent military capability. In short, a settlement of the Crimean question is essential if the conflict is to be resolved in the long term. If bargained cautiously, a resource-rich yet "neutral" and decentralized Ukraine—with sufficient self-defense forces and that does not harbor irredentist claims to Crimea—could begin to defuse tensions between NATO, the European Union, and Russia.[10]

To arrive at a full accord with Moscow, there needs to be formal agreement over NATO expansion, European security, and Ukrainian neutrality. To accomplish this, NATO should formally announce a full suspension of NATO enlargement—but as part of a larger negotiation process that is intended to reach a deal with Moscow over Crimea, eastern Ukraine, and the Caucasus. While NATO has claimed that Article X of the Washington Treaty is "one of the Alliance's great successes," there is nothing in Article X that supports the contention that NATO must expand its membership. NATO members "may" invite other states by unanimous agreement—but there is no necessity to offer an invitation to other states.[11]

Moreover, membership in both the US-led NATO and the Russian-led CSTO are against Ukraine's initial statement of sovereignty. The statement of Ukrainian sovereignty (adopted on August 24, 1991) affirmed that Ukrainian SSR "declares its intention of becoming a permanently neutral state that does not participate in military blocs and adheres to three nuclear free principles: to accept, to produce and to purchase no nuclear weapons."[12] It is furthermore possible that Ukraine could define itself as a permanently neutral country in that its constitution contains principles that state that it will not participate in coalitions.[13]

The United States and NATO would accordingly need to modify NATO's "open enlargement" policy—at least for the Black Sea/Caucasus region. Such a modification of NATO's open-door policy would take place in exchange for the implementation of a new regional, yet internationalized, system of cooperative/collective security for the entire Black Sea and Caucasus regions—much as was envisioned by Turkish proposals for a Caucasus Stability and Cooperation Platform in 2008. Here, Ankara could enter the Minsk talks in order to deal with security issues concerning Crimea and the Caucasus that impact NATO-member Turkey.

In other words, instead of extending full NATO membership to Ukraine, Georgia, or other states, and then attempt to integrate these countries back into NATO's command structure, the United States, Europeans, and Russians would extend overlapping US, European, and Russian security guarantees for states in the entire Black Sea and Caucasus region in the formation of a neutral "peace and development community"—in working with Turkey and other regional powers. The purpose would be to implement a cooperative/collective security approach to the region under the auspices of the Organization for the Security and Cooperation in Europe (OSCE) that seeks to protect "vital" Russian and Ukrainian interests, while at the same time looking for new forms of regional and international cooperation.

A full suspension of NATO enlargement would accordingly be part of a larger negotiation process that is intended to reach a deal with Moscow over Crimea, eastern Ukraine, and the Caucasus—among other issues that are dividing the United States, the European Union, and Russia. The promise of NATO enlargement has done nothing but send mixed signals to Russia, Ukraine, and Georgia. NATO enlargement has antagonized Moscow, while it has been concurrently disingenuous with Kiev and Tbilisi—as full NATO membership for Ukraine and Georgia remains a highly unlikely prospect. Guarantees of Ukrainian neutrality, coupled with a gradual reduction of NATO and Russian forces in the Baltic region, could also minimize the ostensible need to expand NATO membership to EU members Sweden and Finland, given the Russian military buildup in the Baltic region. (See chapters 4 and 5.)

CRIMEA AS A FREE-TRADE ZONE

There are many who argue that the United States and Europe should simply accept the Russian annexation as a *fait accompli*. Yet this position does not address the question of competing claims and the political, economic, energy and legal disputes over Crimea, energy resources, and other issues in the vicinity—and the need to develop and eventually demilitarize the whole Black Sea-Caucasus region that will serve Russian interests as well. To fully develop the region will require international assistance. (See chapter 5.)

The establishment of Crimea as an international free-trade zone with relative autonomy—but under Russian sovereignty—and the opening of Sevastopol to regional security and development cooperation, could open the doors for Russia to cooperate with Ukraine, as well as with the United States and Europeans. This is despite the evident friction over the annexation of Crimea, which shows no signs of dissipating at the time of this writing. The eventual opening of Crimea could, in turn, lead both Russia and Ukraine to forge new forms of memberships with a reformed (and renamed) NATO and the European Union, given deeper security and political-economic cooperation.

One option is to call for a new Crimean referendum. Such a plan was proposed by Andrii Artemenko, who was one of the contacts of President Trump's former National Security Advisor Michael Flynn in Ukraine, before Flynn was forced to resign. Essentially, Artemenko's plan would have required the withdrawal of all Russian forces from eastern Ukraine. Ukrainian voters would then decide in a new referendum whether

Crimea would be leased to Russia for a term of fifty or one hundred years. The plan also outlined a way to lift sanctions on Russia.[14]

Yet, if such a plan could be implemented, it appears unlikely that Moscow would accept the results of a new referendum in Ukraine that could potentially lead Moscow to give up sovereignty over Crimea after having already gone to such great lengths to annex it. On the other hand, it is not entirely impossible that Moscow could accept a way to pay for a lease of the isthmus in a negotiated deal, given the need for a legal accord that would attract foreign investment to Russia in the face of sanctions.[15] As proposed above, a more feasible option might be the establishment of a free-trade zone under Russian sovereignty, or even a system of joint Russian-Ukrainian sovereignty. (See chapter 10.)

Artemenko claimed that he had "compromising" evidence on the Poroshenko government, yet his plan was opposed by a number of Ukrainian politicians, who saw it as capitulating to Russian interests, and who accused Artemenko of treason.[16] Further, it appears highly unlikely that Moscow would have accepted that plan either. Whether the United States and NATO can propose a more feasible plan that Moscow might accept will depend on the evolution not only of relations between the United States, the European Union, and Russia, but also between the Trump administration and Congress. (See chapters 3 and 10.)

PEACEKEEPING IN THE CAUCASUS?

In addition to the potential deployment of peacekeepers under a general UN or OSCE mandate so as to assure security and development prospects in the Donbas region, peacekeepers could also be considered for the states of the southern Caucasus. Instead of demanding that Russia "evacuate Transnistria, Abkhazia, South Ossetia, as well as Crimea and Donbass"[17]—as the hardline position that seeks to isolate Russia advocates and which Moscow would definitely consider as a *casus belli*—joint

NATO, Russian, EU, and international peacekeepers under an OSCE mandate could be deployed in the so-called frozen conflicts in the southern Caucasus. The problem here will be how to engage in joint US, European, and Russian arrangements in an effort to share or internationalize (but not monopolize) those nonvital Russian spheres of influence and security where mutual agreement is possible.

Joint NATO-Russia/CSTO-EU or multinational Partnership for Peace (PfP) peacekeeping deployments (under an OSCE or UN general mandate) could accordingly be deployed in the Donbas region as well as in the frozen conflicts in the Transnistria, Abkhazia, South Ossetia, and Nagorno-Karabakh. These deployments could take place under a joint NATO-EU-Russian command structure in which Russia plays a positive role. These peacekeeping operations would be somewhat similar to joint deployments in the former Yugoslavia in 1995, but Moscow would be truly represented as an equal. Given the fact that the tense situation in Nagorno-Karabakh between Armenia and Azerbaijan appears to be heating up,[18] it seems that joint US/NATO, EU and Russia/CSTO peacekeeping efforts could prove essential to sustaining peace in this region.

The above proposals presume the absolute need to strengthen NATO's Partnership for Peace (PfP) and an EU peacekeeping force that could be deployed under an OSCE or UN mandate and work with UN and Russian/CSTO peacekeepers as well.[19] NATO's PfP and EU peacekeeping is an underused tool that can succeed on the ground in helping to build trust between warring parties—if given the proper resources. And these proposals furthermore provide a real mission for EU foreign and defense policy to cooperate with the local states, Russia, and the United States under a general OSCE mandate. Peacekeepers are real heroes, and they should be considered so by Trump.

WHY SHOULD RUSSIA ACCEPT SUCH A PROPOSAL?

Washington and Moscow need to revisit the Obama administration's failure to "reset" US-European-Russian relations after the 2008 Russo-Georgian War. Both countries need to reexamine both Dmitry Medvedev's June 2008 call for a new European Security Treaty and Turkish President Erdoğan's call for a Caucasus Stability and Cooperation Platform.[20]

With respect to Russia and Turkey, both Medvedev's and Erdoğan's proposals raised critical questions as to whether it was truly necessary to enlarge NATO membership to Ukraine and Georgia, among other states. And both proposals raised questions as to whether there might be other viable options that could provide security for the Black Sea region. The joint US/NATO and EU failure to address these Russian and Turkish diplomatic initiatives—and thus to reconsider the process of enlarging both NATO and EU memberships into Russian-defined spheres of influence and security—represented a major reason for the Russian backlash in early 2014. Moscow consequently took matters into its own hands and decided to annex Crimea and support autonomous movements in eastern Ukraine.

There is a further danger that renewed tensions in Georgia and between Armenia and Azerbaijan, as well as the rise of pan-Islamist movements in Dagestan and elsewhere in the Russian Caucasus, could set off a new series of terrorist acts. Moreover, conflicts in the general Black Sea region and in both the southern and northern Caucasus could begin to interlink with the conflict in Syria and in the wider Middle East—given the return of Islamic State fighters to these regions and given Trump's strong support for Saudi Arabia against Iran. Both Riyadh and Tehran possess interests throughout the region in support of differing Islamist factions that could spark significant conflict. (See chapter 8.)

The establishment of a formally neutral Ukraine, coupled with a negotiated settlement over Crimea and eastern Ukraine, would provide the United States and Europe some bargaining leverage to at least seek a reduction of the ongoing buildup of military forces in the Black Sea region, while likewise seeking to restrain Kiev's demands for a return of the Crimean isthmus. At the same time, it could permit Crimea greater autonomy within the Russian Federation, and help protect non-Russian minorities, including Tatars and Ukrainians.

The Russian Federation is divided into republics, krais, oblasts, cities of federal importance, an autonomous oblast, and autonomous okrugs. In 2014, Sevastopol and the Crimean Republic became the eighty-fourth and eighty-fifth federal subjects of Russia. But could they, along with Kaliningrad, become free-trade and development zones under Russian sovereignty? Or could some form of joint system of sovereignty between Ukraine and Russia be established?

Unless absolutely strapped for cash, it is highly unlikely that Moscow would ever give up total sovereignty over Crimea, much like it is unlikely that it would give the Kuril Islands/Northern Territories to Japan. But for Russia to hold onto Crimea and try to develop it without some form of international investments and backing is already proving quite costly and difficult. (See chapter 5.) Putin needs an economic boost to help him rule, as domestic opposition movements have begun to strengthen. Putin has accordingly pressed for an end of sanctions in order to attract foreign investment and lift the economy out of recession. Russian presidential elections will take place in 2018, and the Trump-Pence administration could possibly try to push for a grand US-Russian compromise just after those elections—that is, if it is possible, given strong domestic US opposition to any accords with Russia. Given the fact that Putin is still seen by the general population as willing to assert presumed Russian interests and to stand up against the pressures of the United States in particular, he will most likely win the 2018 Russian elections—but without as much popular domestic support as in the past given the generally faltering economy. Yet this should not stop the United States and Europeans from engaging in negotiations with Moscow simply in the belief that Putin's rule might soon collapse. (See chapter 4.)

ROLE OF EUROPE

The Ukrainian conflict now holds the key as to whether Russia can ever move closer to the Euro-Atlantic community. On the one hand, if the brutal war in eastern Ukraine continues to rage, it will stimulate a general arms race and destabilize US-EU-Russian and global relations. On the other hand, an overarching geopolitical settlement could help defuse tensions throughout the region and the world.

The dilemma is that even closer political-economic ties to the European Union will not prove to be a panacea for Kiev, given its deep financial crisis. It is accordingly essential that the European Union work out mutual political-economic and financial accords with both Ukraine and Russia as soon as possible once the disputes over eastern Ukraine can be resolved. This can be accomplished in the process of rescinding sanctions against Russia (and vice versa for Russia to rescind sanctions on the European Union and the United States). In addition, the United States, Europeans, and Japanese need to look for ways to reduce the prospects of a US-Russia energy rivalry that could lead to war. One step would be to bring Moscow back into the G8 discussions after Russian membership was suspended in March 2014. The global energy (and environment) question could be one of the main concerns of future G8 talks—even if the May 2017 G7 conference had failed to reach a significant compromise over the issue of global warming with Donald Trump. Both G8 and EU-Russian discussions could likewise lead the European Union to work out a political-economic association accord that better balances both Russian and Ukrainian financial and political-economic interests, given the European Union's failure/refusal to do so in 2013–2014.

Such efforts must be taken to achieve reconciliation between Kiev and eastern Ukraine within Ukraine itself at the national level and at the international level so that a neutral (and non-nuclear) Ukraine could truly serve as a gateway between the United States, Europe, and Russia, much as former Soviet President Mikhail Gorbachev, among others, has proposed.[21] It is in US, European, and Russian interests to prevent Ukrainian state collapse, bankruptcy, and sociopolitical instability from degenerating into a wider sociopolitical conflict. Evidently such an approach can take place only if all sides realize that compromise over presumed "vital" issues is in their mutual interests.

TOWARD A NEW EU DEFENSE AND SECURITY CAPABILITY

Trump's insistence that NATO was "obsolete" has ironically led the Europeans to consider other options—if they can coordinate policies. The possibility that Washington might no longer back NATO has led the French and Germans to consider forging a new post-Brexit European defense entity that would be more autonomous than NATO.

In September 2016, the French and Germans called for a joint and permanent EU command headquarters for its civilian and military missions and a strengthening of the Eurocorps. The initiative would not create a European army as such. But it would seek to advance the European Union's own joint land, air, and sea transport; relief/medical capabilities; peacekeeping; plus its ability to participate in the Global War on Terrorism. It would also initiate a European defense research program that would be funded by the common EU budget by 2021–2027, with France and Germany initiating the program in 2017.[22]

A more unified European defense and security capability, which would pool defense resources, could theoretically engage in peacekeeping, anti-piracy, and anti-terrorism operations, while more effectively handling the waves of immigrants trying to cross the Mediterranean.[23] A new European defense force would represent a coalition of the willing and should be directed only toward defensive and peacekeeping measures. It would be more autonomous and could theoretically work with both NATO and Russia.[24] But to do this, the European Union first needs to implement a

Common Foreign and Defense Policy step-by-step. The European Union has outlined five possible scenarios for its future, but it needs US diplomatic backing if it is to succeed in creating a truly common defense.[25]

Over the years, the Europeans have demanded greater defense autonomy from NATO. Now, following the exit of the United Kingdom from the European Union, the Europeans need to put their money where their mouths are. The United Kingdom, the most powerful military actor in NATO after the United States, had previously blocked a more integrated European defense structure, due to its close defense ties with Washington. At the same time, the political-military dilemma is that Germany has been more supportive of a more federal system of European integration, while France's approach has been more intergovernmental.

If the United States, Europe, and Russia can eventually reach a common accord over defense and security concerns in Europe, NATO can begin to wither way—but it must not totally collapse without first working to put in its place a new Euro-Atlantic security architecture that leads the Europeans to cooperate with both the United States and Russia. If, however, NATO cannot soon find ways to cooperate with Moscow, the defection of Turkey and France, among other states, from NATO is a real possibility.

TOWARD GREATER EU POLITICAL-ECONOMIC COORDINATION

It is also crucial that the Europeans begin to coordinate both its geostrategic and political-economic strategy toward Moscow by looking for ways to incorporate both Russia and the other post-Soviet states, including Ukraine, into new forms of European Associate Partnership agreements. Eventually post-Soviet states could enter the post-Brexit EU as "Associate Members," as to be argued. The European Union likewise needs to work with the United States, Russia, and Turkey to establish a new system of Euro-Atlantic security based on cooperation over the Black Sea region. Such a practical project—the effort to bring peace and development to the Black Sea and Caucasus regions—could in turn provide a means for the Europeans to unify their divergent foreign and security policies, particularly if the conflict between Greece and Turkey over Cyprus can soon be resolved.

Given the real possibilities of the further breakup of the European Union after Brexit, Washington needs to back strong partners, and these actors need to be politically and economically stable and possess governments that are perceived as legitimate. The rise of a number of anti-EU movements that seek to drop the Euro as a currency, dump their creditors, and then exit the European Union, means that the European Union needs to engage in substantial internal reforms and changes in its external policies as well, in order to surmount the financial crisis since 2008. The latter crisis largely stems from low US interest rates since 2001 the US mortgage and toxic-loans crisis, which in turn exacerbated the crises of banking and finance, public debt, and underinvestment in Europe.[26]

The European Union needs to tighten the Franco-German relationship with the rest of its core members, step-by-step, but it also needs forge new kinds of loose linkages with the United Kingdom and other states, such as Russia and Turkey, that do not meet full membership requirements. Here, depending on how the separation between the European Union and the United Kingdom is negotiated (a process that could prove very lengthy and costly), Brexit could possibly provide a new model for forging new EU political-economic relationships with other states that could then develop differing forms of partnership and associated membership with a new, more decentralized, European Union, with a hard Franco-German core and looser appendages.

In effect, a confederal approach to European unity should be pursued that addresses both intergovernmental relations and relations between the different European societies and their values—as opposed to a strong federal approach. The European Union, for example, needs to eliminate its "democratic deficit" and to decentralize some of its decision-making in accord with its own doctrine of subsidiarity, in attempting to better balance local, national, and European interests and concerns—so as to permit greater local and national input into the EU decision-making processes.[27]

One possibility is, thus, for the full or "core" members of the European Union to create a new category of "Associate Membership."[28] European or even non-European states with important financial, trade, or even military interests in Europe—and which are willing to contribute to EU activities and responsibilities—could, if accepted, become Associate Members that possess limited membership rights. This Associate Membership category could possibly include limited voting rights in specific areas of mutual interests (thus going beyond the status of partnership). In such a way, Russia, Ukraine, and Turkey could become Associate Members—particularly if they work with the Europeans and the Americans to establish a new Black Sea regional peace and development community, for example.

Even though Turkey remains a NATO member, it is highly unlikely that it will become a full EU member under present EU rules. But Turkey could become an Associate Member if the European Union begins to reform itself significantly after Brexit. Many politicians on all sides of the political spectrum have argued that it is time to end European hypocrisy and tell Ankara that it will never join the European Union. But this statement implies that the European Union itself will not reform and that it will not eventually morph into a new international regime after Brexit, with core and associate members. Despite President Erdoğan's significant turn toward authoritarianism and repression in Turkey, Berlin, for example, has thus far wanted to keep the door open to Turkish membership in the European Union.[29]

From this perspective, the European Union will need to readjust its EU Partnership program so as to include Russian, Ukrainian, and Turkish political-economic interests. EU political-economic deals with Belarus and other states will also need to find ways to accommodate Moscow's interests as well. The Ukrainian financial crisis will prove almost impossible to resolve without Russian (and Chinese) finance along with European and American funding. This all implies the need for the Trump-Pence administration to work with the Europeans to reform, not abolish, the European Union. Otherwise, there is a real possibility of a new partition of Europe, running through eastern Ukraine.

THE QUESTION OF TURKEY

As argued above, it is highly unlikely that Turkey will become an EU member—unless both the European Union and Turkey begin to reform themselves significantly after Brexit along the lines proposed in this chapter—given the extremely poor relations between the United States, the European Union, and Turkey in recent years. The fact is that Turkey, which is a NATO member but not an EU member, has made it very difficult for NATO and the European Union to fully cooperate. In particular, the need to resolve the intra-NATO dispute between Greece and Turkey over Cyprus, among other issues, is one of the keys to improve Turkish-EU relations.

Turkish-EU relations have been in a bad state for years, given the EU refusal to accept Turkey as a member due to its large population, its predominantly Muslim culture, and its threats to bring back the death penalty. These issues have been made even worse in the aftermath of the immigrant crisis, which began in 2011, following the Arab Spring movements. This crisis led Ankara to threaten that it might unleash thousands of non-European immigrants into the European Union. In addition, since the July 2016 Gülen coup attempt, Turkey's Prime Minister Erdoğan has taken a significant turn toward authoritarianism, or "illiberal democracy," given his still high level of popular support.[30]

Nevertheless, it is crucial that Turkey plays a balancing role between the United States/NATO, Russia, and the Europeans. But here, even if Ankara continues to veer toward authoritarianism and "illiberal democracy," there may still be ways to mitigate its authoritarian tendencies and reconcile Europe and Turkey. One way would be to negotiate a federated accord between Greek and Turkish Cypriots, guaranteed by Greece, Turkey, and the United Kingdom under UN auspices. A UN-brokered deal between Greek and Turkish Cyprus that could resolve property disputes and population displacement could then permit Cyprus to become the first major outlet of maritime trade outside the Suez Canal. And the European Investment Bank/European Bank for Reconstruction and other funds could help develop massive energy reserves in the eastern Mediterranean. If proportioned carefully and fairly, the vast reserves of the eastern Mediterranean could then benefit littoral states, including Greece, Turkey, Israel, Egypt, Palestine, Lebanon, and Syria.[31]

Such an accord could open up Turkey to tremendous trade opportunities with Greece and the European Union, while likewise more closely linking the European Union with NATO member Turkey, in order to limit Turkey from shifting too close to Moscow. Nevertheless, Turkey could still play a key role in bringing NATO, the European Union, and Russia into a closer confederated relationship.[32] After resolving the Cyprus issue, it might prove easier to resolve somewhat-similar disputes in the Caucasus, if not in Crimea as well. Once again, this appears plausible if, after Brexit, the European Union could forge differing membership criteria that would permit Turkey, Russia, and other states to enter the European Union in a new form of associate partnership. As previously argued, Associate Members of the European Union could possess limited voting rights on certain issues that would not be related to their size of population and would possess clearly defined responsibilities related to those issues.

COOPERATION IN THE GLOBAL WAR ON TERRORISM

Donald Trump has made US-European-Russian cooperation in the Global War on Terrorism one of the major themes of his presidency. This is a legitimate goal, if carried out appropriately, but one that has proved very difficult to implement, particularly given the rise of strong anti-Russian sentiment in the United States and the difficulties involved in finding ways for Russia and the United States to agree about what to do with the Assad regime in Syria. Despite the difficulties, a truly concerted approach involving Russia and the other major and regional powers is crucial for preventing the further spread of the Islamic State, al-Nusra, and other anti-state, partisan "terrorist" groups.

This approach seeks ways to put an end to what is essentially a proxy war between Saudi Arabia and Iran throughout the wider Middle East. What is needed is joint US-European-Russian cooperation to press for a cease-fire in Syria and Yemen and to eventually press Saudi Arabia and Iran into cooperation, thus putting an end to their proxy wars and the regional arms race.[33] These steps will require finding ways to balance conflicting domestic socio-political groups, while co-opting some Islamist parties and isolating or destroying others. The key dilemma will be finding an accord with Iran and Hezbollah. If it is given some encouragement and incentives by the European Union, among other incentives from the United States, as argued above, then Turkey could play a key role in helping to mediate between Saudi Arabia and Iran, as well as between Russia and the United States.

One option may be for Syrian leader Bashar al-Assad to take asylum in either Russia or Iran in order to permit the formation of a new Syrian governmental coalition backed by the United States, Europeans, and Russia. This is because most of the Syrian opposition has thus far refused to participate in peace talks that permit the Assad leadership a future role in the governance of the country. On the other hand, a resolution to the Syrian conflict that could result in a loose confederation, or else a possible partition, might mitigate the need for al-Assad to step down, as he would hold power in the Alawite regions along the coast.

Yet the only way Syria could be held together in a confederal arrangement would probably be if some form of joint Arab-Turkish or international peacekeeping force could be deployed under a general UN mandate. The dilemma is that Turkish forces have threatened to move into Syria to check the formation of separate Kurdish enclaves that could, Turkey fears, support Kurdish independence movements inside Turkey. This means the United States, Europeans, and Russia need to find some mutual accords between Syrian Kurds and Kurds in Turkey itself. In this view, Ankara and differing Kurdish movements in Syria, Turkey, and Iraq need to forge Kurdish autonomy agreements, with US, EU, and Russian backing.[34]

Here, instead of demanding full independence, which is nearly impossible to sustain in a highly interconnected world, and particularly as a landlocked society, Kurdish parties in Syria, Iran, and Turkey could opt for autonomy arrangements, much as the Kurds have achieved in Iraq after the 2003 US-led military intervention. Yet the regional situation will prove even more complicated and dangerous if Iraqi Kurds continue to demand independence from the Iraqi federal government due to disputes with Baghdad over the issues of autonomy and taxation in the aftermath of the nonbinding September 2017 referendum on the independence of Iraqi Kurdistan. Iraqi Kurd leader Marwan Barzani claimed victory for independence demands even before the ballots were counted, while Ankara and Baghdad threatened strong sanctions. Baghdad, backed by Iran, then began to seize Kirkuk and other oil-rich territories formerly controlled by the Kurds, potentially opening the door to a new regional conflict.[35] (See chapter 8.)

ISRAEL AND PALESTINE

Trump was furious when the Obama administration had refused to veto the UN Security Council's resolution that condemned Israeli settlements in the West Bank and East Jerusalem.[36] Obama's ambassador to the United Nations, Samantha Power, abstained from voting, on the basis that Israeli irredentist claims and plans to expand settlements in Palestinian territory could undermine any prospect of reaching a possible "two-state" solution to the ongoing conflict. At that time, a neophyte Trump supported not only expanding Israeli settlements but also Israeli claims to Jerusalem as the Israeli capital.

To obtain Jewish American votes, Trump, like many presidents before him, had suggested moving the US embassy to a new Israeli capital in Jerusalem. Trump has, however, appeared to back off on such a position after becoming president, just as he has on so many other questions. King Abdullah II of Jordan purportedly warned Trump that moving the embassy to Jerusalem could threaten the two-state solution, exacerbate the Israeli-Palestinian conflict, and augment recruits for the Islamic State.[37] At the same time, Jordan is concerned that the radicalization of the Palestinian movement might lead to secessionist or Islamist Palestinian movements inside Jordan, due to the large number of Palestinian refugees (more than two million) who have settled there. The president of the Palestinian Authority, Mahmoud Abbas, also warned Trump against supporting Israeli claims to all of Jerusalem.

And while Trump appears to have backtracked on his previous support for the renewed expansion of Israeli settlements in the West Bank, the Trump administration has not yet developed a full-fledged policy—except that it could be secretly pressing for a rapprochement between Saudi Arabia, the United Arab Emirates, Egypt, and Israel.[38] Trump has met with both Israeli Prime Minister Benjamin Netanyahu and President Mahmoud Abbas, the Palestinian leader of the West Bank, but it is still not clear what kind of accord can be achieved. To achieve peace, Trump will need to eventually press both sides into a settlement. Here, however, Trump may be pressing Israel and Saudi Arabia into a deal that would take Palestinian interests only into limited consideration in the effort to forge a united front against Iran. If so, such an unholy alliance could enrage many Islamist groups throughout the Arab/Islamic world.

Yet as an alternative strategy to achieve peace in the long term that would not rely primarily on Saudi Arabia, the United States could reach out to both Saudi Arabia and Qatar for diplomatic support and financing through bilateral and multilateral diplomacy, in an effort to press Israel to accept a modified Arab peace plan with further negotiations. This could open the door to greater Arab investment not only in Palestine (which would also expand Israeli markets) but also in Israel itself. The Arab Gulf states have agreed to set up telecommunication lines with Israel, open trade negotiations, and allow Israeli planes to fly over their airspace. In exchange, Israel would need to freeze settlement construction in the West Bank and relax trade restrictions with the Gaza Strip.[39]

The two-state solution is the Arab and the UN-sponsored approach.[40] There have been reports that the president of the Palestinian Authority, Mahmoud Abbas, might present a plan to the Israelis in which the Palestinians would give up 6.5 percent of their lands to Israel—three times as much as previously offered. The proposal would not include Jerusalem. In exchange, one option is for Israel to return to the Palestinians land equivalent to 5.8 percent of the West Bank, along with lands that would connect the West Bank to the Gaza Strip.[41]

The political dilemma is that Benjamin Netanyahu appears determined to implement a "one-state" solution with Saudi support. President Trump, after his meetings with the Israeli leader, publicly voiced the option of a one-state solution. While it appears feasible that Saudi Arabia, the United Arab Emirates, Egypt, Bahrain, and Jordan might support such an approach, it appears unlikely that the rest of the Arab world, Iran, and the divided Palestinians would acquiesce.

A third option is a confederal solution, but as a slight modification of the two-state concept. This is feasible given the fact that Fatah in the West Bank and Hamas in Gaza have largely separate leaderships and will need to forge power-sharing accords, perhaps like those in Northern Ireland. At the same time, Hamas has been trying to change its image in part due to its own mismanagement of Gaza. Israeli sanctions are not the only factor undermining the full development of the Gaza enclave. The fact that Hamas also opposes groups like the Islamic State also leads it to seek new backers. Concurrently, the rivalry between Saudi Arabia and Qatar impacts Hamas, but also represents a major issue over which Doha and Riyadh could find compromise, particularly if assisted by US and multilateral diplomacy. (See chapter 8.)

An Israeli-Palestinian peace settlement is not a panacea that will suddenly put an end to the Global War on Terrorism, and it will not put a sudden end to the conflicts that have been raging between Shi'a and Sunni, between Kurds and Turks, and among differing Sunni factions. But it would help bring the majority of "moderate" and undecided individuals and groups of Arab/Islamic background (plus others who may support Palestinian rights but not Islamist movements) closer to the positions of the United States, Europeans, and Russia. Concrete steps toward a full-fledged Israeli-Palestinian peace settlement would begin to socially and politically isolate those who continue support violent pan-Islamist movements.

Without concrete progress toward resolving the Israeli-Palestinian conflict, Trump will find it very difficult to forge a concerted approach to the Global War on Terrorism that involves both major and regional powers—including those states most impacted by differing Islamist movements. Trump's rhetoric has only tended to inflame the already-grave crisis.

THE IMPORTANCE OF THE IRAN NUCLEAR ACCORD

What is needed to resolve the crisis with Iran is a new regionally based diplomacy, backed by Washington, that brings Iran into differing multilateral discussions with Saudi Arabia, Turkey, Iraq, the Kurds, the Palestinians, and Israel, if possible, among other states in the region. Placing heavy political and economic sanctions and military pressures on Tehran in the effort to force it to stop developing its ballistic and cruise missile capabilities and to stop it from supporting Hamas, Hezbollah, and the Houthis in Yemen, as Trump has proposed in opposing the Iran nuclear accord or Joint Comprehensive Plan of Action (JCPOA), will not succeed without regional negotiations. Nor will such pressures help deal with the Kurdish independence question. In addition, the possibility that the United States, Saudi Arabia, and Israel will focus primarily on the Iranian "threat" will tend to sidetrack the Global Coalition against Daesh from fully focusing on efforts to destroy the Islamic State and al-Qaeda—while undermining the possibility of a nuclear accord with North Korea.

First, Iran, Turkey, and Iraq need to find ways to compromise with Iraqi Kurdish demands for independence through mediating the formation of loose confederal arrangements among Turkish, Iraqi, and Iranian Kurds, for example, but without engaging in a major alteration of borders. With respect to Iranian support for Hamas, Washington needs to encourage Israel, Saudi Arabia, Qatar, Iran, and other states, to settle their differences with respect to the Palestinian "two-state" solution and toward Hamas in particular. By the same token, the questions of Hezbollah and Houthis need to be addressed in the process of settling the ongoing wars in Syria and Yemen, by means of finding a domestic power-sharing settlement in Yemen, as proposed by the United Nations. (See chapter 8.) Evidently none of these proposals represent an easy process, but they can be dealt with only by diplomacy, not by force.

With respect to the Iranian nuclear issue, it is highly unlikely that Israel would give up its purported "existential" nuclear deterrent, as demanded by most Arab states and Iran. Turkey, Saudi Arabia, and Egypt have all threatened to develop a nuclear weapons capability—particularly if Iran acquires a nuclear weapons capability in addition to Israel. But given Israel's intransigence to even discuss its nuclear weapons capabilities, another possible option is to pursue an agreement involving a "no-first-use" of weapons of mass destruction (WMDs) for all states in the wider Middle East region. Such a "no-first-use" of WMDs accord would permit states in the region to engage in a new strategic dialogue that could eventually result in the control and reduction of conventional weaponry, including ballistic and cruise missiles. Washington could help initiate multilateral negotiations intended to limit missile capabilities through the Missile Technology Control Regime (MTCR), for example, while seeking compromise on a number of geopolitical disputes. And instead of seeking an Israeli-Saudi alliance against Iran, the United States should not drop out of the Iran nuclear accord; it should try to improve the JCPOA verification procedures and its implementation—but gradually, as confidence is restored over time.

A Trump administration and US congressional effort to suddenly try to renegotiate perceived weaknesses in the JCPOA nuclear accord will not succeed—as it will prove very difficult, if not impossible, to restore mutual confidence between the United States and Iran, whose revolutionary guards have threatened war if Washington labels them as a terrorist organization. (See chapter 8.) It is thus up to Washington to build upon the JCPOA, not by undermining that treaty, but by negotiating a new series of multilateral treaties. New multilateral treaties would seek to establish an agreement over the "no-first-use" of WMDs; the control and limitation of ballistic and cruise missile capabilities; joint development of alternative energies, such as solar and geothermal, in an effort to reduce Iran's demand for nuclear power; plus diplomatic agreements that seek to ameliorate regional rivalries (between Israel, Saudi Arabia, Turkey, Iraq, the Palestinians, the Kurds, and Iran, among other states and populations) that have resulted in horrific acts of state-supported and anti-state terrorism.

The JCPOA can significantly reduce the threat of further nuclear proliferation throughout the wider Middle East, but the treaty will only work in the long term if the United States, Israel, Saudi Arabia, and Iran can sustain full confidence. Trump's demands that the JCPOA Iran nuclear accord be renegotiated is doomed to failure and will only exacerbate the conflicts that are now confronting the wider Middle East and the world—and could lead other regional states to develop a nuclear deterrent, in addition to North Korea.

INDIA, PAKISTAN, AND KASHMIR

Areas of mutual US-Russian-Indian interest need to be explored for the development of joint policies: A Taliban victory in Afghanistan, for example, does not appear to be in Russian, Chinese, or US/NATO interests. This represents a major area in which these three sides could potentially find ways to cooperate. India could also engage more effectively in a Contact Group to help resolve disputes in Central and Southwest Asia, if not the Indo-Pacific as well. At the same time, however, Moscow has opened up talks with the Taliban in expectation of NATO withdrawal and an eventual Taliban victory. But India would most likely oppose recognition of the Taliban, given the latter's links to Pakistan. These issues need to be thoroughly discussed in a new Contact Group format.

The fact that India joined the Chinese-led Shanghai Cooperation Organization in 2017,[42] and that India has sought to speed up the signing of a free-trade agreement (FTA) with the Russian-led Eurasian Economic Union, which includes Belarus, Kazakhstan, Russia, Armenia, and Kyrgyzstan in 2017,[43] has raised questions as to whether India will move out of relative neutrality and move closer toward a Eurasian alliance—despite its ongoing disputes with Pakistan and China. Given the development of closer defense ties with the United States and Japan, how India's relations with both Russia and China will develop remains to be seen. (See chapter 7.)

Yet instead of siding with one alliance or the other, India could play a mediating and balancing role. But this will also require India-Pakistan reconciliation over Kashmir and other issues.[44] Here New Delhi has been reticent to engage in such discussions, whether mediated by the United States or more recently by China. As the situation in Kashmir appears to be getting worse,[45] one option is to propose joint Pakistani-Indian sovereignty agreements. But this will prove difficult to implement, given the rise of militant groups that seek total independence—as if total independence would be possible in today's highly interconnected world.

Could India shift toward Russia and China despite the apparent development of even closer Russian-Chinese ties to India's rival Pakistan and to the Taliban? Or could China, as it seeks to develop areas in Pakistani-controlled Kashmir and in Pakistan itself, mediate the Indo-Pakistan dispute over Kashmir, for example, as has been suggested by the Chinese media, but opposed by New Delhi? Or will India continue to tilt toward the United States, Europe, and Japan? Or could New Delhi eventually play a mediating role between the United States, Europeans, and Japan on the one hand, and China and Russia on the other?

TOWARD PEACE IN ASIA

In May 2016, Japanese Prime Minister Shinzo Abe advocated an eight-point plan for Vladivostok that was designed to ameliorate Russia-Japanese tensions. His goal was to "make Vladivostok a city that links Eurasia and the Pacific Ocean. . . . Let's diversify Russia's industry and make it more efficient. Let's turn the Russian Far East into an export base for the entire Asia-Pacific region."[46] As this action seemed to break US- and EU-led sanctions on Russia, it was purportedly opposed by President Obama.

These accords include a joint $1 billion Russian-Japanese investment fund between Russian Direct Investment Bank and Japan's Bank for International Cooperation; a special system for joint economic activity for

Kurile Islands/Northern Territories; and an easing of travel restrictions to the islands.[47] The ultimate goal is to achieve a peace treaty—but there was no accord signed that would resolve the territorial dispute. Nevertheless, Putin did admit, "that the absence of a peace treaty between Russia and Japan is, of course, an 'anachronism.'"[48]

To prevent the real possibility of conflict in the Indo-Pacific, particularly given the North Korean threat, Japanese efforts to seek out a rapprochement with Russia eventually need to be backed (at least tacitly) by the Trump administration with a focus on joint US-Russian-Japanese energy projects on Sakhalin island, among other bilateral Russian-Japanese accords. Given the fact that Tokyo took the first step in engaging in a rapprochement with Russia after the sanctions placed on Moscow in 2014 (after Russia's annexation of Crimea and political-military interference in eastern Ukraine), the first steps toward a US-Russian entente could possibly take place in Asia, and in particular by working cooperatively to resolve the North Korean nuclear crisis. (See chapter 7.) But steps toward a full US and Japanese rapprochement with Russia will prove very difficult without a political and legal settlement with respect to Ukraine and Crimea.

Concurrently, the United States, ASEAN states, Japan, Russia, and China will need to work out new joint development projects over disputed islands in the South China Sea and East China Sea. New multilateral agreements could involve joint naval patrols and combined task forces in combating terrorism, piracy, and trafficking of illicit materials (to North Korea, for example). Trump's offer, on his trip to Asia in November 2017, to negotiate island disputes in the South China Sea between China and its neighbors appears extremely positive—assuming Trump will actually provide the State Department with sufficient resources to do the job correctly.[49]

But the possibility of a concerted approach has thus far been undermined by the buildup of tensions with North Korea and the inability of the United States and China to coordinate strategy, while also involving Moscow. Here, Japanese and South Korean efforts to engage in positive relations with Moscow, through trade and investments in Russia, for example, are crucial to obtain Russian assistance in helping to settle the North Korean crisis. These steps in Asia could eventually open the door to much stronger US-EU-Russian relations in Europe—that is, if Trump does not also inadvertently destabilize relations with South Korea by renegotiating or terminating the US-South Korean free-trade agreement (KORUS FTA) because of a $17 billion US trade deficit with Seoul in 2016.[50] (See chapter 7.)

THE CRISIS OF NORTH KOREA

Finding a common policy among the United States, China, Russia, South Korea, and Japan toward North Korea is absolutely crucial to preventing war on the Korean Peninsula. (See chapter 7.) The United States, Russia, China, Japan, North Korea, and South Korea had already taken part in six-party talks from 2003 to 2009 in an effort to denuclearize North Korea. The problem now is how to reinitiate those Contact Group talks that had stalled in the aftermath of renewed nuclear and missile testing by North Korea, and in the aftermath of the US refusal in September 2005 to provide North Korea with light-water nuclear power plants as Pyongyang requested.[51]

Although North Korea and China are said to possess a closely interrelated relationship of "lips to teeth," Beijing does not support North Korea's nuclear provocations, as it would prefer to preserve its own nuclear hegemony over Pyongyang. In effect, Beijing would prefer the "denuclearization of the peninsula."[52] But this demand might not prove realistic. Beijing has thus far tried to take a balanced position between North Korea and the United States. Beijing fears that an effort to engage in a complete embargo on coal and food supplies or to engage in regime change, polices proposed by the United States, will eventually destabilize the country and thus undermine its sphere of security and influence against Japanese, South Korean, and American political-economic and military influence, while also undercutting Chinese economic interests within the country.

For its part, the United States is prepared to impose sanctions not only on North Korea but also on other countries where companies or individuals are known to have helped North Korea's military programs. This is in accord with UN Security Council Resolution 2270, which Beijing had supported in the UN Security Council, and which gives a mandate to all countries to search every ship and aircraft coming in or out of North Korea to make sure there are no illicit goods and to prevent nuclear proliferation.[53] The latter UN sanctions are important in that they impact the Strategic Rocket Force of the Korean People's Army and systems of illicit financing arranged by the Koryo Bank, in addition to sanctions placed on certain individuals. Both China and Russia did agree to consider even tougher UN sanctions, and they could possibly consider an oil embargo. But so far, sanctions do not seem to be stopping North Korea from testing its missiles.

Beijing signed the UN Security Council Resolution 2270 on sanctions, yet it does not believe sanctions alone are sufficient. China would thus prefer to press Pyongyang to freeze its missile and nuclear weapons programs in exchange for a halt to US-South Korean annual drills and freezing the deployment of missile defense systems—positions thus far opposed by Washington. China does not want war, nor does it want a destabilization of the Korean Peninsula, which could result in a massive refugee crisis. Nor does Beijing want a South Korean buyout of the North in which South Korea, backed by the United States, would dominate North Korea in a way similar to how West Germany, backed by the United States, bought out East Germany. At the same time, Beijing fears that a nuclear North Korea with effective delivery capabilities could provoke Japan and South Korea to obtain nuclear weaponry—as is being proposed by both Japanese and South Korean nationalist groups. Despite Chinese objections, Kim Jung Un appears determined to keep North Korea's nuclear weaponry as a deterrent against any rival, Japan, South Korea, the United States—and potentially China itself.

China's foreign minister, Wang Yi, has been worried that the region is faced with a "precarious situation" in which "one has the feeling that a conflict could break out at any moment. . . . If a war occurs, the result is a situation in which everybody loses and there can be no winner."[54] In addition to urging both North Korea and the United States to calm down, Wang Yi has also urged Moscow to play a diplomatic role as well. Both Beijing and Moscow hope to revive six-party talks over North Korea—if the Trump administration will agree.[55]

Yet the Trump position, as thus far formulated by Rex Tillerson, is that the United States would not negotiate with Pyongyang unless it first gave up both its nuclear and missile programs. This is a nonstarter, as North Korea has already declared itself to be a "nuclear state" much as NATO has declared itself to be a "nuclear alliance." President Trump and his Secretary of State Rex Tillerson have accordingly tried to put the onus on China to resolve the Korean issue through diplomatic pressure and economic sanctions. Here, Trump has hoped to attract China by offering a good trade deal if Beijing helps out with North Korea. At the same time, Trump has threatened to act alone militarily if Beijing does not put sufficient pressure on the North Korean regime to prevent it from expanding its nuclear and missile-delivery programs.[56] In this regard, South Korean government officials and the Pentagon have discussed the option of deploying US tactical nuclear weapons in South Korea to counter the North Korean nuclear threat—an option that could cause a dangerous counter-reaction by Pyongyang.[57]

As previously argued, Trump and Kim have entered into a personal radioactive pissing match without any end in sight. This was indicated by Trump's visit to South Korea in November 2017, during which Trump once again warned North Korea (but in less apocalyptic language) not to test the resolve of *his* administration, which he claimed was tougher than past US administrations. But for Trump, the only way for the United States to begin negotiations with North Korea is for Kim Jung Un to take the first step, by stopping the development of his nuclear missiles and by accepting a "complete, verifiable, and total denuclearization."[58]

Once again, it is dubious North Korea will accept Trump's formula. Nevertheless, from the perspective of China, and possibly for North Korea as well, the option of denuclearization could prove feasible, but only if the United States denuclearizes its own armed forces in the area or if the two sides can engage in step-by-step downsizing of their conventional and nuclear capabilities with international verification. Chinese Foreign Minister Wang Yi has accordingly called for the denuclearization of the entire peninsula and for an end to US-South Korea military exercises: "The use of force does not solve differences and will only lead to bigger disasters. . . . [China should not be] a focal point of the problem on the peninsula. . . . The key to solving the nuclear issue on the peninsula does not lie in the hands of the Chinese."[59]

While Beijing has wanted Washington to engage in quiet talks with Pyongyang, Rex Tillerson has replied that it was up to North Korea to take the first concrete steps, not Washington: "We will not negotiate our way back to the negotiating table. . . . We will not reward their bad behavior with talks."[60] As Tillerson indicated on Trump's tour of the Asia-Pacific in November 2017, the United States has accordingly been reluctant to initiate talks with Pyongyang—as it has not wanted to be seen as caving to North Korea, which could reinitiate nuclear weapons and missile tests unexpectedly, even if peace talks were announced. Tillerson had previously affirmed that the United States is not seeking "regime change" in North Korea, even though it is not absolutely certain that Trump is in full agreement.[61] (See chapter 7.) In his November 2017 trip to Asia, Tillerson then argued that he could envision the possibility that the United States and North Korea could agree to hold talks at some point, but only as a precursor to formal negotiations. Tillerson stated that he would seek a signal from Kim Jong Un himself indicating that he would like to have some type of a meeting, communicating through one of the two or three communication channels that the United States possesses with North Korea. But Tillerson also forewarned that the United States would continue to threaten North Korea as long as Kim did not give up his nuclear weapons program.[62]

US policy is faced with a real conundrum. On the one hand, Washington wants to halt North Korea's nuclear and missile program while also "containing" the ambitions of both China and Russia. On the other hand, Washington also wants Russia to resolve its dispute with Ukraine on Washington's terms and argues that China should be the prime agent in resolving the dispute with North Korea. This evidently makes positive support from both Moscow and Beijing difficult to obtain. Nevertheless, China appears to possess greater incentive to act in the North Korea case because it feels more threatened by a potential war on the Korean Peninsula than Moscow feels threatened by a potentially wider war over Ukraine that could encompass the Black Sea and eastern European regions.

Another dilemma is that the Trump-Pence administration needs to figure out how to demonstrate a minimum show of American force as a deterrent in support of South Korea and Japan, while also engaging in an informal dialogue with Pyongyang—an option that has been urged by Beijing for the last couple of years, but had been refused by the Obama administration, and thus far by the Trump administration. Without real dialogue with Pyongyang, the Trump administration could fail to prevent a nuclear war. Such an initial dialogue, which need not be interpreted as capitulation, could then help strengthen the Chinese position and permit Beijing apply more pressure, including tighter sanctions, on North Korea, if necessary.[63] The problem remains: How much should Washington rely on Beijing to do the negotiating? And how much of the negotiating with Pyongyang should be led by Washington? Beijing has purportedly told Washington that it had informed North Korea "that if they did conduct further nuclear tests, China would be taking sanctions actions on their own."[64] And in November 2017, Chinese President Xi Jinping did say he was unequivocally against North Korea sustaining a nuclear capability.[65]

At some point in the near future, the United States should begin to offer Pyongyang some practical proposals through quiet diplomacy.[66] Washington should promise to normalize US-North Korean relations and no longer threaten preemptive strikes against Pyongyang's nuclear program, if North Korea would agree to a "nuclear freeze," rejoin the Non-Proliferation Treaty, and permit comprehensive inspections by the International Atomic Energy Agency (IAEA), along the lines of Iran JCPOA nuclear accord. (See chapter 8.) Hopefully, North Korea could then promise to eventually eliminate all of its nuclear weapons, but most likely only in exchange for firm joint security guarantees from the six powers. A step-by-step process of gradual demilitarization by both the North and South Koreans, in which both sides would then begin to withdraw their forces from the Demilitarized Zone, could then be matched by a step-by-step withdrawal of US forces and elimination of economic sanctions on North Korea. The United States would be prepared to return to the assistance of South Korea if necessary but would work with all the permanent members of the UN Security Council to provide joint security assurances for North Korea. This would ensure that North Korea remains a "buffer" between China and South Korea and that South Korea (whose economy is fifty times the size of North Korea's) would not buy up the North as West Germany bought up East Germany. Both North and South Korea could then enter into a very loose confederation until other political arrangements could be made. In the meantime, the United States, South Korea, China, Japan, and Russia would fund North Korean energy needs and development, while seeking ways to decommission North Korea's heavy investments in the military (Pyongyang may spend as much as 22 percent of its GDP on the military, at the expense of the population[67]) and convert its economy to more useful and productive consumer activities. Hopefully this approach will prove feasible, as even a very limited and inspected North Korea nuclear deterrent, as perhaps demanded by Pyongyang, appears unacceptable to Washington, Seoul, Tokyo, and Beijing.

Trump could eventually propose something like this in meeting with Kim Jung Un. The realist side of Trump has stated that he would be "honored," to meet directly with Kim Jung Un, but "under the right circumstances." Yet Trump also stated: "There is a chance that we could end up having a major, major conflict with North Korea. Absolutely, We'd love to solve things diplomatically but it's very difficult."[68]

The United States needs to take a less self-righteousness approach and engage in a real and intensive dialogue—which is the only way to end the impasse and prevent the real risks of either a collapse of the North Korean regime or a possible regional war. It seems informal US-North Korean dialogue leading to a direct meeting between Trump and Kim Jung Un could begin to provide North Korea with the international respect and attention that it has been craving in the aftermath of the 1950–1953 Korean War, in which the United States devastated the country with conventional bombs and Napalm while threatening the use of nuclear weaponry.[69] International aid and assistance could then help to develop the country in exchange for step-by-step demilitarization and informal accords between North and South Korea. North Korea would then be backed by mutual security assurances by the United States, Russia, China, France, and the United Kingdom (as outlined above).

The question remains, Will Trump eventually meet with the North Korean leader in direct bilateral diplomacy if North Korea does eventually agree to a freeze on its nuclear and missile tests? Could this result in US capitulation to North Korean demands? Or could it result in a mutual compromise, which could then prevent the real possibilities of a more general conflagration? No one has yet accused Trump of seeking business deals with North Korea or seeking to construct a Trump Tower in the midst of Pyongyang, but would anyone really complain if he is able to make peace with Kim Jung Un by way of eliminating North Korea's nuclear threat? But can he eliminate that threat without provoking war?

Chapter 10
DEFUSING THE GLOBAL CRISIS

Trump's proposed military buildup and American First nationalism appear intended to press from a position of strength Moscow, China, Iran, Syria, and North Korea, among other countries, into a settlement of a number of disputes. But is Peace through Strength to be achieved on American terms, in accord with a posture of power-based bargaining? Or will such power-based bargaining bring about mutual compromise? Will one side or the other capitulate? Or will major power war be the consequence?

Former Soviet President Mikhail Gorbachev has warned that "no problem is more urgent today than the militarization of politics and the new arms race. Stopping and reversing this ruinous race must be our top priority."[1] Gorbachev has proposed "that a Security Council meeting at the level of heads of state adopt a resolution stating that nuclear war is unacceptable and must never be fought. I think the initiative to adopt such a resolution should come from Donald Trump and Vladimir Putin—the Presidents of two nations that hold over 90 percent of the world's nuclear arsenals and therefore bear a special responsibility."

TOWARD NUCLEAR AND CONVENTIONAL ARMS REDUCTIONS/ELIMINATIONS

Because the United States and Russia have entered into a new nuclear and conventional arms race since at least 2002–2008, the dilemma is that the more the Ukrainian crisis blocks Russia from cooperating fully with the

United States and the European Union, the more it will prove difficult to cooperate on other issues of common concern, including the need to reduce arms expenditures, concentrate on social and environmental concerns, and deal with the dangerous crisis unfolding on the Korean Peninsula. (See chapters 5 and 9.)

Nevertheless, as soon as is politically possible, in addition to the need for further discussions on reductions of long-range ballistic missiles going beyond New START (Strategic Arms Reduction Treaty), which was implemented in 2011 and which is hoped to last at least until 2021, there should be full-fledged discussions to reduce, if not eliminate, all tactical nuclear weaponry as soon as politically possible. These arms reduction/elimination talks could take place in the aftermath of a US-Russia summit.

On the one hand, Moscow has been enhancing its A2/AD (Anti-Access/Area Denial) tactics in Kaliningrad by deploying S-400 air defense missiles and tactical, nuclear-capable, Iskander surface-to-surface missiles, plus shore-based cruise missiles, so as to block NATO from potentially resupplying the Baltic states in case of war. Russia has developed a new Satan missile, while Washington has accused Moscow of violating the 1987 Intermediate-Range Nuclear Forces Treaty (INF Treaty) by testing a new intermediate-range missile, which, if true, could set US/NATO-Russian relations back to the 1980s, when NATO opted to counter Soviet intermediate-range SS-20s with the deployment of cruise and Pershing missiles before the 1987 INF accord was signed.

For its part, the Pentagon has been modernizing the B61-12 tactical nuclear weapon and extending its rage, even when the utility of such weaponry has been questioned, and when its deployment could be considered in violation of nuclear non-proliferation treaty.[2] The United States has also been modernizing its launch capabilities for missiles with both conventional and nuclear warheads, such as the Ground-Based Strategic Deterrent and the Long-Range Standoff Cruise Missile. In addition to deployments in Guam, the United Arab Emirates, Turkey, and South Korea, and possibly Japan, the Pentagon has been considering deploying

THAAD missile defense systems and penetrating radar in Europe and Saudi Arabia.

A first step would be to take the roughly two thousand US and Russian warheads off "high-alert" status. Both Moscow and Beijing, in a sign of strategic-nuclear insecurity, have put a large number of their nuclear missiles on hair-trigger alert in order to maintain the survivability of their nuclear weapons against superior US delivery nuclear systems.[3] So as to reduce tensions, Washington and Moscow could furthermore agree to a mutual "no-first-use" of nuclear weapons. These steps could be strengthened if Washington considers eliminating land-based elements of the nuclear triad so as to reduce some pressure on Moscow to feel that it must launch its missiles "on warning." This approach needs to be taken, but without undermining a strong US air- and sea-based deterrent that should remain in the background. Similar confidence measures will prove necessary with Beijing, which opposes the deployment of THAAD defense systems in South Korea and potentially Japan. Both China and Russia fear that the United States can use its missile defense (MD) systems and advanced missiles to launch a preemptive strike.

A thorough US-Russian discussion of tactical and intercontinental nuclear systems could be accompanied by potential compromises on the deployment of US missile defense systems in Europe. The United States could agree to removing all provocative forward-deployed tactical nuclear weapons from Europe, such as the B61-12, in exchange for significant reductions in Russian nuclear weaponry, while also reducing conventional capabilities on both sides. This approach would likewise mean bargaining within NATO—as NATO's consensus-based decision-making process means that small powers most interested in keeping nuclear weapons in Europe, such as the Baltic states, can oppose a decision to remove those weapons.[4]

With respect to MD, the fact that Washington had initially justified MD deployments in eastern Europe based on the fear that Iran would eventually obtain a nuclear weapons and long-range missile capability should open the door to discussions in the aftermath of the Joint Comprehensive Plan of Action (JCPOA) nuclear deal with Iran. (See chapters 8 and 9.) To reach a compromise, the United States and Russia should revisit some of the previous proposals for joint missile defense systems that were proposed before UN-backed Contact Group negotiations pressed Iran to give up on its nuclear program.[5]

There has been almost no strategic nuclear confidence between Washington and Moscow since the United States unilaterally dropped out of the Anti-Ballistic Missile Treaty (ABM Treaty) in 2002 without seeking a substitute treaty on missile defenses with Moscow. Here, the Bush Jr. administration argued that the spread of nuclear missiles made the treaty obsolete but did not discuss the matter with Moscow to see if the treaty could be revised in a new format. This is the major strategic issue that helped set off the new arms race, and it will still take some time to build up trust. And Moscow will not give up unilaterally or even compromise without very tough power-based bargaining. Nevertheless, these proposals are not impossible to implement.

FULLY ABIDING BY THE NUCLEAR NON-PROLIFERATION TREATY

Gorbachev's point that Presidents Vladimir Putin and Donald Trump need to take the first steps toward banning nuclear warfare is well taken, but neither Trump nor Putin appear ready to move in this direction, given mutual imprecations between the United States and Russia, American accusations of Russian meddling and use of cyber-espionage in the US election process, and Russian counteraccusations of US meddling in Russian affairs, among the many other reasons discussed in this book. (See chapters 3 and 9.) The dilemma is that US-Russian mutual imprecations only serve to enhance the power and influence of the US military-industrial-congressional complex and its Russian equivalent, Siloviki—Putin's prime supporters—as they both seek to build more and more powerful weapons in a very unbalanced game of terror.

Nevertheless, this fact should not prevent the world's populations and legislatures from pressing Washington, Moscow, Beijing, France, and the United Kingdom, among the other declared and non-declared nuclear powers, to work toward the reduction, if not the elimination, of nuclear weaponry—as is, in fact, demanded of nuclear-weapons states by Article VI of the Nuclear Non-Proliferation Treaty (NPT).[6] And if the nuclear arms races continues unabated, then Congress should pass an act that would require a congressional declaration of war for the president to authorize a nuclear first strike or else declare that the United States will never use nuclear weapons first.[7] If domestic pressures on governments can achieve global peace, then such steps could ultimately lead to the reconversion of the military-industrial complexes of all countries toward the development of alternative technologies for peaceful social and ecological purposes.

TOWARD DUAL SOVEREIGNTY ARRANGEMENTS

But the problem here is that even if state legislatures and populations do insist that their leaderships take the concrete steps to end the nuclear arms race and to settle international disputes, the devil is still in the details. A general political settlement with Russia, China, Iran, and other states will not be achieved by slogans calling for INSTANT PEACE, but only by a concerted US-European-Japanese strategy that possesses concrete proposals as to how negotiate arms reductions and eliminations—and that, in turn, could result in the withering away of the military-industrial complexes of the United States, Russia, China, and Europe. These proposals need to be coupled with complex negotiations in multilateral Contact Groups that deal with territorial and political-economic disputes as well. Given China's rejection of the Permanent Court of Arbitration ruling in favor of the Philippines in July 2016 (see chapter 7) over island disputes in the South China Sea, Beijing's promise in November 2017 to abide by the nonbinding 2002 Code of Conduct that seeks to peacefully regulate island disputes and prevent conflict represents a tiny step forward toward the possibility of peace in the region.[8]

One concrete proposal to augment the possibility of peace would be to implement an international legal agreement that would work to settle a number of territorial disputes. In some cases, this could be accomplished by either finding ways to establish zones that would be governed by an international administration or through a resurrection of the United Nations' trusteeship administration. Or states could find ways to implement systems of joint sovereignty and power-sharing or free-trade accords that provide certain regions greater autonomy, combined with agreements involving the mutual renunciation of the use of force. What is needed is an international legal agreement that would either establish internationally administered zones or else joint sovereignty agreements over specific territories.[9]

Some of these proposed accords could use a potential Cypriot settlement brokered by the United Nations as a model, in addition to the power-sharing accords that were reached in the 1998 Belfast agreement of Northern Ireland, for example. The approach could seek out free-trade accords or even joint sovereignty and power-sharing agreements, combined with the agreements involving the mutual renunciation of the use of force, for Crimea between Ukraine and Russia; Kaliningrad between Germany and Russia; the Kurile Islands/Northern Territories between Japan and Russia; Senkaku/Diaoyu Islands between China, Taiwan, and Japan; the differing islands in the South China Sea; the islands Abu Musa, Greater Tunb, and Lesser Tunb between the United Arab Emirates and Iran; Gibraltar between Spain and the United Kingdom; and the Falklands Islands between Argentina and the United Kingdom. Such power-sharing accords could also apply to India and Pakistan over Kashmir. These accords could also apply to islands in the French empire or those in the American empire, including Guam, Diego Garcia, American Samoa, and other islands in the western Pacific, along with Puerto Rico and the Virgin Islands in the Caribbean, plus Guantánamo Bay.

In some cases, such accords could also serve to crack down on the island tax havens of the super-wealthy, as was revealed in the Paradise Papers in November 2017,[10] at the same time that a global Tobin tax could be implemented on international financial transactions, among other possible items. In the United States, such a tax could possibly generate as much as $190 billion a year (or 1 percent of GDP). A Tobin tax could additionally help stabilize global financial transactions, but it needs to be accepted by a vast majority of countries, which will then need to close financial paradises.

The funds raised from a global tax base would be invested with strict international regulations and controls as to how and where such funds are to be distributed, with priorities given to assist the development of the poorest regions of the planet. On average—and taking into account population size—income inequality increased by 11 percent in developing countries between 1990 and 2010. A significant majority of households in developing countries—more than 75 percent of the population—are living today in societies where income is more unequally distributed than it was in the 1990s.[11]

The Tobin tax, which had been proposed as a means to assist the underdeveloped world, had been rejected at the 2011 G20 summit. One of the reasons for its rejection was due to already-high taxation in a number of countries. So, to be made more politically acceptable, such a Tobin tax proposal would need to be accompanied by reductions in national taxation, so that international taxation would be given priority in the new era of globalization.[12] The concept of an international Tobin tax should not entirely be an anathema to Trump. One pro-Trump proposal is a tax based on profits made by US overseas corporations as a means to support infrastructure development in the United States itself.[13] Other options could include higher personal income taxes for CEOs—

but Trump would dubiously support such an option. Nevertheless, if it can be shown that certain regions and urban areas in the United States are highly impoverished, there is no reason why a percentage of international tax revenues for regional development and infrastructure could not go to the United States or to other developed countries as well. The political question, of course, is precisely what kind of development and infrastructure assistance would prove most beneficial. (See discussion, this chapter.)

CONTACT GROUP DIPLOMACY

As argued in chapter 9, a grand compromise between the United States, Europeans, and Russia that would seek to draw Russia into a new relationship with NATO and the European Union—by means of establishing a regional system of peace and development for the entire Black Sea and Caucasus region—should be in the interests of all parties. But such a proposal, to be implemented under the auspices of the OSCE (Organization for Security and Co-operation in Europe) or the United Nations, will work only if it is given a real testing by truly engaged diplomacy in which US, EU, Russian, and Ukrainian vital interests are eventually redefined and reconciled.

This is an argument not for global government, but for interacting global, regional, national, and local governance. It is an argument for greater multilateral cooperation within and among states through multilateral accords and through differing international organizations. During his election campaign, Trump stopped short of threatening to leave the United Nations, but he nevertheless denounced the international regime as "just a club for people to get together, talk and have a good time."[14] He asserted that it was an organization that possessed "enormous potential" but did not always live up to its potential, thus wasting time and money. In Trump's view, the United Nations did not always solve problems, but "caused them."

The Trump-Pence administration will probably not leave the United

Nations altogether, but it has already begun to seek ways to cut US funding for a number UN programs, and it has dropped out of UNESCO, which oversees World Heritage Sites, in October 2017 due to mounting arrears and a purportedly "anti-Israeli bias."[15] While international organizations such as the United Nations and the OSCE are far from perfect, they nevertheless provide a forum for dialogue between the United States, Europeans, Russia, China, other states, and non-state actors, when relations between states and peoples are strained. And it is clear that the United Nations is caught up in concepts of bureaucratic hierarchy and cannot implement a new UN Security Council that takes into account the rise of new powers such as India, Brazil, South Africa, and Japan since the end of World War II. The United Nations generally works only when the UN Security Council wants it to work. And UN operations and peacekeeping, for example, can be very complicated if officers on the ground are not given strong political support and assistance for what is needed to accomplish their task.

Nevertheless, UN or OSCE backing for more flexible multilateral Contact Groups can effectively deal with many key issues. One major example is the group of states that negotiated the Iran Joint Comprehensive Plan of Action (JCPOA) nuclear accord that was negotiated by the five UN Security Council members, plus Germany and later the EU. Another is the six-party talks dealing with North Korea's nuclear program, which are negotiated by the United States, China, Russia, Japan, and North and South Korea. Another is the Minsk accords, negotiated by Germany, France, Ukraine, and Russia; but that will eventually need US and Turkish participation, as argued in chapter 9.

The Contact Group formula has proved to be a very effective way to get around UN bureaucratic hierarchy and engage the key state actors involved in the pursuit of peace. The process, even if it may take years to reach a solid accord, helps create international legitimacy for the decisions reached, which should make those accords easier to implement—even if this is not proving the case with Trump's critique of the JCPOA Iran nuclear accord.

TRUMP'S POLICIES TOWARD PEACEKEEPING AND CLIMATE CHANGE

Of concern are Trump's negative attitudes toward UN Peacekeeping and climate change. The United Nations and the OSCE are absolutely essential in order to engage in peacekeeping operations. The deployment of peacekeepers for the protection of refugees and immigrants under UN or OSCE mandates or other international organizations may soon be needed in Syria, eastern Ukraine, the Caucasus, and between Israel and a new Palestine, as well as in other regions, such as the Sudan, the Congo, and possibly North Korea, among many others. This will prove a major endeavor, but it can be compared to the expansion of UN (and NATO) peacekeeping missions at the end of the Cold War.

The Trump-Pence administration plans to cut costs or limit the role of the UN peacekeeping operations represents a major error on the part of the new administration. These proposed cuts (in which the Trump administration was able to cut $500 million, but not $1 billion as it intended, for 2017) are not necessarily in US interests, as UN operations can serve US interests by providing a political buffer between US policy and the differing political and social interests that are in dispute. In short, these international regimes help provide legitimacy for multilateral actions to achieve peace and development. This helps the United States and other countries not to get dragged unilaterally into intractable conflicts. And the burden can be shared to a larger extent.

THE UNITED NATIONS AND PEACEKEEPING

According to the United Nations, the approved budget for UN Peacekeeping operations for the fiscal year July 1, 2016–June 30, 2017, is $7.87 billion. This amount finances fourteen of the sixteen United Nations Peacekeeping missions.[16] By way of comparison, the UN Peacekeeping budget is way below the nominal US defense budget of $639 billion (which, in reality, is probably double that amount—see chapter 2). The United States pays almost three times more than the amount China now pays for UN Peacekeeping operations. It is true that these relative dues could perhaps be better assessed given China's significant sovereign funds. Nevertheless, investing in UN and OSCE peacekeeping could save billions in defense expenditure—if accompanied by effective multinational diplomacy intended to bring lasting resolutions to conflict, or at least working to better manage those conflicts.

For example, UN Peacekeeping proved absolutely necessary for the Democratic Republic of Congo, which became for the focal point for war between major and regional powers in the period between 1994 and 2003.[17] What was once called World War III in Africa, and which resulted in the loss of some five million lives, was sparked, in part, by the genocide that took place in Rwanda, when some two million Hutus fled into the Democratic Republic of Congo. The horrific conflict that ensued eventually drew the Congo, Rwanda, Zimbabwe, Namibia, and Angola into a proxy war.

The issue raised here is that the Trump-Pence administration suspended legislation that was intended to require transparency in the supply chain for "conflict minerals"[18] in April 2017. The Securities and Exchange Commission (SEC) had implemented the Conflict Mineral Rule of 2010 so that companies and consumers knew that they were not contributing to illegal activities in purchasing "conflict minerals" either from the Democratic Republic of the Congo (DRC) or from those countries adjoining the DRC. The minerals found in this region (worth an estimated $24 trillion) include diamonds, gold, copper, cobalt, and zinc, plus tin, tungsten, and tantalum (the 3TGs). The regions also possess coltan, which is used in mobile phones and other electronic gadgets, as well as cassiterite, used in food packaging. The countries involved include Angola, Burundi, the Central African Republic, the Republic of the Congo, Rwanda, South Sudan, Tanzania, Uganda, and Zambia.[19]

Yet under the Trump-Pence administration, the SEC has ruled that it will no longer enforce key parts of the Conflict Mineral Rule. US corporations will no longer be required to conduct a diligence review or an audit regarding sourcing of conflict minerals.[20] In addition to the change in SEC rules—which could set the grounds for renewed conflict over conflict minerals—the Trump-Pence administration is also hoping to reduce the US contribution to UN Peacekeeping—even if renewed conflicts could ultimately hurt both US political and economic interests and actually make it harder for US businesses to invest. The UN Organization Stabilization Mission in DRC (MONUSCO) is the world's largest UN Peacekeeping operation, with about 18,750 uniformed personnel.[21]

In effect, the Trump-Pence administration efforts in late March 2017 to cut the MONUSCO Peacekeeping operation down to only three thousand personnel could open the Congo to new conflicts and exploitation by rival mining industries and additionally exacerbate tensions in other countries in Africa. It was MONUSCO that had fought the M23 rebel group, the largest rebel force in the Congo. The Congolese government itself has spoken out against the potential reversal of this rule.[22] UN Peacekeepers are still necessary, as the conflict is not altogether resolved, particularly in the eastern areas of Congo, where some forty to fifty conflicting rebel groups have been financed by extracting resources with the backing of external states and major corporations. It is true that MONUSCO and other UN Peacekeepers have been accused of sexual abuses, due to improper vetting of individuals involved in the peacekeeping operations. UN Peacekeeping operations have also been accused ineffectiveness; yet such ineffectiveness can be attributed to lack of resources and lack of clear political mandates, plus the need to more carefully vet the political purposes of the countries involved and the need to work more closely with the local population.[23] UN Peacekeeping is run on a shoestring budget: UN Peacekeeping has had its successes and failures, but it is not necessarily worse than NATO or EU peacekeeping, which often interact with the United Nations and have had different kinds of weaknesses.[24]

This rivalry in Africa to obtain access strategic minerals in the Congo region that are needed for the new global communications economy, and for other purposes, could well forewarn of an even more perverse global conflict ahead—one that could use nuclear weaponry if the major and regional powers cannot soon reach accords on the differences that divide them in their own quest for energy and other strategic resources across the planet.

Trump and Global Warming

In addition to his efforts to cut UN Peacekeeping costs, Trump has called global climate change a "hoax" created by and for the Chinese to undercut American business.[25] One of Trump's first acts as president was to sign decrees to cut the funding of the following US governmental agencies: the Environmental and Natural Resources Division of the Department of Justice; the UN Intergovernmental Panel on Climate Change; the Office of Energy Efficiency and Renewable Energy; and the Office of Fossil Energy. In his first G7 meeting on the subject at the end of May 2017, Trump opposed the views of the six major industrial democracies: Germany, France, Italy, Canada, the United Kingdom, and Japan. Of positive note, Trump did agree to "promote multilateralism" in the G7 communique.[26] On the negative side, Trump appeared more concerned with the German trade surplus than with global climate change. A few days later, Trump dropped out of the Paris COP 21 Accords on global environmental issues. Ironically, he claimed that he made his decision against the Paris COP 21 because he was elected by the people of Pittsburgh (which is in the heart of the coal mining and steel industry region of Pennsylvania) and "not by Paris"; yet the mayor of Pittsburgh then tweeted: "Pittsburgh stands with the world & will follow [the] Paris Agreement."[27] Fortunately, American states and cities have declared that they will actively support the goals of the Paris Agreement; for example, in July 2017, the California legislature stated its plans to extend its COP 21 commitments to 2030.[28]

The risk here is that a lack of US support for the COP21 will tend to undermine global cooperation in the struggle against global climate change and carbon pollution in general, which is choking urban areas throughout the world and poisoning the environment. Although not perfect, the COP21 represents an important environmental accord reached in Paris, in which the two major polluters of the planet, the United States and China, finally reached an agreement that brings together most of the countries in the world into cooperation. The Paris environmental accord needs complete interstate and interregional cooperation and implementation if it is to succeed.

Trump appears to have based his decision to drop out of the Paris COP 21 Accords, at least in part, on reports by the right-wing Heritage Foundation and NERA Consulting. The Heritage Foundation report presented a negative assessment of the impact of those accords on American society. According to the report, the Paris COP 21 accord will supposedly result in: (1) An overall average shortfall of nearly 400,000 jobs; (2) An average manufacturing shortfall of over 200,000 jobs; (3) A total income loss of more than $20,000 for a family of four; (4) An aggregate gross domestic product (GDP) loss of over $2.5 trillion; and (5) Increases in household electricity expenditures between 13 percent and 20 percent. The NERA Consulting report argued that "meeting the Obama administration's requirements in the Paris Accord would cost the U.S. economy nearly $3 trillion over the next several decades. So that by 2040, our economy would lose 6.5 million industrial sector jobs—including 3.1 million manufacturing sector jobs."[29] Yet these studies make worst-case assumptions that tend to inflate the cost of meeting US targets under the Paris Accord while largely ignoring the economic benefits to US businesses from building and operating renewable energy projects.[30]

By contrast with the Heritage Foundation and NERA Consulting reports, a number of major multinational corporations strongly support investment in alternative energy. More than 360 major American corporations—including DuPont, General Mills, Levi Strauss, Nike, and

Starbucks—have supported the Paris accord. These major corporations signed a statement called "Business Supports a Low Carbon USA," which urged President Trump to honor the US commitments to the COP 21. These major companies declared that "failure to build a low-carbon economy puts American prosperity at risk," and that the "right action now will create jobs and boost US competitiveness."[31] One pro–alternative energy study by the International Renewable Energy Agency argued that renewable energy could generate over 24 million jobs worldwide by 2030. And that if environmental and human health externalities are priced into the global energy mix over time, the renewable energy transition would result in net savings.[32]

Once president, Trump moved immediately in an antediluvian pro–fossil fuels direction by issuing five executive orders that would start the process of developing the Keystone and Dakota Access Pipelines, which had been blocked by environmentalists and the Obama administration. Trump likewise signed executive actions intended to facilitate the process of obtaining permits for manufacturing projects and to speed environmental reviews for infrastructure projects, while removing a moratorium on coal-mining leases on federal lands. He also began to undermine a number of Obama-era efforts to prevent coal-mining debris from being dumped into nearby waters.[33] It should not be surprising that the coal industry has been one of the major contributors to the Republican Party over many years. And in 2016, Trump and other politicians in the Republican Party received 97 percent out of a total of $13,461,828 of coal-mining contributions to the election campaign.[34]

Yet Trump's own economic adviser, Gary Cohn, has downplayed coal and argued that the United States could export natural gas as "a cleaner fuel" and by investing in wind and solar energy. Cohn was quoted as saying that the country "can be a manufacturing powerhouse and still be environmentally friendly."[35] And both Trump's daughter Ivanka Trump and her husband, Jared Kushner, were said to have pressed Trump to support the COP 21.[36] Coal mining accounts for less than 75,000 US jobs.[37] Fossil fuel generation employment accounts for only 22 percent of total electric power generation employment and supports 187,117 workers across coal, oil, and natural gas generation technologies.

As promised during his campaign, Trump hopes to create a mere 28,000 to 29,000 jobs in the process of producing up to $36 billion annually in increased energy production.[38] Yet the sustainable energy sector already employs far more than the coal or oil or gas industries. Renewable energy—including wind, solar, and biofuels—accounts for more than 650,000 US jobs. Roughly 2.2 million Americans are employed, full- or part-time, in the area of energy efficiency products and services, while almost 1.4 million energy efficiency jobs are in the construction industry. Sustainable energies currently support hundreds of thousands of manufacturing and construction jobs around the country: Wind energy employs 101,738. Solar energy employed 300,192 American jobs in 2015 and grew to 373,807 in 2016, or 43 percent of the electric power generation workforce—more than the fossil fuel and nuclear energy industries. Employment in the US solar industry "grew 12 times as fast as overall job creation in the US economy, and surpassed those in oil and gas extraction (187,200) or coal mining (67,929)."[39] The US Department of Energy has stated that three million Americans worked in the clean energy sector in 2016—a number that would be threatened by a Paris pullout.[40]

There are weaknesses to the COP 21, but Trump is not concerned with them. One of the weaknesses of the COP 21 is not at all the costs of the accord that Trump points out. One problem is that the COP 21 emissions targets are not legally binding and thus there is no guarantee that all countries will be able to curb carbon dioxide emissions soon enough to prevent significant environmental damage. The next concern with the Paris COP 21 Accord is that the agreement does not directly oppose subsidies for fossil fuel industries—even if that is the heart of the problem of global climate change.

For his part, Trump has opposed international governmental subsidies for the COP 21 agreement, which would mount to $100 billion for the developed countries by 2020.[41] Yet, conversely, Trump does not appear to be opposed to fossil fuel subsidies to major energy companies. These latter subsidies, which are intended to lower the price of oil, coal, and gas, cost world governments around US$500–$600 billion per year.[42] Of this amount, the twenty major economic powers (the G20) were responsible for the majority of the subsidies—averaging $444 billion in 2013 and 2014. Russia, the United States, Australia, Brazil, China, and the United Kingdom all had significant national subsidies for fossil fuel production. The United Kingdom has been one of the few G20 countries that has been augmenting its fossil fuel subsidies while cutting back on support for the renewable energy investments.[43] How UK environmental policy might develop after Brexit remains to be seen. South Korea and Germany, and then the United States, Russia, and France, possessed the next largest sources of funding for coal. On the positive side, Japan, South Korea, and Australia have been leading the effort to try to mandate limits on coal subsidies in international discussions.[44]

The problem is that these G20 subsidies enforce the general trend toward high-carbon energy development and thus divert investments away from low-carbon energy alternatives, such as solar power, wind power, and hydropower, among others. President Barack Obama did demand that Congress try to eliminate fossil fuel industry subsidies, but to no avail. If the United States and other major countries do not lead, it is dubious the rest of world will act—except, perhaps, for France and China (the latter, because its major cities are literally choking in coal dust and pollution).[45]

With Trump and pro–fossil fuel Cabinet members in power, ExxonMobil (and other energy companies) could stand to gain as much as $1 trillion overall if the Trump administration does continue to eliminate federal environmental restrictions while also undercutting the Obama's push to develop energy alternatives to fossil fuels.[46] In turn, this could press ExxonMobil to invest in the United States rather than in Russia (See chapters 3 and 5.) Trump is fighting real progress in the name of poisonous, outmoded sources of energy—when the future can create a full-employment, ecologically viable society.

More and more countries have been investing in renewables. It is estimated that global electricity production from renewable sources plus hydropower will increase by nearly 60 percent between 2011 and 2017.[47] In part because of its extremely high levels of urban pollution, China has led investment in alternative non-carbon and renewable energy sources, with the United States, Japan, and Germany following. As costs continue to fall, alternative energies can provide even greater employment in housing, transport, and other needed infrastructure. Ironically, now that he has dropped the United States out of the Paris climate accord, in part to please his American First nationalist supporters and coal and shale energy producers, Trump will be handing sustainable energy innovation, including solar energy, wind power, and carbon-capture technology, over to the China and Europeans—instead of helping American firms take the lead in these very promising industries. In effect, Trump's anti-COP 21 decision will draw Europe and China closer together in political-economic, financial, and technological cooperation—which could effectively isolate the United States from the innovations of two largest economies in the world.

THE SECURITY-ECONOMIC BENEFITS OF DECENTRALIZED ALTERNATIVE ENERGY

Trump intends to reinstate heavily polluting and environmentally destructive coal and to invest in shale oil and gas. This is instead of investing in solar, wind, geothermal, and other less-polluting energies—possibilities that could also create healthier jobs—while concurrently decentralizing energy production in such a way so that the United States would be even less dependent on polluting carbon industries and overseas suppliers. Multiple decentralized energy units with different backup systems in case of supply shortage can better match local needs. This decentralized approach also results in greater energy savings and overall security than dependence on large, centralized nuclear power systems—which, when they break down, can cut power for millions of consumers all at once. In addition, in the new games of cyber-sabotage, large, centralized energy and power systems, such as nuclear power plants, could become the ultimate target that militant hackers could attempt to shut down. Or that terrorists and states may seek to destroy.

Global climate change and pollution is not a joke. Militaries throughout the world have been studying the potential security and political-economic implications of a warming planet. Global climate change has already begun create major humanitarian catastrophes due exceptionally severe weather conditions: climate-related droughts, floods, crop failures, hurricanes, and the like. These catastrophes have resulted in mass migrations and refugees—while directly or indirectly causing social suffering and conflicts. One wonders if the Trump-Pence administration might finally understand the issues involved if Manhattan (or other coastal cities such as Miami, New Orleans, London, Venice, Shanghai, Hong Kong, and Sydney) begin to flood, as predicted in some catastrophic scenarios. All of this is at a time when the Earth's temperature has hit a record high level for three years in a row—with the expected melting of the Arctic and Antarctic ice caps.[48] By 2045, Trump's own "Winter White House" at Mar-a-Lago could be under at least a foot of water for 210 days a year because of increased tidal flooding.[49] But this possibility seems to be too far in the future for Trump to think about.

The fundamental way to deal with this crucial, not-so-long existential threat is by fostering global social-ecological-aesthetic consciousness—in conjunction with the development of self-sustaining alternative-energy infrastructure. This is the true alternative to Trump's antediluvian path.

TOWARD PEACE AND DEVELOPMENT COMMUNITIES

Also as an alternative to Trump's essentially unilateralist and nationalist America First strategy, the policy approach argued in this book demands concerted multilateral efforts to formulate new international geopolitical, defense, political-economic, and environmental accords. The establishment of new regional systems dedicated to peace and development simply cannot be accomplished unilaterally or even bilaterally. Such an irenic peace and diplomacy-oriented strategy needs the support of all the major and regional actors, combined with concerted efforts to prevent "spoilers," such as anti-state "terrorist" groups, from trying to undermine negotiated peace accords.

In this peace-oriented strategy, Washington will need to fully engage in diplomacy with the major and regional actors of the world. Global peace and human development can only be achieved by redefining the US national interest in such a way as to reach compromises not just with US allies and friends but also with American rivals, including Russia, China, and Iran. Rather than asserting presumed national interests first, as the Trump administration appears to believe, each of the actors involved in a dispute or conflict needs to make trade-offs and possible sacrifices. Each state needs to redefine or reframe national interests in such a way that all involved can eventually benefit as much as possible, so that peace, or at least a *modus vivendi*, can be established in a healthy and ecologically balanced global environment.

In an effort to prevent the global system from polarizing into two rival alliances, and in working with the major and regional actors, Washington needs to look toward ways to forge new systems of cooperative-collective security, involving international administrations or agreements of joint sovereignty in both the Euro-Atlantic region (with a focus on the Black Sea and Caucasus region) and in the Indo-Pacific region. In Europe, this means forging a new Euro-Atlantic security pact with Russia, based in large part on a new regional "peace and development community" for the Black Sea region under the auspices of the OSCE.

In the Indo-Pacific, this means supporting Japan's efforts to forge the new rapprochement with Russia that was initiated in 2016, while concurrently finding areas where the United States, Japan, Russia, and India can cooperate with China with respect to North Korea, island disputes, and Taiwan. In addition, despite their apparent reluctance to do so, India and Pakistan, with US, Russian, and Chinese diplomatic backing, need to negotiate their differences over Kashmir, among other issues. Washington likewise needs to back the efforts of the new South Korean leadership to forge a rapprochement with Russia, so that Seoul can pursue a new Sunshine Policy—in the effort to establish a long-term peace between North and South Korea. (See chapter 7.)

Establishing a system of peace in the Indo-Pacific could mean the creation of a new Organization for Security and Cooperation in the Indo-Pacific (OSCIP) modeled after the OSCE and interacting with the Association of Southeast Asian Nations (ASEAN). A proposed OSCIP could find international, legal ways to move toward differing forms of confederation and systems of joint sovereignty over specific regions of contention. All of this implies a US-led multilateral approach to conflict resolution, which means that Washington will also need to make significant compromises, as well as concessions in some cases—if peace is to be sustained in the long term. Here, one of Trump's more positive proposals on his trip to Asia in November 2017 was his offer to negotiate the island disputes in the South China Sea between China and its neighbors.[50] Whether this offer will work out remains to be seen, but it represents a very positive sign that Trump may begin to be actually thinking of the greater good, instead of just America First.

In this perspective, Washington will concurrently need to work collectively through the United Nations, the OSCE and other multilateral Contact Groups with the major powers and regional partners, as well as with the states and certain anti-state actors involved, in order to quell the turmoil throughout the wider Middle East. Here the United States and its partners should engage in a multidimensional strategy designed to co-opt differing Islamist movements, while seeking to isolate and destroy IS and al-Qaeda offshoots where possible. This multidimensional strategy involves concerted multilateral diplomacy that is sometimes US-led and sometimes not. Such diplomacy would be intended to transform issues of dispute and conflicts in a more positive direction, if not resolve them altogether.

With respect to the wider Middle East, there are several increasingly interrelated conflicts that threaten to merge with major power rivalries and explode into war. The first is the ongoing regional conflict between Saudi Arabia and Iran, which manifests itself in Syria, Iraq, and Yemen, and which has begun to implicate Qatar and Lebanon and divide countries and political movements throughout the region. The second is the indirectly related conflict between Turkey, Syria, Iran, Iraq, and the Kurds. The third is the conflict between India and Pakistan over Kashmir, which needs to be resolved through power-sharing accords. And the fourth is the Israeli-Palestinian conflict, which helps fuel pan-Sunni and pan-Shi'a pan-Islamist movements in the background. All of these above regions need the concerted attention of Contact Groups that work with the United Nations and the major actors involved. (See chapter 8.)

Without making reasonable compromises—or even some significant concessions—with both rivals and allies, Trump's nationalistic America First project risks stumbling into a dangerous unilateralism that will result in a dangerous and destabilizing arms race and will further provoke not only US rivals but also those states that are presently US allies as well—and whose pro-American stance cannot be absolutely taken for granted in the future.

TOWARD A REEVALUATION OF "AMERICA FIRST"

Donald Trump may have initially hoped to change the geopolitical map and fulfill many of his campaign promises in his first one hundred days in office, but disputes over Crimea, Taiwan, Iran, and North Korea, among other crucial concerns, including the natural environment, are not issues that can be rapidly altered by threats to use force or hastily conceived real-estate-like "deals." This is because the complex and interwoven geo-strategic, military, political-economic, and even sociocultural and ideological issues that surround these areas represent the tip of the now-melting iceberg.

Each dispute will require very careful attention and patient irenic diplomacy—if they are not to continue to fester and ultimately result in a crisis, like an iceberg that does sink US warships. The problem is that traditional, realistic prudence and the need for careful long-term negotiations is not a trademark of the Trump casino dynasty. Trump definitely needs to sail with greater tact toward these issues and others. He also needs to sail more carefully if he wants to retain US allies, who could either float into neutrality or else look toward either Russia or China, as is the case with Bulgaria, Hungary, the Philippines, Qatar, Turkey, and others, if the United States opts to apply tougher protectionist and other nationalist measures.

It will prove nearly impossible for the United States to reach international agreements if all countries continue to assert their presumed national interests *above* the interests of other states—as Trump put it in his inauguration speech, "It is the right of all nations to put their own interests first." On the one hand, Trump stated his preference for the United States to work positively with all countries; on the other, he has also promised to assert presumed US national self-interests first, with respect to all other states. This means that US interests may be seen as literally trumping the interests of second and third parties, against their will—rather than making fair and equitable compromises or even concessions.

These latter states will generally argue in response to Trump that the United States, as the predominant hegemonic power at least since the end of the Cold War, has always had an unfair advantage over a large number of areas—so his assertions appear completely false even if the United States may appear to be losing some of its economic advantages and ideological support for American-style democracy in recent years. Trump's assertion of an American First doctrine could consequently make international agreements and compromises either impossible to achieve or else very difficult to maintain in the long term.

In response to America First, some US allies could drift into neutrality or else seek out trade, political-economic, and financial deals from China, or seek out energy, resource, and arms deals from Russia—thus ignoring US interests as much as possible. A number of states, including China, could opt to nationalize or even expropriate US or European multinational firms, for example—and then militarize in the assertion of their own presumed vital interests—"first."

If the United States wants to retain its position of global diplomatic leadership, Trump's America First policies are not the right way to do it—that is, unless Trump ultimately proves willing to compromise, if not make concessions, on a number of issues with Russia and China, among other secondary powers, and only if his administration shows a willingness to engage in multilateral processes that involve both states and societies. What is needed is not a rush toward absolute military superiority but prudent steps toward an engaged and concerted US diplomacy that seeks to mitigate, if not resolve, through mutual compromise and concessions, the disputes and conflicts that divide various states and sociopolitical movements. Without engaged and concerted diplomacy that works to defuse significant disputes among both major and regional powers, and that incorporates the interests of both US allies and potential rivals, Russia and China, US military superiority alone will not prove capable of preserving the peace.

Moreover, US global hegemony cannot be sustained if the United States becomes entrenched in conflicts in its own hemisphere. The possibility of conflict in Mexico and the Caribbean region becomes increasingly plausible if the Trump administration tries to repel Mexican and Latin American immigrants (meaning that their remittances would no longer help float the economies of these foreign countries), while threatening to intervene militarily in Mexico's drug wars or in Venezuela's social strife—all without engaging in regional Contact Group diplomacy, that could involve Cuba, for example, in the case of Venezuela. (See chapter 3.)

With respect to immigration, there is another way to deal with that question, through the effective use of the Earnings Suspense File. One factor that needs consideration is that even undocumented workers have often paid into Social Security using fake or stolen Social Security numbers. This money goes into what is called the Earnings Suspense File (ESF). In 2010, unauthorized immigrants worked and contributed as much as $13 billion in payroll taxes to the Social Security Old Age, Survivors and Disability Insurance (OASDI) program; at that time, only about $1 billion in benefit payments during 2010 were attributable to unauthorized work.[51] Moreover, the ESF reached a whopping $1.2 trillion in uncredited wages for the tax years 1937 to 2012—even if the number of W-2s posted to the ESF declined by 36 percent from 2007 to 2012; the latter is in part because of high unemployment, which contributed to the decrease in suspended wage items.[52] And the decline in W-2s was also due to Obama's efforts to crack down on false Social Security numbers. What is to be done with this money needs an open public debate, for it could fund numerous social programs, including helping to pay for better integrating undocumented workers into American society, as well as other educational "infrastructure" projects.

Another issue is the need for a new approach to the War on Drugs that was initiated by President Richard Nixon, and which has spread from Columbia throughout Latin America and the world, much like the Global War on Terrorism has spread beyond the wider Middle East. It is clear that the War on Drugs has failed miserably, whether in Latin America, Afghanistan, or elsewhere.[53] And the November 2016 peace accord between the Revolutionary Armed Forces of Colombia (FARC) and the Colombian government offers some hope for ending the drug wars throughout the region, even though new social and political tensions have come to the surface in the aftermath of that agreement. (See chapter 3.)

An approach that should help stabilize the general Latin American region economically, given the spread of drug production primarily for the American market, would be the legalization of less addictive drugs such as marijuana, hashish, and possibly cocaine, among other drugs—but with clear warnings about health effects, as is already the case for cigarettes and alcohol. There should be very strong laws against driving while under the influence, for example, but not against drug use and drug possession itself. Such an approach would be accompanied by a major police crackdown on more-dangerous drugs, including crack cocaine, PCP, scopolamine, crystal meth, among others. The legalization of some drugs, but not others, would represent an effort to push drug mafias into legal business as much as possible—and to obtain significant tax gains with significant cuts in law enforcement costs as well.[54] At a minimum, drug use and possession should be decriminalized so the police can focus on terrorism and high-level crimes. Ireland, for example, is considering decriminalizing heroin possession, among other drugs.[55] But decriminalization alone would not be sufficient to deal with the depth of the drug epidemic, which should be considered a health, and not a criminal, issue.

As was the case for legalizing alcohol after the Great Depression, which helped to eliminate at least some of the more pernicious influences and crimes of the Mafia, the drug issue is a major social and health issue and needs to be dealt with realistically. Drug legalization would additionally help to reduce gun violence, in that many urban shootings are a result of wars between drug gangs. With 1.5 million arrests for drug infractions, more persons are incarcerated for drug infractions than for all violent crimes combined, so that 50 percent of the US federal prison population comprises narcotics violators. This draws the police and the courts away from other, more vital, concerns.[56] Despite US government efforts since the Nixon administration, drugs continue to flow into the country or else are produced in basement labs. Many dangerous drugs are formulated with the use of readily available chemicals and pharmaceutical products, helping to create the opioid epidemic in the United States, for example, which killed 64,000 people in 2016.[57] A new approach is imperative.

REVIVING US DEMOCRATIC PRINCIPLES AND PRACTICES

Finally, as pointed out in the first chapters of this book, the United States will not be able to continue to engage in global leadership unless it truly begins to practice what it preaches. Trump himself recognized a number of the incongruences in the American system of governance. But instead of attempting to expand democratic practices, he has attempted to shift the country toward a more authoritarian form of governance under his leadership.

In his inaugural address in January 2017, Trump declared that "we do not seek to impose our way of life on anyone, but rather to let it shine as an example for everyone to follow." Yet the very nature of his own presidential victory—in which the billionaire Trump did not possess a clear mandate from the American people themselves—has raised questions as to whether many countries and peoples in the world will follow the American lead on various issues.

Ironically, in 2012, Trump himself had demanded some sort of reform of the democratic process—if not a "revolution"—when he mistakenly believed that Obama had won the electoral college vote but not the popular vote. He declared by tweet: "The phoney [*sic*] electoral college made a laughing stock [*sic*] out of our nation."[58] Trump then called for a "revolution." By revolution, Trump was certainly referring an authoritarian, right-wing revolution that serves the interests of the military-industrial-congressional complex and the major fossil fuel industries. After Trump's victory (during which he lost the popular vote by a colossal 2.8 million votes), the electoral college system has indeed appeared to have made the United States a laughingstock—as Trump himself had put it.

The issue raised here is that the complexity of American governance fuels the propaganda machines of US rivals, terrorist groups, and other enemies—who seek to justify their own forms of illiberal, authoritarian, or theocratic systems of governance—by the failure of the American system of democracy to live up to its own principles and values. Yet it appears highly unlikely that these crucial of issues of democratic governance will be addressed by the Trump administration, which appears more interested in challenging the US judicial system than in tackling problems raised by liberal majoritarian democracy.

Even though it was only the fifth time in US history that a president won the election without winning the popular vote,[59] some form of electoral reforms appear absolutely necessary, given huge imbalances in the population sizes across the fifty American states. One option—which would not require a constitutional amendment—is for every state to cast its votes for whomever won the popular vote within that state.[60] A more radical option would be to reduce the number of states to thirty-eight in such a way as to better balance rural and urban areas.[61] This option would provide fairer local and regional governance, while cutting state and federal governmental costs significantly, given the rising debt crisis. It would help simplify the process of American governance. If the French can reduce the number of regions from twenty-two to thirteen, as it did in 2014–2016,[62] so can the Americans!

Another radical option intended to cut costs, strengthen local regional representation, improve efficiency, and attempt to ameliorate incapacity to act resulting from "vetocracy"[63] (which seems to depict many issues except for defense appropriations), is to eliminate the aristocratic Senate and augment the power of the House of Representatives by making each member run for a single term of office, without chance of reelection, for four to six years, instead of two years. As discussed in chapter 2 in relation to defense appropriations, this would lessen the chances that crucial decisions would be made for demagogic purposes in order for congresspersons to be reelected, and it would also strengthen the role of the House. Because there would be sufficient checks and balances between regions and individual congresspersons inside such a unicameral system, a bicameral system is not necessary. Another proposal would be to limit the presidency to one five-year term of office, once again to minimize election-year demagoguery.

The goal of these proposed constitutional reforms is to make the US government less costly, more effective, and more responsive to the needs and interest of the American people. If the US government is to provide positive leadership for its own citizens, while likewise working in good faith with all other peoples and countries of the world community, it will need to rebuild its credibility and its democratic legitimacy that has been lost in the aftermath of its post–Cold War military interventions abroad, and further desecrated by the unstatesmanlike and untrustworthy nature of Donald Trump's presidency. (See chapters 1, 2, and 3.) The US Constitution has not been altered significantly for more than two hundred years, so it may be time to do so!

Even more crucially, and what should be given priority, is the fact that Trump's domestic policies do nothing to address the crucial issue of growing inequity and gross disproportion in incomes. One way to do this would be a global tax on financial transactions, as previously discussed, coupled with a reduction in national taxation. Another way to do this—which should become part of the national and international debate—is to better distribute the income of major corporations through employee stock-ownership plans combined with greater employee power-sharing in product and investment decisions through shared capitalism and "workplace democracy."[64] There are, after all, times when employees possess more common sense and innovative ideas than their managers do—and they should be better rewarded for their contributions.

The above is, of course, just a sketch of what kind of steps need to be taken domestically and internationally if the United States, and the world with it, is to literally weather through this global financial, geopolitical, and ecological crisis. Given the significant amount of the US budget that is devoted toward defense purposes, the national debt keeps mounting without apparent end, in large part because of costs directly or indirectly related to military spending and military interventions. It is primarily by seeking ways to forge diplomatic and geopolitical compromises that lead to significant reductions in military expenditure and reconversion of the military-industrial complex to peaceful purposes that the United States will eventually be able to truly devote greater attention to the full development of its own citizens, and those of the world.

Trump could prove to be like Richard Nixon, who was forced to step down as president under the threat of impeachment. Or he could possibly prove to be more like Ronald Reagan, who reversed hardline American policies in his second term by seeking to improve US relations toward the Soviet Union and by working to put the conflicts of the Cold War to rest in the ash heap of history. In that era, it was the Soviet Union that made major compromises and concessions over nuclear arms and Germany, for example. In this era, it is the United States that must make major compromises and concessions over nuclear arms and policy toward Ukraine, for example, among other compromises with Russia, China, Iran, North Korea, and other countries discussed in this book.

If the Trump-Pence team or the next administration (whether or not Trump is impeached) does not take a radical about-face away from its present America First course, those nationalist policies will actually accelerate tendencies toward the polarization of Amerian society and the division of the world into rival camps—while concurrently setting the conditions for World War Trump.

Postscript

IT CAN HAPPEN HERE

In the midst of his presidential campaign, Trump denied that he was an isolationist, but he did affirm that he liked the expression, "America First."[1]

It is accordingly not certain whether the Trump campaign's America First slogan was inspired by pre–World War II "isolationism" of the America First Committee, the largest anti-war organization in US history. The organization dissolved after the December 7, 1941, Japanese attack on Pearl Harbor. A number of prominent Americans were associated with the anti-war America First movement, which supported a strong national defense, but which opposed US intervention in the then-ongoing war in Europe. These prominent individuals included future US presidents Gerald Ford and John F. Kennedy, the controversial aviator Charles Lindbergh, who acted as its spokesperson, and many others. But even if the precise meaning of "America First" for Trump and his team is not entirely clear, the term has certainly lost any anti-war significance that it might have had prior to the arrival of the Trump-Pence administration to power.

Trump's conception of America First can nevertheless be ascertained by his choice of individuals whom he considers to be great leaders: General George S. Patton, General Douglas MacArthur, and President Teddy Roosevelt.[2]

In choosing these individuals, who cannot really be considered anti-war, Trump indicates that he possesses a predilection not only for military power and unilateral actions but also for those maverick leaders who act outside of the chain of command and official hierarchy, or who, in some way, challenge established norms and preconceived ideas.

George S. Patton's speech to American soldiers appears to parallel Trump's views of America First and his own philosophy of supporting only "winners," however defined: "All real Americans love the sting and clash of battle. . . . Americans love a winner and will not tolerate a loser. Americans despise cowards. Americans play to win—all the time. I wouldn't give a hoot in hell for a man who lost and laughed. That's why Americans have never lost, not ever will lose a war, for the very thought of losing is hateful to an American."[3]

Trump also venerates General MacArthur. In doing so, Trump advanced the dubious thesis that MacArthur was merely using the *threat* to use nuclear weaponry as leverage to negotiate with the People's Republic of China during the 1950–1953 Korean War.[4] In fact, however, MacArthur had drawn up the actual plans to use such weaponry, after already having used the destructive potential of Napalm and other weapons against North Korean and Chinese forces, which did not possess nuclear weapons at that time. In addition, and contrary to the general understanding, MacArthur was not removed from his position as supreme commander of the US-led UN force as a result of his public threat to use nuclear weaponry against North Korea and China; MacArthur was removed from duty for insubordination. The US Joint Chiefs of Staff were still considering the possible use of nuclear weaponry even after MacArthur's dismissal—an action that could have escalated hostilities with China and could have possibly brought the Soviet Union more directly into the war.

Contrary to Trump's argument, MacArthur's threat to use nuclear weapons did not dissuade Beijing from sending in one million troops across the Yalu River and pursuing the war in support of North Korea after MacArthur had ordered UN forces to attack north of the 38th parallel.[5] And the brutal way in which the United States waged the war—US B-29 bombers had dropped 866,914 gallons of Napalm onto North Korea from June to late October 1950—did not deter either North Korea or China from fighting. These facts help to explain the militant pro-nuclear-weapons policy of the contemporary North Korean regime.

In terms of his favorite US president, Trump points to the Republican maverick Teddy Roosevelt.[6] It was Roosevelt who had established the "Roosevelt corollary" to the Monroe Doctrine that permitted US military intervention in Latin American affairs while also strengthening the power of the presidency. It was Roosevelt who forced Congress to fund the American Great White Fleet so as to augment US naval capabilities across the globe. To his credit, Teddy Roosevelt also helped broker the 1904–1905 Russo-Japanese War. This fact could possibly inspire the Trump-Pence administration to mediate between Russia and Japan in contemporary circumstances—that is, if it will eventually prove possible to engage in a general rapprochement with Russia, given strong domestic American and international opposition to dealing with Russian President Vladimir Putin.[7]

Roosevelt advocated "speaking softly and carrying a big stick." But this represents a maxim that Trump has not fully ingested. Given his loose and combative tongue, his emotional outbursts and reactions to critical media reports, and his apparent inability to control his "tweets" in the new social media that permits him to comment directly to his followers and denounce his critics outside of both governmental and corporate media outlets, Trump appears incapable of speaking softly, or even in a more controlled manner. Trump is well known for his tweeting; in fact, in a French political cartoon, one White House counselor laments to another: "You will see, he [Trump] will end up tweeting the nuclear codes."[8] Further underscoring his seeming inability to control his speech, Trump has also been accused of inadvertently leaking secret information to Moscow in a White House meeting.[9] (See chapter 3.)

The issue raised here is that Trump's tweets oversimplify complex policy issues that require complex behind-the-scenes discussion and debate before bringing them out into the public. If not appropriately articulated, the emotional impact of such simplified policy statements could provoke strong negative reactions among national populations concerned—particularly as Trump is the leader of the most powerful and influential country in the world. It may also prove difficult for Trump's own official spokespersons and leaders of other countries to play down some of Trump's more inflammatory remarks. Popular outbursts abroad against Trump could, in turn, force the leaderships of those countries to take strong stands—even if those leaders may actually prefer possible compromise approaches. Insulting leaders, if not whole populations, can create deep resentment. Yet Trump has done this with Mexico and China repeatedly; with Iran, which he considers the major cause of terrorism; and with North Korea, which he has threatened to "totally destroy." Calls for retribution could take a long time to die out.

Moreover, Trump's contemporary domestic policies appear to be totally at odds with the domestic policies of Roosevelt's era. Teddy Roosevelt had fought fiercely for environmental and consumer protection. Roosevelt doubled the number of US national parks to ten; created eighteen national monuments (including the Grand Canyon), through the 1906 Antiquities Act; and set aside fifty-one federal bird sanctuaries, four national game refuges, and more than 100 million acres of national forests.[10] Yet it is Teddy Roosevelt's legacy and the Antiquities Act that Trump has begun to undermine by opening public lands (which were not entirely closed) to the mining industry. On March 28, 2017, Trump signed an executive order that could allow companies to mine and drill for oil at all national monuments designated after 1996.[11] Companies are now demanding, for example, that the Grand Canyon be opened to uranium mining, in opposition to Obama's 2012 ban on mining. By November 2017, Trump was, in fact, reconsidering the ban on mining in the Grand Canyon.[12]

Teddy Roosevelt had also fought for governmental regulation of industry and anti-monopoly reforms under the Sherman Antitrust act—an issue that Trump has largely ignored. And Roosevelt possessed a generally strong, even if mixed, record in support for the right of women to vote and for the rights of African Americans and minorities; this is in contrast to a number of Trump's outrageously crude remarks about women and his blatant sexism.[13] Moreover, Trump does not even appear to be offering a Roosevelt-like Square Deal that will eventually compress the burgeoning gap between the very, very rich 1 percent (of which Trump and many members of his cabinet are prime examples) and the rest of the American public, including his own blue-collar supporters. (See chapters 2, 3, and 10.)

Trump's form of nationalism and populism—and his inauguration promises to the American people that "your voice, your hopes, and your dreams will define our American destiny"—can be traced back even further, to the frontier populism of Andrew Jackson. President Jackson, to a certain extent like President Trump, had been elected by the vote of the frontiersmen of the western states of that era once suffrage was extended. Jackson had hoped to assert federal government control over Native Americans while starting the brutal process of implementing American coast-to-coast claims of Manifest Destiny. The latter was a term, in effect, used by Jackson as early as 1835 in an editorial affirming that the United States was "manifestly called by the Almighty to a destiny" that would have been envied by Greece and Rome.[14]

One of Andrew Jackson's many negative legacies was his signing of the democidal Indian Removal Act of 1830, which was responsible for the Cherokee Trail of Tears. This action involved the forced removal of and brutal wars with the Five Civilized Tribes (the Chickasaw, Choctaw, Muscogee or Creek, Seminole, and the original Cherokee Nations), in addition to other native peoples.[15] One could argue that Trump, although he is an urban New Yorker, exhibits a frontiersmen mentality somewhat similar to that of Andrew Jackson, but in reference to conflicts overseas against non-European cultures that lie on the "frontier" of the American empire in the wider Middle East. In this respect, the American struggle against the Native American peoples on the US-conquered continent throughout the nineteenth century possesses some key parallels with the contemporary Global War on Terrorism against a number of Islamist movements, but now on a global scale.

In this analogy, the wars between the Texas Rangers (before Texas became a state) and with the US military against the Comanches (with their claims to Comancheria, which ranged from eastern New Mexico to northwestern Texas and parts of Mexico), the Apaches, and other native peoples who opposed American Manifest Destiny have now been replaced by US-led wars with al-Qaeda, the Islamic State, and other Islamist political movements, which generally possess the ultimate goal to create an Islamic caliphate, much like the Ottoman Empire.

In many ways, the ultimate goals of Trump's inauguration call—to "unite the civilized world against radical Islamic terrorism, which we will eradicate from the face of the Earth"—do not appear to have changed that significantly from the brutal democidal anti-Native American campaigns of Andrew Jackson and Texas President Mirabeau B. Lamar. In effect, much as the United States expanded its continental empire into the Wild West, Trump has hoped to expand US global hegemony into the wider Middle East. But this effort to assert control over that region is taking place in a geopolitical situation involving a complex mix of rivalry and collaboration with Russia, China, the Europeans, Israel, Iran, Turkey, and Saudi Arabia, among other powers.

Trump's support for America First nationalism (in large part by means of undermining systems of interstate governance, including the European Union, trade pacts such as NAFTA and the Trans-Pacific Partnership, or TPP), plus his decision to drop out of the Paris climate agreement, could actually work to undermine the very "civilized world" that he has hoped will work together for a number of causes and against a number of potential threats. And, given deeper civilizational divisions that Trump himself has emphasized, there is a real danger that despite his expressed hope that the "three Abrahamic Faiths . . . can join together in cooperation, then peace,"[16] Trump's form of Judeo-Christian messianism—as it clashes with Russian Orthodoxy, Chinese Communist revanchism, and differing apocalyptic pan-Islamist movements—risks provoking World War Trump in a self-fulfilling prophecy.

TOWARD A WORLD EVEN BLEAKER THAN *1984*?

Both *1984* by George Orwell and *It Can't Happen Here* by Sinclair Lewis surged in sales after Trump's victory. In many ways, Trump is more like Sinclair Lewis's demagogic and opportunist con man Buzz Windrip (purportedly based on the real-life US Senator Huey Long), who takes total control of the US government in the establishment of a plutocratic state, than he is like Orwell's omnipresent Big Brother in his novel *1984*. Moreover, Trump's version of political language is more that of "no think" than like Big Brother's more sophisticated and manipulative "doublethink." Trump's often vulgar language—and particularly his inability to articulate the reasons for his frequent policy flip-flops—makes his rule very destabilizing. Unlike Orwell's *1984*, there is no logic or carefully constructed ideology to his often-unpredictable off-the-cuff remarks. He says or tweets spontaneously what he believes his public supporters will believe. At the same time, Trump appears to be expert at manipulating the news media in his own version of "doublespeak" by denouncing "fake news" even when that news is based on fact, while also proclaiming certain things to be "true" when they are, in fact, false. Trump claims to support America First, that is, to speak for presumed American values, but really he is speaking for the interests of an American empire of which he and his plutocratic associates possess a significant portfolio.

Yet let us assume that the militarists of the Trump-Pence administration do possess a more or less carefully conceived foreign and defense policy and that they are correct (or just lucky) that a global war will not result from a major arms race. But let us also assume that no significant steps are taken to defuse political-military and economic tensions throughout the world either. Let us assume that global interstate relations can remain in a precarious position of "no peace, no war," much like that depicted in Orwell's *1984*, more so than Lewis's *It Can't Happen Here*. What will such a world look like? And how long will it last?

Trump had proclaimed in his January 2017 inauguration that he hoped to cultivate "friendship and goodwill with the nations of the world." This appeared to represent a utopian, Mazzini-like vision in which the republics and nations of the world would be able to agree to form a coalition to fight together in the Global War on Terrorism, while somehow also cooperating on other important geostrategic and political-economic issues, despite their differing national interests.

Yet, in accord with the new logic of Trump's version of doublespeak, precisely the opposite is happening. On the domestic side, Trump's inaugural address reflected his own version of doublespeak when he stated: "At the bedrock of our politics will be a total allegiance to the United States of America, and through our loyalty to our country, we will rediscover our loyalty to each other. When you open your heart to patriotism, there is no room for prejudice." Yet Trump's claim that allegiance, loyalty, and patriotism will somehow minimize prejudice is contradictory, as it is not at all grounded in actual historical experience. This is particularly true because appeals to patriotism can be very divisive—and even more so if the so-called patriotic cause is not considered by all to be just. Quite the contrary, it is in historical periods of extreme nationalism and patriotism that prejudice runs rampant.

The question remains: What will happen to those, such as FBI Director James Comey, who do not pledge "total allegiance" to the president or to the US government?[17] And what happens if individuals do find themselves subject to discrimination and prejudice because they are not believed to be upholding "national" or "patriotic" values? What happens to those who do not pledge allegiance to the American flag?[18] And if individuals are subject to discrimination and prejudice, will that fact then lead to dissent, repression, and social conflict at home?

Trump's public support during his presidential campaign for the use of torture and extrajudicial killing is very worrisome in this regard. (Both *1984* and *It Can't Happen Here* deal with themes of torture.) Trump has, for example, stated that he would consider tactics like waterboarding of suspected terrorists—and their families—in the struggle against terrorist groups.[19] He has also threatened to engage in drone attacks on the families of terrorists and other civilians who are not directly involved in hostilities, thus expanding the military's mandate to use extrajudicial force.[20] Trump has consequently promised to go beyond the efforts of the George W. Bush administration to legalize torture under the euphemism of "enhanced interrogation techniques;" by contrast, Senator John McCain, who was tortured as a captured US serviceman during the Vietnam War, vowed to oppose any Trump effort to revive the use of torture against detained terrorism suspects.[21]

Trump's support for torture denigrates traditional American values and constitutional rights. The American military knows that it should not willingly do what is known to be illegal and immoral—and that they should resist illegal orders in order to preserve the civilian control over the military. The use of torture is counterproductive and does not necessarily obtain useful information for "actionable intelligence," despite what its proponents have claimed.[22] A Trump-Pence administration decision to relegitimize the use of torture would furthermore feed into the propaganda machines of the Islamic State, al-Qaeda, and other anti-state sociopolitical movements and countries that oppose US foreign policy and US interests.

On the international side, Trump's calls for "patriotism" and "loyalty" have sounded like President George W. Bush, who declared to the countries and populations of the world, "either you are with us or you are with the terrorists"—in initiating the war against the Iraqi regime of Saddam Hussein in 2003.[23] Yet despite Trump's disclaimers, as long as Washington continues to assert its own hegemonic interests first, the United States will not find itself cultivating the friendship of all countries. Instead, it will soon find itself as acting alone in an even more grotesque geopolitical context—in which conflicts, with unclear or complex causes, could break out unexpectedly.

In such a world, each major country, ruled by plutocratic elites, will be destabilized by the burgeoning gap between the very, very rich and the poor. Millions will be concentrated in overcrowded, highly polluted, and crime-ridden megacities—and those megacities along the coasts will increasingly be impacted by Arctic and Antarctic flooding while other regions will become increasingly arid.[24] In addition to the massive pollution and overheating of the environment caused by carbon emissions, the tons of plastic waste dumped directly into the ocean is already causing unresolvable damage to aquatic ecosystems and to our bodies. As plastic breaks up, it, along with other poisonous pollutions, is ingested by fish and climbs up the food chain and into humans.[25]

It will be a world in which the national security apparatus of states and their cyber wizards possess almost total informational control over their citizens, while seeking to root out more information, from friends and foes alike—in rivalry with "enemy" states and anti-state actors and mad computer hackers. In this global context, each government will seek to control media and information that might delegitimize or oppose the official line and policies.

In such a global situation, "friend-enemy" distinctions will not be as crystal-clear as they at least appeared to be during the Cold War. Enemies in one situation could become friends, and vice versa, much as George Orwell stated in his book *1984*: "The enemy of the moment always represented absolute evil, and it followed that any past or future agreement with him was impossible."[26] Orwell's comment appears to fit the present situation of US-Russian relations.

And, just as anarchists once claimed that sticks of dynamite could equal the score between themselves and the superior force and manpower of the police and military, lesser sociopolitical anti-state actors will continue to undermine reasonable diplomatic efforts to achieve "peace." This will prove particularly true in situations in which those anti-state actors interpret the grandiose claims of major powers to seek peace as actually intended to preserve their own hegemony. Major powers may appear to talk peace, but only in Orwellian doublespeak. Their leaderships may not at all be concerned with actually resolving complex political, economic, and social problems. In such cases, authoritarianism and repression becomes the status quo.

The geopolitical rivalries of such a world could be even more abominable than the fictional dystopia depicted in Orwell's *1984.* In that book, the planet is plagued by potentially nuclear conflicts between three major powers: Oceania, Eurasia, and Eastasia. In the contemporary geopolitical context, in which the world is under the constant threat of hybrid, if not nuclear, warfare, Oceania can be considered the United States, plus the Europeans, Japan, and its remaining allies; Eurasia is Russia and its allies; while an increasingly powerful Eastasia is now China—in a geopolitical rivalry in which Eurasia and Eastasia are presently threatening a full-fledged military alliance against Oceania for control over the world and over outer space as well. Concurrently, each of these powers are also be competing for the political-economic and military allegiance of a fourth power, amphibious India—the rising power of "Southasia," which was not foreseen in Orwell's otherwise-prescient geopolitical vision. In this view, India could play a potentially positive role of mediator, or a negative one of antagonist—that is, if India does not succumb to its own significant internal and regional conflicts.

Such a world is in obvious contrast to the liberal vision of a world of total interdependence.[27] Nevertheless, such a horrific world could become closer to reality if the United States takes an extreme America First position. The Trump administration dumped the TPP accord, which will assist China's rise as a major authoritarian and anti-democratic actor. It also dumped the important COP 21 agreement, which unilaterally relinquishes American leadership in the area of alternative and sustainable energies and carbon emissions control. And it is not impossible for the European Union to break up into nationalist rivalries in the next five to ten years, in part with Trump's blessing. Moreover, Moscow and Beijing could both refuse to accept geo-economic compromises with the United States and Europeans, while the United States and North Korea could continue to threaten nuclear war against each other. And all sides could concurrently refuse to reduce, if not eliminate, their nuclear weaponry. An arms race and buildup of military forces would remain a permanent feature of the highly polluted geopolitical landscape.

In such a global context, any number of overseas conflicts could drag the United States in to protect a strategically significant ally against a presumed threat. But what if an opposing regional major power—or even a lesser state potentially backed by a major nuclear power—decides to call the American bluff? Or what if anti-state terrorist organizations, with differing social and political ideologies, not just Islamist, ostensibly operating alone, purposely seek to spark conflict between major and regional powers—which is even more plausible if alliances continue to polarize?

A self-isolated United States, as it attempts to bully its allies and rivals (and citizens) alike, could then find itself pressed to choose which international conflicts represent an existential priority and which do not. The country would be pushed to engage in a form of strategic triage that would seek to determine which areas and countries might be worth the risk of "hybrid" conflict against rival nuclear powers, and which areas and countries would not.

NOTES

INTRODUCTION: A SELF-FULFILLING PROPHECY

1. See Hall Gardner, *Dangerous Crossroads: Europe, Russia and the Future of NATO* (Westport, CT: Praeger, 1997). The original adage has been attributed to Lord Ismay but probably came from one of his assistants.

2. Stan Resor, "Opposition to NATO Expansion: Open Letter to President Clinton," Arms Control Association, June 26, 1997, https://www.armscontrol.org/act/1997_06-07/natolet (accessed May 22, 2017).

3. On alternatives to NATO enlargement considered in the late 1990s, see Gardner, *Dangerous Crossroads*.

4. See Mikhail Zygar, *All the Kremlin's Men* (New York: Public Affairs, 2016). See also Hall Gardner, *NATO Expansion and the US Strategy in Asia: Surmounting the Global Crisis* (New York: Palgrave Macmillan, 2013); Hall Gardner, "The Genesis of NATO Enlargement and of War 'Over' Kosovo," *Central and Southeastern Europe in Transition: Perspectives on Success and Failure Since 1989*, ed. Hall Gardner (Westport, CT: Praeger, March 1999).

5. Most of my books have addressed the question of Russian revanche since 1994: *Dangerous Crossroads*; *Surviving the Millennium: American Global Strategy, the Collapse of the Soviet Empire, and the Question of Peace* (Westport, CT: Praeger, 1994); *American Global Strategy and the "War on Terrorism"* (Ashgate, 2005; revised and updated, 2007); *Averting Global War: Regional Challenges, Overextension, and Options for American Strategy* (New York: Palgrave Macmillan, 2007); *NATO Expansion and the US Strategy in Asia: Surmounting the Global Crisis* (New York: Palgrave Macmillan, 2013); Hall Gardner, *Crimea, Global Rivalry, and the Vengeance of History* (New York: Palgrave Macmillan, 2015).

6. On the costs of post–September 11, 2001, wars, see the Watson Institute, "Costs of War" Project, http://watson.brown.edu/costsofwar/ (accessed October 17, 2017).

7. Ibid. These huge costs are, to a large extent, due to the new form of post–Cold War "short war illusion" in which the initial military interventions are rapid, but

the peacekeeping and peacemaking have proven to be very long term. See Gardner, *American Global Strategy*.

8. Donald J. Trump, "Remarks of President Donald J. Trump, as Prepared for Delivery, Inaugural Address," Washington, DC, January 20, 2017, https://www.whitehouse.gov/inaugural-address (accessed November 13, 2017).

CHAPTER 1: THE PERILS OF THE NEW "AMERICA FIRST" NATIONALISM

1. Nick Gass, "Trump: Taking Back Crimea Would Trigger World War III," *Politico*, August 1, 2016, http://www.politico.com/story/2016/08/donald-trump-crimea-ukraine-war-226522 (accessed May 22, 2017).

2. Jordan Fabian and Evelyn Rupert, "Trump Promises Chinese President He'll Honor 'One China' Policy," *Hill*, February 10, 2017, http://thehill.com/homenews/administration/318874-trump-to-honor-one-china-policy (accessed May 22, 2017).

3. Austin Ramzy, "Kim Jong-un Called Trump a 'Dotard.' What Does That Even Mean?" *New York Times*, September 22, 2017, https://www.nytimes.com/2017/09/22/world/asia/trump-north-korea-dotard.html (accessed November 5, 2017).

4. Robert Helbig and Guillaume Lasconjarias, "Winning Peace and Exporting Stability: Colombia as NATO's Next Global Partner?" *NATO Research Paper* 138 (May 2017), http://www.ndc.nato.int/news/news.php?icode=1056 (accessed October 17, 2017).

5. Ruth Sherlock, "America's Allies Are 'Ripping Us Off' Says Donald Trump," *Telegraph*, March 27, 2016, http://www.telegraph.co.uk/news/2016/03/27/americas-allies-are-ripping-us-off-says-donald-trump/ (accessed November 5, 2017).

6. Peter Navarro, who was appointed as head of the newly created National Trade Council, blames Beijing for the loss of 57,000 American factories and 25 million jobs. He has called China a "global pollution factory" and "disease incubator." Tom Phillips, "'Brutal, Amoral, Ruthless, Cheating': How Trump's New Trade Tsar Sees China," *Guardian*, December 22, 2016, https://www.theguardian.com/world/2016/dec/22/brutal-amoral-ruthless-cheating-trumps-trade-industrial-peter-navarro-views-on-china (accessed October 17, 2017).

7. On the failure of new technological innovation to produce jobs relative to previous epochs, see Robert J. Gordon, *The Rise and Fall of American Growth: The US Standard of Living since the Civil War* (Princeton, NJ: Princeton University Press,

2016); Elena Holodny, "Trump Vows to 'Crack Down' on Anyone Who Violates Trade Agreements," *Business Insider*, January 20, 2017, http://uk.businessinsider.com/trump-trade-deal-plans-on-whitehousegov-2017-1?r=US&IR=T (accessed October 23, 2017).

8. Ken Moak, "A US-China Trade War Is the Last Thing the World Needs," *Asian Times*, August 9, 2017, http://www.atimes.com/us-china-trade-war-last-thing-world-needs/ (accessed October 23, 2017).

9. Tom Murse, "How Much U.S. Debt Does China Really Own?" ThoughtCo, February 28, 2017, https://www.thoughtco.com/how-much-debt-does-china-own-3321769 (accessed November 5, 2017).

10. "There is surely something odd about the world's greatest power being the world's greatest debtor. In order to finance prevailing levels of consumption and investment, must the United States be as dependent as it is on the discretionary acts of what are inevitably political entities in other countries?" Lawrence H. Summers, "The United States and the Global Adjustment Process," speech at the Third Annual Stavros S. Niarchos Lecture, March 23, 2004 (Washington DC: Peterson Institute for International Economics, 2004), https://piie.com/commentary/speeches-papers/united-states-and-global-adjustment-process (accessed November 16, 2017).

11. President Donald J. Trump, quoted by CNN on its Twitter account @CNN, February 24, 2017, https://twitter.com/cnn/status/835157246212460546?lang=en (accessed November 13, 2017).

12. David Brunnstrom and Matt Spetalnick, "Tillerson Says China Should Be Barred from South China Sea islands," Reuters, January 11, 2017, http://www.reuters.com/article/us-congress-tillerson-china-idUSKBN14V2KZ (accessed October 23, 2017). Tillerson later softened his position; Jesse Johnson "Behind the Scenes, Tillerson Tones down Rhetoric on South China Sea," *Japan Times*, February 7, 2017, http://www.japantimes.co.jp/news/2017/02/07/asia-pacific/behind-scenes-tillerson-tones-rhetoric-south-china-sea/#.WR7k6PqGP8Q (accessed October 23, 2017).

13. Alec Luhn, "Russia Bans Siberia Independence March," *Guardian*, August 5, 2014, https://www.theguardian.com/world/2014/aug/05/russia-bans-siberia-independence-march-extremism-law (accessed October 23, 2017).

14. Ben Aris, "Moscow Blog: Is Russia Seeing the Start of a Colour Revolution?" *Intellinews*, March 26, 2017, http://www.intellinews.com/moscow-blog-is-russia-seeing-the-start-of-a-colour-revolution-118327/?source=blogs&inf_contact_key=a4781fd4783dd3593aaa41c8da6700a29bf3206cfe5b7795c3d64b33000606fb (accessed October 23, 2017).

15. Donald J. Trump Presidential Campaign, "Donald J. Trump Military

Readiness Remarks," press release, September 7, 2016, https://warsclerotic.com/2016/09/07/donald-j-trump-%e2%80%8bmilitary-readiness-remarks/ (October 23, 2017).

16. In Trump's October 2016 debate with Hillary Clinton: "Our nuclear program has fallen way behind and they have gone wild with their nuclear program. Not good. Our government shouldn't have allowed that to happen. Russia is new in terms of nuclear and we are old and tired and exhausted in terms of nuclear. A very bad thing." Staff, "Full Transcript: Second 2016 Presidential Debate," *Politico*, October 10, 2016, http://www.politico.com/story/2016/10/2016-presidential-debate-transcript-229519 (accessed May 22, 2017).

17. Ploughshares Fund, "Obama's Prague Speech: A World Without Nuclear Weapons," Ploughshares Fund, December 8, 2016, http://www.ploughshares.org/issues-analysis/article/obamas-prague-speech-world-without-nuclear-weapons (accessed May 22, 2017).

18. Dov H. Levin, "When the Great Power Gets a Vote: The Effects of Great Power Electoral Interventions on Election Results," *International Studies Quarterly* 60, no. 2 (2016): 189–202, https://www.isanet.org/Publications/ISQ/Posts/ID/5027/When-the-Great-Power-Gets-a-Vote-The-Effects-of-Great-Power-Electoral-Interventions-on-Election-Results (accessed October 23, 2017); Dov Levin, "Database Tracks History of US Meddling in Foreign Elections," interview by Ari Shapiro, NPR, *All Things Considered*, December 22, 2016, http://www.npr.org/2016/12/22/506625913/database-tracks-history-of-u-s-meddling-in-foreign-elections https://academic.oup.com/isq/article-abstract/60/2/189/1750842/When-the-Great-Power-Gets-a-Vote-The-Effects-of?redirectedFrom=fulltext (accessed October 23, 2017).

19. Hall Gardner, "Iranian and Russian Versions of 'Little Green Men' and Contemporary Conflict," NATO Defense College Research Paper 123, December 15, 2015, http://www.ndc.nato.int/news/news.php?icode=885 (accessed November 5, 2017).

20. Darya Korsunskaya, "Putin Says Russia Must Prevent 'Color Revolution,'" Reuters, November 20, 2014, https://www.yahoo.com/news/putin-says-russia-must-guard-against-color-revolutions-135807378.html (accessed October 23, 2017).

21. Brendan I. Koener, "Inside the Cyberattack That Shocked the US Government," *Wired*, October 23, 2016, https://www.wired.com/2016/10/inside-cyberattack-shocked-us-government/ (accessed October 23, 2017).

22. Andy Greenberg, "The WannaCry Ransomware Has a Link to Suspected North Korean Hackers," *Wired*, May 15, 2017, https://www.wired.com/2017/05/wannacry-ransomware-link-suspected-north-korean-hackers/ (October 23, 2017).

23. "At this time, roughly 30 nations employ offensive cyber programs. . . . [The] future is burdened by an irony: Stuxnet started as nuclear counter-proliferation and

ended up to open the door to proliferation that is much more difficult to control: The proliferation of cyber weapon technology." Ralph Langner, *To Kill a Centrifuge: A Technical Analysis of What Stuxnet's Creators Tried to Achieve* (Arlington, Hamburg, Munich: Langner Group, November 2013), http://www.langner.com/en/wp-content/uploads/2013/11/To-kill-a-centrifuge.pdf (accessed October 31, 2017).

24. Hall Gardner, *The Failure to Prevent World War I: The Unexpected Armageddon* (Farnham, UK: Ashgate, 2013).

25. See Hans Morgenthau and Kenneth Thompson, *Politics Among Nations*, 6th ed. (New York: McGraw-Hill, 1985); Hall Gardner, *American Global Strategy and the "War on Terrorism"* (Farnham, UK: Ashgate, 2007).

CHAPTER 2: INAUGURATION TREMORS

1. In addition to expanding sales of George Orwell's 1984, Trump's unexpected presidential victory brought back the book *It Can't Happen Here*, by Sinclair Lewis (Garden City, NY: Doubleday, Doran, 1935). In the book, the "Respectables" (respectable individuals) are unable to accept the fact that "justified discontent . . . against the smart politicians and the Plush Horses of Plutocracy" had permitted the largely unexpected rise to power in the United States of a right-wing authoritarian leader, Buzz Windrip, who bears some resemblance to Trump.

2. Trump won the electoral college votes by 306 to Clinton's 232. Clinton won the popular vote by 48.2 percent to Trump's 46.1 percent, with roughly 58 percent of eligible voters voting. Trump was supported by roughly 58 percent of all white voters, as compared to only 8 percent of African American voters, and 29 percent each of Hispanics and Asian Americans, according to exit polls at the time of the vote. More males voted for Trump than did females (but he still obtained 42 percent of the women's vote); more people over forty and with incomes higher than $50,000 voted for Trump than Clinton; and Trump also obtained more rural and suburban votes than Clinton, who obtained more urban votes. Skye Gould, "7 Charts Show Who Propelled Trump to Victory," *Business Insider*, November 11, 2016 http://nordic.businessinsider.com/exit-polls-who-voted-for-trump-clinton-2016-11?r=UK&IR=T#while-people-living-in-urban-areas-predictably-voted-democrat-and-those-in-rural-areas-voted-republican-its-interesting-to-see-that-trump-captured-more-votes-from-people-living-in-the-suburbs-than-clinton-did-6 (accessed May 23, 2017); Philip Bump, "Donald Trump Will Be President Thanks to 80,000 People in Three States," *Washington Post*, December 1, 2016, https://www.washingtonpost.com/news/

the-fix/wp/2016/12/01/donald-trump-will-be-president-thanks-to-80000-people-in-three-states/?utm_term=.19386fdf51fa (accessed May 26, 2017).

3. Drew DeSilver, "Trump's Victory Another Example of How Electoral College Wins Are Bigger than Popular Vote Ones," Pew Research Center, Washington, DC, December 20, 2016, http://www.pewresearch.org/fact-tank/2016/12/20/why-electoral-college-landslides-are-easier-to-win-than-popular-vote-ones/ (accessed May 26, 2017).

4. Jonah Engel Bromwich, "Felony Charges for Journalists Arrested at Inauguration Protests Raise Fears for Press Freedom," *New York Times*, January 25, 2017, https://www.nytimes.com/2017/01/25/business/media/journalists-arrested-trump-inauguration.html (accessed May 26, 2017).

5. On January 19, 2017, Trump promised that he would cut funding for a large number of governmental programs. For the sixty-six programs he proposed to cut in May, see Niv Elis, "Here Are the 66 programs Eliminated in Trump's Budget," *Hill*, May 23, 2017, http://thehill.com/policy/finance/334768-here-are-the-66-programs-eliminated-in-trumps-budget (accessed October 23, 2017).

6. Andrews Wilson, Kenan Davis, Adam Pearce, and Nadia Popovich, "What Trump's Tax Proposal Will Cost," *New York Times*, April 26, 2017, https://www.nytimes.com/interactive/2017/04/26/us/politics/what-trumps-tax-proposal-will-cost.html?_r=0 (accessed October 23, 2017).

7. "Economic Impact of Immigration: Why Is Labor Important to Farmers?" American Farm Bureau Federation, http://www.fb.org/issues/immigration-reform/agriculture-labor-reform/economic-impact-of-immigration (accessed October 23, 2017).

8. Devin Henry and Timothy Cama, "Trump Using Executive Orders at Unprecedented Pace," *Hill*, April 29, 2017, http://thehill.com/policy/energy-environment/331134-trump-using-executive-orders-at-unprecedented-pace (accessed May 26, 2017).

9. "Global Inequality," Institute for Policy Studies, http://inequality.org/global-inequality/ (accessed October 23, 2017).

10. Lawrence Misahl and Alyssa Davis, "Top CEOs Make 300 Times More than Typical Workers," Economics Policy Institute, June 21, 2015, http://www.epi.org/publication/top-ceos-make-300-times-more-than-workers-pay-growth-surpasses-market-gains-and-the-rest-of-the-0-1-percent/ (accessed October 23, 2017).

11. Tim Mullaney, "Why Corporate CEO Pay Is So High, and Going Higher," CNBC, May 18, 2015, http://www.cnbc.com/2015/05/18/why-corporate-ceo-pay-is-so-high-and-going-higher.html (accessed October 23, 2017).

12. Bill Allison, Mira Rojanasakul, Brittany Harris, and Cedric Sam, "Tracking the 2016 Presidential Money Race," Bloomberg, December 9, 2016, https://www.bloomberg.com/politics/graphics/2016-presidential-campaign-fundraising/ (accessed May 26, 2017).

13. Jared Kushner and Ivanka Trump have each received top secret security clearances for their work in the White House, but purportedly they omitted to mention their meetings with Russian officials in their security-clearance application forms. Nor did they mention their friendship with Russian billionaire Roman Abramovich and his wife, who have close ties to Putin. Eliza Relman, "Kushner Omits Contacts with Russian Officials in Application for Security Clearance," *Business Insider*, April 7, 2017, http://www.businessinsider.com/kushner-omits-contacts-with-russian-officials-in-application-for-security-clearance-2017-4 (accessed May 26, 2017); Marvin Zonis, "The Strange Case of Jared and Ivanka Trump and Their Friendship with Roman Abramovich and Dasha Zhukova and Their Top-Secret Security Clearances," Marvin Zonis, May 12, 2017, http://www.marvinzonis.com/posts/the-strange-case-of-jared-and-ivanka-trump-and-their-friendship-with-roman-abramovich-and-dasha-zhukova-and-their-top-secret-security-clearances (accessed May 26, 2017).

14. Jay Solomon, "Military Brass Fill Donald Trump's National Security Council," *Wall Street Journal*, January 26, 2017, https://www.wsj.com/articles/military-brass-fill-national-security-council-1485478127 (accessed May 26, 2017).

15. Morgan Chalfant, "Worries Mount about Vacancies in Trump's State Department," *Hill*, May 21, 2017, http://thehill.com/policy/international/334327-worries-mount-about-vacancies-in-trumps-state-department (accessed October 23, 2017).

16. Jim Tankersley and Ana Swanson, "Donald Trump Is Assembling the Richest Administration in Modern American History," *Washington Post*, November 30, 2016, https://www.washingtonpost.com/news/wonk/wp/2016/11/30/donald-trump-is-assembling-the-richest-administration-in-modern-american-history/?tid=a_inl&utm_term=.6a6dc4b308fa (accessed May 26, 2017). George W. Bush's disastrous cabinet in 2001 possessed an inflation-adjusted net worth of about $250 million—which is roughly one-tenth the wealth of Donald Trump's nominee for commerce secretary alone or $2.5 billion.

17. Christopher Hayes, *Twilight of Elites: America after Meritocracy* (New York: Crown, 2012).

18. Ismael Hossein-zadeh, *The Political Economy of US Militarism* (New York: Palgrave Macmillan, 2006).

19. Bouree Lam, "Trump's Promises to Corporate Leaders: Lower Taxes and Fewer Regulations," *Atlantic*, January 23, 2017, https://www.theatlantic.com/business/archive/2017/01/trump-corporate-tax-cut/514148/ (accessed October 23, 2017).

20. As Trump claimed that he would not cut entitlements, he will most likely run yet another US government budgetary deficit, as the costs of social services payments mount along with rising interest payments on the national debt, which had crossed over 100 percent of US GDP in 2012. By the end of FY2017, the total government debt in the United States, including federal, state, and local, is expected to reach $23.2 trillion, if not more. David Lawder, "No Cuts to US Entitlement Programs in Trump Budget: Mnuchin," Reuters, February 26, 2017, http://www.reuters.com/article/us-usa-trump-economy-idUSKBN1650LL (accessed October 23, 2017).

21. Mike Lillis, "Dems, Not Trusting Trump, Want Permanent ObamaCare Fix," *Hill*, April 30, 2017, http://thehill.com/homenews/house/331172-dems-not-trusting-trump-want-permanent-obamacare-fix (accessed October 23, 2017); Kate Fritzsche, Sarah Masi, et al., *How Repealing Portions of the Affordable Care Act Would Affect Health Insurance Coverage and Premiums* (Washington, DC: Congressional Budget Office, January 2017), https://www.cbo.gov/sites/default/files/115th-congress-2017-2018/reports/52371-coverageandpremiums.pdf (accessed October 23, 2017).

22. A major issue in the new dynamic workplace means that moving from one job to another can not only result in a loss of insurance, but the issue of preexisting conditions will be reintroduced in the new job—even if one had already paid into insurance premiums at the previous job. Peter Sullivan and Rachel Roubein, "Republicans Go to Battle over Pre-Existing Conditions," *Hill*, May 26, 2017, http://thehill.com/policy/healthcare/335218-republicans-go-to-battle-over-pre-existing-conditions (accessed October 23, 2017).

23. *Congressional Budget Office Cost Estimate: American Health Care Act* (Washington, DC: Congressional Budget Office, March 9, 2017), https://www.cbo.gov/sites/default/files/115th-congress-2017-2018/costestimate/americanhealthcareact.pdf (accessed October 23, 2017); Peter Sullivan, "GOP Hits the Gas on ObamaCare Repeal," *Hill*, March 6, 2017, http://thehill.com/policy/healthcare/322609-gop-releases-bill-to-repeal-and-replace-obamacare (October 23, 2017); Niall Stanage, "THE MEMO: Trump Faces Long War on Healthcare," *Hill*, May 6, 2017, http://thehill.com/homenews/administration/332169-the-memo-trump-faces-long-war-on-healthcare (accessed October 23, 2017).

24. Drew DeSilver, "What the Unemployment Rate Does—and Doesn't—Say about the Economy," Pew Research Center, Washington, DC, March 7, 2017, http://

www.pewresearch.org/fact-tank/2017/03/07/employment-vs-unemployment-different-stories-from-the-jobs-numbers/ (accessed May 26, 2017).

25. Graphics, Reuters, "Anxieties about Racism," Reuters, http://fingfx.thomsonreuters.com/gfx/rngs/USA-TRUMP-POLL-RACE/010040W71X6/index.html (accessed May 26, 2017).

26. According to an eyewitness, it was the white supremacists and neo-fascists, who were shouting "blood and soil" and "Jews will not replace us," who initiated the violence against peaceful counterprotesters promoting antiracism, feminism, LGBTQ rights, and equity. See Jason Wilson, "I Was in Charlottesville. Trump Was Wrong about Violence on the Left," *Guardian*, August 16, 2017, https://www.theguardian.com/us-news/2017/aug/16/charlottesville-violence-right-left-trump (accessed November 5, 2017).

27. Sheryl Gay Stolberg and Brian M. Rosenthal, "Man Charged after White Nationalist Rally in Charlottesville Ends in Deadly Violence," *New York Times*, August 12, 2017, https://www.nytimes.com/2017/08/12/us/charlottesville-protest-white-nationalist.html?mcubz=1 (accessed October 26, 2017).

28. Editorial Board, "Steve 'Turn on the Hate' Bannon, in the White House," *New York Times*, November 15, 2016. Bannon was removed from his position as National Security Advisor to Trump in April 2017, but he remains a confidant of the president. Roberta Costa and Abby Philip, "Stephen Bannon Removed from National Security Council," *Washington Post*, April 5, 2017.

29. Donald Braman, "Stop-and-Frisk Didn't Make New York Safer," *Atlantic*, March 26, 2014, https://www.theatlantic.com/national/archive/2014/03/stop-and-frisk-didnt-make-new-york-safer/359666/ (accessed October 24, 2017); Christina Sterbenz, "Donald Trump Claims Stop-and-Frisk Had a 'Very, Very Big Impact' on New York City's Crime—Here's What the Data Really Says," *Business Insider*, September 27, 2016, http://uk.businessinsider.com/donald-trump-stop-and-frisk-debate-2016-9?r=US&IR=T (accessed October 24, 2017); David F. Greenberg, "Studying New York City's Crime Decline: Methodological Issues," *Justice Quarterly* 31, no. 1 (2014), http://www.tandfonline.com/doi/abs/10.1080/07418825.2012.752026 (accessed May 29, 2017).

30. Trump is on the record for banning assault weaponry: "I generally oppose gun control, but I support the ban on assault weapons and I support a slightly longer waiting period to purchase a gun. With today's Internet technology we should be able to tell within 72-hours if a potential gun owner has a record." "Donald Trump on Gun Control," On the Issues, last updated June 15, 2017, http://www.ontheissues.org/Celeb/Donald_Trump_Gun_Control.htm (accessed May 29, 2017).

31. Trump: "I'm very much in favor of making all concealed-carry permits valid in every state." Ibid.

32. Lois Beckett, "'Our Moment to Go on Offense': NRA Makes Big Plans for Trump Presidency," *Guardian*, November 28, 2016, https://www.theguardian.com/us-news/2016/nov/28/nra-gun-control-donald-trump-republicans (accessed October 24, 2017);

33. Jessica Schulberg, "Trump Sought Military Equipment for Inauguration, Granted 20-Plane Flyover," *Huffington Post*, January 19, 2017, http://www.huffingtonpost.com/entry/trump-military-equipment-inauguration_us_58811f4ae4b096b4a23091f7 (accessed October 24, 2017).

34. Donald J. Trump, "Remarks of President Donald J. Trump, as Prepared for Delivery, Inaugural Address," Washington, DC, January 20, 2017, https://www.whitehouse.gov/inaugural-address (accessed November 13, 2017).

35. South Front, "Trump's Vice President Mike Pence Wants War against Syria and Russia?" Global Research, November 13, 2016, http://www.globalresearch.ca/trumps-vice-president-mike-pence-wants-war-against-syria-and-russia/5556752 (accessed May 26, 2017).

36. *America First: A Budget Blueprint to Make America Great Again* (Washington, DC: Office of Management and Budget, 2018), https://www.whitehouse.gov/sites/whitehouse.gov/files/omb/budget/fy2018/2018_blueprint.pdf (accessed October 24, 2017).

37. Obama administration's Omnibus Spending bill sought over $1.1 trillion, split more or less evenly between defense and domestic spending. William J. Broad and David E. Sanger, "Race for Latest Class of Nuclear Arms Threatens to Revive Cold War," *New York Times*, April 16, 2016, http://www.nytimes.com/2016/04/17/world/europe/atom-bomb-nuclear-weapons-hgv-arms-race-russia-china.html?emc=edit_th_20160417&nl=todaysheadlines&nlid=70196410&_r=0 (accessed October 24, 2017); in addition, Kingston Reif, "Fact Sheets & Briefs: US Nuclear Modernization Programs," Arms Control Association, August, 2017, https://www.armscontrol.org/factsheets/USNuclearModernization (accessed May 23, 2017); Fred Kaplan, "Obama's Whopping New Military Budget: Forget What the GOP Says. Obama Loves Big Military Budgets," *Slate*, February 9, 2016, http://www.slate.com/articles/news_and_politics/war_stories/2016/02/president_obama_s_military_budget_is_still_one_of_the_biggest_ever.html (accessed May 23, 2017); Maj. Gen. James F. Martin, "Department of Defense Briefing by Maj. Gen. James Martin on the Fiscal Year 2016 Air Force Budget in the Pentagon Briefing Room," news transcript, United States Department of Defense, February 2, 2015, http://archive.defense.gov/Transcripts/

Transcript.aspx?TranscriptID=5586 (accessed May 23, 2017); James Drew, "Concept of a Nuclear-Armed F-35C Divides Opinion," FlightGlobal.com, August 4, 1970, https://www.flightglobal.com/news/articles/concept-of-a-nuclear-armed-f-35c-divides-opinion-415353/ (accessed May 23, 2017); James Drew, "US Conducts First Flight Test of Guided B61-12 Nuclear Bomb," FlightGlobal.com, July 10, 1970, https://www.flightglobal.com/news/articles/us-conducts-first-flight-test-of-guided-b61-12-nuclear-414484/ (accessed May 23, 2017).

38. Amy F. Woolf, *The New START Treaty: Central Limits and Key Provisions* (Washington, DC: Congressional Research Service, February 1, 2017), https://fas.org/sgp/crs/nuke/R41219.pdf (accessed October 24, 2017).

39. Michael R. Gordon, "Russia Deploys Missile, Violating Treaty and Challenging Trump," *New York Times*, February 14, 2017, https://www.nytimes.com/2017/02/14/world/europe/russia-cruise-missile-arms-control-treaty.html (accessed November 5, 2017); Franz-Stefan Gady, "Russia Tests Topol-M Intercontinental Ballistic Missile," *Diplomat*, September 28, 2017, https://thediplomat.com/2017/09/russia-tests-topol-m-intercontinental-ballistic-missile/ (accessed November 5, 2017).

40. "Highlights from the 2017 Index," 2017 Index of Military Strength, http://index.heritage.org/military/2017/assessments/ (accessed October 24, 2017).

41. Here, US Secretary of Defense Jim Mattis has discussed the possible deployment of tactical nuclear weaponry with South Korean Defense Minister Song Young-moo, who told his parliament that he had requested that the United States consider the return of tactical nuclear weapons to the Korean Peninsula. No further information was provided. Tara Copp, "Mattis: Use of Tactical Nuclear Weapons Discussed with South Korea," *Defense News*, September 18, 2017, https://www.defensenews.com/news/your-military/2017/09/18/mattis-use-of-tactical-nuclear-weapons-discussed-with-south-korea/ (accessed November 5, 2017).

42. For Trump proposals: Brendan McGarry, "Trump Unveils Plan to Boost Military with More Troops, Weapons," Military.com, September 7, 2016, http://www.military.com/daily-news/2016/09/07/trump-unveils-plan-to-boost-military-with-more-troops-weapons.html (accessed October 24, 2017).

43. Secretary of Defense Mattis was cited as stating that the BCA and sequestration have "done more damage to our readiness than the enemies in the field." "DoD Releases Fiscal Year 2018 Budget Proposal," Release No: NR-192-17, May 23, 2017, https://www.defense.gov/News/News-Releases/News-Release-View/Article/1190216/dod-releases-fiscal-year-2018-budget-proposal/ (accessed November 5, 2017).

44. Adam Taylor and Laris Karklis, "This Remarkable Chart Shows How US

Defense Spending Dwarfs the Rest of the World," *Washington Post*, February 9, 2016, https://www.washingtonpost.com/news/worldviews/wp/2016/02/09/this-remarkable-chart-shows-how-u-s-defense-spending-dwarfs-the-rest-of-the-world/?utm_term=.1df2b5f8eebd (accessed October 24, 2017).

45. Nan Tian, Aude Fleurant, Pieter D. Wezeman, and Siemon T. Wezeman, *Trends in World Military Expenditure, 2016: SIPRI Fact Sheet* (Solna, Sweden: Stockholm International Peace Research Institute, April 2017), https://www.sipri.org/sites/default/files/Trends-world-military-expenditure-2016.pdf (accessed October 24, 2017).

46. Hossein-zadeh, *Political Economy*.

47. For details of budget, see Neta C. Crawford, *US Budgetary Costs of Wars through 2016: $4.79 Trillion and Counting Summary of Costs of the US Wars in Iraq, Syria, Afghanistan and Pakistan and Homeland Security* (Boston: Watson Institute, International & Public Affairs, Brown University, September 2016), http://watson.brown.edu/costsofwar/files/cow/imce/papers/2016/Costs%20of%20War%20through%202016%20FINAL%20final%20v2.pdf (accessed October 24, 2017).

48. After major tax cuts, Alan Greenspan had dropped US interest rates in 2001–2002 after the dot-com 2000–2002 crisis, instead of raising them, and those rates were kept low from 2002 to 2004, which assisted US borrowing for the military interventions after September 11, 2001, while also providing additional cheap money for China's boom. For the view that the crisis was Greenspan's fault for not raising interest rates in 2002: Susan Lee, "It Really Is All Greenspan's Fault," *Forbes*, April 3, 2009, http://www.forbes.com/2009/04/02/greenspan-john-taylor-fed-rates-china-opinions-columnists-housing-bubble.html (accessed May 26, 2017). For the view it was China's fault: Heleen Mees, "How China's Boom Caused the Financial Crisis," *Foreign Policy*, January 17, 2012, http://foreignpolicy.com/2012/01/17/how-chinas-boom-caused-the-financial-crisis/ (accessed May 26, 2017).

49. Yochi Dreazen, "Trump Says He's Boosting Defense Spending by $54 Billion. The Real number Is $18 Billion," *Vox*, February 28, 2017, http://www.vox.com/policy-and-politics/2017/2/28/14765492/trump-pentagon-budget-billion-state-department-misleading-54-billion (accessed May 26, 2017); Kristina Wong, "Trump's Navy Build-Up Comes with Steep Price Tag," *Hill*, January 16, 2017, http://thehill.com/policy/defense/314311-trumps-navy-build-up-comes-with-steep-price-tag (accessed May 26, 2017).

For options to cut budget deficit: "Chapter 3: Discretionary Spending Options," *Options for Reducing the Deficit: 2017 to 2026* (Washington, DC: Congressional Budget Office, February 1, 2017), https://www.cbo.gov/publication/52142; https://

www.cbo.gov/sites/default/files/114th-congress-2015-2016/reports/52142-breakout-chapter32.pdf (accessed May 26, 2017).

50. Catherine A. Theohary, *Conventional Arms Transfers to Developing Nations, 2008-2015* (Washington, DC: Congressional Research Service, December 19, 2016), https://fas.org/sgp/crs/weapons/R44716.pdf (accessed October 24, 2017).

51. Melvin A. Goodman, *National Insecurity: The Cost of American Militarism* (San Francisco: City Lights, 2013).

52. Mike De Bonis, "The Pentagon Found $125 Billion in Waste. Now a GOP Chairman is Asking Other Agencies What They've Found," *Washington Post*, February 10, 2017, https://www.washingtonpost.com/news/powerpost/wp/2017/02/10/the-pentagon-found-125-billion-in-waste-now-a-gop-chairman-is-asking-other-agencies-what-theyve-found/?utm_term=.819a68f3904b (accessed October 24, 2017).

53. John M. Donnelly, "Atomic Arsenal Costs Ballooning by Billions of Dollars," *Roll Call*, January 9, 2017, http://www.rollcall.com/news/policy/atomic-arsenal-costs-ballooning-billions-dollars (accessed October 24, 2017).

54. Geoff Ziezulewicz, "B61-12 Life Extension Program Receives NNSA Approval," UPI, August 2, 2016, http://www.upi.com/Business_News/Security-Industry/2016/08/02/B61-12-life-extension-program-receives-NNSA-approval/3261470147434/ (accessed October 24, 2017).

55. Will Saetren, "3 Nuclear Weapons Programs Obama Should Kill," *National Interest*, September 11, 2016, http://nationalinterest.org/feature/3-nuclear-weapons-programs-president-obama-should-kill-17654 (accessed October 24, 2017).

56. Amanda Macias, "The Legacy of the 2011 Debt Ceiling Fight Is the Biggest Issue the Next President Will Face on Day One," *Business Insider*, August 14, 2016, http://www.businessinsider.com/budget-control-act-2016-8?r=UK&IR=T/#what-is-the-budget-control-act-1 (accessed October 24, 2017).

57. See William Hartung, *Prophets of War: Lockheed Martin and the Making of the Military Industrial Complex* (New York: Nation Books, 2012).

58. Andrea Shalal-Esa, "Exclusive: US Sees Lifetime Cost of F-35 Fighter at $1.45 Trillion," Reuters, March 29, 2012, http://www.reuters.com/article/us-lockheed-fighter-idUSBRE82S03L20120329 (accessed October 24, 2017).

59. *F-35 Strike Fighter: DOD Needs to Complete Developmental Testing before Making Significant New Investments* (Washington, DC: US Government Accountability Office, April 2017), http://www.gao.gov/assets/690/684208.pdf (accessed October 24, 2017); "DoD Releases Fiscal Year 2018 Budget Proposal."

60. Dave Majumdar, "America's F-35 Stealth Fighter vs. Russia's Su-35: Who Wins?" *National Interest*, September 15, 2015, http://nationalinterest.org/blog/

the-buzz/americas-f-35-stealth-fighter-vs-russias-su-35-who-wins-13855 (accessed October 24, 2017); Rakesh Krishnan Simha "Stealth Troubles: Why Leading Air Forces Want More Traditional Warplanes," *Russia Beyond*, January 23, 2017, https://in.rbth.com/blogs/stranger_than_fiction/2017/01/23/stealth-troubles-why-leading-air-forces-want-more-traditional-warplanes_686613 (accessed October 25, 2017).

61. During the Reagan years, the gap between the expanding economy and the shrinking investment in public works/capital meant that the growing private economy augmented demands for public services that could not be supplied by a public sector that was decreasing in size. Hossein-zadeh, *Political Economy*. Here, however, Trump hopes to replace publicly supplied services and infrastructure with private financing.

62. Alex Ward, "What America's New Arms Deal with Saudi Arabia Says about the Trump Administration," *Vox*, May 20, 2017, https://www.vox.com/2017/5/20/15626638/trump-saudi-arabia-arms-deal (accessed October 25, 2017).

63. Lingling Wei, "Push by China's Sovereign-Wealth Fund," *Wall Street Journal*, May 17, 2017, https://www.wsj.com/articles/trump-trade-reboot-spurs-u-s-push-by-chinas-sovereign-wealth-fund-1495022339 (accessed October 25, 2017); Viola Zhou, "China's Sovereign Wealth Fund Wants to Invest in the US Infrastructure Rebuild, Chairman Says," *South China Morning Post*, January 16, 2017, http://www.scmp.com/business/companies/article/2062593/chinas-sovereign-wealth-fund-wants-invest-us-infrastructure (accessed October 25, 2017).

64. Jaclyn Reiss, "Bernie Sanders Rails against Trump after Speech," *Boston Globe*, March 1, 2017, http://www.bostonglobe.com/news/politics/2017/03/01/bernie-sanders-rails-against-trump-after-speech/zFBd9Ff88rSdszRVrdlCJL/story.html?p1=Article_Trending_Most_Viewed (accessed May 26, 2017). According to critics such as Bernie Sanders, Trump also wants to give tax breaks worth as much as $3 trillion to the very rich.

65. This was the case of arms firms who pushed NATO enlargement as a means to expand arms sales in the late 1990s. Katherine Q. Seelye, "Arms Contractors Spend to Promote an Expanded NATO," *New York Times*, March 30, 1998, http://www.nytimes.com/1998/03/30/world/arms-contractors-spend-to-promote-an-expanded-nato.html?pagewanted=all&_r=0US (accessed October 25, 2017).

66. Mike Pence has called for reviving two wasteful weapons programs: the Army's Future Combat Systems and the Air Force's F-22 Raptor fighter jet, which was dumped by the Obama administration. Then Defense Secretary Robert Gates's decision to scrap the F-22 was in part the result of major cost overruns. Austin Wright, "Pence Could Undermine Key Trump War Argument," *Politico*, July 14, 2016, http://www.politico.com/story/2016/07/mike-pence-donald-trump-war-argument-225565

(accessed October 25, 2017); Jeremiah Gertler, *Air Force F-22 Fighter Program* (Washington, DC: Congressional Research Service, July 11, 2013), https://www.fas.org/sgp/crs/weapons/RL31673.pdf (accessed October 25, 2017).

67. Staff, "Trump's Remarks on Military Readiness," *Washington Examiner*, September 7, 2016, http://www.washingtonexaminer.com/text-trumps-remarks-on-military-readiness/article/2601173 (accessed October 25, 2017).

68. McCain's plan would add $430 billion more than FY2017 projections, thus bringing the defense budget to $800 billion in fiscal 2022. McGarry, "Trump Unveils Plan."

69. Daniel Bukszpan, "Why Bernie Sanders Is Backing a $1.5 Trillion Military Boondoggle," CNBC, July 12, 2016, http://www.cnbc.com/2016/07/12/why-bernie-sanders-is-backing-a-15-trillion-military-boondoggle.html (accessed May 26, 2017). Other boondoggles include the excessive expense of the USS *Enterprise* and USS *Zumwald.*

CHAPTER 3: THE NEW BOGEYMAN

1. Ruth Marcus, "Count on Trump to Be a Sore Loser," *Washington Post*, August 5, 2016, https://www.pressreader.com/usa/the-washington-post/20160805/282050506447036 (accessed May 29, 2017).

2. These agencies included the CIA, the National Security Agency, the Justice Department, the Treasury Department's Financial Crimes Enforcement Network, and representatives of the director of national intelligence. Former CIA Director John Brennan testified that he had warned Alexander Bortnikov, head of the FSB Russian intelligence service, against tampering with the US elections in August 2016. Bortnikov, however, denied that Russia was meddling, but said he would raise the issue with President Vladimir Putin. Brennan could not describe Russian-Trump team interactions as "collusion." Tom LoBianco, "Ex-CIA Chief John Brennan: Russians Contacted Trump Campaign," CNN, May 23, 2017, http://edition.cnn.com/2017/05/23/politics/john-brennan-house-intelligence-committee/ (accessed October 25, 2017).

3. Evelyn Rupert, "Senate Intel Panel to Probe Trump Team's Ties to Russia," *Hill*, January 13, 2017, http://thehill.com/policy/cybersecurity/314298-senate-intel-committee-to-probe-russian-interference-in-election (accessed October 25, 2017).

4. Donald Trump (@realDonaldTrump): "Senators should focus their energies on ISIS, illegal immigration and border security instead of always looking to start World War III," Twitter, January 29, 2017, 1:49 p.m., https://twitter.com/realdonaldtrump/status/825823217025691648?lang=en (accessed October 25, 2017).

5. Richard Gonzales, "Senate Panel Plans to Investigate Russian Activities during US Elections," NPR, January 13, 2017, http://www.npr.org/sections/the-two-way/2017/01/13/509762116/senate-panel-plans-to-investigate-russian-activities-during-u-s-elections (accessed October 25, 2017).

6. Ellen Nakashima, "Russia's Apparent Meddling in US Election Is Not an Act of War, Cyber Expert Says," *Washington Post*, February 7, 2017, https://www.washingtonpost.com/news/checkpoint/wp/2017/02/07/russias-apparent-meddling-in-u-s-election-is-not-an-act-of-war-cyber-expert says/?postshare=1741486560691485&tid=ss_mail&utm_term=.ed8edfa98213 (accessed May 29, 2017).

7. Zack Beauchamp and Andrew Prokop, "Robert Mueller's Russia Investigation, and Why Trump Is so Afraid of It," Vox News, August 3, 2017, https://www.vox.com/world/2017/7/24/16008272/robert-mueller-fbi-trump-russia-explained (accessed November 5, 2017).

8. David Voreacos, Stephanie Baker, and Shannon Pettypiece, "Three Trump Associates Charged in Russia Collusion Probe," Bloomberg News, October 30, 2017, https://www.bloomberg.com/news/articles/2017-10-30/trump-s-ex-campaign-chairman-manafort-told-to-surrender-to-u-s (accessed November 5, 2017).

9. "Statement by President Donald J. Trump on the Signing of H.R. 3364," news release, White House, Office of the Press Secretary, August 2, 2017, https://www.whitehouse.gov/the-press-office/2017/08/02/statement-president-donald-j-trump-signing-hr-3364 (accessed October 25, 2017).

10. Steve Mollman, "What Would Actually Happen If Donald Trump Shot That Russian Ship 'Right out of the Water,'" *Quartz*, February 17, 2017, https://qz.com/913443/what-would-actually-happen-if-trump-shot-that-russian-ship-right-out-of-the-water/ (accessed October 25, 2017).

11. Darlene Superville, "Trump Defends Seeking Better Ties with Russia," *Intelligencer*, February 6, 2017, http://www.theintelligencer.net/news/top-headlines/2017/02/trump-u-s-isnt-so-innocent/ (accessed October 25, 2017).

12. Ibid. This answer (which is not very presidential, but crudely honest) enraged a number of political elites, as if they had forgotten CIA/KGB assassinations during the Cold War and after. The grim reality is that the US foreign policy elites must deal with many leaders that are "killers," whether Washington likes it or not, and whether those countries like dealing with the United States.

13. Numerous critics of Putin have died in mysterious circumstances, but it is not clear who paid for the killings. Mary Louise Kelly, "The Curious Deaths of Kremlin Critics," NPR, August 30, 2016, http://www.npr.org/sections/parallels/2016/08/30/491898040/the-curious-deaths-of-kremlin-critics (accessed November 5, 2017).

14. "President Putin 'Probably' Approved Litvinenko Murder," BBC, January 21, 2016, http://www.bbc.com/news/uk-35370819 (accessed November 5, 2017).

15. Noam Chomsky, "On the NATO Bombing of Yugoslavia," interview by Danilo Mandic, RTS Online, April 25, 2006, https://chomsky.info/20060425/ (accessed October 26, 2017).

16. In November 2005, a British newspaper leaked a thus far unconfirmed secret report that purported that Tony Blair was able to convince George Bush not to bomb the Qatari TV station Al Jazeera in Doha in April 2004 during the US siege of Falluja in Iraq. Bush purportedly threatened to bomb Al Jazeera due to the fact that unembedded Al Jazeera journalists had been accusing the US military of atrocities. Jeremy Scahill, "Did Bush Really Want to Bomb Al Jazeera?" *Nation*, November 23, 2005, https://www.thenation.com/article/did-bush-really-want-bomb-al-jazeera/ (accessed October 26, 2017). Seymour M. Hersh, "Chain of Command," *New Yorker*, May 17, 2004. In any case, the purpose of the leak seemed to be to make Blair look like a good guy who stood up to Bush, and not Bush's "poodle," as was often claimed at the time.

17. Veteran Intelligence Professionals for Sanity (VIPS), "A Demand for Russian 'Hacking' Proof," *Consortium News*, January 17, 2017, https://consortiumnews.com/2017/01/17/a-demand-for-russian-hacking-proof/. Here there should be a distinction between "cyber-leaks" and "cyber-hacking," as it is not clear which the Kremlin is allegedly responsible for.

18. "Russia: The 'Cloud' over the White House," BBC News, September 29, 2017, http://www.bbc.com/news/world-us-canada-38966846 (accessed October 26, 2017).

19. Michelle Ye Hee Lee, "Julian Assange's Claim That There Was No Russian Involvement in WikiLeaks Emails," *Washington Post*, January 5, 2017, https://www.washingtonpost.com/news/fact-checker/wp/2017/01/05/julian-assanges-claim-that-there-was-no-russian-involvement-in-wikileaks-emails/?utm_term=.563247ffca74 (accessed May 29, 2017).

20. Andrew Higgins, "Maybe Private Russian Hackers Meddled in Election, Putin Says," *New York Times*, June 1, 2017, https://www.nytimes.com/2017/06/01/world/europe/vladimir-putin-donald-trump-hacking.html?emc=edit_na_20170601&nl=breaking-news&nlid=70196410&ref=cta&_r=0 (accessed October 26, 2017).

21. Sean Gallagher, "WikiLeaks to US Government: Stop Leaking Secrets! WikiLeaks Joins Trump in Decrying NBC 'Exclusive' on Top Secret Intelligence Report," *Ars Technica*, January 6, 2017, https://arstechnica.com/tech-policy/2017/01/

wikileaks-to-us-government-stop-leaking-secrets/ (accessed November 5, 2017). NBC, for example, illegally received a leaked document before Trump saw it, with no threat of punishment; yet Chelsea Manning was accused of "aiding the enemy" by handing over secret documents to Julian Assange.

22. FBI Director James Comey had announced a new inquiry into Clinton's private email server only eleven days before the presidential election, but then he dropped the issue just two days before Americans voted. It is possible that the Kremlin was involved in hacking Democratic National Committee emails, but other groups could have been involved as well, possibly in an effort to make Moscow look like the culprit. Alex Thompson, "Why Nothing Was Done," Vice News, December 16, 2016, https://news.vice.com/story/obama-explains-why-he-didnt-retaliate-against-russia-for-hacking-hillary-clintons-campaign (accessed October 26, 2017).

23. Pamela Engel, "Clinton Never Set Foot in Wisconsin—Then She Lost It, and It Helped Cost Her the Presidency," *Business Insider*, November 9, 2016, http://uk.businessinsider.com/clinton-losing-wisconsin-results-2016-11?r=US&IR=T (accessed October 26, 2017).

24. Jacob Heilbrunn, "It Was Inevitable That Trump Would Fire James Comey," *National Interest*, May 9, 2017, http://nationalinterest.org/feature/it-was-inevitable-trump-would-fire-james-comey-20589 (accessed October 26, 2017). Ali Vitali and Corky Siemaszko, "Trump Interview with Lester Holt: President Asked Comey If He Was Under Investigation."

For an analysis of Trump's interview with Lester Holt on NBC, see Amy Davidson Sorkin, "The Threat in President Trump's Interview with Lester Holt," *New Yorker*, May 12, 2017, https://www.newyorker.com/news/amy-davidson/the-threat-in-president-trumps-interview-with-lester-holt (accessed November 5, 2017).

25. Maggie Haberman, Mark Mazzetti, and Matt Apuzzomay, "Kushner Is Said to Have Discussed a Secret Channel to Talk to Russia," *New York Times*, May 26, 2017, https://www.nytimes.com/2017/05/26/us/politics/kushner-talked-to-russian-envoy-about-creating-secret-channel-with-kremlin.html?emc=edit_th_20170527&nl=todaysheadlines&nlid=70196410&_r=0 (accessed October 26, 2017). Jo Becker, Matt Apuzzo, and Adam Goldman, "Trump's Son Met with Russian Lawyer after Being Promised Damaging Information on Clinton," *New York Times*, July 9, 2017, https://www.nytimes.com/2017/07/09/us/politics/trump-russia-kushner-manafort.html (accessed November 5, 2017).

26. See controversial report written by former British MI6 intelligence agent Christopher Steele, "Company Intelligence Report 2016/080: US Presidential Election: Republican Candidate Donald Trump's Activities in Russia and Com-

promising Relationship with the Kremlin," available at https://www.documentcloud.org/documents/3259984-Trump-Intelligence-Allegations.html (accessed October 26, 2017). This unconfirmed report was passed around Washington before it was placed on *BuzzFeed*'s website: Ken Bensinger, Miriam Elder, and Mark Schoofs, "These Reports Allege Trump Has Deep Ties to Russia," *BuzzFeed*, January 10, 2017, https://www.buzzfeed.com/kenbensinger/these-reports-allege-trump-has-deep-ties-to-russia?utm_term=.mljnBG5rbp#.la3vMX57eJ (accessed November 2, 2017). By November 2017, "Clinton Campaign, DNC Paid for Research That Led to Russia Dossier," *Washington Post*, https://www.washingtonpost.com/world/national-security/clinton-campaign-dnc-paid-for-research-that-led-to-russia-dossier/2017/10/24/226fabf0-b8e4-11e7-a908-a3470754bbb9_story.html?utm_term=.597105078b6b (accessed November 5, 2017).

27. For a critique of the Fusion GPS report, see Philip Bump, "What the Trump Dossier Says—and What It Doesn't," *Washington Post*, October 25, 2017, https://www.washingtonpost.com/news/politics/wp/2017/10/25/what-the-trump-dossier-says-and-what-it-doesnt/?tid=a_inl&utm_term=.a63e2e8cf802 (accessed November 5, 2017).

28. Mikhail Fishman, Daria Litvinova, "Why Putin Fired His Chief of Staff and Longtime Ally," *Moscow Times*, August 25, 2016, https://themoscowtimes.com/articles/why-putin-replaced-head-of-presidential-administration-54978 (accessed October 26, 2017).

29. For a cautious view, see Fydor Lukyanov, "Like Obama, Trump Is Unlikely to Lead as the World's Policeman," *Russia in Global Affairs*, November 18, 2016, http://eng.globalaffairs.ru/redcol/Like-Obama-Trump-Is-Unlikely-to-Lead-as-the-Worlds-Policeman-18466 (accessed October 26, 2017).

30. Bryan Logan, "Nikki Haley Just Delivered the Trump Administration's Most Hawkish Words Yet toward Russia," *Business Insider*, February 3, 2017, http://uk.businessinsider.com/trump-nikki-haley-russia-ukraine-2017-2?r=US&IR=T (accessed October 26, 2017).

31. David M. Herszenhorn and Ellen Barrydec, "Putin Contends Clinton Incited Unrest Over Vote," *New York Times*, December 8, 2011, http://www.nytimes.com/2011/12/09/world/europe/putin-accuses-clinton-of-instigating-russian-protests.html (accessed October 26, 2017).

32. Priyanka Boghani, "Putin's Legal Crackdown on Civil Society," *Frontline*, January 13, 2015, http://www.pbs.org/wgbh/frontline/article/putins-legal-crackdown-on-civil-society/ (accessed October 26, 2017). Former US Ambassador Michael McFaul stated he personally heard Putin complain about Clinton's comments.

Michael Crowley and Julia Ioffe, "Why Putin Hates Hillary," *Politico*, July 25, 2016, http://www.politico.com/story/2016/07/clinton-putin-226153 (accessed October 26, 2017). In an effort to delegitimize Putin before the Russian people, Washington elites accused him of being a billionaire: Stephen Grey, Andrey Kuzmin, and Elizabeth Piper, "Putin's Daughter, a Young Billionaire and the President's Friends," Reuters, November 10, 2015, http://www.reuters.com/investigates/special-report/russia-capitalism-daughters/ (accessed October 26, 2017).

33. "Ukraine Crisis: Transcript of Leaked Nuland-Pyatt Call," BBC, February 7, 2014 http://www.bbc.com/news/world-europe-26079957 (accessed October 26, 2017).

34. Josh Meyer, "DNC Email Hack: Why Vladimir Putin Hates Hillary Clinton," NBC News, July 27, 2016, http://www.nbcnews.com/news/us-news/why-putin-hates-hillary-clinton-n617236 (accessed October 26, 2017).

35. Jon Swaine and Ed Pilkington, "The Wealthy Men in Trump's Inner Circle with Links to Tax Havens," *Guardian*, November 5, 2017, https://www.theguardian.com/news/2017/nov/05/wealthy-men-donald-trump-inner-circle-links-tax-havens (accessed November 6, 2017).

36. Charles Tiefer, "'Paradise Papers' Disclosures of Trump Administration-Russia Ties Warrant Congressional Hearings," *Forbes*, November 5, 2017, https://www.forbes.com/sites/charlestiefer/2017/11/05/new-paradise-papers-disclosures-of-trump-russia-ties-warrant-immediate-congressional-hearings/#720d71d14baa (accessed November 13, 2017).

37. ExxonMobil has lost at least $1 billion on its investments in Russia, as of early 2015. Ed Crooks, "Rex Tillerson, ExxonMobil, and the Separation of Oil and State," *Financial Times*, January 22, 2017, https://www.ft.com/content/2acabb7a-def9-11e6-9d7c-be108f1c1dce (accessed October 16, 2017).

38. Karoun Demirjian, "Tillerson Says US Should Have Used Other Options in Crimea," *Washington Post*, January 11, 2017, https://www.washingtonpost.com/politics/2017/live-updates/trump-white-house/confirmation-hearings-trump-speaks-and-vote-a-rama-analysis-and-updates/tillersons-says-u-s-should-have-used-other-options-in-crimea/?utm_term=.66a0f1f32078 (accessed October 26, 2017).

39. In his testimony before Congress, Rex Tillerson affirmed that he would keep US sanctions in place and consider new penalties related to Russian meddling in the presidential election. Ibid.

40. Crooks, "Rex Tillerson, ExxonMobil, and the Separation of Oil and State"; Samuel Rubenfeld, Lynn Cook, and Ian Talley, "Exxon Sues US over $2 Million Russian Sanctions Fine," *Market Watch*, July 21, 2017, http://www.marketwatch.com/story/exxon-sues-us-over-2-million-russian-sanctions-fine-2017-07-21 (accessed

October 26, 2017); Peter Baker and Sophia Kishkovsky, "Trump Signs Russian Sanctions into Law, with Caveats," *New York Times*, August 2, 2017, https://www.nytimes.com/2017/08/02/world/europe/trump-russia-sanctions.html (accessed October 26, 2017).

41. Flynn was accused of acting illegally as a foreign agent, paid by Russian Television (RT) and by the Turkish government, without registering as a foreign agent during the Trump campaign. It was argued that his actions could lead him to be "compromised" by Moscow. Katie Bo Williams, "Yates Warned Flynn Was Vulnerable to Blackmail by Russia," *Hill*, May 8, 2017, http://thehill.com/policy/national-security/332416-yates-flynn-conduct-created-a-compromise-situation (accessed October 26, 2017). Philip Giraldi put the issue this way: ". . . the destruction of Flynn, involving as it may have a number of leakers coming from all across the intelligence community, might be part of a coordinated effort to narrow the Trump White House's options for dealing with Russia. Many in Washington do not want a comfortable working relationship with Putin in spite of the fact that a reset with Moscow should be the No. 1 national-security objective." Philip Giraldi, "More about Russia and Less about Flynn?" *American Conservative*, February 16, 2017, http://www.theamericanconservative.com/articles/more-about-russia-and-less-about-flynn/ (accessed October 26, 2017).

42. Megan Twohey and Scott Shane, "A Back-Channel Plan for Ukraine and Russia, Courtesy of Trump Associates," *New York Times*, February 19, 2017, https://www.nytimes.com/2017/02/19/us/politics/donald-trump-ukraine-russia.html? (accessed May 29, 2017); Danielle Kurtzleben, "Michael Flynn Left the Trump White House This Week. Here's How That Happened," NPR, February 14, 2017, http://www.npr.org/2017/02/14/515233669/michael-flynn-left-the-trump-white-house-this-week-heres-how-that-happened (accessed May 29, 2017). Other allegations included Trump team efforts to discuss with Moscow a change in US policy toward Syria.

43. "Transcript: Michael Flynn on ISIL," Al Jazeera, January 13, 2016, http://www.aljazeera.com/programmes/headtohead/2016/01/transcript-michael-flynn-160104174144334.html (accessed November 6, 2017).

44. Elana Schor and Nolan D. McCaskill, "Republicans Warn Trump against Lifting Russia Sanctions," *Politico*, January 27, 2017, http://www.politico.com/story/2017/01/trump-russia-sanctions-john-mccain-response-234268 (accessed May 29, 2017).

45. Russia essentially has had three sets of sanctions put on it by the US since Crimea became part of Russia. US sectoral sanctions on Russia (on energy) are due to expire in December 2017 and could be renewed—if the US Senate does not try to

block such a move. "Ukraine/Russia Related Sanctions Program," US Department of the Treasury, last updated September 29, 2017, https://www.treasury.gov/resource-center/sanctions/Programs/Pages/ukraine.aspx (accessed October 26, 2017).

46. Aaron Blake, "Donald Trump Claims None of Those 3 to 5 Million Illegal Votes Were Cast for Him. Zero," *Washington Post*, January 26, 2017, https://www.washingtonpost.com/news/the-fix/wp/2017/01/25/donald-trump-claims-none-of-those-3-to-5-million-illegal-votes-were-cast-for-him-zero/?utm_term=.c260ce102f66 (accessed November 6, 2017).

47. Adam Liptak, "Supreme Court Rejects Challenge on 'One Person One Vote,'" *New York Times*, April 4, 2016, https://www.nytimes.com/2016/04/05/us/politics/supreme-court-one-person-one-vote.html?_r=0 (accessed October 26, 2017). The 2016 Supreme Court decision that states must count all residents in each voting district, whether they can vote or not, tends to enhance the power of urban areas, thus generally benefitting Democrats, while if only eligible voters would be counted in the census, then political power would shift from cities to rural areas, generally benefiting Republicans. In the near future, Trump supporters will be overseeing the 2020 census and could attempt to manipulate redistricting in each state according to Republican interests through gerrymandering.

48. "Remittances to Mexico Jump by Most in 10 Years after Trump Win," Reuters, January 2, 2017, http://www.reuters.com/article/us-mexico-economy-remittances/remittances-to-mexico-jump-by-most-in-10-years-after-trump-win-idUSKBN14M115 (accessed November 5, 2017).

49. The income from remittances reduces poverty in families and discourages their members from engaging in criminal behavior. Remittance flows are an important source of income for many households, communities, and LAC countries. They also enable households to invest more in the education and safety of young people, which helps to prevent crime and provide better job opportunities in the future. Steve Brito, Ana Corbacho, and René Osorio, *Remittances and the Impact on Crime in Mexico* (Washington, DC: Inter-American Development Bank, May 2014), working paper series no. 514, https://publications.iadb.org/bitstream/handle/11319/6482/IFD%20WP%20Remittances%20and%20the%20Impact%20on%20Crime%20in%20Mexico.pdf?sequence=1 (accessed October 26, 2017).

50. Associated Press, "Trump Says He'll Send Military to Mexico to 'Take Care of' 'Bad Hombres,' But Officials Say Comments Were Lighthearted," *Denver Post*, February 2, 2017, http://www.denverpost.com/2017/02/02/trump-mexico-bad-hombres/ (accessed October 26, 2017).

51. See argument of Robert A. Levy, "Reflections on Gun Control by a Second

Amendment Advocate," *National Law Journal*, February 12, 2013, https://www.law.com/nationallawjournal/almID/1202587764936/?slreturn=20171007060056 (accessed November 13, 2017).

52. Ali Vitali, "President Trump Signs New Immigration Executive Order," NBC News, March 6, 2017, http://www.nbcnews.com/politics/white-house/president-trump-signs-new-immigration-executive-order-n724276 (accessed October 26, 2017).

53. The Justice Department insisted that ban on immigrants from certain countries was justified for national security reasons. Unless the law can be proved to be discriminatory, the ban may not violate the Establishment and Equal Protection Clause of the Constitution, but it could violate the Immigration and Nationality Act of 1965, which had banned all discrimination against immigrants on the basis of national origin—unless "countries of concern" can be considered exempt. Nolan Rappaport, "If Immigration Ban Goes to Supreme Court, Trump Is Shoo-In to Win," *Hill*, February 13, 2017, http://thehill.com/blogs/pundits-blog/immigration/319212-if-immigration-ban-goes-to-supreme-court-trump-is-shoo-in (accessed October 26, 2017); Andrew Chung and Mica Rosenberg, "Courts Likely to Probe Trump's Intent in Issuing Travel Ban," Reuters, February 13, 2017, http://www.reuters.com/article/us-usa-trump-immigration-legal-idUSKBN15S14H (accessed October 26, 2017).

54. Trump does, however, appear to believe gun control laws that could impact those "deemed to be a threat to themselves or others" is "something to look into—people with mental health problems are on the streets who shouldn't be." "Donald Trump on Gun Control," *On the Issues*, last updated June 15, 2017, http://www.ontheissues.org/Celeb/Donald_Trump_Gun_Control.htm (accessed May 29, 2017).

55. As of April 2016 (prior to the July 14, 2016, Nice attacks) research found that lone right-wing extremists represent a substantial aspect of the lone-actor threat and must not be overlooked. Clare Ellis, Raffaello Pantucci, Jeanine de Roy van Zuijdewijn, Edwin Bakker, Benoît Gomis, Simon Palombi, and Melanie Smith, *Lone-Actor Terrorism: Final Report*, Countering Lone-Actor Terrorism Series, no. 11 (London: Royal United Services Institute for Defence and Security Studies, 2016), https://rusi.org/sites/default/files/201604_clat_final_report.pdf (accessed October 31, 2017); Tom Keatinge and Florence Keen, "Lone-Actor and Small Cell Terrorist Attacks: A New Front in Counter-Terrorist Finance?" RUSI Publications, January 24, 2017, https://rusi.org/publication/occasional-papers/lone-actor-and-small-cell-terrorist-attacks-new-front-counter (accessed October 26, 2017).

56. For the ideological development of Breivik's anti-Marxist ideology, see his

2011 manifesto: Anders Breivik [Andrew Berwick, pseud.], "2083: A European Declaration of Independence" https://fas.org/programs/tap/_docs/2083_-_A_European_Declaration_of_Independence.pdf (accessed October 26, 2017).

57. Asne Seierstad, "Is Norwegian Mass Murderer Anders Breivik Still a Threat to Europe?" *Newsweek*, May 13, 2016, http://europe.newsweek.com/anders-breivik-neo-nazi-suing-norway-asne-seierstad-447247?rm=eu (accessed October 26, 2017).

58. Sheryl Gay Stolberg and Brian M. Rosenthal, "Man Charged after White Nationalist Rally in Charlottesville Ends in Deadly Violence," *New York Times*, August 12, 2017, https://www.nytimes.com/2017/08/12/us/charlottesville-protest-white-nationalist.html?mcubz=1 (accessed October 26, 2017).

59. Ibid.

60. Joshua Berlinger, "Gavin Long: Who Is Baton Rouge Cop Killer?" CNN, August 4, 2016, http://edition.cnn.com/2016/07/18/us/who-is-gavin-long/ (accessed October 26, 2017). Long stated in a video that he had no affiliation with the Nation of Islam or ISIS.

61. Other issues that could lead to impeachment are based on two clauses in the US Constitution: The foreign-emoluments clause forbids any gifts or benefits from foreign governments and a second that forbids gifts or benefits from the US government or any US state. These concerns have been raised as a result from Donald Trump's refusal to separate himself from his major business interests as past presidents have done. David Swanson, "Why Impeach Donald Trump," *Counterpunch*, January 24, 2017, http://www.counterpunch.org/2017/01/24/why-impeach-donald-trump/ (accessed October 26, 2017).

62. Ken Bensinger, Miriam Elder, and Mark Schoofs, "These Reports Allege Trump Has Deep Ties to Russia," *BuzzFeed*, January 10, 2017, https://www.buzzfeed.com/kenbensinger/these-reports-allege-trump-has-deep-ties-to-russia?utm_term=.qxL4y3W2O3#.ldwb6E173E (accessed May 29, 2017).

63. See controversial report written by former British MI6 intelligence agent Christopher Steele, Fusion GPS report. Interestingly enough, the report indicates that the Russian government did want to sell 19 percent of Rosneft shares to foreigners, which it did, but not all of the names of share owners have been revealed. The Qatar Investment Corporation and the Swiss firm Glencore are listed as purchasers of 19.5 shares of Rosneft, but the figures do not add up. An unknown entity in the Cayman Islands may hold as much as $2.2 billion. Katya Golubkova, Dmitry Zhdannikov, and Stephen Jewkes, "How Russia Sold Its Oil Jewel: Without Saying Who Bought It," Reuters, January 24, 2017, http://www.reuters.com/article/us-russia-rosneft-privatisation-insight-idUSKBN1582OH (accessed October 26, 2017).

64. If Trump receives any special treatment in securing trademark rights, it might be considered a violation of the US Constitution, which bans public servants from accepting anything of value from foreign governments unless approved by Congress. Associated Press in Shanghai, "China Provisionally Grants Trump 38 Trademarks—Including for Escort Service," *Guardian*, March 8, 2017, https://www.theguardian.com/us-news/2017/mar/08/china-approves-trump-trademarks-businesses (accessed October 26, 2017). One of the theories of the secret GPS Fusion report is that Trump's political dealings with Russia were intended to deflect attention from his even bigger business deals with China. If so, the Russia affair has exploded way beyond Trump's expectations!

65. Greg Miller and Greg Jaffe, "Trump Revealed Highly Classified Information to Russian Foreign Minister and Ambassador," *Washington Post*, May 15 2017, https://www.washingtonpost.com/world/national-security/trump-revealed-highly-classified-information-to-russian-foreign-minister-and-ambassador/2017/05/15/530c172a-3960-11e7-9e48-c4f199710b69_story.html?utm_term=.731d6f4738e4 (accessed October 26, 2017).

66. Aristotle, *Politics*.

CHAPTER 4: RISKS OF THE NEW AMERICAN NATIONALISM FOR THE EUROPEAN UNION

1. Lewis Sanders, "World Leaders Tackle Uncertainty at the Heart of Global Order," *Deutsche Welle*, February 17, 2017, http://www.dw.com/en/world-leaders-tackle-uncertainty-at-the-heart-of-global-order/a-37608782 (accessed May 29, 2017).

2. Lionel Barber, "Juncker Tells Trump to Stop 'Annoying' Praise for Brexit," *Financial Times*, March 24, 2017, https://www.ft.com/content/938452b6-1072-11e7-a88c-50ba212dce4d (accessed October 26, 2017).

3. Tom Batchelor, "Donald Trump Says He Is 'Totally in Favour' of 'Wonderful' EU," *Independent*, February 23, 2017, http://www.independent.co.uk/news/world/americas/us-politics/donald-trump-european-union-eu-us-president-totally-in-favour-wonderful-steve-bannon-mike-pence-a7596731.html (accessed October 26, 2017).

4. Gardiner Harris and James Kanter, "Mike Pence, in Europe, Says Trump Supports Partnership with EU," *New York Times*, February 20, 2017, https://www.nytimes.com/2017/02/20/world/europe/pence-european-union-trump.html?rref

=collection%2Fnewseventcollection%2FThe%20Trump%20White%20House&action=click&contentCollection=Politics&module=Collection®ion=Marginalia&src=me&version=newsevent&pgtype=article (accessed May 30, 2017); "Remarks by President Donald Tusk after His Meeting with Vice President of the United States Mike Pence," press release, European Council: Council of the European Union, February 20, 2017, http://www.consilium.europa.eu/en/press/press-releases/2017/02/20-tusk-remarks-meeting-us-vice-president-pence/ (accessed May 30, 2017).

5. Batchelor, "Donald Trump Says."

6. Mathew Nussbaum, "Pence to Europe: We're Still with You," *Politico*, February 18, 2017, https://www.politico.com/story/2017/02/mike-pence-nato-european-leaders-235172 (accessed November 7, 2017).

7. Michael Birnbaum, "Trump's Calls for Europe to Increase Defense Spending Could Force Other Upheaval," *Washington Post*, February 15, 2017, https://www.washingtonpost.com/world/europe/trumps-calls-for-europe-to-increase-defense-spending-could-force-other-upheaval/2017/02/15/fe257b44-efc1-11e6-a100-fdaaf400369a_story.html?tid=a_inl&utm_term=.53f37519044d (accessed October 26, 2017).

8. US Donald Trump, "President Trump's Remarks at 9/11 and Article 5 Memorial Unveiling," US Mission to NATO, May 25, 2017, https://nato.usmission.gov/may-25-2017-president-trumps-remarks-911-article-5-memorial-unveiling/ (accessed October 26, 2017).

9. Germany's foreign minister, Sigmar Gabriel, retorted, "I don't know where Germany can find billions of euros to boost defense spending if politicians also want to lower taxes." Ewan MacAskill, "Pence's Speech on NATO Leaves European Leaders Troubled over Alliance's Future," *Guardian*, February 18, 2017, https://www.theguardian.com/world/2017/feb/18/trump-pence-eu-nato-munich-conference-germany-britain (accessed October 26, 2017); Steve Eder and Thomas Kaplan, "Donald Trump and Mike Pence: One Ticket, Two Worldviews," *New York Times*, July 17, 2016, https://www.nytimes.com/2016/07/18/us/politics/donald-trump-mike-pence.html?_r=0 (accessed October 26, 2017).

10. The United States, the United Kingdom, and France are global hegemonic powers, but Germany is not. Its political-economic influence is largely European, although it does a large business in conventional arms. From 2014 to 2015, German arms sales almost doubled to €7.5 billion, with sales to the United Kingdom but also to Qatar and Saudi Arabia. "German Arms Exports Keep Rising in 2016," Deutsche Welle, July 5, 2016, http://www.dw.com/en/german-arms-exports-keep-rising-in-2016/a-19377912 (accessed October 26, 2017).

11. "Ombudsman: German Army Is 'Short of Almost Everything,'" Deutsche

Welle, January 26, 2016, http://www.dw.com/en/ombudsman-german-army-is-short-of-almost-everything/a-19005841 (accessed May 29, 2017).

12. "Réduite de 50% sous Sarkozy et Hollande, l'armée française est au bord de l'explosion," *Le Salon Beige*, October 27, 2015, http://www.lesalonbeige.fr/reduite-de-50-sous-sarkozy-et-hollande-larmee-francaise-est-au-bord-de-lexplosion/ (accessed May 29, 2017).

13. Ivana Kottasova, "How NATO Is Funded and Who Pays What," CNN, March 20, 2017, http://money.cnn.com/2017/03/20/news/nato-funding-explained/index.html (accessed November 7, 2017). On demands that the Europeans, not the Americans, pay more for defense, see Doug Bandow, "U.S. to Spend More on Europe's Defense: Let the Europeans Pay Instead," *Huffington Post*, February 12, 2017, https://www.huffingtonpost.com/doug-bandow/us-to-spend-more-on-europ_b_9219754.html (accessed November 7, 2017).

14. "Donald Trump: More Countries Will Leave the EU Following Brexit—Video," *Guardian*, June 24, 2016, https://www.theguardian.com/politics/video/2016/jun/24/donald-trump-more-countries-will-leave-eu-following-brexit-video (accessed November 13, 2017).

15. The Greek financial crisis is not only due to excessive covert expenditure, but also a result of the 2008 US financial crisis. On the relationship to the US mortgage crisis and European banking crisis, see "James K. Galbraith: The Final Death (and Next Life) of Maynard Keynes," transcript, *Shadowproof*, August 5, 2011, https://shadowproof.com/2011/08/01/james-k-galbraith-the-final-death-and-next-life-of-maynard-keynes/ (accessed May 30, 2017).

16. Roberto Savio, "Merkel's Defeat Confirms Dismal Trend for Europe," *Other News*, September 29, 2017, http://www.other-news.info/2017/09/merkels-defeat-confirms-dismal-trend-for-europe/ (accessed November 6, 2017).

17. John Mauldin, "Italy's Banking Crisis Is Nearly upon Us," *Forbes*, December 8, 2016, https://www.forbes.com/sites/johnmauldin/2016/12/08/italys-banking-crisis-is-nearly-upon-us/#6c235e6f6c23 (accessed October 26, 2017); Philip Molyneux, "Will Italy's Failing Banks Trigger Financial Collapse across Europe?" *Guardian*, November 28, 2016, https://www.theguardian.com/commentisfree/2016/nov/28/italy-failing-banks-new-japan (accessed October 26, 2017).

18. Nicole Koenig and Marie Walter-Franke, "France and Germany: Spearheading a European Security and Defence Union?" (policy paper; Berlin: Jacques Delors Institut, July 19, 2017), http://www.institutdelors.eu/media/franceandgermanyspearheadingaeuropeansecurityanddefenceunion-koenigwalter-jdib-july2017.pdf?pdf=ok (accessed October 26, 2017).

19. *Joint Declaration Issued at the British-French Summit* (Saint-Malo, France: EU Institute for Security Studies, February 2000), https://www.cvce.eu/en/obj/franco_british_st_malo_declaration_4_december_1998-en-f3cd16fb-fc37-4d52-936f-c8e9bc80f24f.html (accessed October 26, 2017).

20. Daniel Keohane, "Three's Company? France, Germany, the UK, and European Defence Post-Brexit," Real Instituto Elcano, January 5, 2017, http://www.realinstitutoelcano.org/wps/portal/rielcano_en/contenido?WCM_GLOBAL_CONTEXT=/elcano/elcano_in/zonas_in/ari1-2017-keohane-threes-company-france-germany-uk-european-defence-post-brexit(accessed May 30, 2017).

21. Tom Batchelor, "Scotland 'Would Not Get Automatic Membership of NATO If It Voted for Independence,'" *Independent*, March 13, 2017, http://www.independent.co.uk/news/uk/politics/scottish-referendum-nicola-sturgeon-nato-membership-independent-scotland-a7627481.html (accessed May 30, 2017).

22. Rainer Buergin and Toluse Olorunnipa, "Trump Slams NATO, Floats Russia Nuke Deal in European Interview," Bloomberg, January 15, 2017, https://www.bloomberg.com/politics/articles/2017-01-15/trump-calls-nato-obsolete-and-dismisses-eu-in-german-interview (accessed May 30, 2017).

23. Kevin Liptak and Michelle Kosinski, "After Combative Meeting, Trump Tries Phone Flattery to Win over Merkel," CNN, March 28, 2017, http://edition.cnn.com/2017/03/28/politics/donald-trump-angela-merkel-call/ (accessed October 26, 2017).

24. "Donald Trump Slams Angela Merkel's Refugee Policy," Deutsche Welle, January 15, 2017, http://www.dw.com/en/donald-trump-slams-angela-merkels-refugee-policy/a-37141791 (accessed May 30, 2017).

25. "New US Russia Sanctions Bill Risks EU Anger," Deutsche Welle, July 28, 2017, http://www.dw.com/en/new-us-russia-sanctions-bill-risks-eu-anger/a-39867060 (accessed October 26, 2017).

26. Shannon Tiezzi, "China and Germany's 'Special Relationship,'" *Diplomat*, July 08, 2014, https://thediplomat.com/2014/07/china-and-germanys-special-relationship/ (accessed November 7, 2017).

27. Robin Harding, "Japan Fears Brexit Blow to EU Arms Embargo on China," *Financial Times*, https://www.ft.com/content/219af680-41c6-11e6-b22f-79eb4891c97d (accessed October 26, 2017).

28. Daniel Twining, "Leveraging America's Asian Pivot to Reinforce the Transatlantic Alliance and Vice Versa," Asan Forum, June 30, 2016, http://www.theasanforum.org/leveraging-americas-asian-pivot-to-reinforce-the-transatlantic-alliance-and-vice-versa/ (accessed May 30, 2017).

29. For details, see "Migrant Crisis: Migration to Europe Explained in Seven

Charts," BBC, March 4, 2016, http://www.bbc.com/news/world-europe-34131911 (accessed November 7, 2017).

30. "BP-Rosneft Deal," *Russia Beyond the Headlines*, January 15, 2011, http://rbth.com/bp-rosneft (accessed May 30, 2017).

31. Justin Sink, "Trump, Merkel Discussed NATO, Mideast in First Phone Call," Bloomberg, January 28, 2017, https://www.bloomberg.com/politics/articles/2017-01-28/trump-merkel-discussed-nato-middle-east-in-first-phone-call (accessed October 26, 2017).

32. "New CAP Is Still Struggling to Find New Export Markets," *EurActiv: Main Challenges Facing the CAP*, special report, July 25–29, 2016, http://en.euractiv.eu/wp-content/uploads/sites/2/special-report/EurActiv-Multilingual-Special-Report-The-main-challenges-facing-the-CAP-1.pdf (accessed November 7, 2017).

33. Jake Rudnitsky and Ilya Arkhipov, "Putin's Reliance on American Commerce Has Never Been Greater," Bloomberg, June 15, 2016, https://www.bloomberg.com/news/articles/2016-06-15/putin-s-reliance-on-american-commerce-has-never-been-greater (accessed October 26, 2017).

34. David Shamah, "Sanctions Propel Israel, Russia to Expand Agriculture Ties" *Times of Israel*, September 14, 2014, http://www.timesofisrael.com/sanctions-propel-israel-russia-to-expand-agriculture-ties/ (accessed October 26, 2017).

35. Aleksandra Eriksson, *EU Observer*, June 23, 2017, https://euobserver.com/foreign/138334 (accessed November 6, 2017). Daniel P. Ahn and Rodney D. Ludema, "Measuring Smartness: Understanding the Economic Impact of Targeted Sanctions," working paper 2017-01, December 2016, https://www.state.gov/documents/organization/267590.pdf (accessed, November 6, 2017). Sarantis Michalopoulos, "Russia Extends Embargo on EU Food Products," *EurActiv*, June 30, 2016, https://www.euractiv.com/section/agriculture-food/news/russia-extends-embargo-on-eu-food-products/ (accessed May 30, 2017). See impact of sanctions on Russia and the EU. Anastasia Nevskaya, "Russia-EU Economic Relations: Assessing Two Years of Sanctions," *Russia Direct*, June 16, 2016, http://www.russia-direct.org/analysis/russia-eu-economic-relations-assessing-two-years-sanctions (accessed October 26, 2017).

36. Raphaël Proust, "Jean-Luc Mélenchon veut une « conférence sur la sécurité » en Europe," *l'Opinion*, March 31, 2017, http://www.lopinion.fr/edition/politique/jean-luc-melenchon-veut-conference-securite-en-europe-123375 (accessed October 26, 2017).

37. *Wikipedia*, s.v. "German Federal Election, 2017," last modified November 21, 2017, https://en.wikipedia.org/wiki/German_federal_election,_2017 (accessed November 21, 2017).

38. Trump's adviser and strategist Steve Bannon has been seen as organizing a new international order based on "illiberal democracy." His allies include Nigel Farage (United Kingdom Independence Party), Matteo Salvini (Italian Northern League), Beppe Grillo (Italian 5 Star Movement), Marine Le Pen (French National Front), and Geert Wilders (Netherlands Freedom Party)—who, at the beginning of the Trump administration, had Washington (and not so much Moscow) as their point of reference. Roberto Savio, "Trump Marks the End of a Cycle," Inter Press Service, February 21, 2017, http://www.ipsnews.net/2017/02/trump-marks-the-end-of-a-cycle/ (accessed May 30, 2017). Given the shift back toward neoconservativism and neo-liberalism in the Trump administration, whether this alliance can hold together is another question.

39. Dan Stewart, "Donald Trump's Meeting with Nigel Farage Leaves Britain's Leaders Red-Faced," *Time*, Nov 14, 2016, http://time.com/4569416/donald-trump-nigel-farage-meeting-theresa-may/ (accessed October 27, 2017).

40. Ben Jacobs, "Donald Trump: Marine Le Pen Is 'Strongest Candidate' in French Election," *Guardian*, April 21, 2017, https://www.theguardian.com/us-news/2017/apr/21/donald-trump-marine-le-pen-french-presidential-election (accessed October 27, 2017).

41. Fredrik Wesslau, "Putin's Friends in Europe," European Council on Foreign Relations, October 19, 2016, http://www.ecfr.eu/article/commentary_putins_friends_in_europe7153 (accessed May 30, 2017).

42. Gašper Završnik, "Beata Szydło: Poland May Drop Rome Declaration," *Politico*, March 23, 2017, http://www.politico.eu/article/beata-szydlo-poland-may-drop-rome-declaration/ (accessed October 27, 2017).

43. Péter Krekó and Lóránt Györi, "Don't Ignore the Left! Connections between Europe's Radical Left and Russia," *OpenDemocracy*, June 13, 2016, https://www.opendemocracy.net/od-russia/peter-kreko-lorant-gyori/don-t-ignore-left-connections-between-europe-s-radical-left-and-ru (accessed May 30, 2017).

44. Stephanie Kirchgaessner, "Italy's Five Star Movement Part of Growing Club of Putin Sympathisers in West," *Guardian*, January 5, 2017, https://www.theguardian.com/world/2017/jan/05/five-star-movement-beppe-grillo-putin-supporters-west (accessed May 30, 2017).

45. Two major events have worked to further destabilize the region, leading to a mass exodus: French and UK-led military intervention in Libya (backed by NATO) in March 2011 and then the Syrian civil war which began in 2011, but escalated even further with direct Russian military involvement in September 2015.

46. Roberto Savio, "Merkel's Defeat Confirms Dismal Trend for Europe," *Other*

News, September 29, 2017, http://www.other-news.info/2017/09/merkels-defeat-confirms-dismal-trend-for-europe/ (accessed November 6, 2017).

47. IPSOS, Résultats du 2nd tour, 2017, https://www.ipsos.com/fr-fr/presidentielle-2nd-tour-les-estimations-ipsos-sopra-steria-dune-grande-precision (accessed November 6, 2017).

48. Saim Saeed, "US Intelligence Chief: Russia Interfering in French, German Elections," *Politico*, March 30, 2017, http://www.politico.eu/article/us-intelligence-chief-russia-interfering-in-french-german-elections/ (accessed October 27, 2017).

49. Helene Fouquet, Gregory Viscusi, and Henry Meyer, "Le Pen Struggling to Fund French Race as Russian Bank Fails," Bloomberg, December 22, 2016, https://www.bloomberg.com/news/articles/2016-12-22/le-pen-struggling-to-fund-french-race-after-russian-backer-fails (accessed November 13, 2017).

50. Gideon Resnick, "Steve Bannon Knew about Marine Le Pen's Trump Tower Party, Organizer Claims," *Daily Beast*, January 30, 2017, http://www.thedailybeast.com/articles/2017/01/12/steve-bannon-knew-about-marine-le-pen-s-trump-tower-party-organizer-claims.html (accessed May 30, 2017).

51. Eric Auchard and Bate Felix, "French Candidate Macron Claims Massive Hack as Emails Leaked," Reuters, May 6, 2017, http://www.reuters.com/article/us-france-election-macron-leaks-idUSKBN1812AZ (accessed October 27, 2017).

52. Andrew Higgins, "Maybe Private Russian Hackers Meddled in Election, Putin Says," *New York Times*, June 1, 2017, https://www.nytimes.com/2017/06/01/world/europe/vladimir-putin-donald-trump-hacking.html (accessed November 7, 2017).

53. Auchard and Felix, "French Candidate Macron."

54. "Dutch Referendum a Difficult Result for EU and Ukraine," BBC News, April 7, 2016, http://www.bbc.com/news/world-europe-35984821 (accessed May 30, 2017).

55. Jennifer Rankin, "EU Lifts Most Sanctions against Belarus Despite Human Rights Concerns," *Guardian*, February 15, 2016, https://www.theguardian.com/world/2016/feb/15/eu-lifts-most-sanctions-against-belarus-despite-human-rights-concerns (accessed May 30, 2017).

56. See for example, Andrew Wilson, "Europe, Keep an Eye on Minsk: If the Belarus President Is to Survive, He Will Have to Walk a Narrow Path between Pressure from Demonstrators and the Kremlin," *Politico*, March 17, 2017, http://www.politico.eu/article/europe-keep-an-eye-on-minsk-belarus-alexander-lukashenko-vladimir-putin-russia/ (accessed May 30, 2017).

57. Colin Brose, "Serbia Maneuvers between the EU and EEU," Jamestown

Foundation, November 11, 2016, https://jamestown.org/serbia-maneuvers-eu-eeu/ (accessed May 30, 2017).

58. Rikard Jozwiak, "Brussels Notebook: Elections Aren't Only Things Keeping NATO, EU Folks up at Night," RadioFreeEurope/RadioLiberty, January 4, 2017, http://www.rferl.org/a/brussels-notebook-elections-not-only-things-keeping-nato-eu-up-at-night/28214010.html?ltflags=mailer (accessed October 27, 2017).

59. Nick Gass, "Trump: Taking Back Crimea Would Trigger World War III," *Politico*, August 1, 2016, http://www.politico.com/story/2016/08/donald-trump-crimea-ukraine-war-226522 (accessed May 30, 2017).

60. Christina Boyle, "European Council President Includes United States as Threat to Europe," *LA Times*, January 31, 2017, http://www.latimes.com/world/europe/la-fg-europe-trump-20170131-story.html (accessed October 27, 2017); M. Emmanuel Macron, "United Nations General Assembly—Speech by M. Emmanuel Macron, President of the Republic," (speech; New York: United Nations, September 19, 2017), http://www.diplomatie.gouv.fr/en/french-foreign-policy/united-nations/united-nations-general-assembly-sessions/unga-s-72nd-session/article/united-nations-general-assembly-speech-by-m-emmanuel-macron-president-of-the (accessed October 27, 2017).

CHAPTER 5: THE RISK OF WAR OVER CRIMEA, THE BLACK SEA, AND EASTERN EUROPE

1. Nick Gass, "Trump: Taking Back Crimea Would Trigger World War III," *Politico*, August 1, 2016, http://www.politico.com/story/2016/08/donald-trump-crimea-ukraine-war-226522 (accessed October 27, 2017).

2. Bryan Logan, "Nikki Haley Just Delivered the Trump Administration's Most Hawkish Words Yet toward Russia," *Business Insider*, February 3, 2017, http://uk.businessinsider.com/trump-nikki-haley-russia-ukraine-2017-2?r=US&IR=T (accessed May 29, 2017). Christopher Miller, "Anxious Ukraine Risks Escalation in 'Creeping Offensive,'" RadioFreeEurope/RadioLiberty, January 30, 2017, http://www.rferl.org/a/ukraine-russia-creeping-offensive-escalation-fighting/28268104.html (accessed October 27, 2017). See chapter 3.

3. Nikita Vladimirov, "Trump Vows to Restore 'Peace' Along Russia, Ukraine Border," *Hill*, February 4, 2017, http://thehill.com/policy/international/317943-trump-vows-to-restore-peace-along-russia-ukraine-border (accessed May 29, 2017).

4. It is not absolutely clear whether Haley's speech implied a complete end to sectoral sanctions. Russia essentially has had three sets of sanctions put on it by the United States since Crimea became part of Russia. US sectoral sanctions on Russia are due to expire in December 2017. European sanctions are due to expire in January 2018. It is more likely that the Europeans will eventually end sanctions earlier than the Americans, given the impact of sanctions on European agriculture. Kenneth Rapoza, "What UN Ambassador Haley's Comment on Russia Really Means," *Forbes*, February 3, 2017, http://www.forbes.com/sites/kenrapoza/2017/02/03/what-u-n-ambassador-haleys-comment-on-russia-really-means/#63320ee74405 (accessed May 29, 2017).

5. Andrew E. Kramer and Clifford Krauss, "Rex Tillerson's Company, Exxon, Has Billions at Stake over Sanctions on Russia," *New York Times*, December 12, 2016, https://www.nytimes.com/2016/12/12/world/europe/rex-tillersons-company-exxon-has-billions-at-stake-over-russia-sanctions.html?_r=1 (accessed October 27, 2017). For projected benefits of the Trump presidency for Exxon, see Jenny Rowland et al., "How Exxon Won the 2016 Election," Center for American Progress, January 10, 2017, https://www.americanprogress.org/issues/green/news/2017/01/10/296277/how-exxon-won-the-2016-election/ (accessed October 27, 2017).

6. If, for example, the ExxonMobil and Rosneft joint venture is forced to break up, then Exxon and Rosneft could swap assets in the United States and Canada and in Russia. But the gas deposits in the Arctic Circle are probably worth much more than the US/Canadian deposits. And the Bazhenov shale could prove ten times bigger than the Bakken shale of North Dakota. See Christopher Helman, "Why Forcing ExxonMobil out of Russia Isn't Going to Help Anything," *Forbes*, September 14, 2014, https://www.forbes.com/sites/christopherhelman/2014/09/14/why-forcing-exxonmobil-out-of-russia-isnt-going-to-help-anything/#2f7240121a20 (accessed October 27, 2017).

7. Nick Cunningham, "Chevron Pulls out of $10 Billion Gas Deal with Ukraine," OilPrice.com, December 15, 2014, http://oilprice.com/Energy/Natural-Gas/Chevron-Pulls-Out-Of-10-Billion-Gas-Deal-With-Ukraine.html (accessed May 29, 2017).

8. Christopher Hellie, "Should Russia's Internal Issues Scare Long-Term Investors?" *Global Risks Insights*, January 31, 2017, http://globalriskinsights.com/2017/01/russia-internal-issues/ (accessed October 27, 2017); Kenneth Rapoza, "Russia Investors Get No Love From Trump, But . . ." *Forbes*, April 24, 2017, https://www.forbes.com/sites/kenrapoza/2017/04/24/russia-investors-get-no-love-from-trump-but/#787ebf505470 (accessed October 27, 2017); Jason Corcoran, "Russia Set to Remain out in the Cold," *bne IntelliNews Daily*, May 9, 2017, http://online

.flipbuilder.com/myab/ihpb/mobile/index.html?inf_contact_key=fe813ce84d777d1d7ae6e339ad06b82609b749d2ca1cd0f1867aca4c553ba280 (accessed October 27, 2017).

9. Reuters, "The Art of the Deal: Why Putin Needs Trump More Than Trump Needs Putin," *Business Insider*, February 1, 2017, http://uk.businessinsider.com/r-the-art-of-the-deal-why-putin-needs-one-more-than-trump-2017-2?r=US&IR=T (accessed May 30, 2017).

10. There is a statistical dispute as to whether oil and gas account for around 34 percent or 50 percent of government revenues. Jon Hellevig, "Oil and Gas Revenue Accounts for 21% of Russia's Budget Not 50%," *Russia Insider*, March 28, 2016, http://russia-insider.com/en/business/oil-and-gas-revenue-accounts-just-21-russias-budget-not-over-50-routinely-misreported-west (accessed May 29, 2017); Alexander Metelitsa, "Oil and Natural Gas Sales Accounted for 68% of Russia's Total Export Revenues in 2013," US Energy Information Administration (EIA), July 23, 2014, http://www.eia.gov/todayinenergy/detail.php?id=17231 (accessed May 29, 2017).

11. Donald Trump, "Statement by President Donald J. Trump on the Signing of H.R. 3364," press release, White House, Office of the Press Secretary, August 2, 2017, https://www.whitehouse.gov/the-press-office/2017/08/02/statement-president-donald-j-trump-signing-hr-3364 (accessed October 27, 2017).

12. Ibid.

13. James Osborne, "EIA: US Shale Oil Production to Fall Sharply through 2017," *Fuel Fix*, August 22, 2016, http://fuelfix.com/blog/2016/08/22/eia-u-s-shale-oil-production-to-fall-sharply-through-2017/ (accessed May 29, 2017); Reuters, "US Shale Firms Go Back to Work after Donald Trump's Victory," *Fortune*, November 14, 2016, http://fortune.com/2016/11/14/donald-trump-victory-us-shale-oil/ (accessed October 27, 2017).

14. ICMN Staff, "Rosebud Sioux Tribe Calls House Keystone XL Passage an 'Act of War,' Vows Legal Action," Indian Country Media Network, November 17, 2014, https://indiancountrymedianetwork.com/news/politics/rosebud-sioux-tribe-calls-house-keystone-xl-passage-an-act-of-war-vows-legal-action/ (accessed May 29, 2017).

15. Glenn Ellis and Katerina Barushka, "A Very Montenegrin Coup," Al Jazeera, March 2, 2017, http://www.aljazeera.com/programmes/peopleandpower/2017/03/montenegrin-coup-170302060130440.html (accessed October 27, 2017).

16. It is possible that Finland and the Yeltsin administration may have talked about Russia selling Karelia back to Finland, but the idea was dumped. Putin has stated that territorial exchanges are not the best way to bring peace! Martti Valkonen, "President Ahtisaari Unlocked a Door towards Debate about Lost Karjala," *Prokarelia*,

November 28, 2002, http://prokarelia.net/en/?x=artikkeli&article_id=314 &author=1 (accessed October 27, 2017).

17. Rapoza, "What UN Ambassador Haley's Comment"; "Ukraine/Russia Related Sanctions Program," US Department of the Treasury, last updated September 29, 2017, https://www.treasury.gov/resource-center/sanctions/Programs/Pages/ukraine.aspx (accessed October 26, 2017).

18. Kiev could have tried to sustain its nuclear weaponry; Kiev had the missiles, but needed to build the warheads as the control systems were in Moscow (at a cost of $65 billion). Yet the Clinton Administration threatened Ukraine with isolation and sanctions if Kiev sustained the nuclear weapons while Russia threatened preemptive strikes. See Hall Gardner, *Surviving the Millennium: American Global Strategy, the Collapse of the Soviet Empire, and the Question of Peace* (Westport, CT: Praeger, 1994).

19. NATO, "Founding Act on Mutual Relations, Cooperation and Security between NATO and the Russian Federation Signed in Paris, France," North Atlantic Treaty Organization, May 27, 1997, http://www.nato.int/cps/en/natohq/official_texts_25468.htm (accessed May 29, 2017).

20. Ibid.

21. Ibid.

22. Ibid.

23. Dave Majumdar, "Revealed: Russian Invasion Could Overrun NATO in 60 Hours," *National Interest*, February 4, 2016, http://nationalinterest.org/blog/the-buzz/revealed-russian-invasion-could-overrun-nato-60-hours-15112 (accessed May 29, 2017). It was estimated that a proposed deployment of seven brigades to deter potential Russian aggression in the Baltic region could cost about $2.7 billion. But such a force could only slow, not defeat, Moscow—if the latter were truly determined to overrun these countries. Lisabeth Gronlund, "How Much Does It Cost to Create a Single Nuclear Weapon?" Union of Concerned Scientists, November 2013, http://www.ucsusa.org/publications/ask/2013/nuclear-weapon-cost.html#.V9VZ4z595wc (accessed May 29, 2017); On Obama's military buildup: Dov S. Zakheim, "The Great Reversal: Obama's Military Buildup," *National Interest*, February 9, 2016, http://nationalinterest.org/feature/the-great-reversal-obamas-military-buildup-15151 (accessed May 29, 2017).

24. Jeffrey Goldberg, "The Obama Doctrine," *Atlantic*, March 17, 2016, http://www.theatlantic.com/magazine/archive/2016/04/the-obama-doctrine/471525/#3 (accessed May 29, 2017).

25. NATO, "Ukraine Commission," North Atlantic Treaty Organization, May 21, 2014, http://www.nato.int/cps/iw/natohq/topics_50319.htm (accessed May 29, 2017).

26. Emily Tamkin, Dan De Luce, Robbie Gramer, "Ukraine Expects Trump to Approve Arms Deliveries," *Foreign Policy*, October 26, 2017, http://foreignpolicy.com/2017/10/26/ukraine-expects-trump-to-approve-arms-deliveries/ (accessed November 7, 2017).

27. See Hall Gardner, *Crimea, Global Rivalry and the Vengeance of History* (Basingstoke, UK: Palgrave MacMillan, 2015).

28. "Minsk Agreement: Full Text in English," UNIAN, February 12, 2015, http://www.unian.info/politics/1043394-minsk-agreement-full-text-in-english.html (accessed May 30, 2017).

29. Tim Judah, "Will Ukraine Ever Change?" *New York Review of Books*, May 25, 2017, http://www.nybooks.com/articles/2017/05/25/will-ukraine-ever-change/ (accessed November 7, 2017). See also Gordon M. Hahn, "Getting Ukraine Wrong," Gordon Hahn, September 8, 2017, https://gordonhahn.com/2017/09/08/getting-ukraine-wrong/ (accessed October 27, 2017).

30. Mikhail Minakov and Maryna Stavniichuk, "Ukraine's Constitution: Reform or Crisis?" *Open Democracy*, February 16, 2016, https://www.opendemocracy.net/od-russia/mikhail-minakov-maryna-stavniichuk/ukrainian-constitution-reform-or-crisis (accessed November 7, 2017)

31. "Poroshenko's proposal is not approved by the separatists, nor by the Kremlin. It does not really give any 'special status' to separatist areas, and any specific details on autonomous rule in Donbass may later be revised by a simple majority vote in Ukrainian parliament. Moreover, the so-called 'decentralisation' is accompanied by a strengthening of the presidential control over local self-government via centrally assigned 'prefects' with broad powers." Volodymyr Ishchenko, "Ukraine's Government Bears More Responsibility for Ongoing Conflict Than the Far-Right," *Guardian*, September 4, 2015, http://www.theguardian.com/world/2015/sep/04/ukraine-government-svoboda-clashes-conflict (accessed October 27, 2017).

32. "Corruption Perceptions Index 2016," *Transparency International*, January 25, 2017, http://www.transparency.org/news/feature/corruption_perceptions_index_2016 (accessed October 27, 2017).

33. The self-proclaimed Union was established in May 2014. Yet the Novorossiya pan-nationalist movement was not officially recognized internationally, even by Russia, and was labeled as a "terrorist organization" by Kiev. The movement came to a sudden end in May 2015 after meetings between US and European officials with Moscow. Andrei Kolesnikov, "Why the Kremlin Is Shutting Down the Novorossiya Project," Carnegie.ru/commentary, May 29, 2015, http://carnegieendowment.org/2015/05/29/why-kremlin-is-shutting-down-novorossiya-project/i96u (accessed November 14, 2017).

34. Pavel Podvig, "What the Crimea Crisis Will Do to US-Russia Relations," *Bulletin of the Atomic Scientists*, March 27, 2014, http://thebulletin.org/what-crimea-crisis-will-do-us-russia-relations7009 (accessed May 30, 2017).

35. NATO, "Wales Summit Declaration," press release, issued by the heads of state and government participating in the meeting of the North Atlantic Council in Wales, September 5, 2014, http://www.nato.int/cps/ic/natohq/official_texts_112964.htm (accessed October 27, 2017).

36. Joshua Yaffa, "The Unaccountable Death of Boris Nemtsov," *New Yorker*, February 26, 2016, http://www.newyorker.com/news/news-desk/the-unaccountable-death-of-boris-nemtsov (accessed May 30, 2017).

37. Miller, "Anxious Ukraine Risks Escalation."

38. Roman Olearchyk, "Ukraine Imposes Cargo Blockade on Breakaway East," *Financial Times*, March 15, 2017, https://www.ft.com/content/276f3fd8-098c-11e7-ac5a-903b21361b43 (accessed October 27, 2017); Nicolai Petro, "The Bizarre Reason Ukraine Could Be Facing a Legitimacy Crisis," *National Interest*, March 15, 2017, http://nationalinterest.org/feature/the-bizarre-reason-ukraine-could-be-facing-legitimacy-crisis-19787 (accessed October 27, 2017); Miller, "Anxious Ukraine Risks Escalation."

39. Andrew Roth, "Russia Accuses Ukraine of Igniting Border Clash in Crimea," *Washington Post*, August 10, 2016, https://www.washingtonpost.com/world/russia-accuses-ukraine-of-igniting-border-clashes-in-crimea/2016/08/10/f8e1641a-5f00-11e6-84c1-6d27287896b5_story.html?tid=a_inl (accessed May 30, 2017); Nicolai N. Petro and David C. Speedie, "Update from Ukraine," Carnegie Council for Ethics in International Affairs, August 18, 2016, http://www.carnegiecouncil.org/studio/multimedia/20160818b/index.html (accessed May 30, 2017).

40. Nina Sorokopud, *Ukraine UNHCR Operational Update* (Geneva, Switzerland: UN Refugee Agency, January 2017), http://unhcr.org.ua/attachments/updates/2017%2001%20Update%20FINAL%20EN.pdf (accessed October 27, 2017).

41. Halya Coynash, "Russia's Crimea Bridge Could Collapse Anytime," The Atlantic Council (blog), January 10, 2017, http://www.atlanticcouncil.org/blogs/ukrainealert/russia-s-crimea-bridge-could-collapse-anytime (accessed October 27, 2017).

42. Lily Hyde, "Crimea's Water Troubles," *Euromaidan Press*, February 8, 2017, http://euromaidanpress.com/2017/02/10/crimeas-water-troubles/#arvlbdata (accessed October 27, 2017); "Dam Leaves Crimea Population in Chronic Water Shortage," Al Jazeera, January 4, 2017, http://www.aljazeera.com/indepth/features/2016/12/dam-leaves-crimea-population-chronic-water-shortage-161229092648659.html (accessed October 27, 2017).

43. Writer, Staff. "F-35s to Participate in NATO Exercises Near Russian Border," *Popular Military*, April 26, 2017, http://popularmilitary.com/f-35s-participate-nato-exercises-near-russian-border/ (accessed May 29, 2017).

CHAPTER 6: THE GLOBAL IMPACT OF THE CHINA-RUSSIA EURASIAN ALLIANCE

1. Laura Zhou, "China and Russia Criticise THAAD Missile Defence System as Destabilising Region," *South China Morning Post*, July 8, 2016, http://www.scmp.com/news/china/diplomacy-defence/article/1987103/china-and-russia-criticise-thaad-missile-defence-system (accessed May 30, 2017).

2. Bob Savic, "Behind China and Russia's 'Special Relationship'" *Diplomat*, December 7, 2016, http://thediplomat.com/2016/12/behind-china-and-russias-special-relationship/ (accessed May 30, 2017). The revised, official translated name of the initiative is "The Belt and Road Initiative"—with "BRI" as its acronym instead of the "OBOR."

3. China's per capita disposable personal income was $3,469 in 2016. Xinhua, "China's personal Income Rises 6.3% in 2016," *China Daily*, January 1, 2017, http://www.chinadaily.com.cn/business/2017-01/20/content_28010029.htm (accessed November 7, 2017).

4. Franz-Stefan Gady, "China and Russia Conclude Naval Drill in Mediterranean," *Diplomat*, May 22, 2015, http://thediplomat.com/2015/05/china-and-russia-conclude-naval-drill-in-mediterranean/ (accessed May 30, 2017).

5. Joshua Kucera, "Armenia Nixes Pakistan's Ties with CSTO," EurasiaNet.org, November 29, 2016, http://www.eurasianet.org/node/81476 (accessed May 30, 2017). Pakistan not only supports Azerbaijan in its conflict with Armenia over Nagorno Karabakh, but goes so far as refusing to recognize Armenia's existence until it gives Karabakh back to Azerbaijan.

6. Vladimir Radyuhin, "The Dragon Gets a Bear Hug," *The Hindu*, March 7, 2013, http://www.thehindu.com/opinion/op-ed/the-dragon-gets-a-bear-hug/article4485335.ece (accessed May 30, 2017).

7. Charles Clover, "Russia Resumes Advanced Weapons Sales to China," *Financial Times*, November 16, 2016, https://www.ft.com/content/90b1ada2-a18e-11e6-86d5-4e36b35c3550 (accessed November 11, 2017).

8. According to Konstantin Makienko, "the Chinese mainly need the Su-35

to obtain access to the aircraft's new 117S engine, and Russia's latest and extremely powerful aircraft-based IRBIS radar system." Beyond that, Russia has a very limited catalogue of military hardware that it can sell to Beijing at this point. Russia has already sold most everything else. Matthew Bodner, "In Arms Trade, China Is Taking Advantage of Russia's Desperation," *Moscow Times*, November 1, 2016, https://themoscowtimes.com/articles/in-arms-trade-china-is-taking-advantage-of-russian-desperation-55965 (accessed May 30, 2017).

9. Charles Clover, "Russia Resumes Advanced Weapons Sales to China," *Financial Times*, November 3, 2016, https://www.ft.com/content/90b1ada2-a18e-11e6-86d5-4e36b35c3550 (accessed May 30, 2017). In November 2016, China unveiled its own advanced stealth fighter, deployments to come later.

10. China's main focus is indigenizing foreign technologies and systems in order to create a self-sufficient defense industry that can both produce weaponry platforms for the PLA and compete successfully in the global arms market. Stephen Blank, "Moscow Talks Business, Beijing Answers with Geo-strategy," *China Brief* 13, no. 22 (Washington, DC: Jamestown Foundation, November 07, 2013), http://www.jamestown.org/single/?tx_ttnews[tt_news]=41596&no_cache=1#.U3t4EyhauZQ (accessed May 30, 2017).

11. Bodner, "In Arms Trade, China Is Taking Advantage."

12. Stephen Blank and Younkyoo Kim, "Russian Arms Sales and Its Future as an Asian Power," *Asian Politics & Policy* 6, no. 2 (2013): 267–84.

13. Jakobson et al., "China's Energy and Security Relations with Russia: Hopes, Frustrations and Uncertainties," (policy paper; Solna: Stockholm International Peace Research Institute, 2011), pp. 27 and 35.

14. Neal Buckley, "Sino-Russian Gas Deal: Smoke without Fire," *Financial Times*, May 11, 2016, https://www.ft.com/content/eea4f2ec-16c0-11e6-b197-a4af20d5575e (accessed October 27, 2017); Henry Foy and Neil Hume, "CEFC China Energy Buys $9bn Stake in Rosneft," *Financial Times*, September 8, 2017, https://www.ft.com/content/25b18d2e-94a4-11e7-a9e6-11d2f0ebb7f0?mhq5j=e6 (accessed October 27, 2017). The deal reduces the shares of the Swiss Glencore mining and the Qatar Investment Authority.

15. Blank and Kim, "Russian Arms Sales."

16. "China, Russia Sign Joint Statement on Strengthening Global Strategic Stability," Xinhuanet, June 25, 2016, http://news.xinhuanet.com/english/2016-06/26/c_135466187.htm (accessed May 30, 2017). Savic, "Behind China and Russia's 'Special Relationship.'"

17. Robert D. Kaplan is correct to call the ongoing Sino-Soviet disputes in Eurasia

a "quiet rivalry," but this rivalry is going beyond a marriage of convenience, as he argues, that might break up in the near future and toward a proto-alliance due to the US unwillingness to forge an entente with Moscow over Ukraine while concurrently seeking to *channel* China's power potential through a US-China rapprochement, as argued in this book. For Kaplan's views, see "The Quiet Rivalry Between China and Russia," *New York Times*, November 3, 2017, https://www.nytimes.com/2017/11/03/opinion/china-russia-rivalry.html (accessed November 8, 2011).

18. Le Hong Hiep, UNSW ADFA, and VNU, "Defence Cooperation Underpins Vietnam–Russia Push for Renewed Economic Cooperation," East Asia Forum, November 13, 2013, http://www.eastasiaforum.org/2013/11/13/defence-cooperation-underpins-vietnam-russia-push-for-renewed-economic-cooperation/ (accessed May 30, 2017). "China, Russia Sign Joint Statement."

19. Philip S. Golub, *East Asia's Reemergence* (Cambridge, UK: Polity Press, 2016).

20. "SFWI, "Fund Rankings," https://www.swfinstitute.org/fund-rankings/ (accessed November 25, 2017). US and Japanese pension funds rank first and second in terms of total amount of assets.

21. On a number of energy partnerships, see Savic, "Behind China and Russia's 'Special Relationship.'" The economic relationship between China and Russia has been driven by a variety of bilateral intergovernmental commissions, including 26 sub-commissions.

22. Rem Korteweg, "Unfreezing TTIP: Why a Transatlantic Trade Pact Still Makes Strategic Sense," Center for European Reform, May 2017, http://www.cer.eu/sites/default/files/pb_ttip_rk_10.5.17.pdf (accessed November 14, 2017).

23. "Goldman Sachs, China's CIC to Launch up to $5 Billion Fund: Sources," Reuters, November 6, 2017, http://www.reuters.com/article/us-goldman-sachs-cic/goldman-sachs-chinas-cic-to-launch-up-to-5-billion-fund-sources-idUSKBN1D61H7 (accessed November 8, 2017).

24. Prior to Trump's decision to dump the TPP, Australian Prime Minister Malcolm Turnball had stated that the "effectiveness of the TPP will be considerably enhanced by the inclusion of China whose constructive participation in regional elements is a central element in its peaceful rise." Malcolm Turnball, "Assessing the Future of the Asia-Pacific–US/Australia Dialogue," MalcolmTurnball.com, January 31, 2015, http://www.malcolmturnbull.com.au/media/future-of-the-asia-pacific (accessed October 27, 2017).

25. Xi Jinping, "President Xi's Speech to Davos in Full," World Economic Forum, January 17, 2017, https://www.weforum.org/agenda/2017/01/full-text-of-xi-jinping-keynote-at-the-world-economic-forum (accessed May 30, 2017).

26. Barack Obama, "Statement by the President on the Signing of the Trans-Pacific Partnership," press release, White House, Office of the Press Secretary, February 3, 2016, National Archives and Records Administration, https://obamawhitehouse.archives.gov/the-press-office/2016/02/03/statement-president-signing-trans-pacific-partnership (accessed May 30, 2017).

27. Emanuele Scimia, "Taiwan in the TPP: How to Break the Cross-Strait Status Quo," *Asian Times*, July 3, 2017, http://www.atimes.com/taiwan-tpp-break-cross-strait-status-quo/?utm_source=The+Daily+Brief&utm_campaign=68d50bf894-EMAIL_CAMPAIGN_2017_07_03&utm_medium=email&utm_term=0_1f8bca137f-68d50bf894-31523549 (accessed October 27, 2017).

28. According to the Organization of Economic Cooperation and Development (OECD), Chile is the first most inequitable society; Mexico is second; and the United States is third, as compared to other European, North American, and South American states.

29. Steve Benen, "China Is Eager to Capitalize on Trump's Early Missteps," MSNBC, February 7, 2017, http://www.msnbc.com/rachel-maddow-show/china-eager-capitalize-trumps-early-missteps (accessed May 22, 2017).

30. Paul Coyer, "Undermining America While Washington Sleeps: China in Latin America," *Forbes*, February 5, 2016, http://www.forbes.com/sites/paulcoyer/2016/01/31/undermining-america-while-washington-sleeps-china-in-latin-america/#505fca7d6694 (accessed May 30, 2017).

31. "Landbridge Group Connects Three Ports with Acquisition of Margarita Island Port," *ChinaGoAbroad*, May 25, 2016, http://www.chinagoabroad.com/en/recent_transaction/20530 (accessed May 30, 2017); Andreea Brînză, "How a Greek Port Became a Chinese 'Dragon Head,'" *Diplomat*, April 25, 2016, http://thediplomat.com/2016/04/how-a-greek-port-became-a-chinese-dragon- (accessed May 30, 2017). Peter Jennings, "Darwin: Storm in a Port," *Strategist*, November 6, 2015, https://www.aspistrategist.org.au/darwin-storm-in-a-port/ (accessed May 30, 2017); Geoff Wade, "Landbridge, Darwin, and the PRC," *Strategist*, November 9, 2015, https://www.aspistrategist.org.au/landbridge-darwin-and-the-prc/ (accessed May 30, 2017).

32. Suzanne Daley, "Lost in Nicaragua, a Chinese Tycoon's Canal Project," *New York Times*, April 3, 2016, https://www.nytimes.com/2016/04/04/world/americas/nicaragua-canal-chinese-tycoon.html?_r=0 (accessed May 30, 2017). François Lafargue, "China's Presence in Latin America. Strategies, Aims and Limits," *China Perspectives* 68, June 1, 2007, https://chinaperspectives.revues.org/3053 (accessed May 30, 2017); David Z. Morris, "Why China and Nicaragua's Canal Project Is

Floundering?" *Fortune*, February 29, 2016, http://fortune.com/2016/02/29/china-nicaragua-canal/ (accessed May 30, 2017); Jonathan Watts, "Nicaragua Canal: In a Sleepy Pacific Port, Something Stirs," *Guardian*, November 24, 2016, https://www.theguardian.com/world/2016/nov/24/nicaragua-canal-interoceanic-preparations (accessed May 30, 2017).

33. Peter Jennings, "Darwin: Storm in a Port," *Strategist*, November 6, 2015, https://www.aspistrategist.org.au/darwin-storm-in-a-port/ (accessed May 30, 2017); Wade, "Landbridge, Darwin, and the PRC."

34. *Russia and the Caribbean* (London: Caribbean Council, March 24, 2015), http://www.caribbean-council.org/wp-content/uploads/2015/08/Russia-and-the-Caribbean.pdf (accessed October 27, 2017).

35. Karen de Young, "White House Implements New Cuba Policy Restricting Travel and Trade," *Washington Post*, November 8, 2017.

36. Negative economic effects of Chinese investment in Latin America and elsewhere include the hollowing out of manufacturing in the region and the enlarging of regional dependence on raw material exports, which increases the regional economies' sensitivity to fluctuations in commodity prices. The countries can also become dependent on fluctuations of Chinese demand. Paul Coyer, "Undermining America While Washington Sleeps: China in Latin America," *Forbes*, January 31, 2016, http://www.forbes.com/sites/paulcoyer/2016/01/31/undermining-america-while-washington-sleeps-china-in-latin-america/#505fca7d6694 (accessed October 27, 2017). Further, because Chinese firms often bring their own labor, Chinese investments do not always increase job opportunities.

37. Andrew Rosati and Jose Orozco, "Trump Calls Venezuela 'Horrible' as US Expands Sanctions," Bloomberg, May 18, 2017, https://www.bloomberg.com/politics/articles/2017-05-18/trump-calls-venezuela-horrible-as-treasury-expands-sanctions (accessed October 27, 2017).

38. Robert Helbig and Guillaume Lasconjarias, "Winning Peace and Exporting Stability: Colombia as NATO's Next Global Partner?" North Atlantic Treaty Organization Research Division Research Paper 138, May 23, 2017, http://www.ndc.nato.int/news/news.php?icode=1056 (accessed October 27, 2017).

39. "More Than 100 Terrorists in TT," *Newsday*, February 24, 2016, http://archives.newsday.co.tt/news/print,0,224465.html (accessed October 27, 2017). The Financial Intelligence Unit of Trinidad and Tobago observed that suspected terrorist financial transactions had tripled in 2015.

40. Steve Holland and Anthony Boadle, "Trump Says Democracy Must Be Restored in Venezuela Soon," Reuters, September 19, 2017, https://www.reuters

.com/article/us-usa-trump-latin-america/trump-says-democracy-must-be-restored-in-venezuela-soon-idUSKCN1BT2R7 (accessed November 14, 2017).

41. Jorge G. Castaneda, "Trump and Castro Can Save Venezuela," *New York Times*, September 21, 2017, https://www.nytimes.com/2017/09/21/opinion/trump-castro-venezuela.html (accessed November 7, 2017).

42. AFP, "India, Pakistan Edge Closer to Joining SCO Security Bloc," *Express Tribune*, June 24, 2016, http://tribune.com.pk/story/1129533/india-pakistan-edge-closer-joining-sco-security-bloc/ (accessed May 30, 2017).

43. *Joint Communiqué of the 14th Meeting of the Foreign Ministers of the Russian Federation, the Republic of India and the People's Republic of China* (New Delhi: Ministry of External Affairs, Government of India, April 18, 2016), http://mea.gov.in/bilateral-documents.htm?dtl/26628/Joint_Communiqu_of_the_14th_Meeting_of_the_Foreign_Ministers_of_the_Russian_Federation_the_Republic_of_India_and_the_Peoples_Republic_of_China (accessed October 29, 2017).

44. Alexander Korablinov, "China Snubs Russian Request for Trilateral Defense Meeting with India," *Russia Beyond*, April 12, 2017, https://www.rbth.com/international/2017/04/12/china-snubs-russian-request-for-trilateral-defense-meeting-with-india_740367 (accessed October 29, 2017).

45. Mohan Malik, "Balancing Act: The China-India-US Triangle," *World Affairs*, Spring 2016, http://www.worldaffairsjournal.org/article/balancing-act-china-india-us-triangle (accessed October 29, 2017).

46. Wade Shapard, "China's Jewel in the Heart of the Indian Ocean: The Colombo Port City Project Was Conceived by Sri Lanka, But Is Now an Almost 100 Percent Chinese Undertaking," *Diplomat*, May 9, 2016, http://thediplomat.com/2016/05/chinas-jewel-in-the-heart-of-the-indian-ocean/ (accessed October 29, 2017).

47. Brigadier Vinod Anand, "India's Defence Cooperation with South East Asian Countries," *SP's Land Forces*, no. 3 (2013), http://www.spslandforces.com/story.asp?id=258 (accessed May 30, 2017).

48. Nirmala Ganapathy, "India, Thailand to Boost Defence Ties," *Indian Express*, June 18, 2016, http://indianexpress.com/article/india/india-news-india/india-thailand-to-boost-defence-ties-2859804/ (accessed May 30, 2017).

49. "India's Partnership with Southeast Asia Nears Its Limits," *Stratfor Worldview*, September 20, 2016, https://www.stratfor.com/analysis/indias-partnership-southeast-asia-nears-its-limits (accessed May 30, 2017).

50. Russia and India have held annual naval and land exercises since 2003. In 2016 exercises were hosted by Russia which interestingly chose to host them in Ussuriysk, near Vladivostok and very close to the Chinese border.

51. Loro Hort, "From Russia without Love: Russia Resumes Weapons Sales to China," *PacNet*, no. 89 (Pacific Forum CSIS Honolulu, Hawaii, December 12, 2013), https://csis-prod.s3.amazonaws.com/s3fs-public/legacy_files/files/publication/Pac1389_0.pdf (accessed October 29, 2017).

52. Malik, "Balancing Act."

53. Blank and Kim, "Russian Arms Sales."

54. Different experts dispute whether the Indian Rafales to be acquired from France can match the Russian SU-35s. If the SU-35 is better, India might look back to Russia, unless the latter starts backing Pakistan, which is acquiring the JF-17 fighter jet from China. Franz-Stefan Gady, "Pakistan to Order 50 More Fighter Jets in 2017," *Diplomat*, February 8, 2017, https://thediplomat.com/2017/02/pakistan-to-order-50-more-fighter-jets-in-2017/ (accessed November 26, 2017).

55. Ipsita Chakravarty, "Why Has India Been Silent about the Chemical Attacks in Syria?" Scroll.in, April 8, 2017, https://scroll.in/article/834039/why-has-india-been-silent-about-the-chemical-attacks-in-syria (accessed October 29, 2017).

56. Devirupa Mitra, "Pakistan Critical to Defeating ISIS: Russian Special Rep to Afghanistan," *Wire*, December 5, 2016, https://thewire.in/84672/pakistan-isis-afghanistan-russia/ (accessed May 29, 2017).

57. David Brewster, "India Plays the Balochistan Card with China," *Interpreter*, August 22, 2016, https://www.lowyinstitute.org/the-interpreter/india-plays-balochistan-card-china (accessed May 29, 2017).

58. M. Ilyas Khan, "India's 'Surgical Strikes' in Kashmir: Truth or Illusion?" *BBC News*, October 23, 2016, http://www.bbc.com/news/world-asia-india-37702790 (accessed May 29, 2017). About ten million people live in Indian-administrated Jammu and Kashmir and 4.5 million in Pakistani-run Azad Kashmir. There are 1.8 million people in the Gilgit-Baltistan autonomous territory, which Pakistan created from northern Kashmir and the two small princely states of Hunza and Nagar in 1970.

59. "Is India Planning to Cut Off Pakistan's Water Supply?" *American Interest*, September 27, 2016, https://www.the-american-interest.com/2016/09/27/is-india-planning-to-cut-off-pakistans-water-supply/ (accessed May 29, 2017).

60. David Brewster, "India Plays the Balochistan Card with China."

61. "Highlights of PM Modi's Independence Day speech," *Times of India*, August 15, 2017, https://timesofindia.indiatimes.com/india/highlights-of-pm-modis-independence-day-speech/articleshow/60067783.cms (assessed November 7, 2016).

62. "Pakistan Prime Minister Slams India's 'Expansionist Designs' in Independence Day Address," *First Post*, August 16, 2017, http://www.firstpost.com/

world/pakistan-prime-minister-slams-indias-expansionist-designs-in-independence-day-address-full-text-of-his-speech-3932719.html (assessed November 7, 2016).

63. Emanuele Scimia, "India Is Buying 36 Rafale Fighters from France (and Pakistan Should Worry)," *National Interest*, October 3, 2016, http://nationalinterest.org/blog/the-buzz/indias-buying-36-rafale-fighters-france-pakistan-should-17911 (accessed May 29, 2017). Gady, "Pakistan to Order 50 More Fighter Jets."

64. Arif Rafiq, "India's Modi Is Playing the Wrong Game against China and Pakistan," *National Interest*, August 21, 2016, http://nationalinterest.org/feature/indias-modi-playing-the-wrong-game-against-china-pakistan-17411?page=3 (accessed May 29, 2017).

CHAPTER 7: CHINA, NORTH KOREA, AND THE RISK OF WAR IN THE INDO-PACIFIC

1. Will Ripley, "North Korean Official: Take Hydrogen Bomb Threat 'Literally,'" CNN, October 26, 2017, http://edition.cnn.com/2017/10/25/politics/north-korea-us-hydrogen-bomb-threat/index.html (accessed November 14, 2017).

2. Nahal Toosi and David Cohen, "Trump Undercuts Tillerson's Efforts on North Korea," *Politico*, October 1, 2017, https://www.politico.com/story/2017/10/01/trump-tillerson-korea-twitter-243339 (accessed November 14, 2017).

3. Some diplomats argue that Tillerson's advisers have isolated him from State Department expertise and see this restructuring as creating bottlenecks. Eliana Johnson and Michael Crowley, "The Bottleneck in Rex Tillerson's State Department," *Politico*, June 4, 2017, https://www.politico.com/story/2017/06/04/rex-tillerson-state-department-bottleneck-239107 (accessed November 14, 2017). Others see the restructuring as a politically motivated Republican purge against the predominantly Democratic State Department bureaucracy, while still others argue that Tillerson is not downsizing as much as Trump desires. Nahal Toosi, "Diplomats Fear Tillerson Transparency Push Is Linked to Clinton Emails," *Politico*, November 7, 2017, https://www.politico.com/story/2017/11/07/tillerson-state-clinton-emails-244626 (accessed November 14, 2017).

4. Caren Bohan and David Brunnstrom, "Trump Says US Not Necessarily Bound by 'One China' Policy," Reuters, December 12, 2016, http://www.reuters.com/article/us-usa-trump-china-idUSKBN1400TY (accessed May 30, 2017).

5. *Politico* magazine revealed that Bob Dole, the former Senate Majority Leader

and 1996 Republican presidential nominee, had lobbied the Trump team for months on behalf of the Taiwanese government.

6. Tyler Durden, "Chinese Carrier Sails by Taiwan, Enters Contested South China Sea," *ZeroHedge*, December 26, 2016, http://www.zerohedge.com/news/2016-12-26/chinese-carrier-sails-taiwan-enters-contested-south-china-sea (accessed May 30, 2017).

7. Matthew M. Burke and Chiyomi Sumida, "China Reportedly Responds to Trump's Taiwan Call by Flying Nuclear-Capable Bomber," *Stars and Stripes*, December 12, 2016, http://www.stripes.com/news/china-reportedly-responds-to-trump-s-taiwan-call-by-flying-nuclear-capable-bomber-1.443999 (accessed May 30, 2017).

8. David Brunnstrom and Matt Spetalnick, "Tillerson Says China Should Be Barred from South China Sea Islands," Reuters, January 11, 2017, http://www.reuters.com/article/us-congress-tillerson-china-idUSKBN14V2KZ (accessed October 29, 2017).

9. Jordan Fabian and Evelyn Rupert, "Trump Promises Chinese President He'll Honor 'One China' Policy," *Hill*, February 10, 2017, http://thehill.com/homenews/administration/318874-trump-to-honor-one-china-policy (accessed May 30, 2017). Tillerson later softened his statement about stopping Chinese access to the islands, saying that in the event of an unspecified "contingency," the United States and its allies "must be capable of limiting China's access to and use of" those islands to pose a threat. Idrees Ali, "Exclusive: China Finishing South China Sea Buildings That Could House Missiles—US Officials," Reuters, February 21, 2017, http://www.reuters.com/article/us-china-usa-southchinasea-exclusive-idUSKBN161029 (accessed May 30, 2017).

10. "Projected GDP Ranking (2016–2020)," *Statistics Times*, December 16, 2016, http://statisticstimes.com/economy/projected-world-gdp-ranking.php (accessed May 30, 2017); Liyan Chen, "2015 Global 2000: The World's Largest Banks," *Forbes*, May 6, 2015, http://www.forbes.com/sites/liyanchen/2015/05/06/2015-global-2000-the-worlds-largest-banks/#63c5166724f1 (accessed May 30, 2017). In 2015, the top ten productive countries in the world in nominal terms were: the United States, China, Japan, Germany, United Kingdom, France, India, Brazil, Italy, and Canada. In this measure, the US is first and China second; Russia did not even appear in the top ten! But in terms of purchasing power parity (PPP), China came out on top over the US, with Russia in 6th place.

11. Mike Patton, "China's Economy Will Overtake the U.S. in 2018," *Forbes*, https://www.forbes.com/sites/mikepatton/2016/04/29/global-economic-news-china-will-surpass-the-u-s-in-2018/#32bf7839224a (accessed November 8, 2017).

12. Robert D. Kaplan, "Why the South China Sea Is So Crucial," *Business Insider*

Australia, February 20, 2015, https://www.businessinsider.com.au/why-the-south-china-sea-is-so-crucial-2015-2/ (accessed November 8, 2017).

13. Harold Raveche, "How Trump, Tillerson Could Bring Peace to South China Sea," *Hill*, March 23, 2017, http://thehill.com/blogs/pundits-blog/international-affairs/325620-how-trump-tillerson-could-bring-peace-to-south-china (accessed October 29, 2017). Superoptimists claim that it could possess oil reserves as high as 130 billion barrels, which would make it the second largest reserve, under Saudi Arabia. See Kaplan, "Why the South China Sea Is So Crucial."

14. Jesse Johnson, "Behind the Scenes, Tillerson Tones down Rhetoric on South China Sea," *Japan Times*, February 7, 2017, http://www.japantimes.co.jp/news/2017/02/07/asia-pacific/behind-scenes-tillerson-tones-rhetoric-south-china-sea/#.WR7rcvqGP8Q (accessed October 29, 2017).

15. Minnie Chan, "South China Sea Air Strips' Main Role Is 'to Defend Hainan Nuclear Submarine Base,'" *South China Morning Post*, July 24, 2016, http://www.scmp.com/news/china/diplomacy-defence/article/1993754/south-china-sea-air-strips-main-role-defend-hainan (accessed October 29, 2017).

16. Permanent Court of Arbitration, "The South China Sea Arbitration (The Republic of Philippines v. The People's Republic of China)," Case View: Case no. 2013-19, http://www.pcacases.com/web/view/7 (accessed May 30, 2017); see also "PCA Case No. 2013-19: The South China Sea Arbitration Award of 12 July 2016," http://www.pcacases.com/web/sendAttach/2086 (accessed November 2, 2017).

17. Andrew S. Erickson, "China's Blueprint for Sea Power," *China Brief* 16, no. 11 (July 6, 2016), Jamestown, https://jamestown.org/program/chinas-blueprint-for-sea-power/#sthash.iBD4wLgr.dpuf (accessed May 30, 2017). Beijing has been developing "killer" anti-aircraft carrier missiles and other asymmetrical forms of weaponry so as to check US, Japanese, and Taiwanese naval and air forces from moving close to the Chinese mainland in case of conflict.

18. Nidhi Prasad, "Yes, Japan Could Build Nuclear Weapons (But at What Cost?)," *National Interest*, October 12, 2016, http://nationalinterest.org/blog/the-buzz/yes-japan-could-build-nuclear-weapons-what-cost-18019?page=2 (accessed May 30, 2017).

19. Motoko Rich, "Japanese Government Urges Another Increase in Military Spending," *New York Times*, August 30, 2016, https://www.nytimes.com/2016/08/31/world/asia/japan-defense-military-budget-shinzo-abe.html (accessed May 30, 2017).

20. Ibid.

21. Justin McCurry, "Japan Increases Defence Budget Amid Tensions with China," *Guardian*, December 17, 2013, https://www.theguardian.com/world/2013/

dec/17/japan-increases-defence-budget-tensions-china (accessed May 30, 2017).

22. Other recent incidents include the overflight of a Xian H-6 aircraft over the South China sea in March 2016 and two Xian H-6 bombers and two escort planes additionally flying around Taiwan in late November. These flights are largely in response to US efforts to sustain its hegemony over the South China Sea's international waters using its own nuclear-capable bombers. The Pentagon has repeatedly deployed its own nuclear capable B-52 and B-2 bombers to Guam, which is easily in range of the South China Sea, and which are seen as potential threats to both North Korea and China.

23. Reinhard Drifte, "The Japan-China Confrontation over the Senkaku/Diaoyu Islands—Between 'Shelving' and 'Dispute Escalation,'" *Asia Pacific Journal* 12, no. 30/3 (2014); available online at: Global Research, July 28, 2014, http://www.globalresearch.ca/the-japan-china-confrontation-over-the-senkakudiaoyu-islands-between-shelving-and-dispute-escalation/5393760 (accessed May 30, 2017).

24. Burke and Sumida, "China Reportedly Responds."

25. Brunnstrom and Spetalnick, "Tillerson Says China Should Be Barred."

26. These deployments took place just weeks before scheduled talks between Putin and Japanese Prime Minister Shinzo Abe in Yamaguchi Prefecture on December 15. The Bal complex, armed with the X-35 anti-ship missile, can hit targets at a range of 120 kilometers (seventy-five miles). The Bastion complex, however, is equipped with supersonic Onyx missiles and can strike not only battleships but also destroy land-based targets within a range of 600 kilometers. This makes it not only a defensive but also an offensive weapon. Vladimir Mikheev, "Military Build-Up in the Kuril Islands: Bad Timing or a Signal from Moscow?" *Russia Beyond*, November 24, 2016, http://rbth.com/international/2016/11/24/military-build-up-in-the-kuril-islands-bad-timing-or-a-signal-from-moscow_650715 (accessed October 29, 2017). This buildup includes the Borei-class nuclear-powered ballistic-missile submarines (SSBN), test-launching the Bulava intercontinental ballistic missile (ICBM) in the Kamchatka Peninsula.

27. White House, "Fact Sheet: Advancing the Rebalance to Asia and the Pacific," Office of the Press Secretary, November 16, 2017, https://obamawhitehouse.archives.gov/the-press-office/2015/11/16/fact-sheet-advancing-rebalance-asia-and-pacific (November 14, 2017).

28. Douglas H. Paal, "How Trump Should Deal with China," Carnegie Endowment for International Peace, December 12, 2016, http://carnegieendowment.org/2016/12/12/how-trump-should-deal-with-china-pub-66418 (accessed May 30, 2017). Andrew S. Erickson, "China's Blueprint for Sea Power," Jamestown Foundation,

July 6, 2016, https://jamestown.org/program/beijing-talks-tough-new-cold-war-asia/ (accessed May 30, 2017).

29. Not all extrajudicial killing is related to drugs. See "License to Kill," Human Rights Watch, March 2, 2017, https://www.hrw.org/report/2017/03/02/license-kill/philippine-police-killings-dutertes-war-drugs (November 14, 2017).

30. *Phone Call between Trump and Duterte* (Pasas City, Philippines: Office of American Affairs, April 29, 2017), https://www.documentcloud.org/documents/3729123-POTUS-RD-Doc.html#document/p1 (accessed October 30, 2017).

31. Stephen Blank, "Russia's Growing Ties with Vietnam," *Diplomat*, September 19, 2013, http://thediplomat.com/2013/09/russias-growing-ties-with-vietnam/ (accessed May 30, 2017).

32. Phil Stewart and Nobuhiro Kubo, "Trump's Defense Chief Heads to Asia, Eying China, North Korea Threat," Reuters, February 1, 2017, http://www.reuters.com/article/us-usa-trump-mattis-asia-idUSKBN15G3FG (accessed May 30, 2017).

33. Robert S. Litwak, "An Iran-Style Nuclear Deal with North Korea Is the Best America Can Hope For," *Atlantic*, May 4, 2017, https://www.theatlantic.com/international/archive/2017/05/iran-deal-north-korea-jcpoa/525372/?utm_source=nl-atlantic-daily-050417 (accessed May 30, 2017); Wit and Ahn, *North Korea's Nuclear Futures*.

34. Austin Ramzysept, "Kim Jong-un Called Trump a 'Dotard.' What Does That Even Mean?" *New York Times*, September 22, 2017, https://www.nytimes.com/2017/09/22/world/asia/trump-north-korea-dotard.html (accessed November 14, 2017).

35. Zachary Cohen, "North Korea Accuses Trump of Declaring War," CNN, September 26, 2017, http://edition.cnn.com/2017/09/25/politics/north-korea-fm-us-bombers/index.html (accessed November 14, 2017).

36. Steve Holland, "Trump Wants to Make Sure US Nuclear Arsenal at 'Top of the Pack,'" Reuters, February 24, 2017, http://www.reuters.com/article/us-usa-trump-idUSKBN1622IF?il=0 (accessed May 30, 2017).

37. Lily Hay Newman, "All about the US Missile Defense That'll Protect South Korea—and Tick Off China," *Wired*, April 23, 2017, https://www.wired.com/2017/04/missile-defense-will-protect-south-korea-make-china-nervous/ (accessed October 30, 2017).

38. Lily Hay Newman, "South Korea's New Missile Defense Tech Isn't a Cure-All for North Korea," *Wired*, May 5, 2017, https://www.wired.com/2017/05/south-koreas-new-missile-defense-tech-isnt-cure-north-korea/ (accessed October 30, 2017). In its current placement, the THAAD can defend a number of US military bases, like

Camp Walker in Daegu and Kunsan Air Base in Gunsan, along with ports in Busan and the southern tip of South Korea; but it cannot defend Seoul. So Washington will pay for the one that defends US interests, but not all of South Korea. Seoul would need to purchase its own system.

39. Kingston Reif, "Moon Reverses THAAD Decision," *Arms Control Today*, September 2017, https://www.armscontrol.org/act/2017-09/news/moon-reverses-thaad-decision (accessed November 14, 2017).

40. See Hall Gardner, *Averting Global War* (New York: Palgrave MacMillan, 2007).

41. Kristin Huang, "The 10 Minutes with Xi That Changed Trump's Mind on North Korea," *South China Morning Post*, April 14, 2017, http://www.scmp.com/news/china/diplomacy-defence/article/2087518/10-minutes-xi-jinping-changed-donald-trumps-mind-north (accessed May 30, 2017).

42. Gerry Mullany, Chris Buckley, and David E. Sanger, "China Warns of 'Storm Clouds Gathering' in US-North Korea Standoff," *New York Times*, April 14, 2017, https://www.nytimes.com/2017/04/14/world/asia/north-korea-china-nuclear.html?emc=edit_th_20170415&nl=todaysheadlines&nlid=70196410&_r=0 (accessed May 30, 2017).

43. Veronica Rocha, "US Air Force to Launch Test Missile off Central California Coast," *Los Angeles Times*, April 25, 2017, http://www.latimes.com/local/lanow/la-me-ln-missile-test-launch-vandenberg-20170425-story.html (accessed May 30, 2017).

44. Kristin Huang, "China's Nuclear Get-Out Clause over Defence of North Korea," *South China Morning Post*, April 14, 2017, http://www.scmp.com/news/china/diplomacy-defence/article/2087320/china-not-obliged-defend-n-korea-if-its-attacked-say (accessed May 30, 2017).

45. Ryan Pickrell, "What Would Happen If North Korea Fired Off a Nuclear Weapon?" *National Interest*, April 14, 2017, http://nationalinterest.org/blog/the-buzz/what-would-happen-if-north-korea-fired-nuclear-weapon-20205?page=2 (accessed May 30, 2017).

46. "All North Korean Missile Tests," Nuclear Threat Initiative, April 24, 2017, http://www.nti.org/newsroom/news/new-database-documents-all-north-korean-missile-tests/ (accessed May 30, 2017).

47. Litwak, "An Iran-Style Nuclear Deal."

48. "North Korea Demands Recognition as Legitimate Nuclear State," *Guardian*, September 11, 2016, https://www.theguardian.com/world/2016/sep/11/north-korea-demands-recognition-as-legitimate-nuclear-state-pyongyang (accessed November 14, 2017).

49. Merrit Kennedy, "Pence Tells North Korea: 'The Era Of Strategic Patience Is

Over'" (April 17, 2017), http://www.npr.org/sections/thetwo-way/2017/04/17/524316419/pence-tells-north-korea-the-era-of-strategic-patience-is-over (accessed November 16, 2017).

50. Franz-Stefan Gady, "Time to Go 'Huge'? What Will Trump's Defense Policy in Asia Be?" *Diplomat*, November 10, 2016, http://thediplomat.com/2016/11/time-to-go-huge-what-will-trumps-defense-policy-in-asia-be/ (accessed May 30, 2017).

51. Harry J. Kazianis, "Why China Could Declare a South China Sea ADIZ Right about Now," *National Interest*, February 1, 2017, http://nationalinterest.org/blog/the-buzz/why-china-could-declare-south-china-sea-adiz-right-about-now-19273 (accessed May 30, 2017).

52. See realistic pre-war scenario: Michael Auslin, "How China Could Respond to Trump Call," CNN, December 5, 2016, http://edition.cnn.com/2016/12/05/opinions/china-relations-after-trumps-taiwan-call-auslin/index.html (accessed May 30, 2017).

CHAPTER 8: SYRIA AND WIDENING WARS IN THE "WIDER MIDDLE EAST"

1. Syrian Observatory for Human Rights, http://www.syriahr.com/en/ (accessed November 11, 2017). For a skeptical view of death toll estimates, see Alex Ray, "The Death Toll in Syria: What Do the Numbers Really Say?" *Counterpunch*, May 26, 2016, https://www.counterpunch.org/2016/05/26/the-death-toll-in-syria-what-do-the-numbers-really-say/ (accessed November 11, 2017).

2. UN OCHA, "About the Crisis," http://www.unocha.org/syrian-arab-republic/syria-country-profile/about-crisis (accessed October 30, 2017).

3. See the Global Coalition official website: http://theglobalcoalition.org/en/home/.

4. Hall Gardner, "The Geopolitical Convolutions of Fighting the Global War on Terror (GWOT)," in *A New Global Agenda: Priorities, Practices, and Pathways of the International Community*, ed. by Diana Ayton-Shenker (Lanham, MD: Rowman & Littlefield, 2018); Hall Gardner, "The Russian Annexation of Crimea: Regional and Global Ramifications," *European Politics and Society* 17, no. 4, *Ukraine in Crisis*, ed. by Nicolai Petro (March 15, 2016): 490–505, DOI: 10.1080/23745118.2016.1154190.

5. Jordan Fabian, "Trump Hits Obama after Syrian Gas Attack," *Hill*, April 4, 2017, http://thehill.com/homenews/administration/327259-trump-hits-obama-after-syrian-gas-attack (accessed May 30, 2017).

6. The Tomahawk strike took place after national-populist ideologue Steve Bannon was removed from National Security Council staff and after heavy consultation between Trump and his National Security Advisor, H. R. McMaster. Jordan Fabian, "McMaster Shows Clout in Trump's First Crisis," *Hill*, April 8, 2017, http://thehill.com/homenews/administration/327882-mcmaster-shows-clout-in-trumps-first-crisis (accessed May 30, 2017).

7. Gabriel Sherman, "Trump's Syria Strike Is Latest Sign of Steve Bannon's Waning Influence," *New York Magazine*, April 7, 2017, http://nymag.com/daily/intelligencer/2017/04/trumps-syria-strike-is-sign-of-bannons-waning-influence.html?mid=twitter-share-di (accessed October 30, 2017).

8. Claudia Assis, "Here's How Much It Costs to Replace the 59 Tomahawk Missiles Trump Fired on Syria," *MarketWatch*, April 15, 2017, http://www.marketwatch.com/story/this-is-how-much-it-will-cost-to-replace-the-tomahawks-used-in-syria-2017-04-07 (accessed May 22, 2017).

9. White House, "Press Briefing by Secretary of State Rex Tillerson and National Security Advisor General H. R. McMaster," Office of the Press Secretary, June 4, 2017, https://www.whitehouse.gov/the-press-office/2017/04/06/press-briefing-secretary-state-rex-tillerson-and-national-security (accessed November 11, 2017).

10. Brian Barrett, "The US Strike on Syria Underscores Trump's Media-Fueled Worldview," *Wired*, April 7, 2017, https://www.wired.com/2017/04/us-strike-syria-underscore-trumps-media-fueled-worldview/?mbid=nl_4717_p3&CNDID=49332341 (accessed May 30, 2017).

11. Mary Atkinson, "Latest US Arms Sales to Saudi Arabia Raise Eyebrows about IS War," *Middle East Eye*, October 2, 2014, last updated May 11, 2015, http://www.middleeasteye.net/news/saudi-arabia-1295679323 (accessed November 14, 2017).

12. "Daesh Launches New Palmyra Push after US Strike," *PressTV*, April 7, 2017, http://www.presstv.ir/Detail/2017/04/07/517062/Syria-Daesh-Palmyra-US-Russia-airbase (accessed May 30, 2017).

13. Jonathan Steele, "US-Russia Talks: No Love-In, but No Break-Up Either," *Middle East Eye*, April 13, 2017, http://www.middleeasteye.net/columns/us-russia-tillerson-putin-lavrov-trump-moscow-959468392 (accessed October 30, 2017).

14. Euan McKirdy, Jason Hanna, and Barbara Starr, "Syria Strikes: Site of Chemical Attack Hit Again," CNN, April 8, 2017, http://edition.cnn.com/2017/04/08/middleeast/syria-strikes-russia-donald-trump/ (accessed May 30, 2017). "ISIL Takes Advantage of US Attack on Government to Storm Western Palmyra," MEMPSI, April 7, 2017, http://www.mempsi.net/2017/04/07/isil-takes-advantage-of-us-attack-on-government-to-storm-western-palmyra/ (accessed October 30, 2017).

15. Emma Graham-Harrison, "Syria Nerve Agent Attack: Why It Made Sense to Assad," *Guardian*, April 7, 2017, https://www.theguardian.com/world/2017/apr/07/syria-nerve-agent-attack-why-it-made-sense-to-assad (accessed May 30, 2017).

16. "Seventh Report of the Organization for the Prohibition of Chemical Weapons–United Nations Joint Investigative Mechanism," October 25, 2017, https://drive.google.com/file/d/0ByLPNZ-eSjJdcGZUb0hqalFOa0hhdEZ3WlBvZmRnajFRV3pr/view (accessed November 14, 2017).

17. Robert Parry, "Did Al-Qaeda Dupe Donald Trump on Alleged Syrian Sarin Gas Attack on April 4, 2017," *Consortium News*, November 9, 2017, https://www.newcoldwar.org/al-qaeda-dupe-trump-alleged-syrian-sarin-gas-attack-april-4-2017/ (accessed November 14, 2017); Daniel Lazare, "Luring Trump into Mideast Wars," *Consortium News*, April 8, 2017, https://consortiumnews.com/2017/04/08/luring-trump-into-mideast-wars/ (accessed May 30, 2017); Robert Parry, "UN Team Heard Claims of 'Staged' Chemical Attacks," *Consortium News*, September 8, 2016, https://consortiumnews.com/2016/09/08/un-team-heard-claims-of-staged-chemical-attacks/ (accessed May 30, 2017).

18. Human Rights Watch, "Syria: Barrage of Barrel Bombs: Attacks on Civilians Defy UN Resolution," July 30, 2014, https://www.hrw.org/news/2014/07/30/syria-barrage-barrel-bombs (accessed November 14, 2017); *Wikipedia*, s.v. "List of Syrian Civil War Barrel Bomb Attacks," last edited October 9, 2017, https://en.wikipedia.org/wiki/List_of_Syrian_Civil_War_barrel_bomb_attacks (accessed November 14, 2017).

19. Hamidreza Azizi, "Will US Missile Strike Shift Iran-Russia Partnership in Syria?" *Al-Monitor*, April 12, 2017, http://www.al-monitor.com/pulse/originals/2017/04/iran-russia-syria-partnership-us-missile-strike-impact.html#ixzz4eKCz40hj (accessed May 30, 2017).

20. Iran and Russia have had a legal battle over payments involving the S-300 antimissile system. But Moscow proposed the S-400 as an option in 2015. "Russian S-400 Missiles for Iran," Investmentwatchblog, March 20, 2015, http://investmentwatchblog.com/russian-s-400-missiles-for-iran/ (accessed November 11, 2017).

21. Alec Luhn, "Russia Sends Missile Cruiser to Mediterranean as Syria Tension Mounts," *Guardian*, September 12, 2013, https://www.theguardian.com/world/2013/sep/12/russia-sends-ships-mediterranean-syria (accessed May 30, 2017).

22. Senator Joni Ernst, who is on the Senate Armed Services Committee, stated that "this was a one-time attack on the assets that were used in a chemical weapons attack against the people of Syria," and "not an on-going operation." Todd Beamon, "Joni Ernst on Syrian Strike: 'This Was a One-Time Attack,'" *Newsmax*, April 7, 2017,

http://www.newsmax.com/Politics/joni-ernst-syrian-strike-one-time/2017/04/07/id/783224/ (accessed November 14, 2017).

23. Rebecca Savransky, "Top Trump Officials Turn Up Heat on Russia," *Hill*, April 9, 2017, http://thehill.com/homenews/administration/328019-top-trump-officials-turn-up-heat-on-russia (accessed May 30, 2017).

24. Ibid.

25. AFP, Reuters, "Trump Strikes on Syria: How World Leaders Reacted," *Khaleej Times*, April 7, 2017, http://www.khaleejtimes.com/region/mena/trump-strikes-on-syria-how-world-leaders-reacted (accessed May 30, 2017).

26. White House, "Press Briefing by Secretary of State Rex Tillerson and National Security Advisor General H. R. McMaster," June 4, 2017. Peter Baker, Neil MacFarquhar, and Michael R. Gordon, "Syria Strike Puts US Relationship with Russia at Risk," *New York Times*, April 7, 2017, https://www.nytimes.com/2017/04/07/world/middleeast/missile-strike-syria-russia.html?emc=edit_th_20170408&nl=todaysheadlines&nlid=70196410&_r=0 (accessed May 30, 2017).

27. Parvez Jabri, "China Warns of Deterioration in Syria with Xi in US," *Business Recorder*, April 7, 2017, http://www.brecorder.com/2017/04/07/342347/china-warns-of-deterioration-in-syria-with-xi-in-us/ (accessed November 11, 2017).

28. Liu Jieyi, China's permanent representative to the United Nations, said military actions will only worsen the suffering of the Syrian people and called for all countries to support the efforts of UN Special Envoy for Syria Staffan de Mistura to implement a "political solution." "Political Solution Only Way Out for Syrian Issue: Chinese Envoy," Xinhua, April 8, 2017, http://news.xinhuanet.com/english/2017-04/08/c_136191497.htm (accessed November 14, 2017).

29. "Secretary-General Urges 'Restraint' after United States Air Strikes against Syria, Stressing Risk of Escalation, Need for Renewed Commitment to Political Solution," UN Press Release, April 7, 2017, https://www.un.org/press/en/2017/sgsm18487.doc.htm (accessed November 14, 2017).

30. "World Leaders React to the US Attack on Syrian Military Bases," *Gulf News Syria*, April 7, 2017, http://gulfnews.com/news/mena/syria/world-leaders-react-to-the-us-attack-on-syrian-military-bases-1.2007394 (accessed May 30, 2017).

31. Ibid.

32. Tom Miles, "Yemen's Cholera Epidemic Hits 600,000," Reuters, September 5, 2017, https://www.reuters.com/article/us-yemen-cholera/death-toll-in-yemen-cholera-outbreak-hits-nearly-700-who-idUSKBN18X1LG (accessed November 14, 2017).

33. "Death Toll in Yemen Conflict Passes 10,000," Al Jazeera, January 17, 2017,

http://www.aljazeera.com/news/2017/01/death-toll-yemen-conflict-passes-10000-170117040849576.html (accessed November 14, 2017).

34. Patrick W. Ryan, "The Yemen Crisis and the Bab el-Mandeb Maritime Chokepoint," Saudi-US-Relations Information Service (SUSRIS), April 14, 2015, http://susris.com/2015/04/14/the-bab-el-mandeb-maritime-chokepoint/ (accessed November 14, 2017).

35. "Djibouti Naval Base," sinodefence.com, August 20, 2017, http://sinodefence.com/djibouti-naval-base/ (accessed November 14, 2017).

36. Ramin Mostaghim and Shashank Bengali, "Syrian Ally Iran Blasts U.S. Missile Strikes as 'Dangerous, Destructive and a Violation of International Law,'" *LA Times*, April 5, 2017, http://www.latimes.com/world/la-fg-iran-syria-20170407-story.html (accessed November 14, 2017).

37. Jonathan Stempel, "Saudi Arabia Faces $6 Billion US Lawsuit by Sept. 11 Insurers," Reuters, March 24, 2017, http://www.reuters.com/article/us-usa-saudi-sept-idUSKBN16V1ZP (accessed October 30, 2017).

38. Thomas Gibbons-Neff, "Trump's First Arms Sales, Holdovers from the Obama Era, Are Business as Usual," *Washington Post*, January 24, 2017, https://www.washingtonpost.com/news/checkpoint/wp/2017/01/24/trumps-first-arms-sales-holdovers-from-the-obama-era-are-business-as-usual/?utm_term=.de21160e81f6 (accessed May 30, 2017).

39. Aaron Mehta, "Revealed: Trump's $110 Billion Weapons List for the Saudis," *Defense News*, June 8, 2017, https://www.defensenews.com/breaking-news/2017/06/08/revealed-trump-s-110-billion-weapons-list-for-the-saudis/ (accessed November 14, 2017).

40. Baker, MacFarquhar, and Gordon, "Syria Strike Puts US."

41. Michael Flynn, "Transcript: Michael Flynn on ISIL," Al Jazeera, January 13, 2016, http://www.aljazeera.com/programmes/headtohead/2016/01/transcript-michael-flynn-160104174144334.html (accessed November 14, 2017).

42. "US Missile Strike on Syria: Timeline of Reactions," *PressTV*, April 7, 2017, http://www.presstv.com/Detail/2017/04/07/517085/US-military-attack-Syria-timeline (accessed October 30, 2017).

43. Ibid.

44. Patrick Kingsley, "Erdogan Claims Vast Powers in Turkey After Narrow Victory in Referendum," *New York Times*, April 16, 2017, https://www.nytimes.com/2017/04/16/world/europe/turkey-referendum-polls-erdogan.html?mtrref=fr.search.yahoo.com&gwh=D4531B929DC49A1CFB7B39524DD062DF&gwt=pay (accessed November 14, 2017).

45. Zeina Karam and Sarah El Deeb, "Trump Launches US Missile Strike against Syria," *CTVNews*, April 7, 2017, http://www.ctvnews.ca/world/trump-launches-u-s-missile-strike-against-syria-1.3358473 (accessed May 30, 2017).

46. For an outline of Kurdish parties in the region: Rodi Hevian, "The Main Kurdish Political Parties in Iran, Iraq, Syria, and Turkey: A Research Guide," Rubin Center, August 19, 2013, http://www.rubincenter.org/2013/08/the-main-kurdish-political-parties-in-iran-iraq-syria-and-turkey-a-research-guide/ (accessed May 29, 2017).

47. Ryan Browne and Elise Labott, "US 'Deeply Concerned' after Turkey Bombs Allies in Iraq and Syria," CNN, April 25, 2017, http://edition.cnn.com/2017/04/25/politics/turkey-bombs-kurds-iraq-us-concerned/index.html (accessed November 14, 2017).

48. Michael R. Gordon and Eric Schmitt, "Trump to Arm Syrian Kurds, Even as Turkey Strongly Objects," *New York Times*, May 9, 2017, https://www.nytimes.com/2017/05/09/us/politics/trump-kurds-syria-army.html?emc=edit_na_20170509&nl=breaking-news&nlid=70196410&ref=cta&_r=0 (accessed May 29, 2017).

49. Staff, "Iraqi Kurdish Leader Calls for Non-Binding Independence Referendum," Reuters, February 2, 2016, http://www.reuters.com/article/us-iraq-kurds-idUSKCN0VB2EY (accessed May 30, 2017).

50. Nikolai Pakhomov, "Russia and Turkey: The Arms Deal That Signals the Age of Pragmatism," *LobeLog*, September 9, 2017, http://lobelog.com/russia-and-turkey-the-arms-deal-that-signals-the-age-of-pragmatism/ (accessed October 30, 2017).

51. "UN Envoy Urges Russia, Iran, Turkey to Convene Further Syrian Talks," RadioFreeEurope/RadioLiberty, March 25, 2017, https://www.rferl.org/a/syria-un-envoy-urges-talks-russia-iran-turkey/28390318.html (accessed October 30, 2017).

52. Margaret Talev and Jennifer Jacobs, "Trump Praises Erdogan for 'High Marks' amid Crackdown Concerns," Bloomberg Politics, September 21, 2017, https://www.bloomberg.com/news/articles/2017-09-21/trump-praises-erdogan-for-high-marks-amid-crackdown-concerns (accessed November 14, 2017).

53. Ipsita Chakravarty, "Why Has India Been Silent about the Chemical Attacks in Syria?" Scroll.in, April 8, 2017, https://scroll.in/article/834039/why-has-india-been-silent-about-the-chemical-attacks-in-syria (accessed October 30, 2017).

54. Richard Nephew, "How the Iran Deal Prevents a Covert Nuclear Weapons Program," *Arms Control Today*, September 2, 2015; Martin Zonas, "Iran Nuclear Deal: There Is No Alternative," *Economonitor*, April 7, 2015, http://www.economonitor.com/blog/2015/04/iran-nuclear-deal-there-is-no-alternative/ (accessed October 30, 2017).

55. Sarah Begley, "Read Donald Trump's Full Speech to AIPAC," *Time*, March 21, 2016, http://time.com/4267058/donald-trump-aipac-speech-transcript/

(accessed May 30, 2017). Benjamin Netanyahu immediately denounced the Iranian nuclear accord and continued to threaten a potential military strike against Iranian nuclear infrastructure. See, for example, analysis by Ben Caspit, "Netanyahu Threatens to 'Kill Himself' in Order to Stop Iran Deal," *Al-Monitor*, July 15, 2015, http://www.al-monitor.com/pulse/originals/2015/07/benjamin-netanyahu-iran-nuclear-deal-inspection-clauses.html# (accessed May 30, 2017).

56. Bozorgmehr Sharafedin, "Iran Confirms Missile Test, Drawing Tough Response from Trump Aide," Reuters, February 1, 2017, http://www.reuters.com/article/us-usa-iran-missiles-idUSKBN15G3ZO (accessed October 30, 2017).

57. Peter Kenyon, "Did Iran's Ballistic Missile Test Violate a UN Resolution?" NPR, February 3, 2017, http://www.npr.org/sections/parallels/2017/02/03/513229839/did-irans-ballistic-missile-test-violate-a-u-n-resolution (accessed May 30, 2017).

58. As of October 15, 2017, the US Congress is to decide in sixty days whether Iran is actually cheating on the Iran nuclear accord, the JCPOA. On the one hand, President Trump had been urged to decertify the treaty by Senators Tom Cotton, Ted Cruz, David A. Perdue, and Marco Rubio, and by former Ambassador to the United Nations John Bolton, for example. Israeli Prime Minister Benjamin Netanyahu also demanded renegotiation of JCPOA. On the other hand, US Secretary of State Rex Tillerson and US Secretary of Defense James Mattis, and the Chairman of the Joint Chiefs of Staff Gen. Joseph Dunford, have all argued that the maintenance of the JCPOA is in the US national security interest, and have been reluctant to decertify it. Former US Secretaries of State John Kerry and Madeleine Albright have both strongly supported the JCPOA. Uzi Arad, the former National Security Advisor of Israeli Prime Minister Netanyahu, has urged the White House and Congress not to abandon the JCPOA. In addition, a group of over 180 Democrats led by Representatives Ted Deutch (FL) and David Price (NC) sent a letter to President Trump urging him to recertify the Iran nuclear accord to Congress even before the October 15 deadline. It is possible that Congress could decide to maintain the JCPOA. But this possibility appears unlikely due to strong opposition to JCPOA among both Republicans and Democrats. See interview with Hall Gardner and Majid Golpour (in French), "Trois questions sur l'accord nucléaire iranien," *Contrepoints*, October 15, 2017, https://www.contrepoints.org/2017/10/12/300772-trois-questions-laccord-nucleaire-iranien (accessed November 14, 2017).

59. Thomas Erdbrink, "As Iran and US Leaders Trade Barbs, Big Deals Proceed," *New York Times*, May 28, 2017, https://www.nytimes.com/2017/05/28/world/middleeast/iran-nuclear-deal-hassan-rouhani-donald-trump.html (accessed October 30, 2017).

60. Ken Bredemeier, "Iran Warns US of Possible Missile Attack If It Imposes New Sanctions," VOA, October 08, 2017, https://www.voanews.com/a/iran-guard-chief-warns-us-against-imposing-new-sanctions/4061320.html (accessed November 15, 2017).

61. Christopher Woody, "Trump: The US Is Ready to Leave One of its Most Important Military Bases If the Gulf Crisis Worsens," *Business Insider*, July 19, 2017, http://www.businessinsider.fr/us/trump-us-is-ready-to-leave-al-udeid-military-base-amid-gulf-crisis-2017-7/ (accessed November 15, 2017).

62. "How the Battle for Mosul Unfolded," BBC News, July 10, 2017, http://www.bbc.com/news/world-middle-east-37702442 (accessed May 29, 2017).

63. Angela Dewan and Tim Lister, "Mosul Completely Freed from ISIS: What's Next for the City Left in Ruins?" CNN, July 10, 2017 http://edition.cnn.com/2017/07/10/middleeast/mosul-what-next/index.html (accessed November 15, 2017).

64. *SIGAR's High-Risk List* (Arlington, VA: Office of the Special Inspector General for Afghanistan Reconstruction), https://www.sigar.mil/interactive-reports/high-risk-list/index.html (accessed May 29, 2017).

65. Missy Ryan Greg Jaffe, "Donald Trump to Declare War on Taliban in Afghanistan Despite Experts' Concerns," *Independent*, May 9, 2017, http://www.independent.co.uk/news/world/americas/donald-trump-afghanstan-taliban-us-troop-surge-islamist-militants-talks-battle-fight-general-a7725601.html (accessed May 29, 2017).

66. David Corn, "Here's More Evidence That Trump Did Not Oppose the Iraq War Before It Began," *Mother Jones*, September. 2, 2016, http://www.motherjones.com/politics/2016/09/heres-more-evidence-trump-did-not-oppose-iraq-war/ (accessed November 15, 2017).

67. Hallie Jackson and Erik Ortiz, "Trump Weighs Sending as Many as 5,000 More Troops to Afghanistan," NBC News, May 9, 2017, http://www.nbcnews.com/news/world/trump-weighs-sending-many-5-000-more-troops-afghanistan-n756751 (accessed May 29, 2017).

68. Devirupa Mitra, "Pakistan Critical to Defeating ISIS: Russian Special Rep to Afghanistan," *Wire*, December 5, 2016, https://thewire.in/84672/pakistan-isis-afghanistan-russia/ (accessed May 29, 2017).

69. Masood Saifullah, "Trump's Afghanistan Policy Will Face Big Limitations," Deutsche Welle, May 2, 2017, http://www.dw.com/en/trumps-afghanistan-policy-will-face-big-limitations/a-38661290 (accessed May 29, 2017).

70. A high-ranking Russian official, Zamir Kubalov, was quoted as saying that "our (Russian) interests are the same as Taliban in fighting Daesh." Indrani Bagchi,

"Russia's Stand on Taliban Is Trouble for India," *India Times*, December 15, 2016, http://economictimes.indiatimes.com/articleshow/56001501.cms (accessed October 30, 2017). Kubalov is seen as the brains behind the new Russian rapprochement with Pakistan.

71. Tillerson: "The ongoing commitment of NATO Allies and partners to peace in Afghanistan, including to an eventual settlement between the Afghan government and the Taliban, protects this Alliance's interests, and, when successful, ensures that Afghanistan never again becomes a safe haven for terrorists." Rex W. Tillerson, "NATO Foreign Ministerial Intervention Remarks" (speech; Brussels, Belgium: US Department of State, March 31, 2017), https://www.state.gov/secretary/remarks/2017/03/269339.htm (accessed May 29, 2017).

72. Saifullah, "Trump's Afghanistan Policy."

73. Peter Baker and Michael D. Shearmay, "Trump Softens Tone on Islam but Calls for Purge of 'Foot Soldiers of Evil,'" *New York Times*, May 21, 2017, https://www.nytimes.com/2017/05/21/world/middleeast/trump-saudi-arabia-islam-speech.html?_r=0 (accessed October 30, 2017).

74. Zainab Fattah, "Guide to $400 Billion in Saudi-U.S. Deals: Black Hawks to Oil," Bloomberg, May 31, 2017, https://www.bloombergquint.com/markets/2017/05/22/guide-to-400-billion-in-saudi-u-s-deals-black-hawks-to-oil (accessed November 15, 2017).

75. For a Qatari perspective, "Saudi Crown Prince Mohammed bin Salman Widens Purge," Al Jazeera, November 6, 2017, http://www.aljazeera.com/news/2017/11/saudi-crown-prince-mohammed-bin-salman-widens-purge-171106104312835.html (accessed November 15, 2017). For a Yemeni perspective, "Saudi Prince Mohammad bin Salman Consolidates Power & Purges Rivals under 'Anti-Corruption' Pretense Story, Interview with Toby Jones and Afrah Nasser," *Democracy Now*, November 9, 2017, https://www.democracynow.org/2017/11/9/saudi_prince_mohammad_bin_salman_consolidates (accessed November 15, 2017).

CHAPTER 9: PEACE THROUGH STRENGTH? OR WORLD WAR TRUMP?

1. Donald Trump, *The Art of the Deal* (New York: Random House, 1987).

2. The lifting of sanctions on Moscow—without reinforcing NATO's eastern flank—will be interpreted by Moscow "as consent" to "further expansion," and "the result of a policy not to 'aggravate' Russia and instead to seek 'constructive dialogue'

will be war." Przemyslaw Zurawski vel Grajekski, in Kinga Redlowska, ed., *NATO: Rethink, Realign, React* (Warsaw: Institute for Eastern Studies, 2016), p. 9.

3. Gilbert Doctorow, "Trump Quiets Some Russian Doubts," *Consortium News*, January 30, 2017, https://consortiumnews.com/2017/01/30/trump-quiets-some-russian-doubts/ (accessed May 29, 2017).

4. I. William Zartman, "The Timing of Peace Initiatives: Hurting Stalemates and Ripe Moments," *Global Review of Ethnopolitics* 1, no. 1 (September 2001): 8–18.

5. For Minsk II accords: "Full Text of the Minsk Agreement," *Financial Times*, February 15, 2015, https://www.ft.com/content/21b8f98e-b2a5-11e4-b234-00144feab7de (accessed May 29, 2017).

6. Gwendolyn Sasse, "Constitution Making in Ukraine: Refocusing the Debate," Carnegie Europe, April 12, 2016, http://carnegieeurope.eu/2016/04/12/constitution-making-in-ukraine-refocusing-debate-pub-63304 (accessed May 29, 2017).

7. Vladimir Frolov, "Russia Looks On as Ukraine Hangs in the Balance," *Moscow Times*, April 13, 2016, http://www.themoscowtimes.com/opinion/opinion/article/russia-looks-on-as-ukraine-hangs-in-the-balance-op-ed/565762.html (accessed May 29, 2017). See also Brian Milakovsky, "Understanding the 'Under Control' Donbas," Woodrow Wilson Center, *Kennan Cable*, no. 16 (April 2016), https://www.wilsoncenter.org/publication/kennan-cable-no16-understanding-the-under-control-donbas (accessed October 30, 2017); Nicolai Petro, "Bringing Ukraine Back into Focus: How to End the New Cold War and Provide Effective Political Assistance to Ukraine," Carnegie Council, August 19, 2015, https://www.carnegiecouncil.org/publications/articles_papers_reports/742 (accessed October 30, 2017).

8. "Savchenko Meets Russia-Backed Separatist Leaders, Stirring Outrage," RadioFreeEurope/RadioLiberty, December 12, 2016, http://www.rferl.org/a/ukraine-savchenko-meets-separatists-minsk-plotnitsky-zakharchenko/28172257.html (accessed May 30, 2017).

9. Philip Karber and Phillip Petersen, in Redlowska, ed., *NATO Rethink, Realign, React*, p. 36.

10. One proposal is that Russia and the United States and Europeans "agree to disagree" for the indefinite future over the diplomatic status of Crimea; that the status quo in Donbas as part of Ukraine continues, with an effectively enforced cease-fire; and that a multibillion-dollar aid package be assembled from international sources directed to economic recovery in Ukraine. And, finally, a full and frank exchange on Russian involvement in US domestic elections must be addressed. See Jeffrey Burt, James Hitch, Peter Pettibone, and Thomas Shillinglaw, "Trump, Eisenhower

and Russia: A Chance for Peace," *National Interest*, November 5, 2017, http://nationalinterest.org/feature/trump-eisenhower-russia-chance-peace-23051?page=2 (accessed November 15, 2017). In the view of this author, an agreement in which Russia and the West "agree to disagree" for the indefinite future on the diplomatic status of Crimea, just as the Soviet Union and United States did during the Cold War with respect to the Baltic states, will not prove sufficient to guarantee peace as long as Kiev retains its irredentist claims to Crimea and does not adopt a formally neutral stance with respect to NATO and the Russian-led CSTO.

11. The North Atlantic Treaty Organization (Washington DC: NATO, April 4, 1949), http://www.nato.int/cps/en/natolive/official_texts_17120.htm (accessed October 30, 2017). Hall Gardner, *NATO Expansion and US Strategy in Asia* (Basingstoke: Palgrave MacMillan, 2013); Hall Gardner, *Crimea, Global Rivalry and the Vengeance of History* (New York: Palgrave Macmillan, 2015).

12. Verkhovna Rada Staff, "Declaration of State Sovereignty of Ukraine," Verkhovna Rada of the Ukrainian Soviet Socialist Republic, http://static.rada.gov.ua/site/postanova_eng/Declaration_of_State_Sovereignty_of_Ukraine_rev1.htm (accessed May 29, 2017).

13. "Gorbachev: Ukraine Should Sign Neutrality into Constitution," *Moscow Times*, August 18, 2016, https://themoscowtimes.com/news/ukraine-must-sign-neutrality-into-its-constitution-gorbachev-55027 (accessed May 29, 2017).

14. The plan may have been originally proposed by Opposition Bloc, a parliamentary faction that formed in 2014 from remnants of the old party of the ousted pro-Kremlin President Viktor Yanukovych. Nick Paton Walsh, Salma Abdelaziz, and Victoria Butenko, "Lawmaker: Trump Lawyer Discussed Ukraine Deal," CNN, February 24, 2017, http://edition.cnn.com/2017/02/23/politics/trump-lawyer-ukraine-peace-deal/ (accessed May 30, 2017).

The Ukrainian ambassador, Mr. Chaly, rejected a lease of that kind. "It is a gross violation of the Constitution. . . . Such ideas can be pitched or pushed through only by those openly or covertly representing Russian interests." Megan Twohey and Scott Shane, "A Back-Channel Plan for Ukraine and Russia, Courtesy of Trump Associates," *New York Times*, February 19, 2017, https://www.nytimes.com/2017/02/19/us/politics/donald-trump-ukraine-russia.html?hp&action=click&pgtype=Homepage&clickSource=story-heading&module=a-lede-package-region®ion=top-news&WT.nav=top-news&_r=1 (accessed May 30, 2017).

15. This is what the British did after seizing Hong Kong in 1847—and then leasing it for 150 years before returning Hong Kong to China in 1997, a fact which has not pleased all Hong Kong residents. The US had leased the Panama Canal Zone

after supporting and recognizing Panama's independence from Colombia. In the 1921 Thomson–Urrutia Treaty, the US then paid off Colombia and granted it special privileges in the Canal Zone for recognizing Panama's independence.

16. Twohey and Shane, "A Back-Channel Plan"; Julia Ioffe, "The Mystery of the Ukraine Peace Plan," *Atlantic*, February 20, 2017, https://www.theatlantic.com/international/archive/2017/02/ukraine-peace-plan/517275/ (accessed May 30, 2017).

17. Przemyslaw Zurawski vel Grajekski, in Redlowska, ed., *NATO Rethink, Realign, React*, p. 15.

18. Andrew E. Kramer, "Ethnic Conflict between Armenia and Azerbaijan Flares Anew," *New York Times*, April 4, 2016, https://www.nytimes.com/2016/04/05/world/europe/ethnic-conflict-between-armenia-and-azerbaijan-flares-anew.html?_r=0 (accessed October 30, 2017).

19. US Ambassador Vershbow has rightly argued for such deployments, but NATO has done little to develop the PfP. Alexander Vershbow, "Trump to Lavrov: Get Out of Ukraine or Face Stiffer Sanctions," *Newsweek*, May 9, 2015, http://www.newsweek.com/trump-lavrov-get-out-ukraine-or-face-stiffer-sanctions-606246 (accessed May 30, 2017).

20. Eleni Fotiou, "Caucasus Stability and Cooperation Platform: What Is at Stake for Regional Cooperation?" *ICBSS Policy Brief*, no. 16 (June 2009), https://www.files.ethz.ch/isn/104737/PB_16.pdf (accessed October 30, 2017).

21. Henry Kissinger, "How the Ukraine Crisis Ends," *Washington Post*, March 5, 2014. See also Des Browne, Wolfgang Ischinger, Igor S. Ivanov, Sam Nunn, and Adam Daniel Rotfeld, "Ukraine Must Not Become a New Berlin Wall," Nuclear Threat Institute, March 13, 2014.

22. Gabriela Baczynska and Robin Emmott, "Germany, France Seek Stronger EU Defense after Brexit: Document," Reuters, September 12, 2016, http://www.reuters.com/article/us-europe-defense-idUSKCN11I1XU (accessed October 30, 2017).

23. See Sven Biscop, "How the EU Can Save NATO," *Security Policy Brief*, no. 83 (Brussels, Belgium: Egmont Institute, March 2017), www.egmontinstitute.be/wp-content/uploads/2017/03/SBP83.pdf (accessed October 30, 2017).

24. NATO, "Relations with the European Union" North Atlantic Treaty Organization, March 30, 2017, http://www.nato.int/cps/en/natohq/topics_49217.htm (accessed October 30, 2017).

25. *White Paper on the Future of Europe* (Brussels, Belgium: European Commission, March 1, 2017), https://ec.europa.eu/commission/sites/beta-political/files/white_paper_on_the_future_of_europe_en.pdf (accessed October 30, 2017).

26. Y. Varoufakis, S. Holland, and J. K. Galbraith, "A Modest Proposal for Resolving the Eurozone Crisis," *Genius*, https://genius.com/Y-varoufakis-s-holland-and-jk-galbraith-a-modest-proposal-for-resolving-the-eurozone-crisis-annotated (accessed May 30, 2017).

And even this 2008 crisis stemmed, at least in part, from the US Federal Reserve's decision to keep Federal interest rates artificially low (in the view of many economists) in the period from 2002–2004 during the George W. Bush administration.

27. Jorge Rodríguez, "EU's New Thinking on Decentralisation and Territorial Development," European Centre for Development Policy Management, June 2015, http://ecdpm.org/great-insights/territorial-development-2/eus-new-thinking-on-decentralisation-and-territorial-development/ (accessed May 30, 2017).

28. Hall Gardner, *NATO Expansion and US Strategy in Asia* (New York: Palgrave MacMillan, 2013), chap. 7.

29. Ayhan Simsek, "Germany Opposes Call to End Turkey's EU Accession Talks," AA, November 25, 2016, http://aa.com.tr/en/europe/germany-opposes-call-to-end-turkey-s-eu-accession-talks/693243 (accessed November 15, 2017).

30. Christopher De Bellaigue, "Welcome to Demokrasi: How Erdogan Got More Popular than Ever," *Guardian*, August 30, 2016, https://www.theguardian.com/world/2016/aug/30/welcome-to-demokrasi-how-erdogan-got-more-popular-than-ever (accessed May 29, 2017).

31. Paul Tugwell and Selcan Hacaoglu, "Why the World's Watching Cyprus Unification Talks," Bloomberg, January 9, 2017, https://www.bloomberg.com/news/articles/2017-01-08/why-the-world-s-watching-cyprus-unification-talks-quicktake-q-a (accessed October 30, 2017).

32. Patrick Wintour, "Cyprus Peace Talks:—All You Need to Know," *Guardian*, January 9, 2017, https://www.theguardian.com/news/2017/jan/09/cyprus-peace-talks-all-you-need-to-know (accessed May 31, 2017); "Publications," European Union Institute for Security Studies, http://www.iss.europa.eu/publications/detail/article/toward-a-new-euro-atlantic-security-framework/ (accessed October 30, 2017).

33. Laura Rozen, "Syria Talks Pulled Back from Brink," *Al Monitor*, April 18, 2016, http://www.al-monitor.com/pulse/originals/2016/04/syria-talks-geneva-opposition-assad-mistura.html (accessed October 30, 2017). Ian Black, "All Eyes on US and Russia as Syria Deadline Passes," *Guardian*, February 19, 2016, http://www.theguardian.com/world/2016/feb/19/all-eyes-on-us-and-russia-as-syria-deadline-passes (accessed October 30, 2017).

34. "The PKK's Fateful Choice in Northern Syria," *International Crisis Group*, Report 176, May 4, 2017, https://www.crisisgroup.org/middle-east-north-africa/

eastern-mediterranean/syria/176-pkk-s-fateful-choice-northern-syria (accessed October 30, 2017).

35. Chase Winter, "Iraq Sweeps Up More Territories as Kurds Quarrel amongst Themselves," DW, October 17, 2017, http://www.dw.com/en/iraq-sweeps-up-more-territories-as-kurds-quarrel-amongst-themselves/a-40996992 (accessed November 15, 2017).

36. US policy has traditionally supported limited Israeli expansions into the West Bank, but in exchange for trade off of other lands with the Palestinians. John Podhoretz, "Media Gets Trump's Settlements Policy Wrong," *Commentary Magazine*, February 3, 2017, https://www.commentarymagazine.com/foreign-policy/middle-east/israel/israel-settlements-media/ (accessed May 31, 2017).

37. Jack Khoury and Amir Tibon, "Jordan's King Warns Trump against Moving US Embassy in Israel to Jerusalem, State Media Reports," *Haaretz*, February 2, 2017, http://www.haaretz.com/us-news/1.769266 (accessed May 31, 2017).

38. See for example, Stephen Walt, "Making the Middle East Worse, Trump-Style," *Foreign Policy*, June 9, 2017, http://foreignpolicy.com/2017/06/09/making-the-middle-east-worse-trump-style-saudi-arabia-qatar-iran-israel/ (accessed November 15, 2017). See also Ibrahim Fraihat, "Why Saudi-Israeli Normalisation Could Be Dangerous," Al Jazeera, November 19, 2017, http://www.aljazeera.com/indepth/opinion/saudi-israeli-normalisation-dangerous-171119083143078.html (accessed November 22, 2017).

39. Lubna Masarwa and Arwa Ibrahim, "EXCLUSIVE: Abbas to Offer Large Land Swap with Israel in Trump Talks," *Middle East Eye*, May 21, 2017, http://www.middleeasteye.net/news/abbas-propose-unprecedented-land-exchange-israel-during-trump-visit-703500509 (accessed October 30, 2017).

40. See Hall Gardner, *Averting Global War* (New York: Palgrave Macmillan, 2008).

41. Masarwa and Ibrahim, "Abbas to Offer Large Land Swap."

42. For a skeptical view, see Harsh V. Pant, "The SCO Illusion Takes India: As India Joins the SCO, It Must Keep in Mind Certain Geopolitical Realities," *Diplomat*, June 09, 2017, https://thediplomat.com/2017/06/the-sco-illusion-takes-india/ (accessed November 15, 2017).

43. India's trade with the members of the Eurasian Economic Union stands at about $10 billion. "India to Speed Up FTA with Eurasian Economic Union," *Hindu Business Line*, February 28, 2017, http://www.thehindubusinessline.com/economy/india-to-speed-up-fta-with-eurasian-economic-union/article9564225.ece (accessed November 15, 2017).

44. For a clear outline of seven different proposals to resolve the Kashmir

question, thus indicating its complexity, see "The Future of Kashmir?" BBC News, http://news.bbc.co.uk/2/shared/spl/hi/south_asia/03/kashmir_future/html/7.stm (accessed October 30, 2017).

45. Srinagar, "India's Kashmir Problem Is Getting Worse," *Economist*, May 25, 2017, http://www.economist.com/news/asia/21722666-shunning-separatists-will-not-make-it-better-indias-kashmir-problem-getting-worse (accessed October 30, 2017).

46. On May 6, 2016, Prime Minister Abe had traveled to Russia to meet with President Vladimir Putin in Sochi. As this was seen as breaking the G7's policy of isolating Russia in response to the 2014 annexation of Crimea, President Barack Obama purportedly phoned Abe in an effort to dissuade him from making the visit. James D. J. Brown, "Japan's 'New Approach' to Russia," *Diplomat*, June 18, 2016, http://thediplomat.com/2016/06/japans-new-approach-to-russia/ (accessed October 30, 2017).

47. "Putin, Abe Agree on Joint Russia-Japan Activities on Kuril Islands," RT, December 15 2016, https://www.rt.com/news/370452-putin-visits-japan-talks/ (accessed October 30, 2017). See also Hall Gardner, *NATO Expansion and US Strategy in Asia* (New York: Palgrave MacMillan, 2013).

48. Robin Harding in Tokyo and Kathrin Hille, "Russia and Japan Agree Economic Deal on Disputed Islands," *Financial Times*, December 16, 2016, https://www.ft.com/content/1905fc24-c360-11e6-9bca-2b93a6856354 (accessed October 30, 2017).

49. Jennifer Jacobs and Andreo Calonzo, "Trump Offers to Play South China Sea Peacemaker as Trip Wraps Up," Bloomberg, November 12, 2017, https://www.bloomberg.com/news/articles/2017-11-12/trump-offers-to-broker-deal-to-resolve-south-china-sea-dispute (accessed November 15, 2017).

50. Office of US Trade Representative, "U.S. -Korea Free Trade Agreement," Office of the United States Trade Representative, https://ustr.gov/trade-agreements/free-trade-agreements/korus-fta (accessed November 15, 2017).

51. For timeline of diplomacy dealing with North Korea, see *Wikipedia*, s.v. "Timeline of the North Korean Nuclear Program," last edited October 17, 2017, https://en.wikipedia.org/wiki/Timeline_of_the_North_Korean_nuclear_program (accessed October 30, 2017).

52. Ben Kamisar, "Trump Praises China for Abstaining from UN Vote," *Hill*, April 12, 2017, http://thehill.com/homenews/administration/328573-trump-praises-china-for-abstaining-from-un-vote (accessed May 31, 2017).

53. Sam Nunn, "Former Senator Sam Nunn on CNN re: North Korea,"

interview by Wolf Blitzer, *Nuclear Threat Initiative*, April 25, 2017, http://www.nti.org/newsroom/news/former-senator-sam-nunn-cnn-re-north-korea-interview-wolf-blitzer/ (accessed May 31, 2017).

54. "China Warns Conflict Could Erupt 'Any Moment' over North Korea," *South China Morning Post*, April 14, 2017, http://www.scmp.com/news/china/diplomacy-defence/article/2087726/conflict-could-break-out-any-moment-over-north-korea (accessed May 31, 2017).

55. Anna Fifield and Simon Denyer, "North Korea Shows off New Missiles in Huge Military Parade, but Doesn't Test Nuke," *Washington Post*, April 15, 2017, https://www.washingtonpost.com/world/north-korea-blames-trump-and-his aggressive-tweets-for-tensions/2017/04/14/6932c9aa-20e1-11e7-bcd6-6d1286bc177d_story.html?utm_term=.bc5ea434be8f (accessed May 31, 2017).

56. "The way you are going to make a good trade deal is to help us with North Korea. Otherwise, we are just going to go it alone, but going it alone means going at it with a lot of other nations. President Xi, I think he means well and I think he wants to help. We'll see whether or not he does." Alex Lockie, "Trump Says He Put Economic Pressure on China's President to Help with North Korea," *Business Insider*, April 12, 2017, http://www.businessinsider.fr/us/trump-trade-pressure-north-korea-china-2017-4/ (accessed October 30, 2017).

57. Secretary of Defense James Mattis was said to be opposed to deploying tactical nuclear weapons in South Korea. Robert Burns, "James Mattis: North Korea Has 'Accelerated' Threat of Nuclear Attack," *Time*, October 28, 2017, http://time.com/5001305/james-mattis-north-korea-acclerated-nuclear-threat/ (accessed November 15, 2017).

58. "Donald Trump's South Korea Speech: The Key Points," *Guardian*, November 8, 2017, https://www.theguardian.com/world/2017/nov/08/donald-trumps-south-korea-speech-key-points-kim-jong-un (accessed November 15, 2017).

59. Staff, "China Cautions against Use of Force on North Korea," Reuters, April 28, 2017, http://uk.reuters.com/article/uk-northkorea-usa-un-china-idUKKBN17U29C?il=0 (accessed October 30, 2017).

60. AFP, "North Korea Fires Another Missile, Trump Tweets His Anger," *TheJournal*, April 29, 2017, http://www.thejournal.ie/north-korea-trump-2-3365580-Apr2017/ (accessed May 31, 2017).

61. Barbara Plett Usher, "North Korea: US Not Seeking Regime Change, Says Rex Tillerson," BBC, August 2, 2017, http://www.bbc.com/news/world-us-canada-40797613 (accessed November 15, 2017).

62. Nick Wadhams, "Tillerson Says He Envisions US-North Korea Talks,"

Bloomberg, November 10, 2017, https://www.bloomberg.com/news/articles/2017-11-10/tillerson-sees-u-s-north-korea-agreeing-to-start-conversation (accessed November 15, 2017).

63. Nunn, "Former Senator Sam Nunn," interview by Wolf Blitzer.

64. Steve Holland, Stephen J. Adler, and Jeff Mason, "Exclusive: Trump Says 'Major, Major' Conflict with North Korea Possible, but Seeks Diplomacy," Reuters, April 27, 2017, http://www.reuters.com/article/us-usa-trump-exclusive-idUSKBN17U04E (accessed May 31, 2017).

65. Matthew Little, "China 'Unequivocal' on North Korea Not Getting Nuclear Weapons: Tillerson, Trump and Xi Affirm Position on North Korea during State Visit," *Epoch Times*, November 9, 2017, https://www.theepochtimes.com/china-unequivicol-on-north-korea-not-getting-nuclear-weapons-tillerson_2353648.html (accessed November 15, 2017).

66. See Gardner, *Averting Global War*. See also proposals of Rajan Menon, "What Would War Mean in Korea?" *TomDispatch*, June 4, 2017, http://www.tomdispatch.com/post/176291/tomgram%3A_rajan_menon%2C_what_would_war_mean_in_korea/ (accessed October 30, 2017).

67. Eleanor Albert, "North Korea's Military Capabilities," Council of Foreign Relations, September 5, 2017, https://www.cfr.org/backgrounder/north-koreas-military-capabilities (accessed November 15, 2017).

68. Holland, Adler, and Mason, "Trump Says 'Major, Major' Conflict."

69. Bruce Cumings, "Korea: Forgotten Nuclear Threats," *Le Monde Diplomatique*, December 2004, http://mondediplo.com/2004/12/08korea (accessed October 30, 2017). While the US has blamed Soviet- and Chinese-backed North Korea for initiating the Korean War, the security forces of the US-backed government of President Syngman Rhee (1948–1960) were responsible for killing more than 100,000 people, which included between 30,000 to 60,000 in the infamous 1948 Cheju massacre alone, in an effort to eradicate left-wing opposition in the country. Menon, "What Would War Mean in Korea?" The US needs to dialogue with the North Korean regime whether Washington likes it or not!

CHAPTER 10: DEFUSING THE GLOBAL CRISIS

1. Mikhail Gorbachev, "It All Looks as If the World Is Preparing for War," *Time Magazine*, January 26, 2017, http://time.com/4645442/gorbachev-putin-trump/ (accessed October 30, 2017).

2. Julian Borger, "America's New, More 'Usable,' Nuclear Bomb in Europe," *Guardian*, November 10, 2015, https://www.theguardian.com/world/julian-borger-global-security-blog/2015/nov/10/americas-new-more-usable-nuclear-bomb-in-europe (accessed November 15, 2017).

3. Gregory Kulacki, *China's Military Calls for Putting Its Nuclear Forces on Alert* (Cambridge, MA: Union of Concerned Scientists, 2016), http://www.ucsusa.org/nuclear-weapons/us-china-relations/china-hair-trigger#.WNuCRWSGNwc (accessed October 30, 2017).

4. In 2010, the NATO foreign ministers agreed that "no nuclear weapons would be removed from Europe unless all 28-member states of NATO agreed." Amy F. Woolf, *Nonstrategic Nuclear Weapons* (Washington, DC: Congressional Research Service, February 21, 2017), https://fas.org/sgp/crs/nuke/RL32572.pdf (accessed October 30, 2017). See also Ernie Regehr, *Canadian Defence Policy and NATO's Nuclear Weapons* (Vancouver: Simons Foundation, August 23, 2016), http://www.thesimonsfoundation.ca/sites/default/files/Canadian%20Defence%20Policy%20and%20NATO%E2%80%99s%20Nuclear%20Weapons%2C%20Defence%20Policy%20Review%20briefing%20paper%20-%20Aug%2023%2C%202016.pdf (accessed October 30, 2017).

5. Hall Gardner, *NATO Expansion and US Strategy in Asia* (New York: Palgrave MacMillan, 2013).

6. Treaty on the Non-Proliferation of Nuclear Weapons (Department for Disarmament Affairs, United Nations, 2000), http://www.un.org/en/conf/npt/2005/npttreaty.html (accessed October 30, 2017). Article VI: Each of the Parties to the Treaty undertakes to pursue negotiations in good faith on effective measures relating to cessation of the nuclear arms race at an early date and to nuclear disarmament, and on a treaty on general and complete disarmament under strict and effective international control.

7. Katrina vanden Heuvel, "The Escalating Nuclear Threat Finally Has the Public's Attention," *Washington Post*, October 24, 2017, https://www.washingtonpost.com/opinions/the-escalating-nuclear-threat-finally-has-the-publics-attention-now-what/2017/10/24/504fd5c4-b80b-11e7-9e58-e6288544af98_story.html?tid=ss_mail&utm_term=.bf695991b73c (accessed November 15, 2017).

8. James Pomfret, Neil Jerome Morales, "South China Sea Code of Conduct Talks to Be 'Stabilizer' for Region: China Premier," Reuters, November 14, 2017, http://www.reuters.com/article/us-asean-summit-southchinasea/south-china-sea-code-of-conduct-talks-to-be-stabilizer-for-region-china-premier-idUSKBN1DE05K?il=0 (accessed November 16, 2017). But Beijing's promise does not touch the larger questions of North Korea and rivalries between China, Taiwan, and Japan.

9. Martin Kettle, "The World's Powers Have to Resolve Their Remnants of Empire," *Guardian*, December 23, 2017, https://www.theguardian.com/commentisfree/2016/dec/23/post-imperial-territories (accessed October 30, 2017).

10. See Will Fitzgibbon and Scilla Alecci, "Paradise Papers Firm Managed Millions for a Carousel of Millionaires and Fraudsters," International Consortium of Investigative Journalism, November 15, 2017, https://www.icij.org/investigations/paradise-papers/ (accessed November 15, 2017).

11. Dean Baker, "A Job-Killing Robot for Rich People," *Jacobin*, June 27, 2017, https://jacobinmag.com/2017/06/financial-transactions-tax-finance-inequality-bernie-sanders?cn=cmV0d2VldA== UN (accessed October 30, 2017). "Goal 10: Reduce Inequality within and among Countries," United Nations, http://www.un.org/sustainabledevelopment/inequality/ (accessed October 30, 2017).

12. Lesley Wroughton, "G20 Fails to Endorse Financial Transaction Tax," Reuters, November 4, 2011, http://www.reuters.com/article/g20-tax-idUSN1E7A302520111104 (accessed October 30, 2017).

13. Jennifer Epstein and Mark Niquette, "Trump Wants $200 Billion for Infrastructure, Mulvaney Says," Bloomberg, April 20, 2017, https://www.bloomberg.com/politics/articles/2017-04-20/trump-wants-200-billion-for-infrastructure-mulvaney-says (accessed May 26, 2017); Adie Tomer, Joseph Kane, and Robert Puentes, "How Historic Would a $1 Trillion Infrastructure Program Be?" Brookings Institution, May 12, 2017, https://www.brookings.edu/blog/the-avenue/2017/05/12/how-historic-would-a-1-trillion-infrastructure-program-be/?utm_campaign=Brookings%20Brief&utm_source=hs_email&utm_medium=email&utm_content=51917420 (accessed May 26, 2017).

14. John Wagner, "Trump Re-Ups Criticism of United Nations, Saying It's Causing Problems, Not Solving Them," *Washington Post*, December 28, 2016, https://www.washingtonpost.com/news/post-politics/wp/2016/12/28/trump-re-ups-criticism-of-united-nations-saying-its-causing-problems-not-solving-them/?utm_term=.85d14cebfef3 (accessed May 31, 2017).

15. Robert Schroeder, "U.S. Drops Out of UNESCO over Arrears, 'Anti-Israel Bias,'" *MarketWatch*, Oct 12, 2017, https://www.marketwatch.com/story/us-drops-out-of-unesco-over-arrears-anti-israel-bias-2017-10-12 (accessed November 15, 2017).

16. "Financing Peacekeeping," United Nations, http://www.un.org/en/peacekeeping/operations/financing.shtml (accessed October 30, 2017). Percentages of costs: The US and its allies: United States (28.57 %); Japan (9.68 %); Germany (6.39 %); France (6.31 %); United Kingdom (5.80 %); Italy (3.75 %); Canada (2.92 %); Spain (2.44 %); Russia and China: Russian Federation (4.01 %); China (10.29 %).

17. *Democratic Republic of Congo: Background and US Relations* (Washington, DC: Congressional Research Service, July 24, 2015–February 27, 2017), https://www.everycrsreport.com/reports/R43166.html (accessed October 30, 2017).

18. Sarah N. Lynch, "SEC Halts Some Enforcement of Conflict Minerals Rule amid Review," Reuters, April 7, 2017, https://www.reuters.com/article/us-usa-sec-conflictminerals/sec-halts-some-enforcement-of-conflict-minerals-rule-amid-review-idUSKBN1792WX (accessed November 15, 2017). Michael S. Piwowar, "Reconsideration of Conflict Minerals Rule Implementation," (public statement; Washington, DC: US Securities and Exchange Commission, January 31, 2017), https://www.sec.gov/news/statement/reconsideration-of-conflict-minerals-rule-implementation.html (accessed October 30, 2017); for opposing views see: "Implementation of US Dodd-Frank Act Rule on Conflict Minerals: Commentaries, Guidance, Company Actions," Business and Human Rights Resource Center, https://business-humanrights.org/en/conflict-peace/conflict-minerals/implementation-of-us-dodd-frank-act-rule-on-conflict-minerals-commentaries-guidance-company-actions (accessed October 30, 2017).

19. In 2006, the US Senate passed the S. 2125, the Democratic Republic of Congo Relief, Security, and Democracy Promotion Act. See Pub. L. 109-456 (December 22, 2006). This legislation had concluded that disease, war, and desperate poverty in Africa threatens both the United States' core value of preserving human dignity and the United States' strategic priority of combating global terror. The legislation accordingly committed the United States to work toward peace, prosperity, and good governance in the Congo. Securities and Exchange Commission, "Release No. 34-67716; File No. S7-40-10: Conflict Minerals," https://www.sec.gov/rules/final/2012/34-67716.pdf (accessed November 2, 2017).

20. Lynch, "SEC Halts Some Enforcement of Conflict Minerals Rule amid Review."

21. On the UN Organization Stabilization Mission in the DRC (MONUSCO), see https://monusco.unmissions.org/en (accessed November 15, 2017).

22. John Calvelli, "Only Transparency Can Prevent Conflict Minerals from Harming People and Wildlife," *Hill*, April 18, 2017, http://thehill.com/blogs/pundits-blog/energy-environment/329347-only-transparency-can-prevent-conflict-minerals-from (accessed October 30, 2017).

23. *Conflict Minerals and the Democratic Republic of Congo: Responsible Action in Supply Chains, Government Engagement and Capacity Building* (Washington, DC: Business for Social Responsibility, May 2010), https://www.bsr.org/reports/BSR_Conflict_Minerals_and_the_DRC.pdf (accessed October 30, 2017); Tomi Oladipo,

"The UN's Peacekeeping Nightmare in Africa," BBC News, January 5, 2017, http://www.bbc.com/news/world-africa-38372614 (accessed October 30, 2017).

24. In 2007, the United States was spending some $4.5 billion per month to support its military operations in Iraq. This was about the same as the United Nations spent to run all eighteen of its current peacekeeping missions for a year. See James Dobbins, "A Comparative Evaluation of United Nations Peacekeeping," testimony presented before the House Committee on Foreign Affairs, Subcommittee on International Organizations, Human Rights, and Oversight, June 13, 2007, https://www.rand.org/content/dam/rand/pubs/testimonies/2007/RAND_CT284.pdf (accessed November 15, 2017).

25. According to Trump, the concept of global warming was created by and for the Chinese in order to make US manufacturing non-competitive. Jeremy Diamond, "Trump Nominees Say Climate Change Is No Hoax, but Still Invite Skepticism," CNN, January 19, 2017, http://edition.cnn.com/2017/01/17/politics/donald-trump-cabinet-picks-climate-change/ (accessed May 31, 2017).

26. "Donald Trump at Loggerheads with Rest of G7 over Climate Change," *Financial Times*, May 27, 2017, https://www.ft.com/content/d6ad0050-42cd-11e7-ab92-4c27fbc26eed (login required for access).

27. Mayor Bill Peduto issued an executive order a day after pledging Pittsburgh would continue to follow the guidelines of the Paris Climate Agreement. "Pittsburgh Mayor Issues Executive Order in Response to Trump's Paris Climate Decision," CBS Pittsburgh, June 2, 2017, http://pittsburgh.cbslocal.com/2017/06/02/pittsburgh-paris-climate-executive-order/ (accessed November 15, 2017).

28. Jacqueline Thomsen, "Pittsburgh Mayor Fires Back at Trump: My City Will Follow Paris Agreement," *Hill*, June 1, 2017, http://thehill.com/blogs/blog-briefing-room/news/335994-pittsburgh-mayor-fires-back-at-trump-my-city-will-follow-paris (accessed October 30, 2017).

29. On NERA Consulting, see "Factchecking President Trump's Claims about the Paris Agreement," *Fortune*, June 2, 2017, http://fortune.com/2017/06/02/paris-agreement-factchecking-trump/ (accessed November 15, 2017). See also the Heritage Foundation Report, Kevin Dayaratna, Nicolas Loris, and David Kreutzer, *Consequences of Paris Protocol: Devastating Economic Costs, Essentially Zero Environmental Benefits* (Washington, DC: Heritage Foundation, April 13, 2016), http://www.heritage.org/environment/report/consequences-paris-protocol-devastating-economic-costs-essentially-zero (accessed October 30, 2017).

30. "Factchecking President Trump's Claims."

31. Alanna Petroff, "The Heat Is On: President Trump Says He Will Decide

This Week Whether to Stick with the Landmark Paris Climate Accord," CNN, May 29, 2017, http://money.cnn.com/2017/05/29/news/trump-paris-climate-change-business/ (accessed October 30, 2017). Tomás Carbonell, "What Do the 2016 Elections Mean for the Clean Power Plan?" Pardon Our Interruption, December 6, 2016, http://www.renewableenergyworld.com/articles/2016/12/what-do-the-2016-elections-mean-for-the-clean-power-plan.html (accessed May 31, 2017).

32. International Renewable Energy Agency (IRENA), "Rethinking Energy: Renewable Energy and Climate Change," 2015, http://www.irena.org/-/media/Files/IRENA/Agency/Publication/2014/IRENA-_REthinking_Energy_2nd_report_2015.pdf?la=en&hash=35AF7434755915D342D41966EF595175CB0AE738 (accessed November 15, 2017).

33. Timothy Cama and Devin Henry, "Trump Takes Action to Move Forward with Keystone, Dakota Access Pipelines," *Hill*, January 24, 2017, http://thehill.com/policy/energy-environment/315852-trump-orders-keystone-dakota-access-pipeline-applications-to-move (accessed May 31, 2017).

34. "Coal Mining: Long-Term Contribution Trends," OpenSecrets.org: Center for Responsive Politics, https://www.opensecrets.org/industries/summary.php?ind=E1210 (accessed October 30, 2017). In 2016, general mining interests gave Republicans roughly ten times more in direct campaign contributions than Democrats, electrical utilities gave roughly two times more to Republicans; natural gas industries four times more; oil and gas industries gave nine times more, and Republicans even obtained slightly more than Democrats from alternative energy firms.

35. Associated Press, "Trump Has Promised to Revive the Coal Industry, But His Economic Advisor Says That Doesn't Make Much Sense," CNBC, May 26, 2017, http://www.cnbc.com/2017/05/26/donald-trump-and-economic-advisor-gary-cohn-differ-on-coal.html (accessed October 30, 2017).

36. Ibid.

37. Alexander C. Kaufman, "Trump Signs Executive Orders on Keystone XL, Dakota Access Pipelines," *Huffington Post*, January 24, 2017, http://www.huffingtonpost.com/entry/trump-keystone-dakota-access_us_58877e02e4b070d8cad57814 (accessed October 30, 2017).

38. Ibid.

39. *Renewable Energy and Jobs Annual Review (2016)* (Abu Dhabi, United Arab Emirates: International Renewable Energy Agency, 2016), http://www.se4all.org/sites/default/files/IRENA_RE_Jobs_Annual_Review_2016.pdf (accessed October 30, 2017); Linda Pentz Gunter, "Trump Is Foolish to Ignore the Flourishing Renewable Energy Sector," *Truthout*, February 5, 2017, http://www.truth-out.org/

opinion/item/39306-trump-is-foolish-to-ignore-the-flourishing-renewable-energy-sector (accessed May 31, 2017).

40. *US Energy and Employment Report* (Washington, DC: Department of Energy, January 2017), https://energy.gov/sites/prod/files/2017/01/f34/2017%20US%20Energy%20and%20Jobs%20Report_0.pdf (accessed October 30, 2017).

41. Suzanne Goldenberg, "Rich Countries' $100bn Promise to Fight Climate Change 'Not Delivered,'" *Guardian*, June 29, 2015, https://www.theguardian.com/environment/2015/jun/29/rich-countries-100bn-promise-fight-climate-change-not-delivered (accessed October 30, 2017).

42. Elizabeth Bast, Alex Doukas, Sam Pickard, Laurie Van Der Burg, and Shelagh Whitley, *Empty Promises: G20 Subsidies to Oil, Gas and Coal Production* (Washington, DC: Oil Change International, November 2015), https://www.odi.org/sites/odi.org.uk/files/odi-assets/publications-opinion-files/9958.pdf (accessed October 30, 2017); Elizabeth Bast, Sebastien Godinot, Stephen Kretzmann, and Jake Schmidt, *Under the Rug: How Governments and International Institutions Are Hiding Billions in Support to the Coal Industry* (Washington, DC: Oil Change International, June 2015), http://priceofoil.org/content/uploads/2015/05/Under_The_Rug_NRDC_OCI_WWF_Jun_2015.pdf (accessed October 30, 2017).

43. Bast, Doukas, Pickard, Van Der Burg, and Whitley, *Empty Promises.*

44. Ibid.

45. Ibid.

46. Jenny Rowland, Myriam Alexander-Kearns, Erin Auel, Matt Lee-Ashley, and Howard Marano, "How Exxon Won the 2016 Election," Center for American Progress, January 10, 2017, https://www.americanprogress.org/issues/green/news/2017/01/10/296277/how-exxon-won-the-2016-election/ (accessed May 31, 2017). Natasha Bertrand, "Rex Tillerson's Confirmation Hearing Is Today: Here's How His Company, ExxonMobil, Could Benefit from a Trump Presidency," *Business Insider*, January 11, 2017, http://uk.businessinsider.com/how-exxon-mobil-trump-presidency-benefits-2017-1?r=US&IR=T (accessed May 31, 2017).

47. For a study of renewable energies, see Cédric Philibert, "Renewable Energy for Industry: From Green Energy to Green Materials and Fuels," International Energy Agency: Insights Series 2017, http://www.iea.org/publications/insights/insight publications/Renewable_Energy_for_Industry.pdf (accessed November 15, 2017).

48. Nigel Purvis and Joshua Busby, *The Security Implications of Climate Change for the UN System* (Washington, DC: Wilson Center, United Nations and Environmental Security, 2004); Justin Gillis, "Climate Model Predicts West Antarctic Ice Sheet Could Melt Rapidly," *New York Times*, March 30, 2016, https://www

.nytimes.com/2016/03/31/science/global-warming-antarctica-ice-sheet-sea-level-rise .html?_r=1 (accessed October 31, 2017); Ian Urbina, "Perils of Climate Change Could Swamp Coastal Real Estate," *New York Times*, November 24, 2016, https://www.nytimes.com/2016/11/24/science/global-warming-coastal-real-estate.html?module=Promotron®ion=Body&action=click&pgtype=article (accessed May 31, 2017); Justin Gillis, "Earth Sets a Temperature Record for the Third Straight Year," *New York Times*, January 18, 2017, https://www.nytimes.com/2017/01/18/science/earth-highest-temperature-record.html?emc=edit_na_20170118&nlid=70196410 &ref=cta (accessed May 31, 2017).

49. Adam Gabbatt, "How Hurricanes and Sea-Level Rise Threaten Trump's Florida Resorts," *Guardian*, September 9, 2017, https://www.theguardian.com/us-news/2017/sep/09/trump-florida-mar-a-lago-hurricane-irma (accessed October 31, 2017).

50. Jennifer Jacobs and Andreo Calonzo, "Trump Offers to Play South China Sea Peacemaker as Trip Wraps Up," Bloomberg, November 12, 2017, https://www .bloomberg.com/news/articles/2017-11-12/trump-offers-to-broker-deal-to-resolve -south-china-sea-dispute (accessed November 15, 2017).

51. Stephen Goss et al., *Effects of Unauthorized Immigration on the Actuarial Status of the Social Security Trust Funds*, Actuarial Note No. 151 (Baltimore, MD: Social Security Administration Office of the Actuary, April 2013), https://www.ssa .gov/oact/NOTES/pdf_notes/note151.pdf (accessed October 31, 2017).

52. Inspector General, *Status of the Social Security Administration's Earnings Suspense File* (Baltimore, MA: Social Security Administration, September 2015), https://oig.ssa.gov/sites/default/files/audit/full/pdf/A-03-15-50058.pdf (accessed October 31, 2017).

53. "War on Drugs an Epic Fail, BMJ Editors Say," Global Commission on Drug Policy, November 17, 2016, https://www.globalcommissionondrugs.org/reports/war -on-drugs/ (accessed October 31, 2017); *War on Drugs* (Geneva, Switzerland, Global Commission on Drug Policy, June 2011), https://www.globalcommissionondrugs. org/wp-content/uploads/2012/03/GCDP_WaronDrugs_EN.pdf (accessed October 31, 2017).

54. Jeffrey A. Miron, *The Budgetary Implications of Drug Prohibition* (Cambridge, MA: Harvard University, February 2010), https://scholar.harvard.edu/files/miron/files/budget_2010_final_0.pdf (accessed October 31, 2017).

Miron's report estimates that legalizing drugs would save roughly $48.7 billion per year in government expenditure on enforcement of prohibition. $33.1 billion of this savings would accrue to state and local governments, while $15.6 billion would accrue to the federal government. Approximately $13.7 billion of the savings would result from legalization of marijuana, $22.3 billion from legalization of cocaine and heroin, and $12.8 from legalization of other drugs. The report also estimates that drug legalization would yield tax revenue of $34.3 billion annually, assuming legal drugs are taxed at rates comparable to those on alcohol and tobacco. Approximately $6.4 billion of this revenue would result from legalization of marijuana, $23.9 billion from legalization of cocaine and heroin, and $4.0 billion from legalization of other drugs.

55. Kitty Holland, "Decriminalization of All Drugs for Personal Use Considered," *Irish Times*, April 18, 2017.

56. Robert A. Levy, "Reflections on Gun Control by a Second Amendment Advocate," *National Law Journal*, February 11, 2013, available at CATO Institute, https://www.cato.org/publications/commentary/reflections-gun-control-second-amendment-advocate (accessed November 15, 2017).

57. National Institute on Drug Abuse, "Opioid Crisis," last updated June 2017, http://www.drugabuse.gov/drugs-abuse/opioids/opioid-crisis (accessed November 15, 2017).

58. Kim Stephens "Trump's Tweets Return to Haunt Him. Again," News.com.au, January 23, 2017, http://www.news.com.au/technology/online/social/donald-trump-mocks-protesters-four-years-after-unsuccessfully-calling-for-protests-against-barack-obama/news-story/e114739c33fabb80fd34fef91ce238fa (accessed May 26, 2017). Many of Trump's tweets were later deleted.

59. Drew DeSilver, "Trump's Victory Another Example of How Electoral College Wins Are Bigger than Popular Vote Ones," Pew Research Center, December 20, 2016, http://www.pewresearch.org/fact-tank/2016/12/20/why-electoral-college-landslides-are-easier-to-win-than-popular-vote-ones/ (accessed May 26, 2017).

60. Richard Dawkins, "Can the Electoral College System Be Reformed?" Richard Dawkins Foundation, February 9, 2017, https://richarddawkins.net/2017/02/can-the-electoral-college-system-be-reformed/ (accessed May 26, 2017).

61. Carol Orsag, "A 38-State Nation," The Thirty-Eight States, http://www.tjc.com/38states/ (accessed May 26, 2017), originally published in David Wallenchinsky and Irving Wallace, *The People's Almanac* (New York: Doubleday, 1975). This was proposed in 1972 by C. Etzel Pearcy. Other proposals reduce the number to ten to twelve states, but that might give too much power to certain regions.

62. While one might think politicians would not want to give up power, the highly bureaucratic French were able to reduce the number of regions in mainland France from twenty-two to thirteen in the period 2014 to 2016. "La carte à 13 régions définitivement adoptée," *Le Monde*, December 17, 2014.

63. Francis Fukuyama, *The End of History and the Last Man* (New York: Avon, 1993). See my critique of Fukuyama's work in Hall Gardner, *Crimea, Global Rivalry and the Vengeance of History* (New York: Palgrave Macmillan, 2015).

64. For a brief history of the concept of workplace democracy (what the French call "autogestion") which can take different forms from employee management and control to employee stock ownership without control, see Markus Pausch, "Workplace Democracy from a Democratic Ideal to a Managerial Tool and Back," *The Innovation Journal: The Public Sector Innovation Journal* 19, no. 1 (2013), article 3, http://www.innovation.cc/scholarly-style/19_1_3_pausch_workplace-democracy.pdf (accessed October 31, 2017). For a brief positive description of a generally not well-known form of shared-capitalist management that can function effectively, see Jerry L. Ripperger, "How Employee Ownership Benefits Executives, Companies, and Employees," American Management Association, http://www.amanet.org/training/articles/how-employee-ownership-benefits-executives-companies-and-employees.aspx (accessed October 31, 2017). See more detailed analysis, Douglas L. Kruse, Richard B. Freeman, and Joseph R. Blasi, ed., *Shared Capitalism at Work: Employee Ownership, Profit and Gain Sharing, and Broad-Based Stock Options* (Chicago: University of Chicago Press, 2010), available online at: http://www.nber.org/chapters/c8085.pdf (accessed October 31, 2017). I was national office manager of the Association for Workplace Democracy (AWD) in Washington, DC for two years in the early 1980s, which produced the journal *Workplace Democracy*. Unfortunately, AWD soon died out in the Reagan period, but many of its practical proposals are still relevant in today's socio-political and financial crisis.

POSTSCRIPT: IT CAN HAPPEN HERE

1. Trump: "I'm not isolationist, but I am 'America First.' So I like the expression. I'm 'America First.'" David E. Sanger and Maggie Haberman, "In Donald Trump's Worldview, America Comes First, and Everybody Else Pays," *New York Times*, March 26, 2016, https://www.nytimes.com/2016/03/27/us/politics/donald-trump-foreign-policy.html?_r=0 (accessed October 31, 2017).

2. Ibid.

3. "George S. Patton's Speech to the Third US Army," Patton Museum of Calvary and Armor, March 24, 1944, https://web.archive.org/web/20060616031308/http://www.knox.army.mil/museum/pattonsp.htm (accessed October 31, 2017).

4. Sanger and Haberman, "In Donald Trump's Worldview."

5. After dropping "30 or so atomic bombs . . . strung across the neck of Manchuria," MacArthur planned to introduce half a million Chinese Nationalist troops at the Yalu and then "spread behind us—from the Sea of Japan to the Yellow Sea—a belt of radioactive cobalt." MacArthur was certain that the Russians would have done nothing about this extreme strategy: "My plan was a cinch." MacArthur was not removed from duty because he advocated the use of nuclear weapons, but because he could not be fully trusted to carry out orders that might involve their use. See Bruce Cumings, "Why Did Truman Really Fire MacArthur? . . . The Obscure History of Nuclear Weapons and the Korean War Provides the Answer," *History News Network*, January 10, 2005, http://historynewsnetwork.org/article/9245 (accessed October 31, 2017).

6. Sanger and Haberman, "In Donald Trump's Worldview."

7. Trump's November 2017 offer to negotiate disputes between China and its neighboring countries over the South China Sea could prove positive, as would a settlement between the United States, Japan, and Russia, if Trump is truly willing to lead the negotiations. See chapters 9 and 10.

8. Guillaume Bouzard, "Inquiétude à la Maison Blanche," *Le Canard Enchainé*, January 25, 2017, p. 4.

9. David Horsey, "Trump Leaks State Secrets and Self-Incriminating Boasts," *Los Angeles Times*, May 17, 2017, http://www.latimes.com/opinion/topoftheticket/la-na-tt-trump-leaks-20170516-story.html (accessed November 16, 2017).

10. Tatiana Schlossberg, "What Is the Antiquities Act and Why Does President Trump Want to Change It?" *New York Times*, April 26, 2017, https://www.nytimes.com/2017/04/26/climate/antiquities-act-federal-lands-donald-trump.html (accessed October 31, 2017).

11. Presidential Documents, "Promoting Energy Independence and Economic Growth," Exec. Order No. 13, 783, 82 C.F.R. 16093 (March 28, 2017), *Federal Register* 82, no. 61, March 31, 2017, https://www.gpo.gov/fdsys/pkg/FR-2017-03-31/pdf/2017-06576.pdf (accessed November 2, 2017).

12. Timothy Cama, "Trump to Reconsider Grand Canyon Uranium Mining Ban," *Hill*, November 1, 2017, http://thehill.com/policy/energy-environment/358311-trump-admin-to-reconsider-grand-canyon-uranium-mining-ban (accessed November 16, 2017); Joanna Walters, "Grand Canyon at Risk as Arizona Officials Ask Trump to End Uranium Mining Ban," *Guardian*, June 5, 2017, https://www.theguardian.com/environment/2017/jun/05/public-lands-uranium-mining-arizona-grand-canyon (accessed October 31, 2017).

13. Nina Bahadur, "18 Real Things Donald Trump Has Actually Said about Women," *Huffington Post*, October 10, 2016, https://www.huffingtonpost.com/

entry/18-real-things-donald-trump-has-said-about-women_us_55d356a8e4b07addcb442023 (accessed November 16, 2017).

14. John William Ward, *Andrew Jackson: A Symbol for an Age* (New York: Oxford University, Press, 1962).

15. In contemporary circumstances, many Native American peoples will be impacted by mining interests the more that federal lands originally set aside by the Antiquities Act are opened, as has also been the case for the Keystone pipeline. See chapter 10.

16. Donald Trump, "Transcript of Trump's Speech in Saudi Arabia," CNN, May 21, 2017, http://edition.cnn.com/2017/05/21/politics/trump-saudi-speech-transcript/index.html (accessed October 31, 2017).

17. Trump's alleged statement that he expects "loyalty" from the FBI director James Comey, but who promised "honesty" in return, has not only been interpreted by critics of Trump as obstructing justice, but also as undermining the FBI's relative independence. Katie Bo Williams, "Comey's Dramatic Account on Trump Rocks Washington," *Hill*, June 7, 2017, http://thehill.com/policy/national-security/336848-comeys-dramatic-account-rocks-washington (accessed October 31, 2017). Trump's lawyer, has, however, denied that Trump ever told "Mr. Comey, 'I need loyalty, I expect loyalty' in form or substance." "President Trump's Lawyer's Statement on Comey Hearing," CNN, June 8, 2017. http://edition.cnn.com/2017/06/08/politics/marc-kasowitz-statement-trump-comey/index.html (accessed October 31, 2017). If Comey's position can be somehow verified, the incident raises the threat of "loyalty oaths" as during the early Cold War McCarthy period.

18. NFL player Colin Kaepernick's protest against police brutality and racism during the singing of the national anthem in 2016 is a case in point. President Trump challenged the constitutional right of Kaepernick and others to symbolic protest, urging in a tweet that such individuals be "FIRED" for disrespecting the "Great American Flag (or country)." Trump's threats could become reality if waves of dishonest and hypocritical patriotism sweep the country against honest protest of telling truth to power. Bryan Flaherty, "From Kaepernick Sitting to Trump's Fiery Comments: NFL's Anthem Protests Have Spurred Discussion," *Washington Post*, September 24, 2017, https://www.washingtonpost.com/graphics/2017/sports/colin-kaepernick-national-anthem-protests-and-NFL-activism-in-quotes/?utm_term=.88e10ee1ac46 (accessed October 31, 2017).

19. Stephen Feller, "Trump Supports Waterboarding, Says Intel Officials Told Him It 'Works,'" UPI, January 26, 2017, https://www.upi.com/Top_News/US/2017/01/26/Trump-supports-waterboarding-says-intel-officials-told-him-it-works/

4251485406127/ (accessed November 16, 2017). See critique by Vanessa Schipani, "Trump on Torture," FactCheck.org, July 28, 2016, last updated August 1, 2016, http://www.factcheck.org/2016/07/trump-torture/ (accessed November 16, 2017).

20. Igor Bobic, "Donald Trump Says He Would 'Take Out' Families of Terrorists," *Huffington Post*, December 12, 2015, https://www.huffingtonpost.com/entry/donald-trump-families-terrorists_us_565ef81ae4b072e9d1c41f99 (accessed November 16, 2017).

21. Tom LoBianco, "Trump Softens Tone on McCain, Stands by Waterboarding Support," CNN, February 9, 2016, http://edition.cnn.com/2016/02/09/politics/donald-trump-john-mccain-waterboarding/index.html (accessed November 16, 2017). Having supported waterboarding during the Bush administration, CIA Director Mike Pompeo made ambiguous statements in his testimony to Congress as to whether he was open to the use of waterboarding techniques, if legalized. Pompeo was also ambiguous about the collection of phone metadata and other information about Americans, including about their "lifestyle"—by the use of broad powers that were granted through the expansion of the Foreign Intelligence Surveillance Act in 2008. Amy Davidson Sorkin, "Mike Pompeo and the Question of Torture," *New Yorker*, January 12, 2017, http://www.newyorker.com/news/amy-davidson/mike-pompeo-and-the-question-of-torture (accessed October 31, 2017). By contrast, in opposition to Trump's campaign rhetoric, Secretary of State Rex Tillerson, homeland security director John F. Kelly, and Attorney General Jeff Sessions, all rejected reviving the use of torture.

22. Kenneth Allard et al., "Defending the Honor of the US Military from Donald Trump," *Foreign Policy*, March 16, 2016, http://foreignpolicy.com/2016/03/04/defending-the-honor-of-the-u-s-military-from-donald-trump/ (accessed October 31, 2017). "Refusing to carry out such orders will protect the rule of law and the constitutional order, of which civilian control of the military is fundamental."

23. George W. Bush, address to a joint session of Congress, September 20, 2001; a transcript of his address is available at "Transcript of President Bush's Address," CNN, September 21, 2001, http://edition.cnn.com/2001/US/09/20/gen.bush.transcript/ (accessed November 10, 2017).

24. UN, *World Cities Report* (Nairobi, Kenya: UN Habitat, 2016), http://wcr.unhabitat.org/main-report/ (accessed October 31, 2017).

25. While China has been attempting to reduce its use of coal and investing more in renewable energies, Trump has sought to boost the use of coal and shale oil. (See chapter 10.) China is nevertheless responsible for almost one-third of all oceanic plastic waste. It is time for all countries to reduce use of plastics as much as possible.

Chen Ronggang, "China Is the World's Largest Consumer of Fast Food. And It's Causing Major Damage," World Economic Forum, October 25, 2017, https://www.weforum.org/agenda/2017/10/china-is-the-worlds-largest-consumer-of-fast-food-and-its-causing-major-damage (accessed November 16, 2017).

26. George Orwell, *1984* (Planet E-Book), chapter 3, p. 43.

27. Against this Orwellian vision, Russian analyst Andrei Kortunov was more or less correct to argue that "in today's conditions of total interdependence . . . neither the UK's withdrawal from the EU, nor China's non-participation in the Trans-Pacific Partnership (TPP) will have the disastrous economic consequences predicted by those who love geopolitical horror stories." Andrey Kortunov, "The Inevitable, Weird World," Russia in Global Affairs, September 25, 2016, http://eng.globalaffairs.ru/number/The-Inevitable-Weird-World-18385 (accessed October 31, 2017). Yet, this optimistic perspective was articulated prior to the Trump administration's decision to drop out of the TPP and out of the COP 21 Global Climate Agreement. The latter actions could represent just the beginning of the unravelling of other multilateral and international accords.

INDEX